ENGLISH IN EUROPE

ENGLISH IN EUROPE

Edited by

MANFRED GÖRLACH

OXFORD

UNIVERSITY PRESS

OXFORD
UNIVERSITY PRESS

Great Clarendon Street, Oxford OX2 6DP

Oxford University Press is a department of the University of Oxford.
It furthers the University's objective of excellence in research, scholarship,
and education by publishing worldwide in
Oxford New York

Athens Auckland Bangkok Bogotá Buenos Aires Cape Town
Chennai Dar es Salaam Delhi Florence Hong Kong Istanbul Karachi
Kolkata Kuala Lumpur Madrid Melbourne Mexico City Mumbai Nairobi
Paris São Paulo Shanghai Singapore Taipei Tokyo Toronto Warsaw
with associated companies in Berlin Ibadan

Oxford is a registered trade mark of Oxford University Press
in the UK and in certain other countries

Published in the United States
by Oxford University Press Inc., New York

British Library Cataloguing in Publication Data
Data available
Library of Congress Cataloging in Publication Data
Data applied for
ISBN 0–19–823714–6

1 3 5 7 9 10 8 6 4 2

Typeset in Times
by Kolam Information Services Pvt. Ltd., Pondicherry, India
Printed in Great Britain on acid-free paper by
Biddles Ltd., Guildford & King's Lynn

CONTENTS

Contents

LIST OF CONTRIBUTORS

Dr Nevena Alexieva
English Department
Sofia University
Tsar Osvoboditel Blvd 15
1000 Sofia
BULGARIA

Keith Battarbee
Department of English
University of Turku
SF-20014 Turku
FINLAND

Prof. Dr Amand Berteloot
Institut für Niederländische Philologie
Universität Münster
Alter Steinweg 6–7
D-48143 Münster
GERMANY

Prof. Dr Ulrich Busse
Institut für Anglistik und Am.
Martin-Luther-Universität
Dachritzstr. 12
D-06108 Halle
GERMANY

Ilinca Constantinescu
Institutul de Lingvistică
Calea 13 Septembrie Nr. 13
RO-76117 Bucureşti
ROMANIA

Dr Judit Farkas
Department of English Linguistics
Eötvös Lorand University

Ajtosi Dürer sor 19
H 1146 Budapest
HUNGARY

†Prof. Dr Rudolf Filipović

Prof. Dr Manfred Görlach
Englisches Seminar
Universität zu Köln
Albertus-Magnus-Platz 1
D-50923 Köln
GERMANY

Dr art. Anne-Line Graedler
Dept. of British and American Studies,
University of Oslo
PO Box 1003, Blindern
N-0315 Oslo
NORWAY

Prof. John Humbley
UFR EILA
Université Paris 7 Denis Diderot
F75005 Paris
FRANCE

Prof. Veronika Kniezsa
Department of English Linguistics
Eötvös Lorand University
Ajtosi Dürer sor 19
H 1146 Budapest
HUNGARY

Dr Rolf Ködderitzsch
Noldestr. 37
D-53340 Meckenheim
GERMANY

Prof. Dr Guðrún Kvaran
Institute of Lexicography
Neshagi 16
Reykjavik IS 107
ICELAND

Prof. Dr Elżbíeta Mańczak-Wohlfeld
Uniwersytet Jagielloński
Inst. Filologii Angielskiej
Ul. Mickiewicza 9/11
PL-31-120 Kraków
POLAND

Prof. Tamara Maximova
English Department
Volgograd University
2 Prodolnaya 30
40062 Volgograd
RUSSIA

Dr Victoria Popovici
Institut für Romanistik
Fr.-Schiller-Universität Jena
D-07740 Jena
GERMANY

Prof. Virginia Pulcini
Università degli Studi di Torino
Facoltà di Lingue e Letterature
    Straniere
Dipartimento di Scienze del
    Linguaggio
Via S. Ottavio 20
10124 Torino
ITALY

Prof. Félix Rodríguez González
Dep. de Fil. Anglesa
Universitat d'Alacant
Ap. Correus 99
E-03080 Alacant
SPAIN

Ekaterini Stathi
Messogion 73 B
GR 15126 Athens
GREECE

Dr Ariadna Ştefănescu
Institutul de Lingvistică
Calea 13 Septembrie Nr. 13
RO-76117 Bucureşti
ROMANIA

Ásta Svavarsdóttir
Institute of Lexicography
Neshagi 16
Reykjavik 101
ICELAND

Nicoline van der Sijs
Hooghiemstraplein 103
NL-3514 AX Utrecht
THE NETHERLANDS

I

INTRODUCTION

Manfred Görlach

The sixteen chapters in the present collection are a complement to the *Dictionary of European Anglicisms* and the *Annotated Bibliography of European Anglicisms*, all forming part of a single research project devoted to the lexical impact of English on selected European languages. Whereas the *Dictionary* contains the full data on the presence and style value of some 4,000 items and the *Bibliography* condensed information on the state of research, this book provides readable summaries of the influence of English on the sixteen languages covered in the *Dictionary*, chapter by chapter. The sixteen languages selected represent the various regions and language families of continental Europe as faithfully as possible; they allow a maximum of contrasts relating to the cultural history of the speech communities:

Icelandic	Norwegian	Polish	Russian
Dutch	German	Croatian	Bulgarian
French	Italian	Finnish	Hungarian
Spanish	Romanian	Albanian	Greek

It happens too often in the history of dictionaries that more general statements which could have been put forward by the compilers, after many years of dedicated research, are never put together in coherent form: lexicographers tend to become too aware of the danger of generalizing conclusions from thousands of entries which clearly show that every single word has its own history. Such an attitude is, however, too modest: the individual reader cannot be expected to piece together tendencies and recurring features from large numbers of entries, and it is likely that the conclusions drawn from such more superficial analyses will be further off the point than those cautiously formulated by the experienced researcher. While the conclusions presented in this book are obviously based on data from the

Dictionary of European Anglicisms, we have tried to make the arguments in this collection self-explanatory.

There has never been a survey of the type presented here; Viereck and Bald (1986) come closest to the idea, but the chapters in their book are not structured identically, so that it is impossible to base comparative statements on them. Moreover, there has never been an amount of data comparable to that amassed in the work for the *Dictionary of European Anglicisms*—many of our conclusions (however preliminary they still are) would not have been possible before work on it was complete.

The sixteen chapters here included were written by the colleagues who also compiled the data for the *Dictionary* and *Bibliography*; in a few cases, it is not the *first* editor who is responsible, and various helpers or co-authors were employed in order to make the chapters as informative and reliable as possible.

A chapter on German was first drafted by Manfred Görlach and augmented by Ulrich Busse. This was revised twice and then sent round to all authors, as a pattern for the other contributions to follow. This policy indicated to our colleagues the degree of detail envisaged and established an identical structure which makes it possible to compare the history and types of influence, attitudes, and structural conditions for borrowing between all languages represented, with types of data discussed under the same section numbers and headings.

It is obvious that differences in the history of the contact with English and the intensity of the impact and widely divergent linguistic structures have resulted in sections of different lengths. No attempt has been made to standardize the amount of detail provided: each chapter reflects the special situation of the recipient language.

There are two obvious dangers in this procedure: there is a great deal of unavoidable repetition where conditions and results are similar or identical—often as a reflex of shared cultural history among the languages here compared. (There was an intentional restriction to cultures of a European background which permits such comparisons to be meaningful.) The second danger is that the chapter on German might be too much of a model, the characteristics of the other languages not becoming apparent enough, with too much focus on real or seeming similarities. All the authors have seen the problem and combined a clear exposition of their specific situation with comparability.

All the chapters here printed have been revised several times, and all authors have repeatedly seen their own drafts and—on request—those on related languages. This procedure has produced, we hope, a collection of chapters coming as close as possible to what can be achieved, given our present state of knowledge. It will be obvious that some languages have been much more extensively researched than others: the provisional chapter on Albanian illustrates a typical restriction resulting from that country's recent history.

Each chapter is divided into the same set of sections and subsections. I here discuss some trends and generalizations that emerge from the collection as a whole, and some frequently recurring topics.

1.1 History of language contact

1.1.1 Chronology of intensive influences

The periods of massive impact of English on lexis (and in culture in general) are, first, after the Second World War (for all countries outside the Communist sphere of influence) and then from 1990 onwards when the eastern regimes crumbled and western influences came to flood various domains. Whereas the first wave after 1945 is well documented in monographs and particularly in dictionaries (of Anglicisms), the more recent immersion is very much in process—it was absolutely essential to have native speakers *in* the countries as participant observers to provide eyewitness reports—however impressionistic and provisional.

For Western European countries in particular there is a considerable amount of shared history, especially in earlier periods. The role of nineteenth-century France and Germany was particularly relevant since they not only adopted a great amount of English lexis in domains such as sports, clothes, and technology, but also handed it on to neighbouring languages (cf. s. 1.1.8).

1.1.2 Origins of influence

All researchers agree that a distinction between American English (AmE) and British English (BrE) provenance is impossible to make with regard to loanwords in European languages in any consistent way. This is for various reasons: loanwords tend to be adapted in the borrowing process, which deletes the distinctive features in those words which have different forms (in spelling and pronunciation) in the two varieties. Moreover, many 'Americanisms' are either transmitted through BrE, or they are automatically adapted to the model dominating English language teaching on the Continent—the British variety. The only criterion left for assigning a word to BrE or AmE is, then, encyclopedic: the adoption of words together with new inventions, concepts, commodities imported from America can provide a clue, but such indications are not conclusive in many cases. To summarize: whereas American influence is increasing worldwide, British transmission is still effective, and there is not enough evidence to provide more than hunches confirming generally held opinions.

1.1.3 Types of influences

Straightforward adoption (in form of loans) is the most common principle followed in most of the languages investigated. Since spoken English has become much more easily accessible, loanwords are now largely pronounced in a way that approximates to the etymon. This is certainly the case with new borrowings, but is also evident in corrections of earlier loanwords transmitted through texts. Renderings (calques) are, by contrast, rarer—and this is true even of most purist languages in which the proportion of calques is admittedly higher than in 'open' societies. Influences on the morphology, syntax, style, and pragmatics of receiving languages are also discernible but are not the objective of this research. They are recorded in individual entries where applicable, but a comprehensive study would be necessary to do justice to these aspects.

1.1.4 Chronology of purist phases

The languages (or better: the societies) included in the research have experienced various phases of relatively restrictive or open and liberal attitudes towards the influx of foreign words; often purist attitudes were specifically directed against English. It is particularly interesting to see in what ways purism was correlated with totalitarian governments, and how language communities divided into different states have sometimes followed quite different policies in the individual territories (cf. s. 1.1.5).

1.1.5 Regional differences

Differences are less likely to be significant between dialects of a language in an individual state than between language communities divided by political boundaries: German in East Germany as compared to West Germany, Switzerland and Austria, Dutch in Holland as compared to Flanders, French in France as compared to Wallonia, and Albanian in Albania as compared to Kosovo exhibit striking differences with regard to Anglicisms, which can be related to historical attitudes and political systems.

1.1.6 Stylistic differences

The varying cultural and political history of the communities investigated has resulted in quite striking differences in the types of adopted Anglicisms, which may be colloquial, formal, archaic, fashionable, common, technical, etc. The age of the adoptions is obviously a very relevant factor, as illustrated by the fact that modern Anglicisms tend either to be technical (in domains like computing) or to be jargon (in fields like pop music, drugs, etc.). In contrast to earlier periods of adoption these stylistic features tend to be shared across linguistic and cultural boundaries, increasingly including Eastern Europe.

1.1.7 Innovation and obsolescence

The English-based lexis is probably among the fastest-changing sections of the national vocabularies; Anglicisms do not usually become part of the core vocabulary and are therefore open to being quick imports (because of the novelty or fashionable appeal of the concepts and words) and equally to being quickly lost (because the things designated go out of use or the terms are replaced by more trendy and attractive ones). The statistics of replacement and obsolescence remain opaque; although there is some influence of linguistic legislation (as in France) the effect greatly depends on the domain. Well-integrated loans suffer less from 'natural' or prescribed obsolescence.

1.1.8 Mediating languages

Modern borrowing is most often straight from English—whether from BrE or AmE, and from written, spoken, or electronic sources. The channels of earlier loans were often more indirect: borrowing might predominantly or exclusively depend on written sources and might be through the language(s) prevalent in the schools and most prestigious in the society. This was French for most of Europe until at least the 1930s, and German for much of northern and eastern Europe until the Second World War (in Albanian Italian transmission predominated, an influence also found in a much weaker form in Croatian). This mediation left unmistakable traces in the spelling, pronunciation, morphology, and meaning of such Anglicisms, often deleting all English features in their form. Moreover, English words might be pronounced *as if* they were French etc., even where French did not mediate.

On the other hand, English handed on many words from 'exotic' languages, mainly those of America, Africa, Asia, and Australia. They are classified as Anglicisms if they retain something English in their form, most often a contrast between their spelling and pronunciation.

1.1.9 English in education

Language teaching is the major (but certainly not the only) source of language contact and most convincingly accounts for the number of Anglicisms, the form of their integration, and their prestige. It is therefore very important to establish the status of English as a school language (also in relation to other languages taught, such as French, German, or Russian), the methods used, the proportion of students affected, and the need for English in tertiary education. Even where this information does not correlate in any straightforward way with the spread of Anglicisms, it will at least describe the conditions which made the adoption or avoidance of English words likely.

1.2 Pronunciation and Spelling

1.2.1 Pronunciation

The phonological system of the receiving language allows us to formulate certain predictions about how loanwords from English are treated. As far as phonemes are concerned there will be five classes of correspondences or non-matches:

- (*a*) near-identity in form (with minor articulatory differences) and distribution, as is often the case with consonants;
- (*b*) near-identity in form, but divergent distribution (e.g. devoicing of stops at the end of syllables in many languages removes the contrast between [d] and [t] etc.);
- (*c*) non-identity because of different numbers of phonemes and contrasts (frequent in vowel systems where the set /ɪːeːɛːæ/ may be different or the short vs. long vowel contrasts absent);

(*d*) gaps in the phonemic system (frequent absence of /ð, θ, w/);
(*e*) mismatches involving the related writing system (misinterpretations of <c>, <ch>, <j>, <w> etc., sometimes combined with (*a*)–(*d*) above).

In addition, there are differences in word stress and intonation which are likely to be carried over, affecting the pronunciation of loans from English.

Whereas the conditions are obviously set by the structural characteristics of the receiving language, and the closeness with which English sounds are imitated is partly determined by competence and attitudes, the framework sketched is identical for languages borrowing under similar (European) conditions. Differences spelt out in the '2.1' subsections are therefore highly significant in a contrastive analysis of Anglicisms in European languages.

1.2.2 Graphemic integration

A major difference between receiving languages is whether they use Latin script or not. If they do not, as in Russian, Bulgarian, and Greek, Anglicisms will be transliterated into the 'native' writing system. Early on, this was frequently done on the basis of written forms of English words, but today transliteration is more likely to be phonemic. However, there is also an increasing tendency to use Latin letters as a supplementary system for certain functions and in certain domains: shop signs, or advertisements in newspapers and on TV may be entirely in English or have at least the product name spelt as in English. If this development continues, the adoption of Anglicisms may become easier and even less restricted. In this book (and in the *Dictionary of European Anglicisms*) Anglicisms in Russian, Bulgarian, and Greek have all been transliterated to Roman script for ease of English readers. The systems used are described in the relevant chapters.

The other languages have many items in which Latin graphemes correlate with phonemes corresponding closely to their English equivalents. Such words are taken over without changes <bit, fit>. However, there are three problem cases:

(*a*) Certain English graphemes are missing or at least extremely rare in the borrowing language so that grapheme replacement may occur (<k>, <w>);
(*b*) Some English graphemes or combinations are correlated with different phonemes; the receiving language may then:
  (i) respell in order to safeguard a (close-to) English pronunciation—a system now rare even in Polish, but still normally practised in Czech, and now very uncommon in Germanic languages (even though recent spelling reform proposals have affected some long-established Anglicisms in Norwegian and German);
  (ii) retain the English spelling and risk that such words are mispronounced (most pronunciations of this sort are now heavily stigmatized);
  (iii) replace an old spelling (plus pronunciation) by a new 'more correct' adoption.

When the number of loanwords was few and competence in English restricted in the community, various practices were followed, often with typical national characteristics (which also allow us to detect mediation, s. 1.8) but recent loans tend to follow (*b*ii)—so that mediation is not evident on formal grounds and languages are beginning to have variant correlations of graphemes and phonemes (a state of affairs which had existed for words from French for a long time). Only German now employs capitalization to indicate nouns; accordingly, substantival loanwords are capitalized.

1.3 Morphology

1.3.1 Introduction

As far as inflexion is concerned, all European languages categorize nouns (the prevailing class among loanwords) according either to gender or to declension class or both; adjectives often remain uninflected, especially in predicative use; verbs are more or less automatically transferred to the regular class(es). Patterns of word formation greatly diverge between English and most European languages and there is a noticeable impact on the structure of most borrowing languages of calquing.

1.3.2 Nouns

Nouns form the largest class of loanwords (commonly over 80 per cent); most of these are terms taken over as names for new things, inventions, and concepts. Their integration can be seen from their adaptation in the following respects:

(*a*) Gender: European languages tend to have two or three grammatical genders which can, but need not, correlate with natural gender. Only quotation words (outside a syntactical frame) can do without gender allocation; a few words are also used in their plural form only, so that the gender may remain doubtful. Since various formal and semantic factors influence gender allocation, some words alternate, leaving gender open to personal choice or regional preference. In very few cases different genders reflect semantic distinctions (as in German *Single*);

(*b*) Case inflections are attributed more or less automatically after gender and noun class have been assigned. So is plural formation, a category which is more important since it is obligatory even in languages which have reduced or non-existent case marking. Integration appears to have decreased over time or to take some time: for example early loanwords in German are often inflected according to native patterns, whereas recent adoptions mostly retain English *-s* (apart from words ending in *-er*). Other languages have native inflexion throughout.

1.3.3–4 Adjectives and adverbs

Adjectives are normally inflected, especially in attributive use, but they exhibit various restrictions in case inflexion and comparison. Inflectability is often

achieved by addition of native derivative suffixes (or suffix replacement). Uninflected forms survive especially in predicative use (where the distinction from
adverbs may be difficult) and in modification where they are equivalent to first or
(in Romance languages) second parts of compounds.

1.3.5 Verbs

All verbs are transferred to morphologically simple classes so that obligatory
inflexions can be added more or less automatically (compare the identical procedure in the integration of borrowed verbs in English). Note, however, that the
number of verbs borrowed straight from English is comparatively small in all
European languages and that the number of verbs derived (by way of suffixes,
often zero) in the individual languages may well surpass direct loans (a decision on
the origin is often not possible).

1.3.6 Derivation

1.3.6.1 Gender specification

Gender is not only marked by inflexion but—more or less obligatorily—by gender-
specific suffixes, most often contrastively signalling feminines (cf. English *-ess*). For
new loans, the addition of otherwise obligatory suffixes (such as German *-in*,
Bulgarian *-ka*) can sound awkward or facetious; their unnoted use therefore
indicates full integration.

1.3.6.2 Agent nouns

All languages in the study have derivational patterns to express 'somebody who
does something'; denominal formations (E *forester*) are rarer than deverbal ones
(*baker*), and there are ambiguous cases (*fisher*). Loanwords ending in *-er*, *-ist*, and
-man (f. *-ess*) are often taken over unchanged, sometimes without the English
morpheme being recognized. Since *-er* is identical in form and function in Germanic languages, it is often impossible to decide whether *-er* words are borrowed
or independently (back-)derived. In French, *-eur* is normally substituted, an element also used in suffix replacement in Slavic languages. Other replacements (for
instance in French and Balkanic languages) include *-ist* and *-man* which often
result in pseudo-Anglicisms (*futbalist*, *tennisman*).

1.3.6.3 Denominal verbs

As indicated under s. 1.3.5 above, all languages in the sample have relevant
derivational patterns and it is not always possible to decide whether verbs are
derived or borrowed.

1.3.6.4 New adjectives

Some languages have obligatory uses for adjectives; for instance, when calquing
n.+ n. compounds the modifying element must traditionally be rendered by an
adjective in Slavic and Romance languages. Although word-formation structures

are changing under the impact of English, there is still a noteworthy number of new adjectives derived in these languages. In others, their number is much smaller, being mainly restricted to suffix substitutions in English adjectives and a few new derivatives, often of a colloquial or facetious character.

1.3.6.5 Deadjectival nouns

English loanwords in *-ness* are normally taken over complete (though their number is notably smaller than that of the adjectives on which they are based). By contrast, words in *-ity* have a Romance stem and tend to be interpreted as internationalisms, with 'national' pronunciations and forms of the *-ity* suffix employed. Independent derivatives from borrowed adjectives (e.g. Ge *-heit* or Slavic *-(n)ost*) appear to be quite rare.

1.3.7 Compounds and combining forms

Compounds are an ill-defined category in English. Combinations of two or more free morphemes are taken over regardless of their compound status if they form a semantic entity (*football, beach volleyball, new look,* etc.)—unless they are shortened according to national conventions (e.g. to the first element in Romance). Loanwords become available for use in compounds very soon after their adoption if the receiving language has the same pattern—it is therefore useless to provide a full list of recorded *-fan* and *-shop* compounds in, say, German. It is also impossible to say for many English-looking compounds in Germanic languages whether they are borrowed, semi-calques, or independently formed from English elements (or genetically related items in the receiving languages). However, the great number of compound loanwords has begun to change word-formation patterns in Slavic and Romance languages (cf. Picone 1996). The pattern is further strengthened by internationalisms of the *bio* + *graphy* type which are formed on the same principle.

1.3.8 Calques

The adoption of English words is often in translated form, or other renderings through native means; this procedure is preferred by purists and often advocated by language academies. In general, such substitutions can be arranged on a cline of morphological and semantic equivalence with the etymon:

(*a*) loan translation—the perfect rendering of constituents (*weekend* = German *Wochen* + *ende*);

(*b*) loan rendition—a rendering which deviates from the *meaning* (*skyscraper* = *Wolken* ('cloud') + *kratzer*) or morphology, as in n.1 + n.2 compounds in Romance languages which have n.2 + adj.1 or n.2 + *de* + n.1 calques;

(*c*) loan creation—a free rendering which is formally independent of the etymon (but can be proved to be stimulated by it), such as German *Nietenhose*, an unsuccessful attempt to replace (*blue*) *jeans*.

An alternative strategy for avoiding loanwords is to extend the meaning of a native word (simple or compound) by a foreign sense. This will be termed semantic calque, as in frequent uses of native equivalents of the rodent 'mouse' transferred to the computer item.

1.4 How borrowing affects the meaning of loanwords

An item is borrowed in a specific situation and linguistic context. This usually means that only one sense (of polysemic or homonymous etymons) is involved. Since the word is borrowed in a specific situation, the meaning may be further narrowed down semantically (being more specific), referentially (designating a smaller range of objects), stylistically, socially, or connotationally. All these considerations are universal at least in natural speech/borrowing and thus apply to all the languages here treated. What is different is the situation but also the semantic fields into which the new item is adopted and in which it is defined by contrasts with homoeonyms (words of similar meaning).

This accommodation continues after the word is borrowed. Unless the Anglicism remains a synonym to a native word it may develop distinctive semantic features (normally further restricting its meaning) and it may develop new meanings by contextual restrictions, metaphorical and metonymic applications, euphemistic or facetious uses, and other developments also visible in native words.

A partial exception is the terminological use of a loanword in which the borrowing is justified by a terminological gap and language planning is employed to ensure that the meaning remains constant in order to provide a stable translation equivalent (often in a relationship involving more languages than two, as in international institutions).

Meaning is possibly the most difficult aspect to compare across cultures and language boundaries. Strictly speaking, meaning is always established contrastively, i.e. it functions within a (dialect, sociolect of a) language, equivalence being established, at best, through the referents, i.e. objects and concepts. If we want to take such fundamental objections seriously, there can be no translation, and no equivalence in dictionaries, least of all in one involving sixteen languages. On the other hand there is an obvious semantic overlap of senses of English etymons with those found in loanwords which makes it possible to identify (with some qualms) individual meanings with the meaning classifications in the *Concise Oxford Dictionary* (*COD*). And this is the convention we adopt both here and in the *Dictionary of European Anglicisms*. It would, however, distort the evidence to take over the *COD*'s definitions unchanged. (Newly developed meanings of loanwords are outside the *COD* scheme and are noted as additional by the use of a '+' sign, as in the *Dictionary of European Anglicisms*.)

1.5 Usage

The restrictions sketched for meaning above also hold for usage; they are caused by the selective intentions of the borrowing process as well as the integration into the stylistic system of the receiving language. Unless usage is strictly terminological (and thus not affected by borrowing) the very fact that a loanword is 'foreign' determines its special status, thus contrasting with the normal, everyday usage in the source language. This is also true of fashionable imports into the colloquial language or slang in many languages where these new adoptions contrast with the older native lexis.

The compilation of the *Dictionary of European Anglicisms* initially aimed at a documentation of frequent and comparatively neutral items expected to be known to a majority of users of the receiving language. The fact that more and more additions were offered by collaborators from restricted vocabularies has shifted the focus somewhat so that the majority of the words listed can now not be claimed to be actively employed by (or even passively known to) every user, however well educated and widely interested. The special lexis now included to a greater extent than initially intended consists of at least three sections:

(*a*) technical terms from fields like economics, medicine, and especially computing;
(*b*) the jargon of pop music, drugs, etc.;
(*c*) slang.

Another marginal type of lexis is represented by words marked 'archaic' or 'historical'. However, the reasons for their inclusion in the *Dictionary of European Anglicisms* are different. Apart from their interest for cultural history, these items are indispensable for the full documentation of mediating languages: to explain the present-day distribution of, say, *sleeper* 'railway tie' it is relevant to know that the word was found in nineteenth-century German even though it is totally unknown today.

1.6 Forms of linguistic borrowing

For the individual chapters it was thought preferable to extract the discussion of the topic from s. 1.3.8, to present in greater detail illustrative specimens and point to successes and failures. In order to supplement the *Dictionary of European Anglicisms* data which concentrate on loanwords, this selection is focused on calques. Not all of the purist attempts to replace Anglicisms have proved successful, so each category will be subdivided according to the degree to which replacements were accepted by the speech community.

1.7 The future of Anglicisms

All commentators agree that the recent influx of English words is unprecedented in European history—although it can still not compare with the massive impact of French, especially in the eighteenth and nineteenth centuries. It is very likely that Anglicisms will continue to increase, not only in countries that have been retarded by political and ideological restrictions, mainly in Eastern Europe. It is also likely that other linguistic levels outside lexis will be increasingly affected. The impact is already clearly apparent in phonology (where marginal phonemes imported through great numbers of Anglicisms from spoken English have become accepted, such as /ei/ and /ou/ in German) and in morphology (where -s plurals are becoming normal and compounds on the English pattern are losing their foreignness). Even more drastic changes are under way in the import of an additional writing system, with English loanwords promoting the acceptability of Latin script in communities using different alphabets.

1.8 Research

The full documentation of existing research is found in the accompanying *Annotated Bibliography of European Anglicisms*. This reflects how unevenly the field has been covered. Whereas it was impossible to compile any relevant titles for Albanian, the number of publications had to be strictly limited for Dutch or German (from over 1,000 titles in German the most important had to be selected in a difficult and possibly subjective procedure). The present volume will provide a stimulus, we hope, for further research in the field—much spadework still remains to be done and relevant pilot studies can be undertaken with a minimum of technical equipment, possibly in the form of well-supervised MA theses and doctorates in countries which have the greatest need for reliable data.

1.9 Bibliography

PICONE, MICHAEL DAVID (1996), *Anglicisms, Neologisms and Dynamic French* (Amsterdam: Benjamins).
VIERECK, WOLFGANG, and BALD, WOLF-DIETRICH (eds.) (1986), *English in Contact with Other Languages: Studies in Honour of Broder Carstensen on the Occasion of his 60th Birthday* (Budapest: Akadémiai Kiadó).

2

GERMAN

Ulrich Busse and Manfred Görlach

2.1 History of language contact: historical and sociocultural factors

2.1.1 Chronology of intensive influences

(*DtFWb* 1986; Ganz 1957; Stanforth 1968; Stiven 1936; W. Viereck 1986)

Cultural exchange between Britain and Germany has always been intensive—it dates back to the fifth century when the Germanic settlers who conquered England came from what is now northern Germany and southern Denmark, and the eighth century when much of Germany was Christianized by Irishmen and Englishmen (giving us the words *heilig* 'holy' and *Heiland* 'saviour'). English loanwords in the Late Middle Ages were infrequent and restricted to certain domains, e.g. to seafaring. In connection with the Hanseatic League such words as *Boot*, *Lotse* (cf. archaic *lodesman*), and *Dock* came into German. Many of these loans are now completely assimilated and almost unrecognizable as loans to the average speaker of German. Coinciding with the takeover of some terms relating to the English political system in the mid-seventeenth century, Anglo-German language contacts became closer and were followed by six main stages of lexical borrowing:

1. In the eighteenth century the influence of English literature, social practices, historical and philosophical writings, and the cultural impact in architecture, gardening, pottery, etc. and in the sciences/technology were at a peak.
2. In the nineteenth century the Industrial Revolution was led by Britain world-wide, and British technological methods in shipbuilding, railway technology,

The chapter is based on our work on the *Dictionary of European Anglicisms* and on summaries of our earlier research (esp. Busse 1993, 1995, 1998 and Görlach 1994*a*, 1994*b*, 1996, 1997*a*). The text was circulated to other contributors to the dictionary in 1997.

mining, steel production, weaving, and clothmaking became universally accepted, together with their designations, in the greater part of Europe.

3. In the late nineteenth century a certain degree of Anglomania affected all European countries in the domain of social life; this is particularly obvious in various types of sports imported from Britain, like football, golf, tennis, and horse-racing, but is also evident from the large number of designations for breeds of dogs, cattle, drinks, clothing, etc.

4. The early twentieth century saw the entry of AmE in fields like music, dance, motor cars, and aviation.

5. After 1945, as elsewhere in Europe, the impact of English, in BrE or AmE form, became massive. In (western) Germany, this can partly be explained as a reaction to the xenophobic Nazi system, which had tried to be largely self-sufficient economically—and linguistically/culturally (but cf. s. 2.1.4, point 3). The impact of the Anglo-American re-education policy was reflected in newspapers, magazines, plays, films, and popular music. Since the immediate post-war phase the political and cultural orientation towards the United States has led to a broad and steadily growing influx of Anglo-American loanwords (but cf. s. 2.1.5).

6. Since the 1990s the huge impact of American culture and its linguistic reflexes have become more intense. Worldwide communication via the Internet, globalization of national economies resulting in multinational corporations, and commercial television with its advertisements and videoclips have led to a new dimension of lexical borrowings and code-switching, at least in the technical languages of business and commerce, computing, advertising, and youth language. This unabashed influx has partly provoked hostile reactions (cf. s. 2.1.4, point 4).

2.1.2 Origins of influence
(Wächtler 1980)

In the *Dictionary of European Anglicisms* the term 'E' serves as a superordinate term incorporating borrowings from Britain as well as from the United States and from other English-speaking countries. Methodologically it is often impossible to differentiate between Briticisms and Americanisms, especially since the forms of almost all loanwords are identical and many words which originated in America were *mediated* through BrE as a consequence of BrE norms dominating in German schools. Within three phases (up to the First World War, the inter-war years, and after 1945) the impact of BrE steadily declined, so that we can assume a post-war dominance of AmE, but this statement must be based on content and cultural history rather than on formal criteria.

2.1.3 Types of influence

Language contact can influence all levels of language—spelling, pronunciation, morphology, syntax, pragmatics—and, particularly, vocabulary. In lexical borrowing, units of different size (from morphemes to sentences) can be affected. The types of integration can be arranged from 'most foreign' to 'most native', as detailed in s. 2.6 below.

It is usually the case that the importation of loanwords brings with it a change in spelling, pronunciation, and morphology; whether this impact adds permanent features to the receiving language depends on the number of loans and their degree of integration (reflecting the closeness of the contact and attitudes of the affected speech community).

English influences present a special problem where English words are coined from Latin/Greek elements and are commonly treated as 'internationalisms' by the receiver languages, that is, they are fully integrated on the basis of earlier internationalisms from other sources. These loanwords are excluded from the *Dictionary of European Anglicisms* and from our discussion: *telegram, television, telephone,* or *transistor* have nothing English in their German form. Therefore, only words like *teenager* which are characterized by their foreign spelling, pronunciation, and/ or morphology are here named 'Anglicisms'. This definition also excludes the field of calques: *Kreuzworträtsel* is a translation from English *crossword puzzle*—but its form is entirely German.

2.1.4 Chronology of purist phases
(Kirkness 1975)

Languages, or rather their users, can react in very different ways to the influence of other languages. For centuries, Latin was perceived in Germany (and in much of contemporary Europe) as the great model when it came to developing a fully functional and 'polite' standard language with sufficient prestige to replace Latin words in mostly scholarly registers (Munske 1982; Munske and Kirkness 1996)— but there were of course reactions against misuse and overuse of these loanwords. French presented more of a problem to the language-conscious writers who were intent on building a fully developed language, since in the eighteenth century it was on its way to replacing German as a *spoken* means of communication among the well-to-do and educated. Purism in Germany at that time was therefore not perceived as xenophobic or as an academic eccentricity, but was widely accepted as a necessity and a national obligation. By contrast, English as a source of foreignisms entered the field quite late: Kinderling's list of Anglicisms of 1795 contained only twelve words: namely *Bill, Bombast, Dogge, Frack, Guinee, Jury, Lord, Mops, Park, Pudding, Quäker, Spleen* (Dunger 1909: 12).

In Germany the nineteenth century was the heyday of dictionaries of foreign words (*Fremdwörterbücher*), many intended as guides on how best to avoid such words by providing native German equivalents (Kirkness 1984). Dunger (1909: 6) lists eighty-three such books, of which only a handful are known to specialists today, but the question was felt to be urgent enough for the famous Saxon socialist Wilhelm Liebknecht to compile such a dictionary for use among the workers while he was imprisoned for anti-state activities (Liebknecht 1912, 1st pub. 1876, of which 10,000 copies were printed and sold by 1880; 7th edn. 1893, 13th edn. 1912, 22nd edn. 1953, GDR edition).

When von Stephan 'Germanized' the terminology of the Post Office in 1875, replacing some 700 items of French provenance, and Sarrazin followed between 1886 and 1893 with the replacement of some 1,300 designations of railway terminology, mostly from French, there was still apparently little reason to act against English terms (industrialists who might have seen a linguistic threat of Anglicisms in their domain appear not to have been so much concerned). However, when Dunger gave his notorious talk 'Against Anglomania in the German Language' in 1899 (revised and expanded in Dunger 1909), he strongly objected to language mixing and to the excessive use of Anglicisms particularly in terms relating to society, food and drink, dress and clothing, trade, sailors' language, traffic and public life, technology and science. He singled out for special concern the field of sports, discussing in detail football, tennis, cycling, rowing, sailing, motoring, and horse-racing and appending lists of some 165 English tennis terms and 84 football expressions with German equivalents; the latter were suggested by the *Deutscher Sprachverein* and were made available in poster form for display in tennis and football clubs asking members to use the German terms exclusively. It is interesting to find that in football almost all the proposed translations are still in use (unless changes of rules have made the terms superfluous)—but that the Anglicisms under attack largely survive (at least as alternatives) in Austria and Switzerland. In the 1980s most of the tennis terminology was re-Anglicized in Germany.

The massive impact of foreign languages, formerly of French and later of English, on individual European languages led to various allergic reactions which can be correlated with the phases of lexical borrowing mentioned above (cf. s. 2.1.1):

1. German resistance to foreign words was directed mainly against French in the seventeenth and eighteenth centuries, when the purity of German came to be seen as a necessary quality of the emergent standard language. This concern is illustrated by the works of pre-eminent scholars, philosophers, and writers such as Adelung, Gottsched, Klopstock, Leibniz, and Opitz.

2. The 'Allgemeiner Deutscher Sprachverein', founded in 1885, had a clearly purist programme. Hermann Dunger was one of the leading activists who spoke out against the predominance of English in German. Reactions against foreign words came to include English in the fields of sports in particular around 1900 when the earlier purge of French loanwords was extended to domains affected by English. Until the First World War the general tenor was purist, but not nationalistic and chauvinistic—as it later came to be, epitomized in Engel's dictionary programmatically entitled *Entwelschung* 'De-alienization' (1918). However, these differences were in degree, rather than in kind. Ethnic or even racist tenor, of which Engel is an extreme example, starts dominating in the 1920s.

3. In the 1930s the Nazi ideology saw the impact of American lifestyle, mainly in the fields of music, literature, and liberal thought, as particularly dangerous to the German psyche. The aspirations of the Sprachverein and the Nazi regime, however, finally became incompatible, because the Nazi rulers were well aware of the force of foreign words for the purposes of propaganda, and

with the decree of 11 November 1940 Hitler himself prohibited the witch-hunt of foreignisms (cf. von Polenz 1967). As a consequence of this the Anglicisms in the 1941 *Duden* edition were left unscathed (cf. Busse 1993: 63–5).

4. The growing impact of Anglo-American language and culture has recently led to the foundation of a new puristic society, i.e. 'Verein zur Wahrung der deutschen Sprache' (now renamed 'Verein deutsche Sprache') and the 'Gesellschaft für deutsche Sprache', Wiesbaden, has installed a commission to work out guidelines for a 'Better German'. However, it is too early to say whether such reactions will prove to have a permanent effect.

2.1.5 Regional differences

(Lehnert 1986, 1990; K. Viereck 1986)

The fact that Germany was unified as late as 1871 (and came to be divided again, 1949–90), and the existence of German-speaking communities outside the nation state (now mainly in Austria, Switzerland, Liechtenstein, Luxembourg, and Belgium) has meant that loanwords did not spread evenly throughout the German-speaking territories and that purist measures of national(istic) language planning either did not affect communities outside Germany at all, or did so in more restricted and delayed forms. For instance, in Austrian football terminology *corner*, *goal*, *hands*, *out*, and *penalty* are still the usual words—long since replaced by native equivalents in German German. The political regime in East Germany (1949–90) was opposed to Anglicisms, but could not really stop their spread, which was, however, slightly restricted in number and lagging behind in time in comparison to western Germany (Lehnert 1990). In some cases, however, Anglicisms in the GDR developed special meanings that were restricted to eastern Germany.

Table 2.1. Geographical and geopolitical variation (N : S, E : W)

North	South
Schlips 'neck tie'	*Krawatte, (Selbst)binder* 'tie'
Tunnel 'tunnel'	*Tunell* 'tunnel'
Straßenbahn 'tram'	*Tram(-bahn, -way)* 'tram'
Hand [hant] 'hands'	*Hands* 'hands'
Ecke, Eckstoß 'corner, -kick'	*Corner, Cornerkick* 'corner, -kick'
West	**East**
Nietenhosen (>blue jeans)	*Niethose* 'blue jeans'
Fruchtsaft 'juice'	*Juice* 'juice'
Brathähnchen (N) 'roasted ch.'	*Broiler* 'roasted chicken'
Brathendl (S) 'roasted chicken'	
—	*Dispatcher, Festival, Kombine* ('harvester'), *Meeting* (in politics) (special meanings restricted to the former GDR through Russian transmission)

2.1.6 Stylistic differences

(Carstensen and Galinski 1975; Pfitzner 1978)

Anglicisms have from the beginning dominated in two registers—the technical and the colloquial. The first category ranges from terms adopted to designate industrial processes and products in the nineteenth century to sports expressions and nowadays to highly specialized items in pop music, computer technology, and drug vocabulary, whereas fashionable colloquialisms are found in all fields, but are most frequent in journalese (including advertising) and in youth language. Recent years have seen a drastic increase in non-integrated English words, many of which are apparently not intended as loanwords but are to be interpreted as instances of code-switching used by the individual writer (or speaker) to draw attention to the form of the text. Wordplay involving English elements has also become quite common (Görlach 1994b).

2.1.7 Innovation and obsolescence

There has never been a statistical account of how many loanwords there were in any given period of German, but Busse (1993) has provided valuable statistics on the number of Anglicisms included in various editions of the German *Duden* dictionary[1]. His findings can be summarized as follows.

The total percentage of Anglicisms rose from 1.36 per cent in 1880 (385 items out of 28,300 headwords) to a modest 3.46 per cent in the 1986 West German *Duden* (3,746 Anglicisms out of 108,100 entries) and to 2.77 per cent in the 1985 East German *Duden* (2,074 Anglicisms out of 74,900 entries). Only items marked 'from English' and semi-calques were taken into account. If individual editions are compared to each other, particularly high percentages of Anglicisms are found in those of 1915, 1941, and 1973 (FRG).

There were a few losses, too. Anglicisms were no longer needed because

(a) the object or concept they designate had become obsolete (as happened to terms for vehicles like *brougham*, *gig*, *tilbury*);
(b) they were replaced by a calque (nineteenth-century *maiden speech* by *Jungfernrede*); or
(c) they were replaced by another Anglicism (*rookery* by *slum*; *teenager* presently being pushed out by *kids*).

[1] There is no convincing method for describing the diachronic growth of Anglicisms. Large text corpora of sufficient time depth and distinguished according to text type are not available (not even for German) to account for the increasing token frequencies, nor is the use of dictionaries unproblematic in a count of types. Busse's (1993) solution was to compare successive editions of the *Duden*, a reference book whose data can be considered as representative in a normative/prescriptive sense. However, obsolete items tend to be carried over from earlier editions, and *Duden* does not distinguish carefully enough between loanwords on the one hand and foreignisms/quotation words on the other. (Compare the interesting attempt in Liebknecht 1912 to distinguish the two groups by way of typeface—but the reasons for Liebknecht's classification and the reliability of his sources remain opaque.) However, the chronological register of the *DtFWB* (vii. 433–528) does provide a worthwhile insight. Von Polenz (1991–9) has used it and the other registers to good effect in his new language history (cf. 1994: ii. 78–9, 1999: iii. 391–411, esp. 393).

Older dictionaries (like Liebknecht 1912) and monographs devoted to Anglicisms (like Dunger 1909) provide valuable information about the lexical turnover in the area under investigation. Thus, of the 148 Anglicisms mentioned as current by Dunger (1909: 12), some 28 are no longer common in German, 11 are rare, 11 are foreignisms, and at least 14 are not felt to be English. This leaves us with some 94 survivors (= 63.5 per cent)—many of which have by now lost much of their Englishness in spelling and pronunciation.

It also happens that a word becomes obsolete at one point in time, but that the same item is reborrowed with a different meaning (e.g. *twist*)—similarly a word long replaced by a native term can reappear as a fashionable equivalent (as has happened to some German football and tennis terminology, consider the re-importation of *[goal]keeper*).

2.1.8 Mediating languages

Anglicisms were often not borrowed straight from English but transmitted via French ('Ge' indicates that the secondary transmission was through German):

	Ge	Nw	Rm	Rs	Po	Gr
beefsteak	x	—	x	x	Ge	x
budget	x	x	x	x	—	x
jury	x	x	x	x	x	—
riding coat	x	x	x	x	x	x
wagon	x	x	x	Ge	—	It

German also served as a transmitter of English terms to other languages:

	Rm	Rs	Po	Cr	Bg	Hu
cake(s)	x	x	x	x	x	x
coke(s)	x	x	x	x	x	—
drop(s)	x	—	x	x	x	x

2.1.9 English in education

(Christ and Hüllen 1995; Christ 1995; Lehberger 1995)

The notable rise of English loanwords in the nineteenth century was also connected with the increase of English as a school language in Germany. French was still dominant in the nineteenth century (and remained the obligatory first modern language until 1935 in *Gymnasien* (grammar schools)), but the impact of English grew from the 1830s on. It is significant that J. E. Gailer's important polyglot book, *Neuer Orbis Pictus* of 1833, did not include English versions, but the second edition of 1835 did, pushing Latin from its parallel-column position. In the late nineteenth century English rose to a central position in modern language teaching.

The 'modern' methods of Ollendorf, Becker, Toussaint and Langenscheidt, Son-
nenschein, Plate and Plötze were widely copied for textbooks on French and
German in Britain and elsewhere, and Mätzner's monumental English grammar
was accorded the rank of the best of its kind ever written.

These developments did not necessarily lead to many new loans, but they
certainly contributed to a much enlarged section of the educated German population accepting English as a language on a par with French and becoming ready to
adopt Anglicisms as part of a fashionable lifestyle.

The general introduction of English as the first foreign language in most German
schools after 1945 led to an unprecedented proportion of speakers of English in the
(West) German community. From the 1960s on, all students, in all types of
German schools, had some English taught to them between the ages of 10 and
19. Although this does not mean that all these are fluent speakers of English, they
certainly have sufficient competence to analyse complex loanwords and to adopt a
near-native pronunciation—if they choose to.[2]

Although English teaching was much more limited in the East, the popularity of
the language, and its ubiquitousness in domains like pop music, technology, and
the media (e.g. on western TV), meant that the linguistic deficits arising from a lack
of formal education had not resulted in conspicuous differences as far as Anglicisms were concerned when German unity came in 1990.

2.2 Pronunciation and spelling

2.2.1 Pronunciation

The pronunciation of English loans in German is a complex problem to unravel,
but the following factors seem to be most relevant: the age of the loan, its degree of
popularity, whether the source is written or acoustic (and often, but not necessarily
as a consequence, its orthographic and/or phonemic assimilation), and sociolinguistic criteria such as the age of the language users and their knowledge of
English.

The phonological system of the two languages and the articulation of individual
sounds differ quite considerably. Older loans tend to be fully assimilated, that is,
English phonemes are replaced by their nearest German equivalents. More recent
(and more special) loanwords normally retain the English pronunciation as far as
possible, which can result in the acceptance of peripheral phonemes, as in *laser*
[leiza] in contrast to *Leser* 'reader' [le:za] and in *soul* [soul] in contrast to *Sole*
'brine' [zo:lə].

---

[2] No reliable statistics are available to compare the relative national competences in English;
impressionistically, Norway, Sweden, Denmark, and the Netherlands appear to lead the field, followed
by Germany, with Romance and Slavic languages trailing behind at a distance. At least a partial
explanation may be seen in the fact that the Scandinavian countries and the Netherlands show
Anglo-American TV programmes in the original language, rather than in dubbed versions as in
Germany. This extended 'vicarious' exposure to authentic English may further a more native-like
pronunciation. (However, see recent statistics adduced in Graddol 2001.)

Apart from differences in the inventory, the following phonotactic differences are important:

1. stops and fricatives are regularly devoiced at the end of German words, so that /-d/-t/, /-b/-p/, /-g/-k/ are merged;
2. initial /z-/ and word-final /-s/ do not contrast; only medially is there an opposition of /s/ vs. /z/;
3. English morpheme-initial /s-/ combinations correspond to German /š-/ in /sl-, sm-, sn-, sp-, st-, sw-/.

There are relatively few differences between English and German in word-stress patterns.

As far as articulation is concerned, standard German lacks the allophony of /l/ (as in *all* vs. *lord*), has different forms of /r/, and lacks unaspirated stops in environments like /sp-/ etc. These subphonemic differences present problems for language teaching but they do not affect the borrowing process and the subsequent integration. Adoption of English variants of /l, r/ in a German context is largely considered a mark of affectation.

Misleadingly, the German grapheme <w> stands for /v/, whereas <v> represents both /v/ and /f/; since German has no /w/, adaptation as /v/ is common in English loanwords.

Since German is r-full, postvocalic /r/ is normally pronounced at least in older and more popular loans in stressed syllables. Most other phonetic adaptations are below the level of speaker/listener awareness.

The pronunciation of early (pre-1914) loans tends to exhibit one of the following characteristics:

1. The loanword was borrowed from written English, and the pronunciation is German as in *Puck* or *Humbug* [u];
2. the English form fully agreed with German sound structure so that no difficulty arose, as in *Test*;
3. in words with minor differences in phonemes, these were automatically identified with their German equivalents, as in *hot* [o].
   Note that English /ɑ/ was variously interpreted as /a/ or /o/ as in *Frack* and *baxen* > *boxen*, and /ʌ/ as /ö/ or /a/—the /ö/ pronunciation was suggested by eighteenth-century German grammarians and popularized by the dominant position of Langenscheidt dictionaries which indicated [ʌ] as [œ] (*Bluff*, *Curry*, *Cutter*; this pronunciation is now obsolescent except in a few words);
4. un-German combinations were often adapted to the German system: thus *Schlips* [šl-], formerly also spelt *Shlips*, from *slip(s)*; cf. the spelling in *Schal*, formerly *shawl*; *cakes* became *Keks* and *coke(s)* became *Koks*;
5. word-initial /dʒ/ is often pronounced [ʒ, tʃ, ʃ] or, according to the spelling, [j] as in *Jockey*, *Job*, *Joker*;
6. word-final /b, d, g/ are devoiced, as is /dʒ/; in a few cases (*plunger*, Ge *Plunscher*) this process is reflected in spelling; both *Dredge* and *Dretsche* are attested in German dictionaries;

7. some words were adopted via French, as revealed in their pronunciation (*Budget* [bydʒeː], *Beefsteak*, formerly [bœfʃtek] (cf. the forms transmitted through German to Polish and Russian), *Jury* [ʒyriː] *Tunell* and *Waggon* [vagɔn]).

When spoken English became more widely accessible, many pronunciations which were felt to be mistakes were replaced by those closer to the source ([kloːn] > [klaun] *clown*), but less obvious deviances are still quite common—thus [oː] is the only form for *Bowle* 'punch', *Koks* 'coke', and still an option for *Soul* [oː ~ oʊ]; [eː] only is found in *Keks* ('biscuit', from *cake*), and is still possible for *Laser* [eː ~ eɪ]. In fact, /oʊ/ and /eɪ/ are still marginal phonemes in present-day German, being restricted to contrasts involving loanwords and distinguished by educated speakers in pairs like *Laser* vs. *Leser* 'reader' or *Pole* (*Position*) vs. *Pol* (in electricity or geography).

Other marginal phonemic changes are possibly under way with speakers beginning to use English distributions of sounds. Thus *Spott* [špot] 'derision' now contrasts with *Spot* [spot] 'commercial', and *Sound* [zaunt] is now increasingly pronounced [saund], i.e. the English way.

Note that the rules given do not apply to all German dialects in the same way: many have no exact equivalence of the /s/ : /z/, or /p/ : /b/ contrast, and [sl-] etc. is common morpheme-initially in Low German in northern Germany.

Since adaptation is always possible, it is difficult to say how much the adoption of a word may be delayed by its phonological structure. Such blocking seems to be the case with German *Thriller*: since /θ/ is not available, /sr-/ is preferred, although it is an un-German cluster (and stigmatized); the alternative /tr-/ is not widely used.

2.2.2 Graphemic integration

(Langner 1995)

Since German uses the same alphabetical system as English and there are no modified letters in the English alphabet, the adoption of the English spelling was possible in principle for all Anglicisms. The foreignness of English loanwords results, then, from unusual combinations of letters such as <sh, wh, oa>, but especially from the sounds they signify in an un-German way.

Early loans may have been borrowed from written texts so that problems did not arise (the words are then pronounced according to German rules): *Puck* [puk]. Moreover, in many cases spelling, or its normalization according to German rules, can indicate the age of the loan. Germanized spellings particularly occur in three areas (Busse 1993: 180–205):

1. word-initial German <k> for E <c>
   substitution: *Keks* < *cakes*, *Koks* < *coke(s)*, *kraul(en)* < *crawl* (older loans)
   coexistence: *Cord/Kord, Clan/Klan, Go-cart/Go-kart*
   reborrowing: *Clipper/Klipper* 'aeroplane'/'ship', *Cutter/Kutter* [œ/a] in film industry/[u] 'ship'
   retention: *Camping, Callgirl, Cartoon, Cocktail* (comparatively recent loans)

2. word-initial German <sch> for E <sh>
   substitution: *Schock, Schal, Schelf* (older loans)
   coexistence: *Shredder/Schredder, Shampoo/Schampon*
   retention: *Show, Shopping, T-Shirt* (recent loans)
3. word-final German <ß> for E <ss>
   Business, Cleverness, Dress, Fitness, and *Stress* are now more common than
   the forms ending in <-ß> (and <-ss> is now the only choice—for all words—
   after the latest spelling reform of 1997). In the latest *Duden* edition (1996) all
   orthographic changes are highlighted by means of red print. Heller (1996)
   provides a succinct wordlist of items (including Anglicisms) affected by the
   spelling reform.

   The use of specifically German graphemes is restricted: <ä> appears in the old
loan words *Quäker*, and *dränieren* and (as an obsolete spelling) *tränieren*. Plurals in
words ending in *-y* vary: *Babies/Babys* (Carstensen 1982: 200–15; Busse 1993:
170–9). The spelling reform now prescribes the *ys*-plural; i.e. *Partys, Shantys,
Whisk(e)ys*, etc.
   Where the pronunciation of a word did not agree with the phoneme–grapheme
relations in German, the spelling was commonly adapted to German conventions
in early loans: *strike* was adopted as *Shtreik* (a strange quasi-German spelling
recorded in Dunger 1909: 12) > *Streik; punch* to *Punsch*. Various early spellings are
also attested for *Koks* (*Cokes, Coaks, Kohks*). After 1945, the English spelling was
commonly retained, so that the correlation between spelling and pronunciation is
felt to be highly irregular: if German rules were rigorously followed *butterfly*
should be pronounced [bụtafli:] or be spelt *Batterflei*. This divergence has led to
a few spelling pronunciations which are, however, now stigmatized as uneducated
(*Worcestersauce* [wortʃestazo:sə]) and accordingly avoided; note that *Jazz* has had
various alternating phases of German [jats] and near-English [dʒes] pronunciation.

2.3 Morphology

2.3.1 Introduction

German inflects for case, number (and gender) in nouns, pronouns, adjectives, and
articles, and for person, number, tense, and mood in verbs. Loanwords are
normally integrated to the extent that they fit into any syntactic environment
without restrictions. During the period of integration there may be an uninflected
stage, or uncertainty especially about gender attribution.

2.3.2 Nouns

(Busse 1993; Carstensen 1980, 1981; Gregor 1983; Schlick 1984)

Gender. The attribution of gender is obligatory for German. The topic has been the
object of several studies; while the results are not fully predictable for each
individual item, it is clear that the choice depends on:

1. phonology (monosyllables ending in consonants are mainly M/N; bisyllabic words in -e are F, and those in -er M);
2. morphosemantics (bisyllabic words in -er are M if an interpretation of 'agent'—person or implement—is possible);
3. semantics ('natural' gender is preferred with names for persons; the gender of near-synonyms is normally adopted in other cases).

However, these criteria can be in conflict at times so that the outcome may be unexpected if judged on the basis of one criterion only (*der Job* M, but *die Arbeit* F). In the three meanings of *Single*, the gender marks the distinction between the tennis term (N, *das Einzel*), the bachelor (M, *der Junggeselle*—no specific designation being available for female singles), and the music record (F, *die Schallplatte*)—obviously all allocated according to the nearest German equivalents.

Case. The expected endings are attached, i.e. those regular in the respective class.

Number. The English plural is normally retained; this applies even to the majority of early loans which are otherwise integrated (*Streiks*, very rarely *Streike* 'strikes'). The major exception is the use of zero inflexion with words ending in -er (*ein Manager*, *zwei Manager*; *ein Computer*, *zwei Computer*), even with otherwise little integrated forms (*ein Teenager*, *zwei Teenager*); rare exceptions are *Papers* and *Poster(s)*.

Note that -s is regular for German words ending in a vowel (*Uhu+s* 'owl+s'), and is frequent as a dialect feature in the north (*Jungs* 'boys'); the takeover of the English pattern can therefore be interpreted as strengthening an existing category. By contrast, older loans tend to be fully adapted (*Boote*, *Filme*, *Lotsen*). In very few cases plural forms can indicate geographical variation as in German German *Parks*, *Parke* (rare): Swiss German *Pärke*.

2.3.3 Adjectives

There is some hesitation about using new loanwords in attributive position (where they must be inflected): *die coole/hotte Musik*. Thus many adjectives remain restricted to predicative functions (where they are not inflected): *die Musik ist in/out/hip*, or develop substitute forms as in: *ein pinkfarbenes Kleid* vs. *das Kleid ist pink(farben)* 'the dress is pink'; these restrictions also apply to participles (s. 2.3.5). Morpheme substitution (e.g. -y replaced by -ig) can indicate a high degree of integration (note the competing forms *trendy* and *trendig*). Semantic *and* morphological reasons can limit the adjective's capacity to form comparatives and superlatives (*in, out*) (cf. Zimmer 1997: 59).

2.3.4 Adverbs

Since in German adverbs are identical with uninflected adjectives no problems arise; no loanword with the English adverbial morpheme -ly appears to be recorded in German.

2.3.5 Verbs

Earlier loans were taken over with the derivational morpheme -*ier*- so that they are automatically inflectable (*boykottieren*); there are a few doublets with different meanings (*testieren* 'to attest the presence' from Latin vs. *testen* 'to put to the test') or which are regionally restricted (*parkieren* Swiss German = *parken* 'park your car'; *grillieren* = *grillen* 'to roast something on a gridiron').

Past participles are more difficult to accommodate morphologically. Monosyllables are normally inflected by means of *ge*- and -*t*; uncertainty is reflected in mixtures of English and German morphological rules: *getimt/-met/-med* 'timed'; *gesettlet/-led*, *recycelt/-clet/-cled/-kelt* 'recycled'. Since participles are also inflected for case, forms can result which are not fully acceptable or which are at least awkward: ?*recycletes Papier* 'recycled paper', ?*gestyletere Mode* 'more stylish fashion'. This uncertainty has led to the alternative form *rezyklieren* (with 'French' pronunciation), a coinage which has, however, not been successful (cf. Zimmer 1997: 59–61).

2.3.6 Derivation (selection)

Gender specification. German personal nouns often distinguish between masculine and feminine forms, most often by adding -*in* (*Student: Studentin, Lehrer: Lehrerin*). Loanwords are subject to the same adaptation, although the results may look odd and will in consequence be avoided (they are accepted in cases like *Designer: Designerin*)—and what is the designation for the male counterpart to a *Hostess* ('traffic warden')? In other cases both gender-specific terms are borrowed wholesale from English: *Steward—Stewardess*, which in the process of political correctness are increasingly replaced by *Flugbegleiter(in)* (calqued on E *flight attendant*).

Agent nouns. The equivalence of German and English -*er* leads to identical solutions so that it cannot be decided on morphological grounds whether individual -*er* derivations were coined in German or borrowed wholesale (*toaster, tester*); the alternative -*ist* is very rarely used, and -*man* practically not used at all (Görlach 1999).

Denominal verbs. Zero derivation is common in German and English so that words like *toasten* and *testen* can be taken over without problems—or coined in German. The earlier adaptation by way of -*ier*- (*boykottieren*) does not seem to be productive any more (contrast -*isieren* (= *ize*) in internationalisms).

New adjectives. These are rarely coined, especially since there seems to be little need for them. English -*able* translates into -*bar*, but the number of such German derivatives is limited, and more limited still are coinages with -*ig* (= English -*y*) like *trendig, peppig, poppig*.

Deadjectival nouns. The few adjectives borrowed from English do not tend to permit native derivations; in consequence, English items are normally adopted: *Coolness, Cleverness, Fairness, Fitness*.

In cases where the English word has a Romance base, the derivation is interpreted as an internationalism and pronounced as if Latinate and hence excluded from the *Dictionary of European Anglicisms*. Romance suffixes are replaced by their German equivalents (*Thatcherismus*), but hybrids are normally avoided.

2.3.7 Compounds and combining forms

When a loanword enters into German word-formation it is freely used in compounding (although the frequency tends to be low during the first stages of integration). Acceptability can also be restricted for phonological reasons, because the hybrid character of a new compound is too evident, or because the need for it is not apparent; all the more surprising are 'ugly' words like compounds ending in *-shop* such as *Badshop*, *Brotshop*, *Fleischshop* (in advertising *-shop* and *-centre* are preferred to German *Laden*, *Geschäft*, or *Zentrum*). Zimmer (1997: 22 f.) provides a host of hybrid compounds. In many cases it is impossible to say whether a compound is a German coinage, or whether the hybrid item arose as a partial translation in the process of integration. Other examples are *-boy* 'household utensil' (metaphorically developed from the 'servant' sense), *-centre*, *-lady* with numerous combinations, most of which are German coinages.

In addition, there are combining forms such as *afro-*, *bio-*, and *micro-* followed by a Greek or Latin morpheme. As these are in international use and have nothing English in their form, they are excluded from the *Dictionary of European Anglicisms* for the reasons spelt out in s. 2.1.3 (cf., however, Carstensen and Busse 1993–6).

2.3.8 Calques (loan translations) (cf. section 2.6 below)

Since the morphological structure of English and German is very similar, translations are normally easy. This is particularly true for n. + n. or adj. + n. compounds, as in German *Froschmann* from *frogman* and *Wochenende* from *weekend* (calquing can go both ways, cf. English *loanword* from German *Lehnwort*, *ball lightning* from *Kugelblitz*, and the series English *popular song* (Bishop Percy, 1765) > *Populärlied*, *Volkslied* (Herder, 1773) > English *folksong* (1847, *OED*) > German *Folk*(*song*). In addition, in the 1960s English *pop*, *popular music*, *song* were borrowed again into German, as *Pop*, *Popmusik*, or *Popsong*. The principle works well with synthetic compounds and derivations, too: German *Außenseiter* from *outsider*, contrast *Insider* but there is no **Innenseiter*; cf. English *backformation* from *Rückbildung*. Many equivalents are not total matches, for various reasons (German *Wolkenkratzer* 'cloud-scraper' from *skyscraper*) or the rendition is formally independent (German *Marschflugkörper* for *cruise missile*).

Often it cannot be established beyond doubt that the equivalence is really based on translation: German *Fernsehen* appears to be independent of English *television*; in other items (*chain smoker* = German *Kettenraucher*, *wire puller* = German *Drahtzieher*) the direction of influence is disputed.

2.4 Meaning

Lexical meanings cannot be fully compared across language boundaries since they are contrastively established in relation to other members of a semantic field in the individual languages; we cannot, therefore, strictly say that a meaning is retained in the borrowing process. However, the reference can of course be the same, as with borrowed terminologies: it is the explicit purpose in such cases that the reference should be identical, i.e. translation be possible without the danger of misunderstanding.

In a looser sense, meanings can be accepted as comparable; the following principles hold and can be exemplified with German loanwords from English:

1. Only one sense will be taken over in each case of borrowing. This means that a selection is made from the range of meanings of homonymous or polysemous items in a particular contact situation, and it is unlikely that the whole range of meanings will ever be borrowed even with repeated cases of borrowing: German took over two senses of *twist* as names for 'drink' and 'yarn' in the nineteenth century, and another for the dance in the twentieth century; *Set* in German refers to a combination of tools etc., to a part of a tennis match, and to a place-mat and, in the use of specialists, to 'film set(ting), location', 'jazz or pop concert', and 'group of people' (after the model of *jet set*). In all cases these represent a small selection of the meanings available in English (for *single* see s. 2.3.2 above).

2. After borrowing, the loanword is integrated into the semantic field(s) of which it now forms part. This will entail accommodation, which may involve a change of its original meaning (in denotation or connotation). If its status as a loanword remains transparent, it will take part in the evaluation of loanwords from the respective donor language: i.e. its connotation will be affected. For instance, it may be a 'fashionable' word in contrast to its neutral or humble origins in the source language, as in *Know-how*, which in German with its collocates from the field of technology implies a certain prestige that is largely absent from the informal English term.

Since every word has its own history (especially as far as meanings are concerned) it is not easy to make generalizations about types of semantic change, but the following types of change can be pointed out for German loanwords from English:

1. The range of meanings is reduced from a larger number to a smaller one; if we take the *COD* (1995) definitions as a basis, the range of English *set* is reduced from twenty-four to five in German.

2. An individual meaning is narrowed in the receiving language or restricted to a specific domain (i.e. it acquires further specifying features): German *Barrel* is used only in relation to crude oil; *fighten* is used in German almost exclusively in relation to sports.

3. The range of an (often monosemous) English item is extended or shifted to new domains because new meanings develop (e.g. from metaphoric or metonymic uses in the receiving language): *Start* (of an aeroplane or spacecraft) for English *take-off*; *Striptease* ('geistiger Striptease, Seelen-Striptease') for English 'baring of one's soul'.

4. A meaning is generalized by being applied to a wider range of referents in the receiver language: in German *sprint(en)* and *spurt(en)* may be used outside the sphere of sports with reference to persons, motorcars, etc.

Note that in all such statements accommodation in the borrowing process and its impact on the meaning should be distinguished from the loanword's later semantic development in the receiving language. The interrelation of borrowing and semantic constraints can be illustrated by *Camp*, which was first borrowed with the specification 'for prisoners of war'. The later meanings of 'training camp' and 'holiday camp' were only able to develop (or be borrowed) after the term had lost its negative POW connotations. Other, more extreme forms of semantic change, such as the meaning of a loanword arising from a total misunderstanding of a foreign item, are very rare.

2.5 Usage

(Fink 1983; Görlach 1997a, 1997b)

Comprehensive sociolinguistic and stylistic analyses of Anglicisms in German are largely lacking. It is quite obvious that the present impact of English on German is unevenly spread in the vocabulary as far as domains, degrees of formality, technicality, frequency, and social variables (age, education, region) are concerned. The great number of items which would have to be tested for pronunciation, spelling, morphology, and 'correct' meaning (comprehension) in a representative cross-section of the population in various parts of the German-speaking community makes it unlikely that we will ever have a full account—especially as the data (lexical, stylistic, social, and attitudinal) are continually changing at great speed. Only a sketch of the problems, categories, and linguistic documentation will, therefore, be given here.

In West Germany, research in this area began around the mid-1960s—since when interest in sociolinguistic aspects of borrowing has steadily increased. For the research carried out up to 1980 cf. W. Viereck (1980: 237–321, 1986: 123–5).

Results from the data-gathering for the *Dictionary of European Anglicisms* have confirmed what had been known more impressionistically before: in German, most of the loanwords are

1. 'technical' (restricted to the terminologies of sciences, technologies, and other jargons); these tend to be infrequent, incompletely integrated, written, and attitudinally neutral; or
2. 'colloquial/slang'; these tend to be frequent only in youth language, journalism, and advertising and more typical of spoken use; the degree of integration is somewhat unpredictable, with lack of competence in English in some speakers being partly compensated for by the fashionable prestige of near-English pronunciation. In contrast to the terms in (1), the meaning of colloquial items is often vague.

2.6 Forms of linguistic transfer and their categorization

(Carstensen and Busse 1993–6: *53–*66; Busse 2001*a*)

Language contact can lead to various forms of expansion in the receiver language; the most frequent type is borrowing, i.e. the takeover of the form and (parts of) the content of the foreign word:

1. *Borrowing*
    (*a*) Totally unadapted and not felt to be part of German (quotation words, code-switching, foreignisms);
    (*b*) words still looking foreign in form or entirely unadapted (= *Fremdwörter*, *aliens*);
    (*c*) fully integrated items (= *Lehnwörter*, *denizens*).

There is a continuum between the categories 1 (*a*) and 1 (*b*), and 1 (*b*) and 1 (*c*), words being placed closer to one of the two ends (with differences between individual users). However, there are various other ways of rendering the foreign concept using the resources of the recipient language; all these types can be subsumed under:

2. *Replacement*
    (*a*) Translation (*Lehnübersetzung*), reflecting the morphologic structure of the English complex item as closely as the structure of the receiving language permits. In many cases, only part of the foreign word is translated and the other is taken over in its original form (*semi-calque*). (For examples cf. group A 1–3 below.)
    (*b*) Rendering (*Lehnübertragung*), translating only part of the foreign item but providing looser equivalents for others. (Cf. group B below.)
    (*c*) Creation (*Lehnschöpfung*), a formally independent equivalent whose coinage was, however, prompted by the foreign item. (Cf., however, Höfler 1980 and cf. group C below.)
    (*d*) Semantic loan (*Lehnbedeutung*), with an existing German item taking over one meaning of the foreign partial equivalent. (Cf. group D below.)

3. *Pseudo-loans*
Incomplete competence in the donor language (or a failure to accept its prescriptive norms for borrowed items) can lead to English-looking items which do not exist in English itself. For this reason such un-English coinages should better be explained as indicating the integration of the constituents (which can, then, become productive as elements of the receiving language) rather than as borrowings.
    (*a*) *Lexical pseudo-loans* made with (combinations of) English word material into new linguistic units that do not exist in the donor language, namely compounds (German *Dressman, Go-in, Longseller*).
    (*b*) *Morphological pseudo-loans*, i.e. the shortening of items in the recipient language ranging from simple words (German *Profi* < E *professional*, *Pulli* < E *pullover*) over compounds (German *Happyend* < E *happy ending*) to phrases

and phraseologisms (German *last not least* < E *last but not least*, German *Gin Tonic* < E *gin and tonic*) and to blends made from German and English elements (*Dämmershoppen* 'late-evening shopping', cf. Görlach 1994*b*).

(*c*) *Semantic pseudo-loans* where the Anglicism develops a meaning in German that is absent from English (cf. 5.2.4): German *Slip*~E *briefs, (under)pants, panties*, German *Gag*~E *gimmick*, German *Gangway*~E *steps, ramp*.

The categories 2(*a*)–2(*d*) can be illustrated with German specimens, distinguishing between successful attempts and proposals which were not accepted:

A *Translations*

1. Successful

brainwashing < *Gehirn+wäsche, maiden speech* < *Jungfern+rede, penalty-kick* < *Straf+stoß, pacemaker* < *Schritt+macher, semi-conductor* < *Halb+leiter, to scent the morning air* < *Morgenluft wittern, meals on wheels* < *Essen auf Rädern*

2. Coexisting

basketball = *Korb+ball, Big Brother* = *der Große Bruder, bodyguard* = *Leib+wächter, Grand Old Lady* = *Große alte Dame*

3. Failures

beefsteak > (*Rind+stück*), *white-collar->* (*Weiß+kragen-*), *ghostwriter* > (*Geister+schreiber*), *sweater* > (*Schwitzer*), *have a good time* > *eine gute Zeit haben, selfmade man* > *selbstgemachter Mann, do-it-yourself* > *mach es selbst*

B *Renderings*

1. Successful

centre-forward < *Mittel+stürmer, backwoodsman* < *Hinter+wäldler, roller-skate* < *Roll+schuh, voting cattle* < *Stimm+vieh, skyscraper* < *Wolken+kratzer, matter of fact* < *Tat+sache, dead heat* < *totes Rennen, be in the same boat* < *in einem Boot sitzen, lose face* < *sein Gesicht verlieren, greenfield site* < *auf der grünen Wiese*

2. Coexisting

space shuttle = *Raum+gleiter, big bang* = *Ur+knall, keep smiling* = *immer nur lächeln, public relations* = *Öffentlichkeits+arbeit, boat people* = *Boots+flüchtlinge*

3. Failures

pipeline > *Fern+rohr+leitung*

C *Creations*

1. Successful

steeplechase < *Hindernis+rennen, non-aligned* < *block+frei, air conditioning* < *Klima+anlage, black box* < *Flug+schreiber, do-it-yourselfer* < *Heim+werker, work-to-rule* < *Dienst nach Vorschrift, topless* < *oben ohne*

2. Coexisting

(*Blue*) *Jeans* = *Nieten+hose, Dimmer* = *Helligkeits+regler, Public relations* = *Meinungs+pflege, Hovercraft* = *Luftkissen+boot*

3. Failures

Keks (<cakes) > Knusperchen, Reschling, pullover > Über+schwupper, crawl > Kriech+stoß, (Fosbury) flop > Tauch+wälzer, do-it-yourself > handwerkliche Selbsthilfe

D *Semantic loans*

1. Successful

mouse = Maus (comp.), *bottleneck = Flaschen+hals* 'restriction', *to fire = feuern* 'dismiss'(a person), *to feed = füttern* 'data', *have a bad press* trans. *eine schlechte Presse haben, make money* trans. *Geld machen, to hire and fire* trans. *heuern und feuern*

2. Coexisting

butterfly = Schmetterling (swimming)

3. Failures

fall in love trans. *in Liebe fallen < sich verlieben*

Relative frequency. Since calques are inconspicuous and the fact of their foreign origin is in consequence not known to the general public or this information may be quickly lost, it is almost impossible to compare figures in any statistically relevant sense. It is certainly true that the number of calques tends to be higher in purist phases, while these account for a lower number of loanwords.

Impressionistically we can say that present-day German is open to Anglicisms to an extreme degree in comparison with other languages in modern Europe. This is reflected in the huge number of direct borrowings from English and the comparatively low number of calques—even though the structural similarity of English and German would make calquing easy. Additional evidence is the great number of hybrids (only some of which are modelled on English = semi-calques). These impressions are confirmed by the comprehensive dictionary of Carstensen and Busse (1993–6), in which the number of borrowed items greatly exceeds that of translations.

2.7 The future of Anglicisms

A linguist should not try to prognosticate; the social and political developments of the past few years demonstrate how wide of the mark predictions about Anglicisms in continental Europe made in, say, 1986 would have been. However, from the 1950s onwards quite stable trends in English influences on German have been evident, and this permits us to formulate a few possibilities. Busse's statistical figures based on the coverage of Anglicisms in *Duden* (Busse 1993) can be extrapolated into the future: the increase from Kinderling (1795: twelve Anglicisms) to an early *Duden* (1880: 385 = 1.36 per cent) to Dunger (1909: *c.*900) and *Duden* 1986 (1986: 3,746 = 3.46 per cent) leads one to expect that the number of English loanwords considered dictionary-worthy will pass the mark of 5,000 in the next century (which would make the figure still only a fraction of loans from French or Latin/Greek). This prognosis assumes that there will be no significant factors restricting the adoption of loanwords from English, such as:

1. saturation because all the lexical gaps have been filled;
2. a dramatic reorientation of cultural, economic, or political life;
3. linguistic purism including legislation.

There is no indication that any of these factors are relevant so far. It is quite clear that the importance of English as a second language will further increase as far as numbers of speakers and their competences are concerned. This means that English words will become more easily intelligible to an even wider section of the speech community. Note, however, that this does not necessarily mean that the number of Anglicisms and the frequency of their use will increase. Although there are no reliable figures to prove the hypothesis, it seems that the best speakers of English in Germany are not the most frequent users of Anglicisms—they appear to have sufficient *Sprachgefühl* to keep the two languages apart.

As stated above, the number of Anglicisms in German is still comparatively small, if contrasted with words of native origin and with those of French and neo-Latin/Greek provenance. The close similarity between the linguistic structures of English and German makes many loanwords inconspicuous and easy to integrate, which explains the uncomplicated adoption of most words. The future development of the other type of fashionable borrowings which are used *because* they are notably English in form and content is more difficult to predict, but we do not see, in 2001, any drastic changes of attitude taking place in this area—however much public attention purist demands to avoid Anglicisms have received in the past few years. (In some domains, especially in advertising, there is an increasing use of code-switching involving English).

2.8 Research

German Anglicisms have been a focus of research for German anglicists and foreign 'Germanists' for a very long time. The list of titles in the *Annotated Bibliography of European Anglicisms*, though only a selection of publications, is truly impressive, especially when contrasted with the very patchy information available for some other European languages. Research has concentrated on the following topics:

1. corpus-related analysis often based on a certain run of issues of particular newspapers and journals;
2. the compilation of items current in special vocabularies (pop music, the drug scene, sports, advertising, etc.);
3. the stylistic analysis of items taken from studies of types (1) and (2);
4. the compilation of dictionaries of Anglicisms;
5. the analysis of Anglicisms contained in dictionaries;

6. historical studies of the growth of English influence on German lexis;
7. a (not sufficiently large) number of sociolinguistic investigations exploring the correlations between social variables and the number of loanwords known and used, correctness, attitudes, etc.

2.9 Bibliography

The list includes the titles mentioned in the chapter and the most important works not mentioned. For full evidence the *Annotated Bibliography* should be consulted, where the titles here mentioned are accompanied by short annotations relating to the content and quality of the publications.

BUSSE, ULRICH (1993), *Anglizismen im Duden: Eine Untersuchung zur Darstellung englischen Wortguts in den Ausgaben des Rechtschreibdudens von 1880–1986*, RGL 139 (Tübingen: Niemeyer).

—— (1995), 'Drinks und Dinks: Correctness auf gut Deutsch', in Bernd Polster (ed.), *Westwind: Die Amerikanisierung Europas* (Cologne: DuMont), 140–7.

—— (1996), 'Probleme der Aussprache englischer Wörter im Deutschen und ihre Behandlung im *Anglizismen-Wörterbuch*', in *Symposium on Lexicography VII: Proceedings of the Seventh International Symposium on Lexicography May 5–6, 1994 at the University of Copenhagen*, Lexikographica, Series Maior 76 (Tübingen: Niemeyer), 83–92.

—— (1998), 'A Dictionary of Anglicisms: An Outline of its History, Content and Objectives', in *Festschrift for Rudolf Filipović*, Suvremena lingvistika (Zagreb: Institute of Linguistics), 103–14.

—— (1999), 'Keine Bedrohung durch Anglizismen', *Der Sprachdienst*, 43: 18–20.

—— (2001*a*), 'Typen von Anglizísmen: von der heilago geist bis Extremsparing—aufgezeigt anhand ausgewählter lexikographischer Kategorisierungen', in Gerhard Stickel (ed.) *Neues und Fremdes im deutschen Wortschatz : Aktueller lexikalischer Wandel* (Berlin: de Gruyter), 131–55.

CARSTENSEN, BRODER (1965), *Englische Einflüsse auf die deutsche Sprache nach 1945* (Heidelberg: Winter).

—— (1980), 'The Gender of English Loan-Words in German', *Studia Anglica Posnaniensia*, 12: 3–25.

—— (1981), 'Zur Deklination aus dem Englischen entlehnter Substantive im Deutschen', in Jürgen Esser and Axel Hübler (eds.), *Forms and Functions: Papers in General, English and Applied Linguistics Presented to Vilém Fried on the Occasion of his Sixty-Fifth Birthday*, Tübinger Beiträge zur Linguistik 149 (Tübingen: Narr), 103–22.

—— (1982), '"Babys" oder "Babies"? Zum Plural englischer Wörter im Deutschen', *Muttersprache*, 92: 200–15.

—— (1988), 'Loan-Translation: Theoretical and Practical Issues', *Folia linguistica*, 22: 85–92.

—— and BUSSE, ULRICH (1993–6), *Anglizismen-Wörterbuch: Der Einfluß des Englischen auf den deutschen Wortschatz nach 1945*, established by Broder Carstensen, continued by Ulrich Busse with the collaboration of Regina Schmude, 3 vols. (Berlin: de Gruyter).

—— and GALINSKY, HEINZ (1975), *Amerikanismen der deutschen Gegenwartssprache: Entlehnungsvorgänge und ihre stilistischen Aspekte*, 3rd edn. (Heidelberg: Winter).

CHRIST, HERBERT, and HÜLLEN, ERNER (1995), 'Geschichte des Fremdsprachenunterrichts seit 1945', in Karl-Richard Bausch, Herbert Christ, and Hans-Jürgen

34 **Ulrich Busse and Manfred Görlach**

Krumm (eds.), *Handbuch Fremdsprachenunterricht*, 3rd edn. (Tübingen: Franke), 565–72.

CHRIST, INGEBORG (1995), 'Fremdsprachenunterricht an Schulen', in Karl-Richard Bausch, Herbert Christ, and Hans-Jürgen Krumm (eds.), *Handbuch Fremdsprachenunterricht*, 3rd edn. (Tübingen: Franke), 523–8.

Deutsches Fremdwörterbuch (*DtFWb*) (1913–88), begun by Hans Schulz, continued by Otto Basler, rev. Gabriele Hoppe, Alan Kirkness, Elisabeth Link, Isolde Nortmeyer, and Gerhard Strauß, 7 vols. (Berlin: de Gruyter).

——(1995–), fully revised by Gerhard Strauß, Elke Donalies, Heidrun Kämper-Jensen, Isolde Nortmeyer, Joachim Schildt, Rosemarie Schnerrer, and Oda Vietze, 2nd edn. (Berlin: de Gruyter).

DUNGER, HERMANN (1899), 'Wider die Engländerei in der deutschen Sprache', *Zeitschrift des Allgemeinen Deutschen Sprachvereins*, 14: 241–51.

——(1909), *Engländerei in der deutschen Sprache*, 2nd edn. (Berlin: Verlag des ADSV F. Bergold); repr. together with Dunger's *Wörterbuch von Verdeutschungen entbehrlicher Fremdwörter* (1882), introd. W. Viereck (Hildesheim: Olms, 1989).

ENGEL, EDUARD (1918), *Entwelschung: Verdeutschungswörterbuch für Amt, Schule, Haus, Leben* (Leipzig: Hesse & Becker).

FINK, HERMANN (1983), *Amerikanisch-englische und gesamtenglische Interferenzen der deutschen Allgemein- und Werbesprache im aktiven und passiven Sprachverhalten deutscher Grund-, Haupt- und Oberschüler*, Europäische Hochschulschriften, series 14, no. 113 (Frankfurt am Main: Lang).

GAILER, JACOB EBERHARD (1835), *Neuer Orbis Pictus für die Jugend*, 2nd edn. (Reutlingen: Mäcken; repr. Dortmund: Harenberg, 1979).

GANZ, PETER F. (1957), *Der Einfluß des Englischen auf den deutschen Wortschatz 1640–1815* (Berlin: E. Schmidt).

GÖRLACH, MANFRED (1994a), 'A Usage Dictionary of Anglicisms in Selected European Languages', *International Journal of Lexicography*, 7: 223–46.

——(1994b), 'Continental Pun-Dits', *English Today*, 37: 50–2.

——(1996), 'Is Airbagging Hip or Mega-out? A New Dictionary of Anglicisms', in Martin Pütz (ed.), *Language Choices* (Amsterdam: Benjamins), 91–111.

——(1997a), 'The *UDASEL*: Progress, Problem and Prospects', in Zygmunt Mazur and Teresa Bela (eds.), *New Developments in English and American Studies, Continuity and Change* (Krakow: University), 561–79.

——(1997b), 'Usage in the *UDASEL*', in Jacek Fisiak (ed.), *Festschrift für Roger Lass*, Studia Anglica Posnaniensia 31 (Poznań: University), 67–77.

——(1998), 'Purism and the *UDASEL*', in *Festschrift für Rudolf Filipović*, Suvremena lingvistika (Zagreb: Institute of Linguistics), 163–82.

——(1999), 'Morphological Problems of Integration: English Loanwords Ending in -*er* and -*ing* in Selected European Languages', in Uwe Carls and Peter Lucko (eds.), *Form, Function and Variation in English: Studies in Honour of Klaus Hansen* (Frankfurt/Main: Lang), 117–25.

GRADDOL, DAVID (2001), 'The Future of English as a European Language', *The European English Messenger* X\2: 47–55.

GREGOR, BERND (1983), *Genuszuordnung: Das Genus englischer Lehnwörter im Deutschen*, LA 129 (Tübingen: Niemeyer).

HELLER, KLAUS (1996), *Rechtschreibung 2000. Die aktuelle Reform: Wörterliste der geänderten Schreibungen*, 2nd edn. (Stuttgart: Klett).

HÖFLER, MANFRED (1980), 'Für eine Ausgliederung der Kategorie "Lehnschöpfung" aus dem Bereich sprachlicher Entlehnung', in W. Pöckl (ed.), *Festschrift zum 70. Geburtstag von Mario Wandruszka* (Tübingen: Niemeyer), 149–53.

KINDERLING, J. F. A. (1795) *Über die Reinigkeit der deutschen Sprache und die Beförderungsmittel derselben, mit einer Musterung der fremden Wörter und anderen Wörterverzeichnissen* (Berlin: Maurer).

KIRKNESS, ALAN (1975), *Zur Sprachreinigung im Deutschen 1789–1871: Eine historische Dokumentation*, 2 vols., Forschungsberichte des Instituts für deutsche Sprache 26.1, 26.2 (Tübingen: Narr).

——(1984), 'Aliens, Denizens, Hybrids and Natives: Foreign Influences on the Etymological Structure of German Vocabulary', in Charles V. J. Russ (ed.), *Foreign Influences on German: Proceedings of the Conference 'Foreign Influences on German: Past and Present', held at the University of York, England, 28–30 March 1983* (Dundee: Lochee Publications), 1–26.

LANGNER, HEIDEMARIE C. (1995), *Die Schreibung englischer Entlehnungen im Deutschen*, Theorie und Vermittlung der Sprache 23 (Frankfurt am Main: Lang).

LEHBERGER, REINER (1995), 'Geschichte des Fremdsprachenunterrichts bis 1945', in Karl-Richard Bausch, Herbert Christ, and Hans-Jürgen Krumm (eds.), *Handbuch Fremdsprachenunterricht*, 3rd edn. (Tübingen: Francke), 561–5.

LEHNERT, MARTIN (1986), 'The Anglo-American Influence on the Language of the German Democratic Republic', in Viereck and Bald 1986: 129–57.

——(1990), *Anglo-Amerikanisches im Sprachgebrauch der DDR* (Berlin: Akademie-Verlag).

LIEBKNECHT, WILHELM (1912), *Volksfremdwörterbuch*, 13th edn. (Leipzig: Genossenschafts-Buchdrucker). (1st edn. *Volksstaat-Fremdwörterbuch* (1874).)

MUNSKE, HORST-HAIDER (1980), 'Germanische Sprachen und deutsche Gesamtsprache', in Hanspeter Althaus, Helmut Henne, and Herbert Ernst Wiegand (eds.), *Lexikon der Germanistischen Linguistik* (Tübingen: Niemeyer), 661–72.

——(1982), 'Die Rolle des Lateins als Superstratum im Deutschen und in anderen germanischen Sprachen', in Per Sture Ureland (ed.), *Die Leistung der Strataforschung und der Kreolistik: Typologische Aspekte der Sprachkontakte. Akten des 5. Symposiums über Sprachkontakte in Europa, Mannheim 1982*, LA 125 (Tübingen: Niemeyer), 237–63.

—— and KIRKNESS, ALAN (eds.) (1996), *Eurolatein: Das griechische und lateinische Erbe in den europäischen Sprachen*, RGL 169 (Tübingen: Niemeyer).

PFITZNER, JÜRGEN (1978), *Der Anglizismus im Deutschen: Ein Beitrag zur Bestimmung seiner stilistischen Funktion in der heutigen Presse*, Amerikastudien/American Studies 51 (Stuttgart: Metzler).

POLENZ, PETER VON (1967), 'Sprachpurismus und Nationalsozialismus: Die Fremdwort-Frage gestern und heute', in B. von Wiese and R. Henß (eds.), *Nationalismus in Germanistik und Dichtung: Dokumentation des Germanistentages in München vom 17.–22.10.1966* (Berlin: E. Schmidt), 79–112.

——(1991–9), *Deutsche Sprachgeschichte vom Spätmittelalter bis zur Gegenwart*, 3 vols. (Berlin: de Gruyter).

SCHLICK, WERNER (1984), 'Die Kriterien für die deutsche Genuszuweisung bei substantivischen Anglizismen', *German Quarterly*, 57: 402–31.

STANFORTH, ANTHONY W. (1968), 'Deutsch-englischer Lehnwortaustausch', in Walter Mitzka (ed.), *Wortgeographie und Gesellschaft: Festgabe für L. E. Schmitt zum 60. Geburtstag am 10. Februar 1968* (Berlin: de Gruyter), 526–60.

STIVEN, AGNES BAIN (1936), *Englands Einfluß auf den deutschen Wortschatz* (Zeulenroda: Sporn).

VIERECK, KARIN (1986), 'The Influence of English on Austrian German', in Viereck and Bald 1986: 159–77.

VIERECK, WOLFGANG (1980), 'Empirische Untersuchungen insbesondere zum Verständnis und Gebrauch von Anglizismen im Deutschen', in Wolfgang Viereck (ed.), *Studien zum Einfluß der englischen Sprache auf das Deutsche. Studies on the Influence of the English Language on German*, TBL 132 (Tübingen: Narr), 237–321.

—— (1986), 'The Influence of English on German in the Past and in the Federal Republic of Germany', in Viereck and Bald 1986: 107–28.

VIERECK, WOLFGANG and BALD, WOLF-DIETRICH (eds.) (1986), *English in Contact with Other Languages: Studies in Honour of Broder Carstensen on the Occasion of his 60th Birthday* (Budapest: Akadémiai Kiadó).

WÄCHTLER, KURT (1980), 'Was ist ein Amerikanismus—heute?', *AAA* 5: 145–58.

ZIMMER, DIETER E. (1997), 'Neuanglodeutsch: Über die Pidginisierung der Sprache', in Dieter E. Zimmer, *Deutsch und anders: Die Sprache im Modernisierungsfieber* (Reinbek: Rowohlt), 7–85.

3

DUTCH

Amand Berteloot and Nicoline van der Sijs

3.1 History of language contact

3.1.1 Chronology of intensive influence

(Bense 1924; Gerritsen 1986; Koenen and Smits 1992; Posthumus 1986; De Vooys 1925, 1946–56, 1951; Zandvoort 1964)

The oldest contacts between the Netherlands and England date back to the Middle Ages. In the eighth century the Netherlands were Christianized by Anglo-Saxon monks such as Willibrordus and Bonifatius. English loanwords from this period are *delgen* 'delete', *ootmoed* 'humility', and *bisschop*. About the year 1000 English colonists settled along the Flemish coast. They are, according to Heeroma (1952), responsible for approximately twenty loanwords, such as *brijn* 'brine', *kreek*, and *wulk* 'whelk'. However, Dutch immigrants also came to England from the Netherlands, in particular from Flanders. Thus the oldest Dutch sentence 'Hebban olla vogala nestas hagunnan . . . ' (Have all the birds started their nests . . .) was written by a West Flemish monk in an English monastery. Economic contacts between England and the Netherlands were intensive, too. The cloth industry in the southern part depended strongly on English wool and this repeatedly led to political conflicts. Craftsmen from the Continent settled in England and English traders visited Dutch towns. One of the earliest English printers, William Caxton, learned his trade in Cologne and in Bruges, and the texts he printed included some works which he himself translated from Dutch.

Marriages between the Dutch and English nobility also exerted some linguistic influence. However, the import of English loanwords remained restricted to certain domains such as seafaring, with words like *dok* 'dock', *dreg* 'drag' , *loods* 'pilot',

---

This chapter is based for a major part on Sijs (1996, in particular 294–353); the work will not be mentioned any further.

and *praaien* 'hail'. Trade contacts brought in words such as *bill, factor, money*, and *okshoofd*, a measure rendering English *hogshead*. Many of these words are completely assimilated today and thus hardly recognizable as loanwords.

During the war against Spain many refugees from the Netherlands crossed the Channel in order to continue their fight from the British Isles. When Antwerp was lost in 1585, the southern part of the Netherlands fell to the Spaniards and was governed alternately by the Spaniards, Austrians, and French. Consequently, direct English influence declined considerably and up to the twentieth century nearly all English loanwords were imported via French.

In contrast, the northern part retained independence, which was consolidated in the so-called 'Peace of Münster' in 1648. The republic attracted various Englishmen like Sir Philip Sidney and Ben Jonson, but also traders, scholars, and refugees. About the year 1600 English actors who were travelling on the Continent performed plays in Holland. Nevertheless, the number of English loanwords remained very small and they were not permanent.

The English and the Dutch competed all over the world in the seventeenth century. As a consequence, the English language started to influence Dutch and continued to do so for a long period. Many loanwords entered Dutch from Britain and from the languages of the English colonies. Increasing tensions between Britain and the 'Verenigde Nederlanden' on the world market resulted in the wars of the seventeenth and eighteenth centuries. Despite the close dynastic relations with the royal family, English influence remained restricted to the nobility while French predominated at the Dutch court. In the seventeenth century the first Dutch–English/English–Dutch dictionaries were published.

In the eighteenth century, English culture, fashion, and literature started to influence continental societies. The economic ideas of scholars such as Adam Smith and American democratic thoughts entered the scene. However, the total number of loanwords was still fairly small, probably because of the existence of many familiar French equivalents. Religious designations from the seventeenth and eighteenth centuries include *quaker, methodist*, and *puritan*. Fashionable words of the time are *flip, hornpipe* (later *horlepijp* or *horlepiep*), *nonsens, rosbief, sociëteit*. Other words from the same period are *kerrie* 'curry', *port* 'port-wine', and *koffiehuis*, a translation of English *coffee-house*.

Apart from Romantic literature, which gave Dutch a few loanwords such as *ballade, bombast, essay(ist), folklore, humor(ist)*, English influence in the nineteenth century increased all over Europe in other domains, too. Dutch borrowed English words mainly in four domains – from shipping: *alle hens* (*all hands*), *coaster, klipper, pier, reling*; industry: *hendel*; railways: *buffer, cokes, lorrie, rails, tender, tram, trein, trolley, tunnel*; and parliamentary affairs: *boycotten, budget, club, debating-club, jury, lobbyen, meeting, platform*.

After 1840 English began to invade private and informal spheres. English names such as *Betsy, Mary, Nelly, Bob*, and *Willy* came to be preferred to French ones. Non-technical words started to be borrowed, such as *beauty, bluf, blunder, dandy, down, plenty, puzzel, shocking, snob, spleen, tipsy*, and *would-be*. At the end of the nineteenth century the English influence was still unimportant, as is illustrated by te Winkel (1901), who devoted only one page to English loanwords, claiming that 'although the words which Dutch has taken over from English are directly imported from the language, their number is smaller than one might expect'.

From the end of the nineteenth century onwards the influence quickly extended to other domains and the number of loanwords increased rapidly. Important domains affected were: sports, trade, insurance business, advertising, literary scholarship, publishing, office equipment and organization, and various fields in the informal sphere.

After 1945 'the American way of life' became a model for the rest of the world, America spreading its culture (music, film, literature), its political and economic ideas, and technology. English became the common language of international organizations and companies as well as of science and an obligatory subject at school, taking over the position of French as a prestigious international language. Old and new domains include: transportation and tourism, technology and chemistry, academic and scientific terms, photography, film and television, domestic words (housing, nutrition, clothing, hygiene, physical culture, and 'lifestyle'), drug users' jargon, music, business, politics, and military terms.

3.1.2 Origins of influence

Due to the great similarity of BrE and AmE and the fact that BrE is influenced by AmE, it is hardly possible to discover from which variety an individual word was borrowed. A distinction will here be made only where this is relevant. Words which were recently borrowed from America very often come from specific fields such as music, drugs, computer technology, telecommunication, or words from informal speech.

3.1.3 Types of influence

English influence is mostly in form of loanwords (but cf. ss. 3.3.8 and 3.4.2).

Some English loanwords have come to be restricted to the first or second position in Dutch compounds, often forming hybrids: *-burger* (*baconburger*, *cheeseburger/kaasburger*), *-freak* (*filmfreak*, *milieufreak*), *-minded* (*kunstminded*, *sportminded*), and *-stop* (*loonstop* 'wage-freeze'), as against *all-in-* (*all-in-prijs*), *baby-* (*babypiano*), *budget-* (*budgethotel*), *disco-* (*discomode*), *fancy-* (*fancyprijzen*), *fitness-* (*fitnesscentrum*), *indoor-* (*indoorbaan*), *instant-* (*instantpoeder*), *live-* (*live-optreden* 'live performance'), *top-* (*topattractie*), and *wild-west-* (*wild-westverhaal* 'wild west story'). Swearwords are used in a completely novel way in compounds: *fuck-* (*fuckmuziek*), *shit-* (*shitfilm*); also note the Latin-derived elements *mini-*, *maxi-*, and *video-* which are largely transmitted through English.

Four translated English words have become productive first elements in Dutch: *bijna-* as a translation of English *near-* in: *bijna-akkoord* ('near-agreement'); *doe-het-zelf-* as a translation of *do-it-yourself* in: *doe-het-zelf-centrum*, *doe-het-zelf-winkel*; *eersteklas-* as the translation of *first class* in: *eersteklassigaren* ('first class cigars'); and *zelfbedienings-* as the translation of English *self service* in *zelfbedieningsbedrijf*.

English influence is also responsible for compounds no longer being written in one word, names in particular, as in *Rijks Inkoop Bureau* for *Rijksinkoopbureau*.

The fact that many of these names are abbreviated (e.g. *RIB*) probably contributed to their separation. Computer terms are also frequently written as two words: *beeldscherm emulatie* ('screen emulation'). Today, one can even buy a *kogel bief-stuk* ('round steak') and *braad worst* at the butcher's.

Two kinds of compounds were prompted by German, but their productivity is now mainly due to English influence: noun participle combinations, such as *zonverbrand*, are possibly borrowed from German *sonnenverbrannt*, but have an equivalent in English *sunburnt*. Dutch *handgemaakt* was probably calqued on *handmade*. The popularity of these compounds is caused by the fact that they are precise and short, whereas alternatives (*met de hand gemaakt* etc.) are much too cumbrous. The second type are compounds like *Afrika-reizen*, *het Hite-rapport* which consist of a name and a noun.

Productive idioms which developed under English influence include: *ik ben bang dat* ('I am afraid...') and *er werden* [by a hurricane] *drie mensen gedood* ('three people were killed')—originally Dutch used *gedood worden* ('to be killed') only in the sense 'to be killed by a crime'. A very popular idiom is *de...-ste ooit* ('the... ever'): *de warmste novembermaand ooit* ('the warmest November ever').

There are also translations from English using past tense instead of present perfect; whether these will result in a change of the Dutch system is impossible to say.

3.1.4 Chronology of purist phases

Since the sixteenth century there have been occasional objections to the use of foreign words, as in the two dictionaries *Vocabularius van sommighe utlantsche woorden* by Jan van Mussem and the *Tresoor der Duytscher Talen* by Jan van de Werve (both 1553). Various other authors were involved in the battle against the 'corruption' of the Dutch language, Latin and French words forming the main butt of their activities.

In the nineteenth century the great number of German loanwords caused reactions, but not so much in Flanders, where French influence was felt to be most dangerous. English was of no great importance before the end of the nineteenth century although the number of loanwords was no longer small. In his *Bastaard-woordenboek* (Dictionary of Foreign Words) of 1895 Jan Broeckaert registered only 47 real English loanwords out of an estimated total number of 81,000 foreign words (0.06 per cent); these included *beefsteak, boksen, clown, club, coke, dandy, fancy-fair, high life, interview, lunch, meeting, partner, punch* (> *pons*), *rail(way), square, ticket, toast, tunnel, waggon*.

In the twentieth century, particularly during and after the Second World War, the purist movement also turned against English. The main butt was so-called 'anglicismen': words, expressions, or constructions which conflict with Dutch structural principles, such as (NEN 5050 1994): *frontpagina, onderlijnen, pijplijn*. Some words are only rejected because their meaning expanded under English influence, like *conservatief* 'careful', *typisch* 'representative', and *uitvinden* 'choose'. The resistance to numerous other loanwords appears to be rather ineffectual.

Many of the suggested replacements of English loanwords had no chance of success due to their complexity or vagueness: *bulkcarrier* was to be replaced by *vrachtschip voor stortgoed* or *massa-goedschip*, and *botsballon* was recently tried for *airbag*.

3.1.5 Geographic differences
(Cohen 1996)

The southern Dutch language area was exposed to massive French influence for centuries. The number of English loanwords in Flanders has been smaller than in the north for a long time and most of these were borrowed via French; in consequence they differ in pronunciation and intonation from English as well as from northern forms. Such imports included quasi-English words from French like *living* 'living room'. Some words differ in meaning in north and south: *flat* (in the north pronounced as [flɛt] and in the south as [flat]) is in the north used for an apartment in which all rooms are located on one floor and which is part of a multi-storey building; in the south a *flat* has only one sleeping room. *Camera* in the south only denotes a film- and not a photo-camera. In addition, English loanwords are considerably less popular in Flanders, especially colloquial words and words from the drug scene such as *shit, shot, (drug)scene, coffeeshop*. By contrast, there are a few words which are used in Flanders but do not occur in the Netherlands (or are rare), such as *holdup, baxter*, and some derivatives ending in *-ing* (*building, roofing, scouting, dispatching*).

The plural of nouns in *-en* is more frequent in Flanders than in the Netherlands, whereas verbs are more often assimilated by using the (originally French) suffix *-eren*: *boycotteren, recycleren, handicapperen, relaxeren*. The latter makes the formation of past participles more 'Dutch' than in the north: *gedeleteerd* vs. *gedeletet*.

Reactions to foreign words in Flanders are still dominated by a rejection of French words, and much less of German and English words. It is commonly held in Flanders that the people from the north adopt English words too easily.

3.1.6 Stylistic differences

In the beginning, terms relating to industrial processes and products and sports were borrowed from English. Although many technical terms continue to be taken over, particularly from the field of pop music, computing, and drugs, from 1840 on colloquial words were taken over in ever increasing numbers (de Vooys 1951: 24). They are now encountered in all fields, but especially in journalism and youth language. Recently it has become fashionable to use ephemeral, non-integrated loanwords: *die danst bad!* ('he dances badly'), *dat kun je wel shaken* ('forget it'). Additionally, funny 'translations' are popular among teenagers: *hear you* becomes *hoor je*, *heavy* becomes *heftig*, *peanuts* becomes *pinda's* 'trifle', and *see you* becomes *zie je*. Most of these words quickly make way for other new English fashionable expressions.

Popular words in yuppie language are: *bingo!, commitment, cool, deal, dammit, fake, loser, overstatement/understatement, relaxed, stressen*. Homosexuals use

English words in many contexts: *backroom* and *darkroom*, *buddy*, *buggerie* (besides the Dutchified form *bogger* 'sodomite'), *cockring*, *dijk* and *dyke* 'lesbian', the invective *fruitcake*, *gay*, *gesbian* (a combination of *gay* and *lesbian*), *nursing* 'play doctor', *one night stand*, *piercing*, *queer*, *safe-seks*, *spanking*, *straight*.

English influence on Dutch slang dates to the beginning of this century. The relevant Dutch dictionary by Endt (1974) mentions the following words: *afnokken* (from *to knock off*, sailor's slang), *aftaaien* (from *to tie (up)*), *bietsen* (from *beachcomber*), *'t (helemaal) maken* (from *to make it*), *te mats* 'too expensive, too crazy' (possibly from *too much*), *stuf* 'drugs', and *tipsie*.

3.1.7 Innovation and obsolescence
(Claus and Taeldeman 1989)

Before 1945 the Dutch knew far fewer English than French and German loanwords. The number of Anglicisms began to rise from the 1970s on. However, many English loanwords are ephemeral; the words tend to disappear after some time; they are either translated, or replaced by a Dutch equivalent, as *football* was by *voetbal*.

The number of English loanwords has recently become a matter of some concern. The Dutch language, it is feared, may lose its identity. Claus and Taeldeman (1989) showed that the number of English words in Dutch dictionaries rose from 0.16 per cent between 1898 and 1924 to 0.75 per cent between 1971 and 1976, and there was a sudden increase to 2.95 per cent between 1977 and 1984 (partly reflecting greater tolerance in the lexicographers). The number of words which are used only for a short period is probably much greater. However, the fear that Dutch is being flooded by English words is clearly not justified.

The latest developments show that some English loanwords push out older French ones: greeting formulas such as *adieu*, *au revoir* are being replaced by *bye*, *so long*; *boetiek/boutique* by *shop*; *coiffeur* by *hair stylist*; *dejeuneren* by *lunchen*; *hausse* by *boom*; *pardon* by *sorry*; *potpourri* by *medley*; *verifiëren* by *checken*. Some words which were originally borrowed from French are now pronounced the English way, like *agent*, *compatibel*, *relaxen*, *service* and *surprise*. Others have acquired, together with an English pronunciation, an additional meaning: *abstract*, if pronounced the English way, is equivalent to 'excerpt' in Dutch.

The same English word can be borrowed more than once in different forms: *kerrie—currie*. English *cake* was even borrowed four times, each time in a different form and meaning: in the seventeenth century as *keeks* 'a kind of pancake', in the eighteenth century as *kaakjes* 'a kind of spiced nuts', after that as *cake* and finally as *(honde)kaakjes* 'dog biscuits' (De Vooys 1925: 111).

Some words look like pseudo-English, but are in fact items which have disappeared in the source language, but are still alive in the borrowing language. Such fossils are (according to Posthumus 1996a): *fancy-fair* (present-day E *bazaar*), *butterfly* (now *bow-tie*), *goalgetter* (now *finisher*), *Browning* 'pistol', *plumpudding* (now *Christmas pudding*), *all-risk(s)polis* (now *comprehensive policy*). The word *crack* 'brilliant person' has certainly not disappeared from English but is now restricted to the first part in compounds: *a crack shot*.

3.1.8 Mediating languages

English words are normally directly imported into Dutch. In Flanders French has functioned as an intermediate language in the past.

A number of words were borrowed by Dutch twice, the first time via French and the second time straight from English, as one can see from the form: *akte—act, ballade—ballad, ballon—balloon, cadet—caddie, karton—cartoon, dessin—design, muzikaal—musical, salon—saloon, speciaal—special*. The French forms are always completely assimilated. Many Latin words were also borrowed twice: *bul—bill, kamer—camera, koor—chorus, ons—inch*.

In modern times many new English words were formed from Latin/Greek roots. Most of these words, such as *deodorant* and *insuline*, have become international and hence occur in Dutch as well. Since these items have nothing English in their form, they are excluded from the *Dictionary of European Anglicisms* collection.

3.1.9 English in education

(Kobayashi 1995)

Three modern languages—French, German, and English—were taught in secondary education until 1968. In 1968 the so-called 'mammoth-law' made English obligatory for all types of schools; other foreign languages were optional. In 1986 a new type of an integrated primary school was introduced for children from 4 to 12 with English as the only obligatory foreign language. In 1993 the school system changed again; for children from 12 to 15 primary education now prescribes two obligatory languages: English plus French or German. In secondary education (from 15 to maximally 18) children have to choose one language no matter which; most children opt for English.

Until the end of the 1960s French was the first foreign language in all Flemish schools. The pupils learned English only to a lesser extent and at a later stage. When the choice became free English pushed French quickly into second position.

Dutch and Flemish universities and colleges use English as one of the media for academic teaching. In various disciplines scientific publications are predominantly written in English. In 1989 the Dutch Minister of Educational Matters Jo Ritzen himself favoured lectures in English in order to serve the needs of foreign students and to improve the chances of students who finish their study abroad. The Dutch and Flemish reacted furiously, and in 1992 the Dutch Parliament included a proviso in the law which made Dutch the language of higher, academic education. Other languages can be used under certain circumstances. In line with this agreement the Faculty of Economy of the University of Tilburg decided in February 1997 to switch over to English completely, using it for announcements, invitations, and reports.

3.2 Pronunciation and spelling

(Posthumus 1986, 1988, 1991*a*, 1995)

3.2.1 Pronunciation

A number of common rules apply for spelling and pronunciation. Technical loanwords which were primarily borrowed via oral contacts in the nineteenth and at the beginning of the twentieth century are, as far as spelling and pronunciation are concerned, completely assimilated so that their English origin is hardly recognizable: *kroet* (English *crude*), *piekijzer* (*pig-iron*), *weespijpe* (*waste-pipe*), *wijer* (*wire*). Although these words are found in the dictionary of Van Dale (Geerts and Heestermans 1995), most (native) speakers no longer know them, and in a short time they will probably be totally lost.

Post-1945 loanwords are frequently less thoroughly assimilated, partly because the words became familiar in spoken as well as in written language (via the media, in advertising, as trade names, in films, etc.) and partly because the knowledge of English has increased. Younger speakers now tend to adopt loanwords in their original phonetic form. This practice, if exaggerated, can sound conceited. Additionally there is a big difference between northern and southern varieties of Dutch: people in the Flemish area use spelling pronunciations more often than people in the north, partly reflecting less exposure to spoken English and partly French mediation. However, words are now borrowed increasingly in their English form—only a few younger people consider it funny to pronounce English loanwords the Dutch way.

It is not significant whether words are borrowed from the spoken or written language. A word clearly borrowed from the written form is *folklore*, whose constituents were not recognized, so that the stress moved to the second syllable and the word is now divided into 'fol-klore'.

Whether loanwords are pronounced as in English or are assimilated to Dutch pronunciation (partly based on spelling) depends on a number of factors such as regional origin, the educational standard of speakers, analogies, the phonetic structure, the frequency of the word, and the date of its adoption (van Bezooijen and Gerritsen 1994: 154). In active use the context or interlocutor can influence pronunciation.

The differences in phonemic structure and in pronunciation between English and Dutch are fairly great. However, in most cases there are no phonetic obstacles against the borrowing of an English word. One can always find an appropriate Dutch sound to replace an English one.

3.2.1.1 Consonants

- Fairly great differences exist in the realization of /r/, which varies a great deal in Dutch. Also *w(h)* is realized differently from English. However, this has no negative consequences for borrowing.
- There are no /θ, ð/ in Dutch. The phonemes are mostly realized as [d] (*to the point*), sometimes as [t] (*thinner*), and rarely as [s] (*thriller*).

- English [-ʃ] (*finish*) is realized as [sj] and sometimes as [s], but the latter is commonly regarded as highly colloquial 'plat') in the north of the Netherlands.
- Plosives and fricatives are always devoiced word-finally, a rule which is extended to English words (*trend, club*).
- English < g > is rendered in different ways. A study of the pronunciation of *drugs* and *goal* (van Bezooijen and Gerritsen 1994) showed three ways of pronunciation: pronunciation as in English [g] (especially in words like *goal*), assimilated Dutch [k] (especially for *drugs*, cf. *brik* instead of English *brig*), and assimilated [x] (one third of the occurrences for both *drugs* and *goal*). The latter can be due to spelling pronunciation since < g > is commonly pronounced as /x/. It is remarkable that [x] often occurs in Flanders, possibly caused by a purist rejection of 'alien' elements, a reaction which obviously includes French and English elements. The pronunciation of English < ch > and < j > is sometimes simplified by cluster reduction: from [tsj] to [sj] and from [dzj] to [zj]. *Cheque, chips, choke, jam* are pronounced [sjek], [sjips], [sjook], [sjem] (contrast *charter* [tsjartər]) and *jury* is realized as [zjuriə] (contrast *jingle* [dzjingəl] and *jungle* [dzjungəl]). *Joker, jumbo, jumper* have spelling pronunciations with [j]. However, the number of adaptations is comparatively small in the north (apart from a few everyday words), and it is unlikely that it will rise due to the widespread knowledge of English.
- Concerning the pronunciation of consonants at morpheme boundaries the normal Dutch rules apply: in *zakdoek* as well as in *breakdown* one can find assimilation to simple [d], and in *roadtest, snack country* simple /t/, /k/.

3.2.1.2 Vowels

In most recent loans English pronunciation and spelling are taken over together, with the exception of < u >; because [ʌ] does not exist in Dutch, it is replaced by the normal pronunciation of Dutch *u*. The English spelling–pronunciation correlation often differs from Dutch: for instance, < a > is pronounced as [a(a)] in Dutch. This does not stop most Dutch speakers from pronouncing *a* as [e:] or [ε] in English loanwords. A few words have spelling pronunciation, for example in *kaak* 'cake', *claxon, overlappen*, or vary [tram] vs. [trem], [traktor] vs. [trektor].

3.2.1.3 Stress

In most English loanwords the stress is on the first syllable (as in Dutch), whereas French loanwords are normally end-stressed. The position of the word stress can thus indicate whether a word is borrowed, and from which language. Sometimes the stress of an English loanword is shifted to the end of the word to adapt it to Dutch conventions (*columnist, deodorant, snobisme*) or if the speaker takes it for a French loanword: *attachékoffer* (influenced by the older French loan *attaché*), *budget, comfort, corduroy, essay, pamflet*—a feature shared with other continental languages.

3.2.2 Graphemic integration

Recent English words are borrowed in their original spelling. This has led to spelling pronunciation in some of the oldest loans with reference to vowels (cf. cases such as 'tram'). Only in a few cases is an English *a* or *ai*, which is pronounced [ɛ] or [e:], realized as < e(e) > as it is in *flens* ('flange'), *hendel* ('handle'), *reling* ('railing'), *pleet* ('plate'). Even more sporadically English < e(e) > is pronounced [iə], spelt *ie*: *kien* (English *keen*). We also find *sien*, *wiet* and *scene*, *weed*, where the assimilated Dutch spellings occur exclusively in the language of teenagers or drug users. There is variation also in *moven*, *looken* and *moeven*, *loeken*; in older loanwords *y* was changed to *i* or *ie* (*herrie*) and *(o)u* to *oe* (*hoela*, *toerist*), whereas in more recent loanwords *y* and *ou* are retained (*hurry*, *discount*).

The spelling of the consonants is assimilated only in older loanwords and in colloquial words: < c > was changed into < k > (*kapseizen*, *kluts*), < x > to < ks > (*seks*), <sh-> to <sj-> (*sjekkie* next to *shag*), and <-ch> to <-s> (*kluts*, *pons*).

The Dutch use of diaeresis is commonly not applied to English loanwords where the two vowels are pronounced separately: *efficiency* and not *efficiëncy*.

Dutch has borrowed letter combinations which were formerly not known in native words such as <wh-> (*whiskey*), <sh-> (*shampoo*), <sc-> (*scalp*), <oa > (*coach*), <ea> (*leasen*), and <-ll> (*baseball*).

The growing familiarity with English has also led to a few orthographical interferences. In English the genitive singular is indicated by *'s*; in Dutch this realization is only used after long vowels (*Ada's overwinning*), in other cases *-s* is used. However, *'s* is increasingly used to indicate the genitive of a proper name: *Pietje's tas*, *Vondel's werken*. This is sometimes regarded as an English influence, but it is supported by the fact that *'s* helps to indicate that the *s* is not part of the name.

Plural forms of English loanwords which end in *-y* are now often spelt *-ies* instead of *-y's*: *babies* versus the official *baby's* (cf. *ie*, s. 3.3.2). It is unlikely that this will affect usage in dictionaries and grammars.

3.2.3 Homonyms and homographs

Due to the close relationships between English and Dutch the number of homonyms and homographs has increased. Homographs include *boom* 'tree' and, with an English pronunciation, [bu:m] 'rise, boom', *brand* 'fire' and [brent] 'brand name'. In sports one finds the verb *passen*, with an English pronunciation, and the term *post* from basketball; *putten* is used in the stock exchange business and in golf. Homonyms are words with identical spelling and pronunciation, such as *dribbelen*, which means in Dutch 'to walk with small steps' and which has received an additional meaning from English ('move the ball forward with slight touches'). At the same time the number of homonyms is growing because words which were borrowed from Romance languages (French or Latin) before, are reborrowed from English, mostly in another meaning (see s. 3.4.2): *data* 'dates' adopted the meaning 'facts, data' from English. And finally a loanword can be identical with a native word at the moment of adoption, such as *hall*, which changed into *hal*.

3.3 Morphology

3.3.1 Introduction

Dutch nouns are uninflected for case apart from an old genitive ending in -*s*; only plural is indicated. Gender distinctions are expressed in the definite article. The inflectional system of adjectives and nouns is reduced to a minimum. Verbs vary according to person, number, tense, and mood. Loanwords are commonly integrated in this process so that they can be combined syntactically with the rest of the vocabulary without any problems. This process of adoption sometimes involves a state of uncertainty. Concerning the infinitives of verbs this process normally occurs quickly; by contrast the inflection of verbs can cause considerable spelling problems; cf. s. 3.3.5.

3.3.2 Nouns

3.3.2.1 Gender

(Geerts 1970, 1975; Koenen and Smits 1992: 10; Poplack, Pousada, and Sankoff 1982; Posthumus 1996*b*; Verhoeven and Jansen 1996)

Dutch has two grammatical genders, which can be identified by the use of the definite article: '*het*' (neuter) and '*de*' (masculine and feminine = 'common'). In new loanwords the allocation of a gender is obligatory. Most English loanwords are treated as 'common' (words designating persons have natural gender—*steward* is masculine, *stewardess* is feminine). If neuter *het* is chosen, this can be explained by grammatical, semantic, and analogical reasons:

1. *Grammar*. The suffix determines article and gender: all words starting with *ge-* and ending in -*ment* are neuter *(gerace, management)*; words on -*ing* have the article *de* (*dancing, hearing*), analogous to Dutch *mededeling*; however, if they correspond to a Dutch infinitive in the function of a noun they often have *het*. For these Dutch infinitives occur as alternatives, cf. *het ballroomdancing* vs. *het ballroomdansen*, *het bodybuilding* vs. *het bodybuilden*, and *het brainstorming* vs. *het brainstormen*.
2. *Meaning*. All names of materials, sports and games, languages, and collective terms are neuter; consequently it is *het plastic, het hockey, rugby, tennis; het basic, het panel, sample, design*.
3. *Analogy*. If the sound pattern and meaning of the loanword are identical with those of a native word, the loanword has the same article and gender as the native word: *het dashboard* is modelled on *het bord*. As a consequence of a shared meaning *het concern* is modelled on *het bedrijf*, *het image* on *het beeld*, *het label* on *het etiket*, *het ticket* on *het kaartje*. However, *de creditcard* is analogous to *de kaart*, *de approach* to *de aanpak*, *de club* to *de vereniging*. Analogy is the least predictable factor, for it is often not clear which native word is considered equivalent. Of native Dutch words about 75 per cent have the article *de*, and only 25 per cent *het*. It is striking that the number of loanwords with *het* is even smaller. Thus the increasing number of English

loanwords contributes to making the article *het* more and more marginal (Geerts 1975).

3.3.2.2 Number

(Hoppenbrouwers 1978, 1980; Posthumus 1989*b*)

Most Dutch nouns form their plural in -*en*, but -*s* is a minority option. In consequence, English plurals in -*s* are normally retained. A minority of English loanwords have two plural forms: *budgetten* and *budgets*, *testen* and *tests*, *trams* and *trammen*. Words ending in a sibilant often retain the English -*es*: *coaches*, *sketches*; however, dictionaries often give alternative plural forms: *lunchen/lunches*, *matchen/ matches*, *speechen/speeches*. By contrast, *boxen*, *faxen*, *pieren*, *sporten*, *telexen* have -*en* exclusively. Most English words in -*tor* also have two plural forms -*s/-en*: *tractors/tractoren*, *transistors/transistoren*; older loanwords often prefer -*en*, and more recent ones -*s*: *boxen—black boxes*, *doggen—underdogs*, *liften—face-lifts*, *pluggen—drugs*, *stewardessen—hostesses*, *strippenkaart—strips*; and also those with the suffix -*ing*: *puddingen—happenings*.

English *knickerbockers*, *overalls*, *pyjamas*, *shorts* are regarded as plural forms in Dutch; this has led to non-English 'singulars': *knickerbocker*, *overall*, *pyjama*, *short* (this does not apply to *jeans*).

Some loanwords ending in -*y/-ie* are regarded as diminutive forms, which follow the vulgar Dutch pronunciation in -*ie* as [jə]: *koekie*, *vissie*. This has led to hypercorrected forms such as *flopje*, *gupje*, *pupje*; also forms like *flop*, *gup*, *junk*, and *yup* have been coined through backformation.

3.3.3 Adjectives

(Royen 1952)

Adjectives are inflected in -*e*; this applies to borrowed adjectives: *clever—clevere*. However, adjectives ending in a vowel are unchanged (*heavy*). Comparatives and superlatives follow Dutch rules: *clever/cleverder*, *trendyer/trendyste*.

3.3.4 Adverbs

Uninflected adjectives can be used as adverbs in Dutch; this includes borrowed adjectives. English adverbs ending in -*ly* are not borrowed, with the possible exception of *recentelijk* (from *recently*); the adjective *recent* is borrowed from French.

3.3.5 Verbs

The adaptation of English infinitives proceeds fairly quickly: English *to dim*, *to fix*, *to film*, *to flirt*, *to relax*, *to settle* have -*en* added: *dimmen*, *fiksen*, *settelen*. Some English verbs add -*eren*, a suffix which is borrowed from French. *Alloceren* (pronounced as [allokerən] with [k], as in English), *formatteren*, *implementeren*, *shockeren* are Dutch derivations of English verbs or nouns. The -*eren* ending makes the conjugation of the verbs easier; it is more popular in the south.

The conjugation of English verbs is easy in the spoken language, but it can cause considerable problems in written forms. Some people use English morphemes as in *finishede, gefinished; screenede, gescreened* instead of the Dutch forms *finishte, gefinisht; screende, gescreend*. In particular English verbs in *-e* cause problems in spelling, since Dutch verbs do not have base forms with an *-e*. These verbs vary between *-et* (*racete, geracet*) and *-ed* (*savede, gesaved; timede, getimed*). Dictionaries contradict each other in such cases.

In 1995 a new version of the *Woordenlijst van de Nederlandse Taal* was published, in which the spelling of Dutch words was codified. Verbs of English origin are treated as follows:

1. If the base form ends in a vowel, the simple past has *-de* and the past participle *-d* (*rugbyen, rugbyde, gerugbyd*).
2. If the base form ends in a voiceless consonant, the simple past is formed with *-te* and the past participle with *-t* (*faxen, faxte, gefaxt*); in all other cases *-de/-d* is used (*scrabbelen, scrabbelde, gescrabbeld*).

In English the *-e* sometimes indicates the pronunciation of the preceding vowel or consonant. This *-e* in the root remains in the conjugation (*barbecue, barbecuede, gebarbecued*). However, in combination with [o], as in *scoren*, the *e* disappears and the *o* is doubled in closed syllables: *scoren, scoorde, gescoord*.

In English spelling the duplication of a consonant often indicates a short preceding vowel; this double consonant grapheme is reduced in Dutch clusters: *volleyballen, volleybalde, gevolleybald*. Sometimes there is variation in the final sounds. Some speakers pronounce an [s] in *leasen*, others a [z]. In *briefen* and *golfen* some people pronounce an [f], others a [v]. In such cases both conjugations are possible: *leaste/leasde, gegolft/gegolfd* (Nederlandse en Belgische regering 1995; Timmers 1993).

3.3.6 Derivation (selection)

In most cases English loanwords can easily form derivatives such as *bunkeren, egotrippen, filmisch, fitheid, geflirt, gehandicapten, trendmatig, verfilmen*. It is not always possible to decide whether a derivation was formed in Dutch or whether it was borrowed from English because some suffixes are identical in both languages, especially *-er* and *-ing*. Furthermore, there are many loans attested in derivational word families, for example noun and verb: *boycot—boycotten, interview—interviewen, mailen—mailing*.

Gender specification. In Dutch, words for males can be adapted for females by derivation: *de typist* (M) vs. *de typiste* (F); *barkeeper* (M) vs. *barkeepster* (F). Sometimes a Dutch word is used for both genders as in English (a *manager* can be a woman as well as a man), and sometimes a word is taken over with the English suffix indicating the gender: *steward—stewardess, host—hostess*.

Agent nouns. Since both Dutch and English use the suffix *-er* for agent nouns and tools, it is often not possible to determine whether a particular word is borrowed from English or formed in Dutch. Are words like *manager* and *voetballer*

borrowed, or derived from *managen, voetbal(len)*? Sometimes there is no English
model, which means that they must have been formed in Dutch: *filmer, hockeyer,
lifter*.

Denominal verbs. A verb can be freely converted into a noun (or a noun into a
verb) in both Dutch and English, that is, zero derivation is a very productive
process in the two languages. Whether such verbs are borrowed or formed in
Dutch is not always clear. This holds true for *liften* 'search for a free lift' and
squashen 'play squash', which must be derived in Dutch because English uses *to lift,
to squash* in other meanings. In Dutch the agent noun *lifter* is again derived from
liften. *Baseballen, basketballen, brunchen, golfen, pingpongen, puzzelen, speechen,
volleyballen* are Dutch derivations of the borrowed English nouns. In addition,
there are many backformations on the basis of English nouns in *-ing*: *aquaplaning,
bodybuilding, powerlifting* gave rise to Dutch *aquaplanen, bodybuilden, powerliften*.
Zero derivation can also be used to form nouns out of English verbs which do not
exist in English; e.g. the noun *flirt* in Dutch is derived from *flirten*, whereas English
uses *flirtation*.

New adjectives. There are only a few adjectives derived from borrowed nouns:
filmisch, freakerig, trendmatig 'according to the trend'.

Deadjectival nouns. Hardly any new derivatives are formed from borrowed
adjectives; a possible exception is *fitheid*, which can be explained as derived from
fit, or which can be borrowed from *fitness* with suffix replacement.

3.3.7 *Compounds, combining forms, and idioms*

Compounds made with English elements are very frequent: *arbeidspool, bungalow-
tent, campingbeheerder, cocktailjurk, efficiencybeurs, gasfitter, gordijnrail, intakege-
sprek, lease-auto, modeshow*, etc. *F-side* was invented in Dutch; the expression
designates uncontrollable Ajax supporters who were always led into block F of
the Ajax stadium in Amsterdam. There are also hybrid compounds combining an
English and a French loanword: *fraudeteam, privé-club, recherchebijstandsteam,
weekendretour*. The verbs *in-/uitchecken, in-/uitfaden, in-/uitloggen, in-/uitzoomen*
are compounds which translate English *to check in/out, to fade in/out, to log in/out,
to zoom in/out*; also cf. *afchecken, afkicken, inpluggen, oppeppen, opstarten*, and
overrulen. By contrast, *inplannen, intapen, omturnen, opboksen*, and *uittesten* were
coined in Dutch.

The spelling of English compounds often raises problems. In English compounds can be spelt in three ways: separate, in one word, or hyphenated: *ghost
writer, ghostwriter, ghost-writer*. In Dutch compounds are written in one word, at
least as far as accepted loanwords are concerned. As long as loanwords are still
'alien', English spelling conventions can be followed. This results in different kinds
of treatment in the dictionaries. Additionally English supports the spelling of
compounds as two separate words; this also influences Dutch compounds (*computer systeem*; cf. s. 3.1.3). Language purists vehemently oppose these developments.

English idioms can be borrowed into Dutch or be translated: *after all, business as
usual, dos and don'ts, grand old man, in no time, in the long run, last (but) not least,*

missing link, never mind, of all people/places, off the record, on the rocks, point of no return, red tape, safety first, self-fulfilling prophecy, total loss, up to date, ups and/en downs.

Translated expressions include *als regel* ('as a rule'), *de tijd doden* ('to kill time'), *het kost een fortuin* ('it costs a fortune'), *gemengde gevoelens* ('mixed feelings'), *hoeksteen van de samenleving* ('cornerstone of society'), and *het groene licht geven* ('to give the green light').

3.3.8 Calques (loan translations)

Two types of calques can be distinguished in cases where two closely related languages are in contact. A loan formation is a translation of a compound or derivation using cognate elements like *diepvries, luidspreker, vrijdenker* for English *deep-freeze, loudspeaker, freethinker*. By contrast, if unrelated (but equivalent) words are used, we may call the process and the result a loan translation (thus *blauwdruk* for *blueprint*, *draaitafel* for *turntable*, in which *druk, draai* are the translation equivalents of *print, turn*). A remarkable word is *welvaartsstaat* for *welfare state*—this must be a loan formation, since Dutch *welvaart* has a different meaning from English *welfare*, namely 'wealth'.

There are also semi-calques like *bantamgewicht* for *bantam weight, dataverwerk-ing* for *data processing, loopbaanplanning* for *career planning, praatshow* for *talk show*, and *teamgeest* for *team spirit*. However, such words can also be original combinations of an English and a Dutch word, not following an English example.

Sometimes an English loanword is in due course replaced by a calque. Think of *football*, which was used for a short period in the past, but which has now been definitely replaced by *voetbal* (except for the special form of *American football*, and in *FC* as the abbreviation of *Football Club* in names of soccer clubs). Occasionally, a loanword coexists with a loan translation: *feasibility study* with *haalbaarheidsonderzoek, space-shuttle* with *ruimteveer, verdunner* with *thinner*.

3.3.9 Abbreviations, syllable words, and contractions

The use of abbreviations and acronyms has increased enormously since the nine-teenth century; this is largely due to English influence. In the twentieth century this kind of word flourished in politics, especially in totalitarian states such as Germany after 1933 and the USSR.

English and Dutch prefer acronyms to words combined from syllables. A few abbreviations were borrowed from English: *c.d., l.p., w.c.* (originally a taboo word), and (in pronounceable form) *aids, ECU, laser, radar, sonar, VIP*, and names of organizations such as *NATO, UNESCO*.

Borrowed blends are somewhat rarer: *faction* for *fact + fiction, infotainment* for *information + entertainment, smog* for *smoke + fog*. Compare clippings: *ad* (*adver-tisement*), *airco* (*air conditioning*), *fan* (*fanatic*), *hifi* for *high fidelity, prefab* (*prefab-ricated*), *tram* (*tramway*), *vamp* (*vampire*).

3.4 Meaning

Loanwords retain only one or a few meanings of polysemic items. Thus *keeper* is borrowed only in a sports context. Sometimes two different meanings are successively borrowed, often from different domains, such as *film* ('membrane' and 'pictures') and *chip* (relating to potatoes and computers). Furthermore, sometimes the 'real' meaning of the loanwords can become opaque; this explains Dutch *paardebiefstuk* (literally 'horsebeefsteak') because there is no association of *biefstuk* with 'beef'. After a word is borrowed, it can add meanings, sometimes including senses not recorded in English.

Many recent words have borrowed a meaning from English, as in *doen* as 'deal with superficially': *in twee dagen Parijs doen* (E *to do*); *brug* as 'dental bridgework'; *edelmoedig* as 'magnanimous'; *flessehals* as 'choke point' (*bottleneck*); *haan* on a rifle (*cock*); *heet* as 'recent': *heet nieuws, hete informatie* (*hot*); *mol* as 'spy' (*mole*); *spotten* as 'see' (*to spot*), *schaduwen* as 'follow unobtrusively' (*to shadow*); *ster* as 'famous person' (*star*).

3.5 Usage

Claus and Taeldeman (1989) found that the number of English words had increased in all domains, even though the growth in the last decades had been most spectacular in the fields of technology and music. In some domains nearly all innovations are expressed by English words, but after some time a number of these English words disappear or are replaced by another (sometimes another English word, sometimes a loan translation or a new formation: *beeldscherm* for *monitor*). English words are definitely more popular among the young than among older people.

More and more annual reports, product and job advertisements, and titles of films and books are formulated in English. A study of advertisements for products (Gerritsen 1996) has shown that 19 per cent of the corpus contained some English, being completely (15 per cent) or partly (85 per cent) in English. Gerritsen then studied the attitudes towards these advertisements and the comprehension among younger (younger than 25 years) and older (above 45) people all chosen from the higher social classes. The study showed that the informants valued the use of English positively (the older having a more negative attitude), and that they strongly overestimated their own knowledge: many informants were not able to produce a correct translation of the English. Gerritsen concludes that Dutch is less Anglicized than one is inclined to think; English is often used, but not always understood. Current research at the University of Nijmegen reflects a unanimously more positive attitude towards English, particularly among pupils. Certainly nobody wants to see Dutch disappear, and the position of Dutch is not seen as being directly threatened by English (De Bot 1997).

3.6 Forms of linguistic loans and their categorization

1. *Borrowing*

As we have seen above all sorts of lexical loans occur. Loanwords borrowed according to form and meaning are the biggest group. They can be divided according to the degree of their adaptation in Dutch.

> (*a*) The loan is not adapted and not regarded as a part of the Dutch vocabulary (code-switching, foreignisms).
> (*b*) The loan is foreign or not adapted in its form, i.e. *meeting* and *thriller*.
> (*c*) The loan is completely integrated, i.e. *basketbal*, *dimmen*.

2. *Replacement*

> (*a*) The foreign word is adopted in meaning but not in its form (a loan translation): *belastingvrij* for *tax-free*, *draaitafel* for *turntable*.
> (*b*) Only a part of the compound is translated: *praatshow* for *talk show* and *teamgeest* for *team spirit*.
> (*c*) The foreign word is replaced by cognate items (loan formation): *diepvries* for *deep-freeze*.
> (*d*) A foreign word is rendered by a free translation, i.e. *gemeenschapszin* for *public spirit*, *koppensneller* for *head-hunter*, and *verstekeling* for *stow-away*; *hoorzitting* for *hearing* (to which *zitting* is added); *vouwblad* for English *folder*.
> (*e*) An existing Dutch word adds a meaning from English (semantic calque): *controleren* meaning 'to control'.

Loanwords are much easier to discover than replacements, since their form remains identifiable as foreign.

3. *Pseudo-loans*

(Posthumus 1991*b*, Van der Sijs 1994)

When loanwords are completely accepted they can diverge from the development in the source language. A loanword can be shortened in Dutch as in *baby doll* for English *baby-doll pyjamas*, *camping* for English *camping site*, *detective* for *detective story*, *pocket* for *pocketbook*, *gin-tonic* for *gin and tonic*, *panty* for *panty-hose*, *strip* for *comic strip*, *living* for *living room* (spread via French and Flemish). *Twen* as a short form of English *twenty* was coined in German and handed on to Dutch. *Professional* is shortened to *prof* in Dutch and to *Profi* in German; the English say *pro*. Further examples are *happy end* for *happy ending*, *mixdrink* for *mixed drink*, *stationcar* for English *estate car*, AmE *station wagon*, and possibly *jack* for *jacket*. Such pseudo-loans are of three types.

Lexical pseudo-loans are combinations of English words or morphemes used to form new linguistic items which do not exist in the donor language, i.e. *babybox* (English *playpen*), *speakerbox* (English *speaker*), *city-bag* (English *holdall*), *dumpshop* (English *army surplus store*), *hometrainer* (English *home exerciser* or *exercise machine*), *rally-paper* (English *paper-chase*), *ribcord* (English *corduroy*), *showcaravan* (English *demonstration model*). There are no English equivalents for *ladyshave*, *showmaster*, or *talkmaster* either. Many of these words are intentionally coined in advertising or fashion.

A separate category is words borrowed from English ending in *-ing*. In English these are originally present participles or verbal nouns. In English *dancing* means 'the action of dancing', in Dutch 'an occasion/site for dancing'; in English *doping* means the action, in Dutch also 'drugs'; Dutch uses *franchising* where English uses *franchise*. Many of the above-mentioned pseudo-English words seem to be more or less international (and many have been transmitted through French).

Many pseudo-borrowings develop a non-English meaning; Dutch *Manchester* designates a type of cloth which is called *corduroy* or *velveteen* in English.

3.7 The future of Anglicisms

Despite reactions from purists, the number of English loanwords is likely to increase in the near future. The study by Gerritsen (1996) shows that the attitude towards the use of English in advertising is not particularly positive and that the knowledge of English among addressees is sometimes overestimated. Will the two factors help to slow down the influx of English words?

3.8 Research

In the past a great deal of research into loanwords (including Anglicisms) was carried out by De Vooys. English loanwords were studied in the Anglistisch Instituut te Groningen by Zandvoort, Gerritsen, and in particular Posthumus. There is little systematic research apart from this; it is striking that Koenen and Smits (1992), a book which has no scholarly aim, is the only dictionary of 'Anglicisms' in Dutch. Most contributions on English loanwords are published in popular journals such as *Onze Taal*, and are often biased by a purist point of view.

3.9 Bibliography

BENSE, J. F. (1924), *The Anglo-Dutch Relations from the Earliest Times to the Death of William the Third* (The Hague: Nijhoff).

BEZOOIJEN, RENEE VAN, and GERRITSEN, MARINEL (1994), 'De uitspraak van uitheemse woorden in het Standaard-Nederlands: Een verkennende studie' (The Pronunciation of Foreign Words in Standard Dutch: A Contrastive Study), *De Nieuwe Taalgids*, 87: 145–60.

BOT, K. DE (1997), 'Nederlands en Engels kunnen goed naast elkaar bestaan' (Dutch and English can Coexist well Enough), *Taalschrift*, 1: 28–9.

CLAUS, P., and TAELDEMAN, J. (1989), 'De infiltratie van Engelse (leen) woorden in het Nederlands en in Nederlandse woordenboeken' (The Infiltration of English Loanwords in

Dutch and Dutch Dictionaries), in S. Theissen and J. Vromans (eds.), *Album Moors*, 11–30.

COHEN, HARRY (1996), 'Coca versus Cola: Verschillen tussen Nederland en België in het gebruik van Engelse leenworden' (Coca vs. Cola. Differences between the Netherlands and Belgium in the Use of Loanwords from English), in Van der Sijs 1996: 307–12.

ENDT, E. (1974), *Bargoens woordenboek* (Amsterdam: Rap).

GEERTS, G. (1970), 'De nominale klassifikatie van ontleningen' (The Nominal Classification of Loanwords), *De Nieuwe Taalgids* (Van-Haeringen-nummer), 43–53.

——(1975), 'Het genus van Engelse leenwoorden in het Duits en in het Nederlands' (Grammatical Gender of English Loanwords in German and Dutch), in R. Jansen-Siebens, S. de Vriendt, and R. Willemyns (eds.), *Spel van zinnen: Album A. van Loey* (Brussels: Éditions de l'Université).

—— and HEESTERMANS, H. (eds.) (1995), *Van Dale's Groot woordenboek der Nederlandse taal* (Van Dale's Big Dictionary of the Dutch Language), 12th edn. in new spelling (The Hague: Nijhoff).

GERRITSEN, JOHAN (1986), 'Dutch in Contact with English', in Wolfgang Viereck and Wolf-Dietrich Bald (eds.), *English in Contact with Other Languages* (Budapest: Akadémiai Kiadó), 51–64.

GERRITSEN, MARINEL (1996), 'Engelstalige productadvertenties in Nederland: Onbemind en onbegrepen' (English-Language Commercial Advertising in the Netherlands: Unliked and Misunderstood), in R. van Hout and J. Kruijsen (eds.), *Taalvariaties: Toonzettingen en modulaties op een thema*, Feestbundel voor Toon Hagen (Dordrecht: Foris), 67–83.

HEEROMA, K. (1952), 'Oudengelse invloeden in het Nederlands' (Old English Influences in Dutch), *Tijdschrift voor Nederlandse taal- en letterkunde*, 70: 257–75.

HOPPENBROUWERS, COR (1978), 'Regels voor de meervoudsvorming in het Nederlands' (Rules for Pluralization in Dutch), in *Proeven van Neerlandistiek aangeboden aan prof. dr. Albert Sassen* (Groningen: Nederlands Instituut).

——(1980), 'De meervoudsvorming in het Nederlands', in Th. Janssen and N. F. Streekstra (eds.), *Grenzen en domeinen in de grammatica van het Nederlands* (Groningen: Nederlands Instituut), 159–79.

KOBAYASHI, SAYURI (1995), *The Role of Foreign Language Education in the Netherlands* (Osaka).

KOENEN, LIESBETH, and SMITS, RIK (1992), *Peptalk: De Engelse woordenschat van het Nederlands* (Peptalk: The English Vocabulary of the Netherlands), 2nd edn. (Amsterdam: Nijgh & Van Ditmar). (The 1st edn. had the authors' names reversed.)

Nederlandse en Belgische regering (1995), *Woordenlijst van de Nederlandse taal* (Wordlist of Dutch), 2nd edn. (The Hague: Sdu Uitgevers). (1st edn. 1954.)

NEN 5050 (1994), *Goed woordgebruik in bedrijf en techniek: Woordenlijst met taalkundige aanwijzingen* (Good Usage in Technics: Wordlist with Linguistic Advice) (Delft: Nederlands Normalisatie Instituut).

POPLACK, SHANA, POUSADA, AILICIA, and SANKOFF, DAVID (1982), 'Competing Influences on Gender Assignment: Variable Process, Stable Outcome', *Lingua*, 57: 1–28.

POSTHUMUS, JAN (1986), *A Description of a Corpus of Anglicisms* (Groningen: Anglistisch Instituut).

——(1988), 'De uitspraak van Engelse leenwoorden' (The Pronunciation of English Loan-words), *Onze Taal*, 57: 112–13.

——(1989a), 'Over floppy's, guppy's en yuppies: Schijnbare verkleinwoorden uit het Engels' (On *floppies*, *Guppies*, and *Yuppies*: Seeming Diminutives from English), *Onze Taal*, 58: 123.

56   **Amand Berteloot and Nicoline van der Sijs**

POSTHUMUS, JAN (1989*b*), 'Hybridische woorden: Engels-Nederlandse samenstellingen' (Hybrids: English-Dutch Compounds), *Onze Taal*, 58: 219.

——(1991*a*), 'De acceptatie van Engelse leenwoorden in het Nederlands' (The Acceptance of English Loanwords in Dutch), *Terminologie et traduction*, 1: 163–93.

——(1991*b*), 'Hoe komen wij tot "namaak-buitenlands?"' (How Do we Get to 'Imitation-Foreign'), *Onze Taal*, 60: 11–13.

——(1995), 'Describing the Pronunciation of Loanwords from English', in Jack Windsor Lewis (ed.), *Studies in General and English Phonetics: Essays in Honour of Professor J. D. O'Connor* (London: Routledge).

——(1996*a*), 'Fossielen' (Fossils), in Van der Sijs 1996: 338–9.

——(1996*b*), 'Het woordgeslacht van Engelse leenwoorden' (Grammatical Gender of English Loanwords), *Onze Taal*, 11: 279.

ROYEN, GERLACH (1952), 'Fleksie van uitheemse adjektieven' (Inflexion of Foreign Adjectives), *De Nieuwe Taalgids*, 35: 224–6.

SIJS, NICOLINE VAN DER (1994), 'Pseudo-ontleningen' (Pseudo-loans), *Onze Taal*, 63/5: 99–101; 63/10: 228–9.

——(1996), *Leenwoordenboek: De invloed van andere talen op het Nederlands* (Dictionary of Loanwords: The Influence of Other Languages on Dutch) (The Hague: Sdu Uitgevers).

SMITS, R., and KOENEN, L. (1989), *Peptalk & Pumps: Engels woordgebruik in de Nederlandse taal* (*Peptalk & Pumps*: English Usage in the Dutch Language) (Amsterdam: Rap). (Review: Nicoline van der Sijs, 'Engelse woorden in het Nederlands' (English Words in Dutch), *Onze Taal*, 58 (1989), 216–17.)

TIMMERS, CORRIEJANNE (1993), *Faxen, faxte, gefaxt: De juiste spelling van ruim 700 aan het Engels ontleende werkwoorden* (To Fax, Faxed, Faxed: The Correct Spelling of about 700 Words Borrowed from English) (Apeldoorn: Auctor).

VERHOEVEN, GERARD, and JANSEN, FRANK (1996), 'Het woordgeslacht van Engelse leenwoorden' (Grammatical Gender of English Loanwords), *Onze Taal*, 6: 156–7.

VOOYS, C. G. N. de (1925), 'Engelse invloed op het Nederlands' (English Influence on Dutch), in *Verzamelde taalkundige opstellen* (Collected Linguistic Articles) (Groningen: J. B. Wolters), ii. 71–119. (Summary: 'Hoe zijn anglicismen te beschouwen?' (How to Treat Anglicisms), *De Nieuwe Taalgids*, 8 (1914), 124–31, 161–81, 225–35.)

——(1946–56), 'Engelse invloed op het Nederlands' (The English Influence on Dutch), *De Nieuwe Taalgids*, 34: 145–9, with (almost) annual updatings in 40: 172–3, 41: 175–6, 42: 72–3, 43: 93–6, 46: 82–5, 47: 285–7, 49: 3–9.

——(1951), *Engelse invloed op de Nederlandse woordvoorraad* (English Influence on the Dutch Vocabulary), Verhandelingen der Koninklijke Nederlandse Akademie van Wetenschappen, afd. Letterkunde, NR LVII, no. 5 (Amsterdam: North Holland).

WINKEL, JAN TE (1901), *Geschiedenis van de Nederlandsche taal* (History of the Dutch Language) (Culemborg: Blom & Olivierse).

ZANDVOORT, R. W. (1964), *English in the Netherlands: A Study in Linguistic Infiltration* (Groningen: J. B. Wolters).

4

NORWEGIAN

Anne-Line Graedler

4.1 History of language contact

4.1.1 Chronology of intensive influences

(Haugen 1976, 1978; Norsk språkråd 1982)

Contacts between England and Norway are well documented at least from the Viking Age onwards, but although this contact resulted in some lexical borrowing from Old English into Old Norse (mostly words of Latin origin), a much more extensive contribution was made with the introduction of Christianity during the tenth and eleventh centuries. The early missionaries to Norway came from the British Isles, and brought with them a host of words, often Greek or Latin in origin, and more or less directly related to the Christian faith, the clergy, and the Church, such as *prest* 'priest, vicar' and *kirke* 'church'. These early English loans are no longer conceived of as foreign.

The rise of the Hanseatic League introduced a long period in which Norwegian contacts with the Continent were more important than those with Britain. Middle Low German, and after the Reformation High German, with Danish as the intermediary language, took over as the main sources for borrowing.[1]

This chapter is based on parts of my doctoral dissertation (Graedler 1995), and on the Introduction to *A Dictionary of Anglicisms in Norwegian* (Graedler and Johansson 1997). I would like to thank the following persons: Stig Johansson for kindly reading the whole chapter, Endre Brunstad for comments on the section on Purism, and Deborah Strutt for proofreading the manuscript.

[1] Norway was under Danish rule from 1380 to 1814, and during this period no official independent Norwegian linguistic norm existed. Norwegian and Danish are linguistically closely related, and for the most part mutually intelligible, and Danish continued to be used as the written standard, with minor modifications, during the century following 1814 (Norway was in union with Sweden between 1814 and 1905). Developments in the official language in Norway prior to 1814 are thus really developments in Danish. As an indirect result of this historical fact, Norwegian is now codified in two closely related written standard forms, with equal official status. An attempt to create a new national standard based

From the nineteenth century onwards, three main developments can be distinguished: these are discussed below in chronological order.

In the nineteenth century the technical and industrial revolution reintroduced the English language on the scene. Flourishing trade contacts are reflected in dictionaries of foreign words and expressions, which include terms for British units of measure, textiles, and other imported products, in addition to words directly associated with financial transactions. A number of English terms for food and drink, articles of clothing, and other words related to the social life of the privileged classes, as well as leisure-time activities, like card games and sports, were also adopted. New inventions from England or the USA carried English names, and there are also a number of English terms and expressions associated with maritime life, and reflecting British dominance in world trade and shipping.

Around the turn of the century, borrowing was still basically a means to provide the language with necessary new terminology, and English loans are characteristically technical terms. Otto Jespersen (1902) compiled a list of English loanwords which he divided into domains including the public sphere, the life of the upper classes (including articles of clothing), sports, card games, the railway, agriculture, maritime, literary, and other cultural terms. A number of these new terms indicate changes in society, such as terms associated with industrial life, and with various sports activities.

Aasta Stene (1945), who studied the situation immediately prior to the Second World War, makes use of ten major categories in her classification of English loans: sports and games; transport, travel, and holiday-making; the sea, ships, and sailors; trade; dress, fashion, personal appearance; food, drink, hospitality; cultural life; religion; politics; society. Sports and games is the dominant category, representing more than one fifth of the material. There is a relatively large number of soccer terms, suggesting that this sport had become both popular and widespread, and a number of Anglicisms used in connection with other sports introduced from English are also included, such as bandy, ice hockey, tennis, golf, boxing, and racing. Stene also shows how the mechanization and motorization of the shipping fleet require a new terminology. A number of Stene's categories indicate the increasing dominance of the USA in matters both technical and cultural, such as the motor trade and air travel, photography and film. In view of later developments, the group of words associated with music and dancing is small, but the impact of American cultural expressions is evident.

The bulk of the English vocabulary in Norwegian has come in, however, after 1945. One dictionary estimates that 80–90 per cent of all post-war Norwegian words of foreign origin, including translation loans and semantic extensions of Norwegian words, can be traced back to English influence (Norsk språkråd 1982: 15). Exposure to English language is high, through education, travel and tourism, television, movies and popular music, magazines and books, and the Internet, and English loans are encountered in all forms of modern cultural and scientific

on the Norwegian rural dialects was made around 1850 by Ivar Aasen, resulting in the modern written standard of *Nynorsk*. Parallel to this, a Danish-based variety was adapted, through a series of reforms, resulting in the modern written standard of *Bokmål*.

communication in Norwegian, as well as in subcultures and slang. In some text types, notably scientific prose, pop music lyrics, and lifestyle advertising, English is taking over as the major language at the expense of Norwegian, to the extent that one may speak of a loss of entire domains to English.

4.1.2 Origins of influence

Because of the relationship with Britain described in the previous section, it is safe to assume that most of the earlier English loans came into Norwegian from BrE. Norwegian immigration to America resulted in some new words, but these are mostly foreignisms, and are used with unique reference to things or phenomena specifically associated with the USA.

At a later stage, however, and especially following the Second World War, many of the new words have come from AmE. This reflects the increasingly dominant role of the USA as a world power, in terms of economy, politics, and culture. No formal criteria exist whereby the origins of influence may be determined.

A very few loans have their origin in English-speaking societies outside Britain and the USA. Again, these are mostly foreignisms, such as *homeland* (South Africa).

4.1.3 Types of influence

(Stene 1945; Graedler 1998; Graedler and Johansson 1997)

Lexis. As seems to be the case in most distant contact situations, the most widespread type of influence from English in Norwegian is lexical borrowing. Many different types of lexical elements are borrowed: bound elements (*-minded*), simplexes (*show*), compounds (*paperback*), phrases (*sitting duck*, *shake hands*), and longer expressions (*if you can't beat them, join them*).

Orthography. Indications of borrowing on the level of spelling are not as obvious as those on lexis, but some tendencies may be observed. The letters *c*, *q*, *w*, *x*, and *z*, not normally used in Norwegian words, are sometimes used for effect in non-English words, presumably because of the association of English vocabulary with the modern and trendy. An example is a former TV youth programme called *Kluzz* (Norwegian *kluss* means 'mess; trouble'). A similar phenomenon may be noted in cases where old loans like *box*, normally <boks> in Norwegian, occur in ads and elsewhere with a reversion to the English spelling. English is also frequently blamed for other orthographic tendencies, such as the separate writing of compounds, which should be written as one word according to Norwegian rules, and the use of *'s* as possessive marker *-s*.

Pronunciation. As English is by far the best-known non-Nordic foreign language in Norway today, even foreign words and names of non-English origin sometimes seem to be perceived as English, at least in terms of English rules for pronunciation. Thus, one may hear a German named David introduced on the radio as ['deɪvɪd], and the painter Klee spoken of as [kliː]. Some old Latin loans seem to be changing in pronunciation; for instance, words like *volum* and *massiv*, traditionally pronounced with stress on the second syllable, are today more often heard with stress on the first, and this, too, can possibly be attributed to English influence.

Morphology. Typically, word classes differ with respect to the freedom with which they adapt to the morphological system of the borrowing language. Whereas verbs, almost without exception, are instantaneously integrated, borrowed nouns often carry with them elements from the English system, notably the plural -*s*. The ending -*s* is used in Norwegian as one way of forming the possessive in nouns, but not as a plural marker. However, with the increasing English lexical influence, the association of -*s* with the category of plural seems to be catching on. The plural -*s* is sometimes used for humorous effect with Norwegian words, and is also occasionally found with foreign words of non-English origin, as in the authentic examples *saunas* and *anoracks* [*sic*].

A curious morphological phenomenon which seems to have English origins, but which has taken on a life of its own in Norwegian, is the ending -*ings*, which is presumably a combination of -*ing* + plural -*s*. The ending serves as a stylistic marker to make the base form more informal, and is productive with a wide variety of words, from different word classes: *rullings* 'hand-rolled cigarette', *dritings* 'dead drunk', *mornings* 'good morning', *skjerpings* 'concentrate!, shape up!'

Syntax. Even syntactic influence from English may be said to occur, although the evidence here is less clear. Some verbs show a development in transitivity, such as the Norwegian intransitive verb *gro* 'grow', which is increasingly heard in transitive uses: *gro skjegg* 'grow a beard', *gro vekster i hagen* 'grow plants in the garden'. Another type may be connected to translationese, where we find expressions like Norwegian *Ja, det er* 'Yes, it is' (normally Norwegian *Ja, det er det*).

4.1.4 Chronology of purist phases

(Brunstad 2001)

Purist ideas have a relatively long tradition in Norway, but up until the Second World War efforts were mostly directed towards the Latinate and, in the case of *Nynorsk*, the Danish- and German-derived vocabulary. After the war, however, the influence from English has received increasing attention. During the 1960s and 1970s, Alf Hellevik spoke of the borrowing from English in terms of a linguistic 'invasion' (Hellevik 1963, 1970).

Recently, at least two national campaigns have been initiated partly with the express purpose of protecting the Norwegian language from the increasing and harmful English influence. The most important of these, called 'Aksjonen for språklig miljøvern' (The Campaign for the Protection of the Linguistic Environment), was launched in 1990 by the Norwegian Language Council, whose members feel that the impact of English has been such that it constitutes a genuine threat to the characteristics of the Norwegian language:

The fact that influence from English creates disorder in Norwegian is clearly demonstrated. No one benefits from disorder in the system. Communication is made more difficult, and so is writing correctly. *The loanwords that we admit into our language should not be so numerous that we cannot adapt them to Norwegian.* (Norsk språkråd 1990: 13; my translation)

Purism with reference to English is not restricted to the lexicon, but also includes orthography and morphology. Thus, a list of suggested Norwegianized spellings for a number of English loans, such as <sørvis> for earlier <service>, was issued by the Norwegian Language Council in 1996 (see Blaauw, Vernegg, and Langslet 1996). Articles on the topic can also be found in a number of periodicals whose chief concern is the state of the Norwegian language, and it is a favourite topic of contributors to the newspapers' letters columns. While many writers treat the phenomenon of borrowing from English as a problem, the issue has been hotly debated, and the above-mentioned campaign has also received criticism. The arguments against borrowing may be summarized as follows:

1. English spelling conventions and its sound system make Anglicisms difficult to integrate and use within the Norwegian system.
2. An extensive use of English loans can lead to a widening of the gap between groups of the population (those who know English and those who do not).
3. Using Norwegian rather than English words in a given subject area has an important symbolic function, and helps to maintain the status of Norwegian as a living language.
4. Some domains of language use may be taken over completely by English, and Norwegian, being a small language, needs protection.

4.1.5 Regional differences

Only occasional geographical differences are discernible in the Norwegian written standard language (no official standard norm exists for spoken Norwegian), but the standard of *Nynorsk* (see n. 1 above) has traditionally been more purist than the standard of *Bokmål*. A few old and characteristically oral loans may be typical of one region or town, due to specific sociocultural factors, such as the expression *gå te pisis*, allegedly from English *go to pieces*, which is used in Western Norway, but is unknown elsewhere.

4.1.6 Stylistic differences

As in most European countries, early English loanwords in Norway were of a predominantly technical kind. This has continued to the present time, not surprisingly, since one of the main motives for borrowing from English seems to be to introduce new things, concepts, or phenomena, and these, in turn, often come from the English-speaking world. The use of English loanwords in a text thus produces particular stylistic effects: the text appears technical, professional and authoritative, objective and precise.

Other, more recent motives for borrowing are closely linked to the status of English as a prestige language. English elements are extensively used in advertising and in texts promoting new trends and ideas. Here, the stylistic effect achieved may be one of modernity, urbanity, and internationalization.

Oral usage often reflects a different type of Anglicism. Influence that reaches Norway through commercial and technical channels can frequently be detected in writing, but influence as manifested in the subculture of, for instance, teenage groups rarely finds its way into published written sources, although it may be an important feature of the language behaviour of such groups. Slang is usually associated with group identity, but even slang expressions have a tendency to seep into the standard language after a while.

4.1.7 Innovation and obsolescence

There have only been a few attempts to measure the English element in Norwegian. The proportional increase of English lexical items in the standard vocabulary can be estimated by comparing various editions of dictionaries, but since Norwegian lacks the equivalent of an *OED* or a *Duden*, the comparison must be between different dictionaries rather then different editions of the same dictionary.

One dictionary of foreign words from the mid-nineteenth century (Hansen 1842) contains just over 200 English entries, which is less than 2 per cent of the total. In another dictionary of foreignisms dating from the same time, the English component is less than 0.5 per cent, which illustrates the problem of quantifying lexical influence. By comparison, English entries in a relatively recent dictionary of foreign words (Berulfsen and Gundersen 1986) amount to slightly more than 7 per cent. The proportion in a modern standard dictionary of Norwegian (*Bokmåls-ordboka*; Landrø and Wangensteen 1993) is 3.4 per cent, counting all words that in one way or another originated from English. This represents slightly more than 10 per cent of all the words with foreign etymologies in this dictionary (Gundersen 1990: 1923).

There has been no systematic investigation of the rate or the causes of obsolescence. Many words are no longer in regular use because the object, concept, or phenomenon they designate has gone out of use or is no longer of public interest. Also, because a number of loans function as slang expressions, they tend to go out of fashion, and be replaced by new words after a period of time. Moreover, a conscious policy to introduce Norwegian substitutions and calques for English loanwords has caused many loans to disappear. Recent examples of successful substitution include *datamaskin* for *computer* and *nakkesleng* (literally 'neck-toss') for *whiplash injury* (more examples appear below in s. 4.6).

4.1.8 Mediating languages

Since first Denmark, and later Sweden, have been dominant in Norway (see n. 1), it is safe to assume that many foreign words have entered Norwegian with these languages acting as intermediaries. But Norway has also had direct contact with Britain, notably as a seafaring nation (see s. 4.1.1). Many words first borrowed into French, and characterized by their French pronunciation, like *budsjett* (< E *budget*), have kept this feature on entering Norwegian, but may well have travelled via German and Danish on their way north. It is difficult to describe precisely the routes for individual words, and little research has been done in this area. The following loans have reasonably well-attested routes:

(a) through French
    beefsteak   ? (later simplified to *biff*)
    budget   x (*budsjett*—evidence: pronunciation)
    riding coat   x (*redingot*—evidence: form)
    wagon   x (now obsolete—pronounced as if from French)

(b) through German/Danish
    cakes   ? (*kjeks*)
    coke(s)   ? (*koks*)

4.1.9 English in education
(Gundem 1986, 1989; Sandved 1998)

English first received a place in Norwegian secondary schools with the Education Act of 1869, and in 1896 it was made compulsory as the second foreign language in secondary schools. However, it did not become the first foreign language until 1935, and although English was well established as a school and university subject before 1939, the war accelerated a shift in emphasis from German to English. English played an important role in the democratization process in Norwegian primary education in the 1950s, under the slogan 'English for everyone', and Norwegian children now receive at least seven years of compulsory English in school, and usually more after that. Today, a majority of Norwegians have had at least some formal training in English.

Education prepares the ground for the introduction of a number of English words and expressions through, for instance, the press and the media. Education in English has often been mentioned as one of the main obstacles to Norwegianizing English loans, and it has been suggested that awareness of the English original or source word affects the pronunciation of established loans.

Parallel with developments in Norwegian schools, an increasing number of Norwegians get some of their education abroad, often in an English-speaking country. An international education is highly valued, and during the 1980s some Norwegian schools and universities started offering international qualifications modelled on the British and American systems.

4.2 Pronunciation and spelling

4.2.1 Pronunciation
(Stene 1945; Schmidt 1982; Grønvik 1990a, 1990b)

The pronunciation of English loanwords in Norwegian displays a wide range of variation. Since no official standard of pronunciation exists for Norwegian, the information given in this section is based on the variety sometimes called Standard Eastern Norwegian, which is spoken by many Norwegians living in and around Oslo.

The following factors seem to be relevant to the pronunciation of loanwords in Norwegian:

1. The age of the speakers, their level of education, geographical background, acquaintance with and exposure to English, and their attitude towards English.
2. The age of the loan, its frequency, length, and complexity, its degree of integration on various levels (spelling, morphology), and the type of style in which it is used.

4.2.1.1 The English and Norwegian sound systems compared

Consonants

There are many similarities between the two consonant systems, and the majority of English consonants represent few problems. Minor differences are: the English alveolar sounds /t, d, s, n/ have more dental counterparts in Norwegian, and whereas English /v/ is a fricative, Norwegian /v/ is often classified as a frictionless continuant. Norwegian /r/ also differs from the RP realization, in that the Norwegian sound is either a 'rolling r', or uvular in parts of southern and western Norway. Postvocalic <r> is almost invariably pronounced in English loans, probably reflecting the orthography of the words. A number of English consonant sounds have no Norwegian equivalents. These are often replaced by existing Norwegian sounds in speech:

E [tʃ]	>	Nw [ʃ] *chips*, occasionally [ç] *kjommi* (< E *chummy*)
E [dʒ]	>	Nw [j] *jobb* (< E *job*)
E [θ]	>	Nw [t] *thriller*
E [ð]	>	Nw [d]
E [z]	>	Nw [s] *old boys*
E [w]	>	Nw [v] *web*

Norwegian consonant sounds that do not exist in standard English pronunciation are sometimes heard in English loans. This applies to digraphs with <r> as the first element: <rt>, <rd>, <rn>, <rl>, <rs>, realized as retroflex sounds [ʈ], [ɖ], [ɳ], [ɭ], [ʃ]; and to consonant clusters containing <s>, such as <sl> and <rts> realized as [ʃl], and [tʃ], or [ɭ], respectively. The last variant is found especially in loans that have entered via oral channels. Occasionally [k] before front vowels is realized as [ç], as in *kjeks* (< E *cakes*).

Vowels

The vowel systems of English and Norwegian, though similar in many respects, also display a number of important differences, as illustrated in Fig. 4.1 (*a–d*) (the chart for English is based on the standard variety known as Received Pronunciation or RP). In cases where the systems do not match, there are no hard and fast rules by which Norwegian vowels replace the English ones in adapted loans, and the channel of borrowing (oral or written) probably plays an important role here.

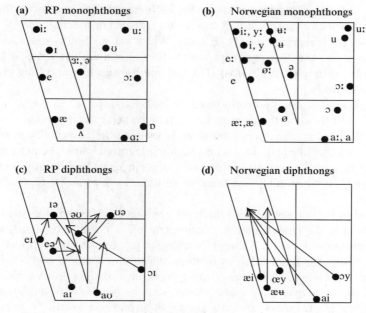

Fig. 4.1

Monophthongs

1. English [iː] is almost always pronounced as Norwegian [iː], as in *green*. The same is mostly true of the short [ɪ], which is usually Norwegian [i], as in *image*. When spelt <y>, the pronunciation may be [y] in Norwegian, as in *pyjamas*, and when spelt <e>, it is sometimes pronounced [e], as in *revolver*.

2. English [ɑː] is usually pronounced as Norwegian [aː], as in *half*. When followed by an *r* we get both [aːr] in *hard-disk* and [ar] in *farm*. The word *Derby* is sometimes pronounced with a spelling pronunciation ['dærby].

3. English [ɔː] is usually pronounced as Norwegian [ɔː], a fact which is sometimes reflected in the spelling with <å> of highly integrated elements, such as *trål* (< E *trawl*) and *ålreit* (< E *alright*). Some earlier loans show less consistency, and we find [a] in *stopp en hal!* (< E *stop and haul*, an expression used at sea) and [aː] in *sjal* (< E *shawl*). The vowel [ʉː] occurs in *eksos* (< E *exhaust*). In *sport* the vowel is shortened as a result of the following consonant cluster. The short [ɒ] is usually pronounced as Norwegian [ɔ], as in *rock*, but it has a spelling pronunciation with [a] in *watt*. *Yacht* is usually pronounced with long [ɔː] in Norwegian.

4. English [uː] is usually pronounced as Norwegian [ʉː], as sometimes reflected in spelling: *kul* (< E *cool*), *turist* (< E *tourist*), *stuert* (< E *steward*), *jus* (< E *juice*), or with [jʉː] in *deuce*. In *sjampo* (< E *shampoo*), stress has been shifted to the first syllable, and the second syllable is an unstressed [u] in Norwegian. The short English [ʊ] is usually pronounced as Norwegian [ʉ], as in *putte* (< E *put*).

5. The closest equivalent to English [ɜː] is Norwegian [ø], and this is the sound that is usually substituted, as sometimes reflected in spelling: *flørt* (< E *flirt*), *sørvis* (< E *service*), *tørn* (< E *turn*). When the spelling is <er>, or in one case <ir>, the Norwegian pronunciation in some older loans is [æ]: *bermuda-*, *sjirting* (< E *shirting*). The old loan *turnips* has a spelling pronunciation with [ʉː].

6. English [e] is usually pronounced as Norwegian [e], as in *essay*, but when followed by <r>, the pronunciation may be [æ(r)], as in *terrier*.

7. English [æ] is often pronounced as Norwegian [æ], especially in relatively recent loans like *acid*. In old and highly integrated loans, the pronunciation may be a spelling pronunciation with [a], as in *jazz*. Occasionally, a narrower sound, Norwegian [e], has been substituted, as in *pledd* (< E *plaid*), *hands*, *back*.

8. English [ʌ] is a sound for which no obvious Norwegian equivalent exists. Probably the closest match, Norwegian [a], is hardly ever used, with the exception of *karri* (< E *curry*). Norwegian [ø] seems to be the most popular substitute for English [ʌ], as is often reflected in spelling: *bløff* (< E *bluff*), *dønn* (< E *done*). A number of older loans have spelling pronunciations with [ʉ], such as *klubb* (< E *club*); others, such as *jungel* (< E *jungle*), have [u]. *Robber* (< E *rubber*, in card games) is pronounced with Norwegian [ɔ]. *Country* is sometimes pronounced with [ɔ] or [au], presumably as a combined result of spelling and hypercorrection.

9. English [ə] can in principle be pronounced as any vowel sound in Norwegian, depending on the spelling in English, as Norwegian does not have the reduced sounds of English. We may thus get [ʉ] in *supporter*, [u] in *propell* (< E *propeller*), [ɔ] in *nylon*, [a] in *festival*, etc.

Diphthongs

10. English [eɪ] in recent loans is usually pronounced as either [eɪ] or Norwegian [æi], depending on the degree of integration, the latter being the most highly integrated. Thus, *tape* can be either [teɪp] or [tæip]. In older loans, there is a wider range of variation, and a number of words have [eː], such as *baby* and *trene* (< E *train*). Short [e] occurs in *kjeks* (< E *cakes*).

11. English [aɪ] is usually pronounced as Norwegian [ai], as in *haike* (< E *[hitch]hike*), but some highly established loans have [æi], such as *streik* (< *strike*) and *ålreit* (< E *alright*). Spelling pronunciations also occur, with [i] in *pilot* (with a shift in stress), and [yː] in *nylon*.

12. English [ɔɪ] is pronounced as Norwegian [ɔy], as in *royalty*.

13. English [əʊ] is usually pronounced as [ou] in recent loans, such as *soul*. In older loans the vowel may be [ɔ], as in *koks* (< E *coke(s)*) or [ɔː], as in *båle* (< E *bowl*).

14. The same is true of English [au], where most recent loans have [au], such as *sound*, but where an old loan like *cowboy* is pronounced with Norwegian [ɔ].

15. The English diphthongs [ɪə, eə, ʊə] are usually not pronounced as diphthongs in Norwegian, but as [ir, er, ʉr], respectively, as in *pir* (< E *pier*), *fair*

and *tour*. English [eə] is also sometimes pronounced as [æːr], as in *skvær* (< E *square*).

In the guide to pronunciation given in the *Dictionary of European Anglicisms*, regular substitutions that occur when a loanword is pronounced with Norwegian sounds have not been marked. Thus the code '=E' is used even though the sounds are not strictly speaking 'English sounds'. For more unpredictable substitutions full or partial indications of pronunciation have been given.

Tonemes

Norwegian also distinguishes words on the basis of two different tonemes in stressed syllables. Most loanwords get toneme 1, a rising tone marked by the symbol [ˈ], but some forms, notably verb forms, invariably get toneme 2, a falling-rising tone. This is the case with all infinitives, and has been marked in the pronunciation with the symbol [ˮ] occurring immediately in front of the stressed syllable. Norwegian derivations forming agent nouns ending in *-er*, like ˮ*bokser* 'person who boxes', and action nouns ending in *-ing*, like ˮ*doping* 'the act of taking or administering drugs', also get toneme 2. This allows for a differentiation between these Norwegian derivations, which are conceived of as intimately connected to the action described by the verb, and any similar forms taken over directly from English, which may have more specific and less predictable meanings. Thus, ˈ*boxer*, with toneme 1, can only be used to refer to the breed of dog, and ˈ*doping*, with toneme 1, may be used to refer to the actual drug. Designations for concrete objects, such as English instrument nouns with the *-er* suffix, often seem to retain their foreign pronunciation, even when a corresponding verb has also been borrowed. Thus, *printer*, used in connection with computers, is usually pronounced with toneme 1, even though the verb *printe (ut)* 'print out' is fairly frequently used.

4.2.2 Graphemic integration

(Sørland 1993; Blaauw, Vernegg, and Langslet 1996; Sandøy 2000)

As is well known, English is a language with a particularly complex (and, from the point of view of the learner, poor) correspondence between orthography and pronunciation. The problem with respect to the integration of loanwords, if the Norwegian system is to be upheld, is whether to keep the English spelling, or something close to it, and try to approach the pronunciation to the written form, or to alter the spelling to fit the pronunciation as it is realized in Norwegian. Both strategies are used; in *jungel* [juŋel] (< E *jungle*), *nylon* [nyːlɔn] and the verb *grabbe* [ˮgrabe] (< E *grab*), spelling and pronunciation correspond. The importance of spelling is also shown in s. 4.2.1, where the choice of substitution vowels may differ according to the orthographic form of the English word. In other loans, many of which have probably entered via oral channels and slang, we find adapted spelling forms: *tøff* (< E *tough*), *ålreit* (< E *all right*), *grønsj* (< E *grunge*).

As mentioned in s. 4.1.4, one of the tasks of the Norwegian Language Council has been to promote Norwegianized spellings for loanwords. Two different and conflicting views seem to lie at the base of language planning in this area:

1. the principle that etymologically foreign words should also reveal their foreignness in form, and that the energy of language planners should be directed at inventing good replacements, rather than integrating foreign word material, and
2. the principle that loanwords likely to remain in the language should be adapted at an early stage, avoiding an entrenchment of the foreign form.

There is a wide range of variation with respect to spelling, and usage as well as official norms sometimes involve more than one form. Some general tendencies, in addition to those noted under s. 4.2.1, are:

Consonants

1. English word-initial <c> becomes Norwegian <k>, as in *kardigan* (< E *cardigan*).
2. English <ch> [k] becomes Norwegian <k>, as in *psyke opp* (< E *psych up*).
3. English <sh> and <ch> [tʃ] become Norwegian <sj>, as in *sjanti* (< E *shanty*) and *sjekke* (< E *check*).
4. English <qu> becomes Norwegian <kv>, as in *kvasar* (< E *quasar*).
5. English <x> becomes Norwegian <ks>, as in the verb *takse* (< E *taxi*, used of aeroplanes).
6. English word-final <gh>, pronounced [f], may become Norwegian <ff>, in *tøff* (< E *tough*) and *røff* (< E *rough*).

Vowels

English <a>

7. pronounced [e(:)] may become Norwegian <e> in old loans like *blezer* (< E *blazer*) and *brekk* (< E *(hand)brake*);
8. pronounced [æi] may become Norwegian <ei>, e.g. in *teip* (< E *tape*);
9. pronounced [æ] may become Norwegian <æ> in informal writing, e.g. in *kræsje* (< E *crash*) and *ræpp* (< E *rap*);
10. pronounced [ɔ] may become Norwegian <å>, e.g. in *trål* (< E *trawl*) and *ålreit* (< E *alright*).

English <i>

11. pronounced [æi] may become Norwegian <ei>, e.g. in *streik* (< E *strike*) and *ålreit* (< E *alright*) pronounced [ai] may become Norwegian <ai>, e.g. in *haike* (< E *(hitch)hike*).
12. English <ir>, <er>, and <ur> pronounced [ø:r] may become Norwegian <ør>, e.g. in *flørt* (< E *flirt*), *sørvis* (< E *service*), and *tørn* (< E *turn*).
13. English <oo>, <ou>, and <ui> pronounced [ʉ] may become Norwegian <u>, e.g. in *kul* (< E *cool*), *turist* (< E *tourist*), and *jus* (< E *juice*).
14. English <ou> pronounced [ø] may become Norwegian <ø>, e.g. in *tøff* (< E *tough*).
15. English silent word-final <e> is often dropped, e.g. in *teip* (< E *tape*), *sørvis* (< E *service*) , and *jus* (< E *juice*).

4.3 Morphology

(Graedler 1998)

4.3.1 Introduction

Norwegian nouns are inflected for the categories of gender, number, and definiteness; Norwegian adjectives for agreement with plurality and definiteness in nouns, and for comparison, and Norwegian verbs for tense and voice. Case inflection and occasional relics of number inflection for verbs are found in some dialects only.

4.3.2 Nouns

Gender. Historically, Norwegian has a three-gender system, with feminine, masculine, and neuter gender. This is reflected in most of the traditional dialects and in *Nynorsk*, where the natural or pronominal and the grammatical gender systems correspond. Agreement forms indicating a three-gender system are also found in *Bokmål*, where masculine nouns characteristically end in -*(e)n* in the definite form, feminine nouns in -*a*, and neuter nouns in -*(e)t*. One result of the complex historical situation is that two different gender systems, one natural or pronominal and one grammatical, coexist in *Bokmål*, and the choice between the feminine -*a* and the masculine -*en* endings is sometimes motivated by other concerns than the purely grammatical, for instance stylistic or social reasons.

The unmarked gender in present-day Norwegian is masculine,[2] and between 80 and 90 per cent of the borrowed nouns are assigned to this class. Gender assignment seems to be based mainly on semantic principles; for instance, animacy almost invariably results in masculine gender in new words, irrespective of the natural sex of the referent. Hence, *he-man*, *call girl*, and *pitbull* are all grammatical masculines. A few formal features, such as word endings and syllabicity, also have an impact on gender assignment, but in cases of conflict, semantic features seem to overrule the formal ones. For nouns with inanimate referents, the principle seems to be a type of assignment by analogy, in that loanwords take the same gender as a native equivalent. Thus, the loan *cover* is presumably neuter because of the native Norwegian equivalent *omslag*.

Number. Norwegian marks plural number with the endings -*er*, -*e*, the choice largely depending on the gender, and to some extent on the syllable structure of the noun. Although many loans occur regularly with a Norwegian plural, it is quite common for English loans to retain the English plural -*s*, an ending which is not found for Norwegian plurals.

The choice between the native plural form and -*s* seems to be largely influenced by three factors. The likelihood of a native plural inflection increases if the noun is of long standing in the language, if the suffix of a noun has a counterpart in Norwegian, such as -*er* and -*ing*, and if the noun is adapted in spelling. Other

---

[2] Endings for the masculine and the feminine gender are often the same, and some like to operate with a common gender class for *Bokmål*, where the class of feminines has been collapsed into the class of masculines. Specific feminine gender endings hardly ever occur with new loans from English.

factors which seem to correlate with the occurrence of the *-s* plural are distance marking (such as the use of inverted commas), textual support (such as an explanation of the meaning of the loan), and the length and complexity of an expression.

Definiteness. In Norwegian, the singular indefinite is the unmarked form, with zero inflection. Singular definite forms are marked by a suffix which was, historically, an enclitic article. Once a noun has been assigned its gender, the singular definite form follows automatically (see above under the section on gender). Some, mainly neuter nouns, have an optional plural definite form ending in *-a*. In addition to these definite forms, Norwegian nouns with definite reference may occur without an ending expressing definiteness. This represents the less common, and stylistically marked, choice. Interestingly this choice seems to occur more often with loanwords than with others; this may be a strategy for avoiding the problem of choosing an inflectional pattern.

4.3.3 Adjectives

Norwegian adjectives, as in English, can be inflected for comparison. There are three forms: the unmarked, or positive form, the comparative form which ends in *-ere*, and the superlative form, which ends in *-est*. Furthermore, gender, number, and definiteness agreement with the noun modified by an adjective may be expressed morphologically. The unmarked form is used when the adjective modifies a singular indefinite noun of masculine or feminine gender, either attributively, or in predicative position. The ending *-t* marks agreement with a neuter noun, and the ending *-e* marks agreement with a plural or definite noun. Whereas inflection for comparison is not obligatory, inflection for agreement with the noun often is. There are a number of restrictions on the occurrence of inflectional endings with domestic adjectives, and this sometimes makes it difficult to assess the extent to which a borrowed adjective is integrated. The tendency is for monosyllabic adjectives to be fully integrated. This group includes very recent and older loans, unless they are in some way restricted to idiomatic expressions or collocations, such as *fair* in *fair spill* 'fair play'. Adjectives of more than one syllable seem to be less well integrated morphologically. Most disyllabic adjectives remain uninflected, *ålreit* (< E *alright*), which frequently occurs with the *-e* ending, being a notable exception. Whereas adjectives ending in *-y* seem to be only sporadically inflected in writing, the situation is different in speech, where integrated forms are often heard. Adjectives of more than two syllables, compounds, and phrasal expressions are usually not inflected, as many native adjectives of this type are. Past participles frequently assume adjectival function, and in a number of cases the English form has been retained, sometimes with an adjectival inflectional ending, but often without.

4.3.4 Adverbs

Some adverbs may also be inflected for comparison, in which case the same rules apply as with adjectives. When adjectives are used adverbially, they usually have a *-t* ending.

4.3.5 Verbs

In contrast to English, standard Norwegian does not express progressive (continuous) aspect through inflection, nor does it make person or number distinctions in verbs. On the other hand, voice is expressed by inflection in Norwegian. Verbs have a passive form which ends in -s, in addition to periphrastic passive constructions which employ auxiliaries. As in English, only the present and past tense are expressed by inflection; other tense distinctions are formed with the help of auxiliaries.

Norwegian has three classes of regular verbs, distinguished on the basis of the past tense and past participle form. Only two verb classes seem to be productive with borrowed English verbs, Class 1, with the endings -et or -a in the past tense and past participle forms, and Class 2, which is rarely used, with the endings -te in the past tense form and -t in the past participle.

In the majority of cases, verbs are inflected according to Norwegian rules, which is to be expected, in view of the central role played by the verb in the syntax of the language: the verb is inextricably linked with the syntactic structure of the sentence in a sense that the other parts of speech are not. Borrowed verbs are also accommodated into the system in the sense that they enter into phrasal verb constructions. English and Norwegian are very similar in this respect and the English particles *in, out, over*, and *up* have close Norwegian formal and semantic parallels: *inn, ut, over, opp*. Hence, the transference is straightforward in most cases, as in *dress up*, which becomes Norwegian *dresse opp*.

Unintegrated verbs fall into two broad categories: participle forms and longer phrases. The English form is sometimes kept in the former, notably in passive constructions. In such cases, the borderline between verbal and adjectival functions is sometimes fuzzy.

4.3.6 Derivation (selection)

Action and agent nouns. The action noun derivation form with -*ing* and agent noun formations with -*er* are highly productive. Lexicalization of derived forms in -*ing* and -*er* is common; thus, *boksing* (< E *box*) may designate a particular sports event, as well as the action specified by the verb, and *dribling* (< E *dribble*) is a noun designating a specific activity in a soccer match, in addition to its more general action noun meaning. Similarly, *rafter* may either designate a sportsperson, or just anybody engaged in the activity specified by the verb.

As a result of the parallelism in form between English and Norwegian derived nouns in -*ing* and -*er*, there are word pairs where the derived Norwegian form with toneme 2 stresses the action of the verb, whereas the corresponding borrowed English form with toneme 1 may denote the concrete result of the verbal activity, or sometimes involve a more abstract meaning (see s. 4.2.1).

Conversion. The origin of nominal forms resulting from conversion (zero derivation), is often difficult to determine with any certainty, since multiple word class membership is common in English and the pattern is a productive morphological process in present-day Norwegian. However, where the meaning has more in common with the Norwegian borrowed verbs than with equivalent English nouns, such forms may be assumed to be Norwegian derivations, rather than direct loans, for instance *flørt* (< E *flirt*) 'flirtation' and *haik* (< E *[hitch]hike*) 'free ride'.

Denominal verbs. Norwegian nouns may be turned into verbs with an infinitive form based on the noun + *-e*. As in German, it may be difficult to decide whether verbs of this type have been borrowed, or are derived in Norwegian from borrowed nouns. In cases where the form and meaning are closely related to the borrowed noun, and far removed from a corresponding English verb, we may assume that the verb is a Norwegian derivation; this is the case with *handse* (< E *hands*) 'touch the ball with the hands (in soccer)', and *stresse* (< E *stress*) 'act in a nervous, busy manner'.

Verbs of Greek or Latin origin are usually adapted to Norwegian by a direct substitution of endings: E *-ate* > Nw *-ere*, E *-ize* > Nw *-isere*. Some verbs derived from English nouns have the longer ending *-ere*, and there are sometimes pairs of short and long forms existing side by side, such as *campe—campere* and *filme— filmatisere*, often as a result of earlier borrowing via French or German and later native derivations. Such pairs may give rise to differences in meaning.

New adjectives. The adjectival suffix *-bar* occurs in isolated instances, such as *diggbar* 'cool, groovy' (< Nw *digge* 'to like' <E *dig*), which is probably a loan mediated through Swedish. Participle forms often function as adjectives, even in some cases where an underlying base verb is hard to find. The present participle form *storscorende* 'scoring a lot of goals' lacks an infinitive form **storscore*, as does *trendsettende*. Rather, these forms seem to be based on corresponding agent nouns (*storscorer*, *trendsetter*). Some past participle forms, too, seem to be derived from verbs that never or rarely occur with other verbal endings, such as *handikappet* (< E *handicapped*) and *frika* (< E *freak*).

Deadjectival nouns. Adjectives may be nominalized by adding an *-ing* ending. This type is restricted to person-characterizing adjectives, and is colloquial in character, as with *tøffing* 'tough guy' (< Nw *tøff* < E *tough*). The ending *-het*, which produces abstract nouns, also occurs occasionally, for instance in *røffhet* 'roughness; the quality of being rough' (< Nw *røff* < E *rough*). A 'vocative' definite form ending in *-en* is highly colloquial, and probably restricted to only a few adjectives, for example *teiten* '(you) stupid person' (< Nw *teit* 'idiotic, stupid, boring' < E *tight*).

4.3.7 Compounds and combining forms

Norwegian, being a Germanic language, forms compounds easily. It is theoretically possible to compound an unlimited number of words, and the restrictions on compounding seem to be very few. The most common type of compound involving an English loan is where an English element occurs as the first constituent. Compounds of the Nw + E type are less frequent. The type E + E, where two English elements have been compounded after being borrowed into Norwegian, is a third option. Most compounds are nouns.

There is sometimes a classificatory problem with regard to constructions with nouns as premodifying elements (premodifying noun + noun), versus genuine compounds (noun + noun). English phrases often correspond to Norwegian compounds, but in translationese, phrases with premodifying nouns may be found, which violate Norwegian rules. A way of avoiding the sometimes awkward decision regarding the orthography of longer compounds, such as *heavy metal-gruppe* ('heavy metal group'), is to resort to ellipsis of one of the elements, as in *heavy-gruppe* or *metal-gruppe*.

In some instances, Norwegian makes use of a linking *-e-* or *-s-* (remnants of the case system), as in *jappekultur* 'yuppie culture' (Nw *japp* < E *yuppy*) and *sportslig* 'pertaining to sport'. Usage varies a great deal here, and no strict principles seem to be observed.

Compounding serves various functions in connection with loanwords. First, it is a means of introducing new words into the language: some English elements initially occur only in compounds and not as independent elements, which may facilitate integration into a Norwegian syntactic environment. Likewise, compounding with semantically relatively empty Norwegian elements may be a way of avoiding certain types of formal integration, such as inflection with plural *-s*. This strategy might also account for the occurrence of some pleonastic compounds such as *service-tjenester* 'service services', or *picnic-utflukter* 'picnic outings'.

In other examples a Norwegian cognate form is substituted for an English compound-final constituent, producing 'mixed paradigms'. *Gentleman* often occurs as *gentlemannen* in definite form, *punch-drunk* may become *punch-drukne* when agreement inflection requires an *-e* ending, and *tax-free* occurs as *tax-fritt* when used adverbially.

Compounding may also be regarded as a symptom of morphological integration, especially in cases where the English element occurs as the last constituent.

4.3.8 Calques (loan translations)

Calques and translation loans, modelled more or less closely on the English original, occur fairly frequently: *ansiktsløftning* (< E *face lift*), *kroppsbygging* (< E *body-building*), *skyskraper* 'cloud-scraper' (< E *skyscraper*). Finding suitable translations, or other Norwegian substitutes for the English loans, is often considered to be a better strategy in language planning than integrating the direct loans, and the Norwegian Language Council actively suggests new 'replacement words' (*avløserord*), as well as promoting ones that are already in use.

While there have been no systematic studies of the acceptance of suggested replacement words, it seems that descriptive Norwegian words with little or no formal dependence on the English loan are often more successful than direct translations, which may appear comical. A case in point is the loan *whiplash* (*injury*), for which two different replacements were suggested at an early stage, the direct translation *piskesnert*, and the independent creation *nakkesleng* ('neck-toss'). Only the latter has survived, perhaps because it was more transparent and easily understood. (For more examples, see s. 4.6.)

Whereas the translation of single words is often considered a good solution, the translation of longer expressions is often condemned as translationese.

4.4 Meaning

How borrowing affects the meaning of loanwords. In most cases, borrowing implies a selection of, or a restriction in, meaning in relation to the English original. The frequency of such examples, together with the fact that many loans seem to have a distribution restricted to particular topics or subject areas, emphasizes the role of borrowing in contexts where some kind of specialist language or terminology is required. Although some kind of restriction seems to be the rule, the possibility that 'the whole dictionary entry' may be taken over is theoretically present in cases where the word has a highly restricted and well-defined meaning in English, and where the contextual range is narrow and there is a low degree of polysemy. This is often the case with compound nouns like *t-shirt* and *skateboard*, but also with English neologisms such as *grunge*, and possibly also with words which are themselves loanwords in English, such as *chopsuey*.

When words are borrowed, it is typical with polysemous etymons that one or two or three senses or shades of meaning are taken over. Thus the 'family ties' that bind the different meanings of a lexeme together in the source language are severed when the lexeme is transferred to the borrowing language. This is clearly seen in the phenomenon sometimes referred to as reborrowing or double loan: word forms that have been borrowed more than once, with different meanings, and where the connection between the words is no longer evident. A Norwegian example is the loan *pickup*, meaning 'needle and arm of a record player', which later reappeared with the meaning 'small van'. In some cases the distance in time and context of borrowing between each loan has resulted in not only semantic, but also formal differences, as with *stuert* (< E *steward*) 'ship's cook' and *steward* 'person who serves passengers on a ship or plane', *sjappe* (< E *shop*) 'small shop' and *shop* 'speciality shop'.

Loanwords are borrowed as isolated units, and usually do not come with a family of derived and related forms; they are therefore, at an initial stage at least, relatively isolated elements in the vocabulary of the receiving language. This isolation is clearly demonstrated in two phenomena that may at first blush appear as the result of opposing tendencies: 'underspecification', in the form of ellipsis or shortening, and 'overspecification', in the form of apparently tautological expressions and compounds (see s. 4.3.7).

Ellipsis, or the dropping of part of a stem form or a compound, without a change in meaning, is quite common. It may be difficult to decide in which of the languages the ellipsis has taken place, and also sometimes whether it is an English or a Norwegian element that has been dropped. Only a few words show what may be called reduction of the stem, such as the old loan *trikk* (< E *electric [tramcar]*) and the more recently borrowed verb *sponse* (< E *sponsor*). As in some other European languages, the words *aircondition* (< E *air conditioning*) and *happy end* (< E *happy ending*) are frequently used without the *-ing* ending of the English originals. Examples of shortened compounds are numerous, and are also often shared by other languages. It seems that ellipsis is especially likely with borrowed compounds where the constituents are not as a rule associated with separate meanings in

Norwegian, and there is no loss of information content in the dropping of an element. Thus, *basket* may take on the meaning of the compound *basketball*, or the even more complex *basketball shoe*, the context reducing the possibility of misinterpretations.

Secondary developments. Established loans are, in principle, eligible for the same types of semantic change as other words in the vocabulary. Metonymic extension, such as the use of *jeans* to refer to the type of fabric, 'denim', and metaphorical extension, such as the use of *fullrigger* to denote a 'large, elaborately dressed woman' are documented. The process of metaphor often involves comparing items from different semantic fields. However, more subtle shifts are perhaps just as common. *Bestselger* in Norwegian may be used about, say, a bestselling TV show, in addition to bestselling books or authors, which is what is usually implied in English definitions of the word. Metaphorical extension also seems to be a relatively common development with verbs.

Collocational meaning may be said to have influenced many adjectives, which largely depend upon the meaning of the nouns they occur with.

The use of English as a source of re-lexification in Norwegian is particularly noticeable in slang, where there is a wide selection of emphatic and intensifying expressions. In cases where words are primarily used for their novelty, denotative meaning may not be of primary importance; rather, it is the newsworthiness of the form that counts. Thus, we may get meanings in Norwegian that differ quite substantially from those of the source words in E, like *teit* 'idiotic, stupid, boring' (< E *tight*). New constellations may develop between loanwords in the borrowing language that differ from their relationships in the source language. In Norwegian, *cool* and *hot* function as near-synonyms in their usual slang meanings, whereas *cool* and *kjip* (< E *cheap*) function as virtual antonyms in teenage culture and slang, which sets great store by evaluating things and phenomena as either 'in, trendy, and fashionable' (*cool*), or 'out and hopelessly passé' (*kjip*).

The explanation for certain types of semantic development must be sought beyond the two languages that are directly involved in the transfer. The relationship between a loan and its source word may be obscured due to the indirect route of borrowing, via one or more intermediary languages. What appears to be interference from a separate word is also found. The borrowed English adjective *cool*, often spelt *kul* in Norwegian, has a homophone and homograph in Swedish *kul* 'funny, amusing', and, as Swedish represents an important source of linguistic influence on Norwegian, we may suppose that the Swedish adjective has had some influence on the use of the English loanword. The Danish adjective *sjov*, which also, incidentally, means 'funny, amusing', is an even more convincing candidate for such interference, since the English loanword *show* is sometimes used as an adjective in Norwegian, a usage for which there is no foundation in English.

Contact-induced developments. In a situation of continued language contact and widespread bilingualism, loanwords are likely to be influenced by related words in the source language. Arguably, the borrowing of related English forms like *smartness* in addition to *smart*, or the derivation *snobbisme* in addition to *snobb*, shares traits with native word formation, in that a lexical element may be associated with different words, with a common element of meaning. More commonly, lexical entries are complemented and enriched by the continued borrowing of new meanings. Reborrowing, often of compounds where one element has already become established in Norwegian, may cause a word gradually to develop in meaning and even to approach the English source word in lexical richness. The loan *bag* in Norwegian means basically 'relatively large strong container made of cloth, plastic, leather, etc., with handles', as illustrated in a number of compounds such as *flybag* 'carry-on bag', *skulderbag* 'shoulder bag', and *treningsbag* 'sports bag'. In addition, *baby-bag* 'portacrib' and *trillebag* 'shopping-bag on wheels' are special kinds of bag, but still essentially covered by the definition above. A number of more recent examples, however, show *bag* being used in Norwegian in senses that are closer to the more general definition 'container made of thin paper or plastic': *te-bag, punching-bag, airbag, oljebag, doggy-bag, bag lady*. As a result of continuing influence from English, in the form of new compounds that contain the old loan, the meaning of *bag* in Norwegian may be undergoing a gradual development and expansion, from 'relatively large strong container made of cloth, plastic, leather, etc., with handles' to the more general meaning 'container made of cloth, paper, plastic, leather, etc., with or without handles'.

4.5 Usage
(Masvie 1992; Ljung 1985 [on Swedish])

Channels. The area of culture and entertainment, including music, seems to be a major channel for English loans in the daily press today, accounting for more than a quarter of all examples according to a recent study (Graedler 1998). The field of sports also accounts for a large proportion of the English loans. In comparison the impact of, for instance, the oil industry, or even technical language in general, seems almost insignificant in the daily press (this may depend on the type of publication studied). It is noteworthy that many of the subject areas that contain the largest number of English loanwords are those often associated with the cultural expressions of young people, such as rock music, fashion, and sport. Age is the factor which correlates most strongly both with the amount and intensity of contact with the English language, and with attitudes towards and acceptance of the use of English or English-influenced material. In both cases young people are in the lead. A number of recent studies of borrowing in Norwegian have concentrated on areas that are often associated with the younger generation, such as pop music, fashion and beauty, film and television. Common to all studies is the observation that besides words belonging to the professional terminology of the various industries, writers on these subjects also use numerous loans with more general meanings. The language associated with an increasing number of subcultures, for instance hip-hop and graffiti, computer games, virtual reality, and skateboarding, is also often heavily influenced by the English language, and by British and North American culture.

The role of translation as a channel for English influence on Norwegian is also often mentioned, but little research has been done in this area.

Specific areas of usage. As a result of the spread of multinational corporations, English is used extensively in the commercial sphere. It functions as a trade and managing language in several areas, notably the Norwegian oil industry, and is increasingly used as a lingua franca in inter-Nordic communication, where this was previously often carried out in one of the Scandinavian languages.

The fact that English is used for purposes other than the mere designation of objects and ideas is evident in advertising language. In the global village, advertising campaigns may be the same all over the world. But the use of English in advertising is not restricted to international or multinational companies: even purely Norwegian companies sometimes address their target consumer groups in English.

4.6 Forms of linguistic borrowing and their categorization
(Graedler 1998)

The most frequent visible result of language contact between English and Norwegian is lexical borrowing, or the direct transfer of linguistic form. The following types may be distinguished:

1. *Borrowing*
   (a) Words that are totally unadapted and in no way felt to be part of the Norwegian vocabulary (quotation words, code-switching, foreignisms/exotica);
   (b) words that look foreign in form; words that have been only partly adapted;
   (c) words that are more or less completely adapted/integrated.

2. *Replacement*
   (a) Translation: (mostly compound) words translated component by component from English to Norwegian.
   (b) Rendition: words that are looser renderings on the basis of the English original.
   (c) Creation: words that are formally independent in Norwegian, coined in order to render the meaning of an English word.
   (d) Semantic loan: Norwegian words that take on a new meaning held by an English formal equivalent.

Examples of all these are found below. A final category is pseudo-loans, divisible into three types:

3. *Pseudo-loans*
   (a) Lexical pseudo-loans: *snacksy* 'tasty; attractive', *stressless* (a type of reclining chair, orig. brand name), *cityshorts*, *collegegenser*, *joggedress* 'tracksuit'.
   (b) Morphological pseudo-loans: *basket* (< E *basketball*), *body* (< E *bodysuit*), *gin-tonic*, *happy end*.
   (c) Semantic pseudo-loans: *binders* 'paper clip', *briefe* 'brag, show off' (< E *brief*), *doping* 'drugs'.

A *Translations*

1. Successful

blood bank < blodbank,   do-it-yourself < gjør-det-selv
dead man button < dødmannsknapp   hot potato < het/varm potet
fringe benefit < frynsegode   throw in the towel < kaste inn håndkleet
welfare state < velferdsstat
skyscraper < skyskraper   on the air < på lufta

2. Coexisting

bodybuilder = kroppsbygger   Big Brother = storebror
covergirl = omslagspike   hard facts = harde fakta

3. Failures

whiplash (injury) > piskesnert(skade)
walkman > gåmann
deadline > dødstrek
fastfood > snøggmat

B *Renderings*

1. Successful

after shave < etterbarberingsvann   go down the drain < gå i vasken
teenager < tenåring   kick somebody upstairs < sparke noen
                                            oppover
blowout < utblåsning

2. Coexisting

bodyguard = livvakt   slow motion = sakte kino
output = utdata   prime time = beste sendetid

3. Failures

hang-gliding > hengeflyging?
compact disc > kompaktplate
PC > PD

C *Creations*

1. Successful

walkman < lommedisco
whiplash < nakkesleng
computer < datamaskin
flight recorder < ferdsskriver

2. Coexisting

designer = formgiver
disc jockey = plateprater
fast food = ferdigmat
keeper = målvakt

D *Semantic loans*

1. Successful

freeze < *fryse*
adopt < *adoptere*
buy 'accept' < *kjøpe*

2. Coexisting

hot 'trendy' = *het*
light 'low calorie' = *lett*

4.7 The future of Anglicisms

In the post-war period, borrowing from English in Norwegian seems to have steadily increased, and there is at present no sign of any dramatic reversal in this development. Rather, the high degree of exposure to English in popular culture and the media would seem, if anything, to speed up the pace of borrowing. At the same time, not only workplaces and schools, but also homes are being computerized, enabling and facilitating English-based communication across the world. However, what appears as a massive influence has also inspired counter-reactions, and bodies such as the Norwegian Language Council have it as their express policy to cultivate new Norwegian lexical elements to replace foreign ones. This, along with the fact that many loans seem to be part of trends and waves that make a lot of noise, but are relatively soon forgotten, may indicate that the 'invasion' is not quite as overwhelming as sometimes feared, and certainly that Norwegian is not endangered, but will survive as a language into the foreseeable future.

4.8 Research

Relatively little research has been done on the topic of Anglicisms in Norwegian, and it is noteworthy that much of what has been written has been the work of scholars specializing in English, rather than those studying the Norwegian language. Aasta Stene was the first to address the topic in a larger study, finished before the Second World War, but published in 1945. Much of the work that has followed after Stene has been in the form of unpublished *hovedfag* theses, or shorter articles. In recent years, an umbrella project called 'English in Norway', initiated and headed by Professor Stig Johansson at the Department of British and American Studies at the University of Oslo, has generated a large number of theses, with topics ranging from studies of specific fields of borrowing, and specific aspects of the borrowing process and its linguistic impact, to sociolinguistic studies of the usage aspect of borrowing. This project has also, so far, resulted in two monographs, Graedler (1998) and Graedler and Johansson (1997).

4.9 Bibliography

BERULFSEN, B., and GUNDERSEN, D. (eds.) (1986), *Fremmedordbok* (Dictionary of Foreign Words), 15th edn. (Oslo: Kunnskapsforlaget).

BLAAUW, K., VERNEGG, T., and LANGSLET, L. R. (eds.) (1996), *Engelske ord med norsk rettskrivning? Seks seminarforedrag 1996* (English Words with Norwegian Orthography? Six Seminar Lectures 1996) (Bergen: Bergens Riksmålsforening, Riksmålsforbundet and Det Norske Akademi for Sprog og Litteratur).

BRUNSTAD, ENDRE (2001) 'Det reine språket. Om purisme i dansk, svensk, færøysk og norsk' (The Pure Language : Purism in Danish Swedish, Faroese, and Norwegian), Dr. Art. thesis.

GRAEDLER, A.-L. (1998), *Morphological, Semantic and Functional Aspects of English Lexical Borrowings in Norwegian*, (Oslo: Universitetsforlaget).

—— and JOHANSSON, S. (1995), '*Rocka, Hipt* and *Snacksy*: Some Aspects of English Influence on Present-Day Norwegian', in G. Melchers and B. Warren (eds.), *Studies in Anglistics*, Stockholm Studies in English 85 (Stockholm: Almqvist & Wiksell), 269–87.

—— (1997), *Anglisismeordboka: Engelske lånord i norsk* (A Dictionary of Anglicisms: English Loanwords in Norwegian) (Oslo: Universitetsforlaget).

GRØNVIK, O. (1990*a*), 'Lånordproblemet i norsk: Guppering og systematisering av lånord og ulike måtar å ta stilling til dei på i normeringa' (The Loanword Problem in Norwegian: A Classification of Loanwords and Various Ways of Dealing with Them in Terms of Standardization), unpub. manuscript (University of Oslo).

—— (1990*b*), 'Oversyn over lånte ordformer i norsk' (A Survey of Borrowed Word-Forms in Norwegian), unpublished manuscript (University of Oslo).

GUNDEM, B. B. (1986), *School Subject—School Reform: The Emergence and Redefining of 'English' as Part of School Reform and Curriculum Revision*, English summary of a report presented as a doctor's thesis at the University of Oslo, 1987 (Institute for Educational Research, University of Oslo).

—— (1989), *Engelskfaget i folkeskolen: Påvirkning og gjennomslag fra 1870-årene til først på 1970-tallet* (English as a School Subject: Influence and Effect from the 1870s to the Early 1970s) (Oslo: Universitetsforlaget).

GUNDERSEN, D. (1990), 'Norwegian Lexicography', in F. J. Hausmann, O. Reichmann, H. E. Wiegand, and L. Zgusta (eds.), *Dictionaries: An International Encyclopedia of Lexicography*, vol. ii (Berlin: de Gruyter), 1923–8.

HANSEN, M. C. (1842), *Fremmed-Ordbog* (Dictionary of Foreign Words) (Christiania: Guldberg & Ozwonkowski). (2nd enlarged and improved edn. 1851.)

HAUGEN, E. (1976), *The Scandinavian Languages: An Introduction to their History* (London: Faber & Faber).

—— (1978), 'The English Language as an Instrument of Modernization in Scandinavia', in R. Zeitler (ed.), *Det moderna Skandinaviens framväxt. Bidrag till de nordiska ländernas moderna historia* (Uppsala).

HELLEVIK, A. (1963), 'Den engelsk-amerikanske påverknaden på norsk' (The English-American Influence on Norwegian), in *Lånordproblemet: To foredrag i norsk språknemnd, Norsk språknemnd småskrifter.* (Oslo: Cappelen), ii. 15–25.

—— (1970), 'Engelsk-amerikanske lånord og språklig sjølvhjelp' (English-American Loanwords and Linguistic Self-Help), in *Det rette ordet: Ord og ordlegging i skrift og tale* (Oslo: Det norske samlaget), 48–54.

JESPERSEN, O. (1902), 'Engelsk og nordisk: En afhandling om låneord' (English and the Nordic Languages: A Treatise on Loanwords), *Nordisk tidskrift för vetenskap, konst och industri*, 500–14.

JOHANSSON, S. (1992), 'Engelsk—et *must* i norsk? On the Role of English in Norwegian Language and Society', in A.-M. Langvall Olsen and A. M. Simensen (eds.), *Om språk og utdanning: Essays in Honour of Eva Sivertsen* (Oslo: Universitetsforlaget), 65–84.

LANDRØ, M. I., and WANGENSTEEN, B. (eds.) (1993), *Bokmålsordboka*, 2nd edn. (Oslo: Universitetsforlaget).

LJUNG, M. (1985), *Lam anka—ett måste? En undersökning av engelskan i svenskan, dess mottagande och spridning* (Lame Duck—A Must? A Study of the English Element in Swedish, its Reception and Spread), EIS Report No. 8 (Stockholm: University of Stockholm).

MASVIE, I.-L. (1992), 'English in Norway—a Sociolinguistic Study', unpub. *hovedfag* thesis (University of Oslo).

Norsk språkråd (ed.) (1982), *Nyord i norsk 1945–1975* (New Words in Norwegian 1945–1975) (Oslo: Universitetsforlaget).

—— (1990), *Ja til norsk! Informasjons-og debatthefte om engelsk i norsk* (Yes to Norwegian! Information and Discussion Leaflet about English in Norwegian) (Oslo: Norsk språkråd).

SANDØY, H. (2000), *Lånte fjører eller bunad? Om importord i norsk* (Foreign Chic or National Costume? On imported words in Norwegian) (Oslo: LNU/Cappelen).

SANDVED, A. O. (1998), *Fra 'kremmersprog' til verdensspråk. Engelsk som universitetsfag i Norge 1850–1943*. (From 'Shopkeepers' Language' to World Language: English as a University Subject in Norway 1850–1943) (Oslo: Universitetet i Oslo, forum for universitetshistorie).

SCHMIDT, K. A. R. (1982), 'The Adaptation of English Loanwords in Norwegian', in R. Filipović (ed.), (1982), *The English Element in European Languages, Vol. 2: Reports and Studies* (Zagreb: Institute of Linguistics, University of Zagreb), 338–77.

SØRLAND, S. A. (1993), ' "Trick", "Trikk", or "Triks"? Some Aspects of Orthographic Adaptation of English Loanwords in Standard Norwegian', unpub. *hovedfag* thesis (University of Oslo).

STENE, AASTA (1945), *English Loanwords in Modern Norwegian: A Study of Linguistic Borrowing in the Process* (London: Oxford University Press).

VALBERG, INGER (1990), ' "The Perfect Look": A Study of the Influence of English on Norwegian in the Area of Fashion and Beauty', unpub. *hovedfag* thesis (University of Oslo).

5

ICELANDIC

Guðrún Kvaran and Ásta Svavarsdóttir

5.1 History of language contact

5.1.1 Chronology of intensive influences

In the first centuries after the settlement of Iceland in the late ninth century, there was little contact between Iceland and Britain. The sagas only mention a few journeys to Britain, partly to the regions inhabited by Norse-speaking settlers. The influence of English was negligible, even though a few loanwords can be traced to Old and Middle English. In most cases, it is difficult to determine with certainty to which of the old West Germanic languages words in the Nordic languages should be traced (Halldórsson 1970). Many factors must be taken into consideration, such as the age of the words, their meaning, and their social and cultural history. Most loanwords from Old English were religious terms, e.g. *biskup* 'bishop', *djákni* 'deacon', *kaleikur* 'chalice', *kirkja* 'church', *klerkur* 'cleric', *prestur* 'priest'; others were words for merchandise brought back from journeys abroad, such as *sokkur* 'sock' and *blek* 'ink'. Research on Middle English loanwords in Icelandic has shown that around thirty of them can be found in old Icelandic sources (Eiríksson 1981). Some of them never became a part of the vocabulary, whereas others are now completely assimilated.

In the fifteenth century, English sailors started visiting Iceland for fishing and trading, and for a century there was close contact between the nations. This period has been called 'The English Century' in Icelandic history, and it has left several English loanwords related to new merchandise, sailing, and fishing in the vocabu-

The Icelandic part of the *Dictionary of European Anglicisms* project was supported by a grant from the University of Iceland's Research Fund which made it possible to employ an assistant for the gathering and registration of data. We thank the fund for its support and our assistant, Guðmundur Erlingsson, for his part in the project. Furthermore, we are indebted to our colleagues, Kristín Bjarnadóttir and Þórunn Blöndal, who read and commented on the manuscript of this article.

lary of Icelandic. Most of these words were assimilated to the extent that most native speakers are not aware of their origin, and would not even recognize them as loanwords; therefore etymological knowledge is necessary to determine their origin.

The Hanseatic League drove the English away from Iceland in the middle of the sixteenth century, and subsequently dominated trade in Iceland to the end of the eighteenth century. Foreign influence was therefore mostly German and Danish during that period, Iceland being a colony of Denmark for centuries.

In the nineteenth century, when restrictions on trade had been lifted, the close contact to Denmark meant that Danish was the main source of linguistic impact. At that time, English influence in the domain of social life increased throughout Europe, but the majority of English loanwords in Icelandic in the period were borrowed via Danish. Many books were translated from English in the latter half of the nineteenth century, but in accordance with the prevailing language purism, new Icelandic words were coined for English expressions, and fewer English terms in the fields of science and technology found their way into the vocabulary of Icelandic than into the languages of the neighbouring countries. Towards the end of the century, there was an increasing contact with English-speaking nations. Considerable emigration of Icelanders to Canada and the United States took place in the late nineteenth century, and at the same time trade and other business contacts with Britain increased. As a consequence, travel to Britain and North America became more frequent, a number of people spent some time in English-speaking countries for work or studies, and this led to increasing interest in the English language and a better and more widespread knowledge of it in the late nineteenth and early twentieth centuries.

Intensive and direct influence of English only started during the Second World War. Iceland was occupied by British troops in 1940, and as a consequence many of the inhabitants came into daily contact with a large group of English-speaking foreigners. The connection to Denmark and Germany was interrupted during the war, but at the same time the connection with the English-speaking world became closer. From 1941 US forces took part in the defence of Iceland, and from 1945, when the British soldiers left, the US Army has maintained military bases in Iceland, from 1951 under the auspices of NATO. After the war, the direct contact between the foreign troops and the native population was, however, greatly reduced.

Ever since the war there has been growing influence from the Anglo-American countries, direct as well as indirect. One consequence of the occupation was a number of marriages between British and American soldiers and Icelandic women, and many of them moved abroad with their husbands at the end of the war, but kept in contact with relatives at home. An increasing number of Icelanders have attended British and North American universities for some part of their higher education, and they have thus spent several years in these countries, often with their families, and obtained good knowledge of the language. Travelling has become more frequent and widespread among the population of Iceland and has brought many people to English-speaking countries, as well as bringing English-speaking tourists to Iceland. Within the country the main influence has come from English and American films and other forms of entertainment. A large part of the nation was able to listen to American broadcasting from the military base, and for some time in the 1950s and 1960s it was possible to watch American military television too, until the Icelandic authorities demanded a restriction of the transmission for cultural and language political reasons.

During the occupation many English words found their way into the language, e.g. words for food, clothing, music, and entertainment, and the continuing English influence after the war has led to linguistic borrowings of various sorts.

5.1.2 *Origins of influence*

In later times, the influence has been both from Britain and North America, and it is seldom possible to determine with any certainty whether individual words were adopted from British or American English. As Icelandic is a highly inflected language, most foreign loanwords undergo morphological, as well as phonological and graphemic adaptation, and thus what formal differences there are between British and American English are deleted. Sometimes the meaning of an Anglicism reveals its origin, in cases where the semantic content and usage of the word differs across the Atlantic. In other cases the origin can be inferred from external evidence, especially the time of borrowing and the domain to which the word belongs. Older Anglicisms, introduced before the Second World War, are more likely to originate in British than in American English, and in some domains there has been closer contact with Britain and in others with North America. Words relating to certain sports, such as golf and football, as well as Anglicisms in the nautical vocabulary, are almost certainly borrowed from British English, whereas words connected to aviation or computer technology are more likely to derive from American English, not to mention domains like jazz.

5.1.3 *Types of influence*

A contact between two nations usually calls for mutual influence on their languages. In the case of Icelandic the influence is in one direction, from English to Icelandic. It appears on all linguistic levels through lexical borrowing of individual words and parts of words, as well as collocations and phrases. Graphemically, some of the words have been adapted to Icelandic spelling, others clearly show their foreign origin. Many of the more recent borrowings are only used colloquially, and do not really have an accepted written form. As the inflectional system of Icelandic is very productive, nouns usually receive grammatical gender and are assigned to one of the declensional classes so that their foreign origin becomes less obvious (see s. 5.3). English influence on syntax, especially in the collocation of words, can easily be found in written sources, notably in translations and in advertisements (Árnason 1989); however, this field has not been studied carefully enough to draw any accurate conclusions.

5.1.4 *Chronology of puristic phases*

In many small language communities, people tend to be well aware of foreign influence. In Iceland this has always been the case. Books were written in the mother tongue as early as the twelfth century, and, when needed, they were also translated from other languages. Inevitably, the translations had some influence on the vocabulary. Most of the texts published in Iceland in the sixteenth century were translations from German, in connection with the Reformation, such as the Lutheran Bible, or Danish, and their foreign origin was obvious. Later, direct German influence decreased, but the influence from Danish was maintained because of the close contact between the countries. In the sixteenth and seventeenth centuries, English loanwords were borrowed via Danish, which in turn had frequently borrowed them from German or Middle Low German, as for example *jakt* 'yacht' and *jolla* 'yawl'.

In the late eighteenth century, the spirit of the European Enlightenment was reflected in the creation of numerous Icelandic neologisms for new and foreign terms in fields that were more or less new in Iceland. In 1779, an association was established with the goal of removing all foreign words and phrases from the language. The implications of the association's language policy became fully apparent only in the early nineteenth century, in connection with the Romantic movement. The battle was mainly directed against Danish, as there was not much direct influence from English at the time. As can be seen from the *Dictionary of European Anglicisms* material, most Anglicisms that entered Icelandic before the early twentieth century were borrowed via Danish.

In the early nineteenth century, a Danish–Icelandic dictionary (Oddsson 1819) was published in Iceland with the purpose of making it easier for people to express themselves in Icelandic on subjects they read about in Danish books. To achieve this, many neologisms were needed. Another Danish–Icelandic dictionary was published in the middle of the nineteenth century (Gíslason 1851) in which the author tried to avoid all loanwords and thus preferred to define the meaning of the Danish words instead of using as a translation words that did not count as Icelandic. This dictionary was used a great deal, and the author is well known, as much for being a competent linguist as for his language policy. The first English–Icelandic dictionary was published in 1896 (Zoëga 1896). Very few English loanwords were used in the translations, except for fully adapted words that were already borrowed in Old Icelandic. An Icelandic–English dictionary by the same author first appeared in 1904 and there the situation was much the same. In the 1920s, an Icelandic–Danish dictionary was published which was to become the main dictionary of the Icelandic language for the next forty years (Blöndal 1920–4). In this book undesirable loanwords and meanings are marked with a question mark, affecting around 1,000 words or 0.9 per cent of the entries. Among these there are some of English origin—*skáti* 'scout', *landa* '(to) land', *trolla* 'trawl', and *trollari* 'trawler', etc. (Óskarsson 1997: 29)—but the majority of the marked words are Danish in origin. This dictionary was partly replaced by the first monolingual Icelandic dictionary (Böðvarsson 1963). It follows the Icelandic–Danish dictionary in using a question mark to indicate undesirable words and wordforms, especially foreignisms. The question mark has, however, been removed from some of the older Anglicisms listed in both dictionaries, but other Anglicisms have been added, some of them with the question mark, as for example *keis* 'the rear part of a trawler, especially a structure over the engine-room', and *skvísa* 'a girl'.

In consequence of the intensive influence on the language caused by the direct contact with the military during and after the Second World War, the interest in neologisms increased greatly. An official Icelandic Language Council was founded in 1964 under the aegis of the Ministry of Education as the official body responsible for language planning and preservation. In 1985, the Icelandic Language Institute was opened as the secretariat of the council. The aim of Icelandic language policy is to keep the language system as intact and free from foreign influence as possible, and to maintain the characteristics of the vocabulary by using native words and neologisms from native stems and affixes rather than loanwords (Halldórsson 1979). Public institutions are expected to follow the official language policy and standards, and the public mass media are required to be models of good language use. Much work has been done in recent years in terminology. Groups of specialists are working on the formation or translation of new terms in their fields of science and technology, many of them in cooperation with the Icelandic Language Institute. Recently published terminological dictionaries include works on computer science and technology, mathematics, physics, aviation, and pedagogy. In addition, the institute has recently opened a word bank on the Internet including many of the above-mentioned terminological dictionaries.

5.1.5 Geographic differences

There are approximately 280,000 inhabitants in Iceland, more than 60 per cent of them living in and around Reykjavík, the capital. The population is ethnically homogeneous, and Icelandic is the native language of the vast majority of the inhabitants. Dialectal variation is insignificant, though there are minor phonological and lexical differences in different parts of the country. The phonological variation is no doubt reflected in the Anglicisms, in the same manner as in the rest of the vocabulary, but there is no indication of a varying geographical distribution of individual words, though this has not been investigated.

5.1.6 Stylistic differences

Very little research has been done on the stylistic distribution of Anglicisms in Icelandic, and indeed of foreign borrowings in general. The *Dictionary of European Anglicisms* material shows, however, that a considerable part of the Anglicisms in Icelandic belong to colloquial speech and many of them are technical terms or specialized vocabulary of some sort. Most of them were borrowed in the twentieth century, and they are from various fields, e.g. sports (such as golf (*birdie*, *caddie*, *green*, etc.), which is a relatively young activity in Iceland), computer technology (*backup*, *bit*, *modem*, etc.), music and dancing (*bíbopp*, *breik*, *freestyle*, etc.). Most of the words connected to narcotics, such as *stöff* 'stuff', *krakk* 'crack', *gras* 'grass', *djönt(ur)* 'joint', etc., are exclusively used by a small group of people and should be counted as slang, and the same is true of many Anglicisms mainly used in the language of youngsters, such as the exclamations *come on* and *fökk* 'fuck'. Other words from youth language are more in the nature of colloquialisms, for example *oh-boy*! and *proffi* (< E *prof*). Colloquialisms of a more general nature belong to various semantic fields, such as cosmetics (*eyeliner*, *aftershave*, etc.), and sports (*bowling*, *body-building*, etc.).

In some cases an Icelandic synonym exists beside the Anglicism, usually a neologism formed by native means, as in computer terminology which has the verb *vista* besides the Anglicism *seifa* (< E *save*), *disklingur* besides *disketta*, etc. In such cases the neologism is usually preferred in writing and other formal language use, as many Anglicisms are not considered acceptable in the more formal registers. Therefore, they are rarely used in writing outside specialized magazines on the subject, even if the words are quite common in colloquial speech.

5.1.7 Innovation and obsolescence

No quantitative studies have been carried out on the English impact on Icelandic, or on other foreign influences on the modern language, notably from Danish and German, and most articles on the subject have dealt with loanwords from a historical or language political point of view. Furthermore, no dictionaries of foreign words in Icelandic have been published, and Anglicisms are rarely entered in general Icelandic dictionaries, either monolingual or bilingual ones, partly for reasons of language policy and partly because most of the words are comparatively new. It is, therefore, impossible to give accurate information on the number of Anglicisms current in the language, though the *Dictionary of European Anglicisms* material, which is so far the most extensive registration of Anglicisms in Icelandic, gives some indication of their number.

New Anglicisms are constantly being introduced, though many of them never acquire any permanent status in the vocabulary. Some words are not long-lived, even though they are used for a certain period of time, and a number of the older Anglicisms have become obsolete. Some have been replaced by Icelandic neologisms, for example *krol* 'crawl' by *skriðsund*, *face-lift* by *andlitslyfting*, *escalator* by *rúllustigi*, *pace-maker* by *gangráður*, etc. Others have become obsolete with the disappearance of the things they designated, especially words for clothes that have gone out of fashion, such as *kokkteildress* 'cocktail dress', *petticoat*, *baby doll*, etc. No examples were found of an Anglicism being replaced by another Anglicism.

5.1.8 Mediating languages

Many of the Anglicisms attested in the *Dictionary of European Anglicisms* material, especially the older ones, were not borrowed directly from English, but were transmitted via other languages, especially Danish, which had in turn sometimes borrowed them via High, Low, or Middle Low German (see s. 5.1.4). In a few cases, external evidence indicates that Anglicisms derive from other mediating languages than Danish, usually Norwegian, e.g. *aðventisti* 'Adventist'.

Some of the words attested in the material are only mediated through English, for example *mokkasína* (< E *moccasin*). In other cases there is no direct connection between the words in Icelandic and English except the common origin, i.e. they are loanwords in both languages, either borrowed directly from the source language or via different mediating languages. Examples are the Icelandic word *braggi*, which corresponds to the English *barrack*, both deriving from French but borrowed independently, the Icelandic word via Norwegian, and the word *jakki* 'jacket' in Icelandic and the corresponding English *jacket*, both again originating from French but borrowed individually, the Icelandic word via Danish.

5.1.9 English in the schools

In the second half of the nineteenth century, contacts with England, and later also with North America (cf. s. 5.1.1), led to increased interest in the English language. The first English textbook was written in 1863 (Gíslason 1863), and another, intended for elementary schools, was published in 1875 (Briem 1875). Others were soon to follow, including textbooks for the emigrants (Ólafsson 1882, 1888), as well as English–Icelandic and Icelandic–English dictionaries (Zoëga 1896, 1904).

English has been part of compulsory education in Iceland for several decades. It used to be the second foreign language children learned, after Danish, and was normally taught from the age of 12. Recently the order of teaching these languages was changed, however, and now all children learn English from the age of 10. In the schools, the emphasis is on British English, with reference to differences in American English. In addition to these two, most young people learn at least one more foreign language in secondary school, usually German or French.

In consequence of the status that English has in Icelandic schools, almost all adults have some knowledge of the language. The linguistic influence of English, which is now by far the strongest foreign impact on the Icelandic language, can, however, not be based entirely on the fact that it is taught as a foreign language in schools, as we would then expect comparable influence from other languages, especially from Danish. A more likely source of Anglicisms is the daily contact with English through music, films, foreign magazines, television, computers, etc., which also accounts for the fact that many children have obtained considerable knowledge of English before they start learning it at school.

5.2 Pronunciation and spelling

5.2.1 Pronunciation

All Anglicisms are subject to some phonological adaptation to Icelandic, to a greater or lesser extent, and this even applies in instances of code-switching—in fact, a certain influence of the Icelandic phonological system can usually be traced even in the pronunciation of Icelanders speaking English. The adaptation is of three main types and is fairly regular: (1) the replacement of an English sound, without correspondence in Icelandic, with a similar sound or sound sequence, usually because English makes a systematic differentiation between sounds that do not have phonemic status or do not even exist in Icelandic; (2) the reinterpretation of an English sound as one of two Icelandic phonemes, in cases where

Icelandic makes a systematic differentiation not present in English; (3) the application of phonological processes, regular in Icelandic, but non-existent in English, to the Anglicisms.

The phonological system of Icelandic is briefly outlined in Tables 5.1 and 5.2. It consists of thirteen vowels, eight monophthongs and five diphthongs, and thirty consonants.

All the vowels, diphthongs as well as monophthongs, have a long and a short variant with roughly the same quality, their length depending on the context. The main rule is that the vowel is long in an open syllable or before a single consonant, and short before a long consonant or a consonant cluster. This rule applies in stressed syllables, the main stress regularly falling on the first syllable of words. In unstressed syllables, on the other hand, length is not distinctive.

Most of the consonants can be either short or long in medial and final position. In writing, the long sound is represented with a geminate, such as <-bb-, -dd-, -gg-> representing a long stop, and <-mm-, -nn-, -ll-, -rr- > which usually represent a long sound. It should be noted, however, that this is not always the case, as geminates do in some cases represent consonant clusters; <-pp-, -tt- , -kk-> stand for the clusters [hp, ht, hc, hk], known as preaspiration, and <-nn-, -ll-> represent the pronunciation [tn, tl] in some contexts.

Other distributional features that need mentioning are the unvoiced quality of nasals, laterals, and drills when preceding a [p, t, c, k] in most dialects, yielding the clusters [m̥p, n̥t, l̥c, r̥k], etc., for example in *svampur* 'sponge', *vanta* 'lack', and the palatalization of stops before a front, unrounded vowel, as well as the unrounded diphthongs [ei] and [ai]; thus the words *kýr* 'cow', *gifta* 'marry', *gefa* 'give', as well as *keyra* 'drive' and *(i) gær* 'yesterday', all start with a palatal stop. In medial positions a nasal preceding the stop will also be palatalized; words like *birki* 'birch' and *fangelsi* 'jail' thus have a palatal stop, and in the latter the palatalization also applies to the nasal, yielding the cluster [ɲc].

In the process of adaptation, vowels normally acquire the vowel quality in Icelandic that most closely resembles the original English sound. There are cases, however, where the influence of the written language can be detected, as in *country* which is rendered as *kántrí* reflecting the diphthong [au] instead of the expected [œ], which is the usual correspondence to the English [ʌ]; the reason, no doubt, is the

Table 5.1. Vowels

	Front		Central (unround)	Central-Front (unround)	Central-back (unround-round)	Back (round)
	Unround	Round				
Monophthongs						
High	i					u
Mid-high	ɪ	ʏ				
Mid-low	ɛ	œ				ɔ
Low			a			
Diphthongs	ei	øy		ai	au	ou

Table 5.2. Consonants

	Labial	Dental/ alveolar	Palatal	Velar	Glottal
Stops					
Aspirated	pʰ	tʰ	cʰ	kʰ	
Unaspirated	p	t	c	k	
Fricatives					
Voiced	v	ð	j	ɣ	
Unvoiced	f	θ	ç	x	h
Sibilant					
Unvoiced		s			
Nasals					
Voiced	m	n	ɲ	ŋ	
Unvoiced	m̥	n̥	ɲ̊	ŋ̊	
Lateral					
Voiced		l			
Unvoiced		l̥			
Trill					
Voiced		r			
Unvoiced		r̥			

spelling <ou> normally indicating a diphthong, as in *sound* which becomes *sánd* [saunt] in Icelandic.

The Icelandic stress pattern, with the main stress on the first syllable of words, is normally applied to Anglicisms. This also affects the length of sounds, as the first vowel of each word has to be interpreted as being either long or short. In Icelandic, a vowel followed by a consonant cluster is automatically short; an originally long vowel will thus be reinterpreted as short in this position, yielding a short diphthong in *sánd* (< E *sound*). There are, however, exceptional cases where the diphthong retains the length, as in *AIDS* and *slæds* (< E *slides*); it should be noted that the resulting string, i.e [V:ts], indeed exists in native words, though only where there is a morpheme boundary between the consonants, e.g. in *bát-s* (gen. of *bátur* 'boat'). In cases where a single vowel is followed by a single consonant the length of the original English vowel is crucial; if it is long the length is usually retained in Icelandic, which can be seen from the fact that in most Anglicisms diphthongs are long, and in the same way originally short vowels are also short in the Anglicisms. This, however, calls for another kind of adaptation as the syllable structure VC, i.e. a short vowel followed by a single short consonant, is non-existent in Icelandic, and thus one of the sounds must always be long. The result is a lengthening of the consonant, which is either realized as a long sound, e.g. in *boddí* [pɔt:i] (< E *body*), *hedd* [hɛt:] (< E *head*), *húdd* [hut:] (< E *hood*), *halló* [hal:ou] (< E *hallo/hello*), or as the cluster known as preaspiration, e.g. *popp* [pɔhp] (< E *pop*), *rokk* [rɔhk] (< E *rock*), *húkka* [huhka] (< E *hook*).

In the process of adaptation, certain consonants that are non-existent in most of the comparative languages cause no problem in Icelandic, notably the dental fricatives [θ] and [ð]. Therefore, in the adoption of a word like *thriller* only a minor phonetic adaptation is needed. Other consonants, on the other hand, have no direct counterparts in the Icelandic phonological system. These are most notably the voiced stops, the affricates, some of the sibilants, and [w].

All stops are voiceless in Icelandic, the difference between <p t k> and <b d g> lying in the aspiration to the extent that they are kept apart, which is mainly in initial position. The same is true of the Anglicisms.

The absence of affricates in Icelandic calls for a reinterpretation of these sounds in the Anglicisms, usually as a cluster of a dental stop plus the voiced palatal fricative [j], either with aspiration, [tʰj-], as in *tékka* (v.; < E *check*), *tjalli* (< E *Charley*), and *tjakkur* (< E *jack*), or with an unaspirated sound, [tj-], as in *djass* (< E *jazz*), *djús* (< E *juice*), etc. The adaptation is not completely regular, as the examples indicate, especially not in the older borrowings, where the influence of the English spelling is also to be found, indicating that some of them, at least, were borrowed from the written language. A good example is the pair *jóker* 'a playing card' and *djóker* 'a joking person', both from English *joker*; the older word, probably borrowed via Danish around the turn of the century, has [j], which would be a normal Icelandic pronunciation according to the spelling, whereas the younger one, introduced much later, has [tj-], which points to a borrowing of the spoken form. Some of the older borrowings also have a sibilant, normally [sj-] but sometimes [s-], where English has an affricate, such as *séns* and *sjans* (< E *chance*) and *sivjot* (< E *Cheviot*). In medial and final position the usual rendering of an English affricate is simply [s], as in *bridds* (< E *bridge*).

Icelandic has only one phonologically distinctive sibilant, the dental unvoiced [s], whereas English also has the voiced [z] and the palatal [ʃ]. The former is simply adopted as [s], e.g. in *súmma* (< E *zoom*), and the latter is normally rendered as the cluster [sj-] in all positions, e.g. in *sjal* (< E *shawl*), *sjoppa* (< E *shop*), and in words with the suffix *-sjón* (< E *-tion*).

As there is no rounded [w] in Icelandic, the original English sound is regularly replaced by the voiced fricative [v], yielding e.g. *viskí* (< E *whisky*), *vá!* (< E *wow*), and *tvist* (< E *twist*).

Some of the phonological processes active in Icelandic are quite regularly applied to Anglicisms. These include preaspiration, already mentioned in connection with sound length. Two other processes, connected to the stops, should also be mentioned. A phonemic differentiation between aspirated and unaspirated stops is only made in initial position; in other positions stops are either all unaspirated, which is the case in the most widespread dialect, or there is a complementary distribution between the pairs [pʰ] and [p], etc. In the former case, the difference between words of pairs like *vandi* and *vanti*, *gildi* and *gilti* lies in a voiced vs. unvoiced nasal or lateral, but not in the pronunciation of the stop as indicated in the spelling. Anglicisms follow the pattern of native words in the pronunciation of such clusters, i.e. of a nasal, a lateral or a drill preceding a stop, and words like *kántrí* (< E *country*), *sjampó* (< E *shampoo*), *milksjeik* (< E *milkshake*), and *partí*

(< E *party*) thus have an unvoiced [n̥ m̥ l̥ r̥]. Another feature worth mentioning is the palatalization of stops and, where appropriate, also nasals, when followed by a front vowel. This is carried out regularly in Anglicisms, with the exception of words like *gæ(i)* (< E *guy*), which shows that this is not an active process before <æ>, even though native words also have a palatal stop there for historical reasons. Words like *gír* (< E *gear*), *gin* (< E *gin*), *gel* (< E *gel*), *kinkí* (< E *kinky*), etc., all have a palatal stop, [c] or [cʰ], and the last one also the cluster [ɲc] in medial position.

5.2.2 Graphemic integration

Due to Icelandic language policy, Anglicisms, and lexical borrowings in general, are not welcome in the language. They are, however, quite frequent in colloquial speech, but do not find their way as easily into the written language. The consequences are that many Anglicisms used in speech are very rarely found in writing, and thus have not acquired a graphemic form. Words of this kind have, as a rule, been used for quite some time and undergone considerable phonological and morphological adaptation before they enter the written language; when they finally do, they usually follow the normal rules of spelling with respect to the pronunciation valid for Icelandic.

Even though English and Icelandic both use the roman alphabet, there are minor differences in its use. Icelandic does not make use of the letters <c, q, w>, normally replacing them by <k/s, k, v> respectively, as in *kók* (< E *Coca-Cola*), *sent* (< E *cent*), *kvekari* (< E *Quaker*), *vatt* (< E *watt*), etc. Furthermore, the English <ch>, representing an affricate, is replaced in various ways depending on the pronunciation (cf. s. 5.2.1), most frequently by <s(j)-, t(j)->: *séff(i)* (< E chef), *sjans* (< E *chance*), *tékka* (< E *check*), etc.; note that the Icelandic letter <é> represents the sound sequence [jɛ]. Some other letters, even though they are used in both languages, have different values. The letter <y> represents a vowel in Icelandic, most often the sound [i]; it is rarely seen in Anglicisms, where the letter <i> would be used for the sound in question. English <y> is normally rendered as <j> in Icelandic in accordance with the pronunciation: *jójó* (< E *yo-yo*). English <j>, on the other hand, denoting an affricate that does not exist in Icelandic (cf. s. 5.2.1), is replaced by the letter or letters that reflect the pronunciation in Icelandic, normally the sequence <dj->. As mentioned before, the sounds [θ] and [ð] are common to both languages, but they are represented differently in spelling, Icelandic using the letters <þ> (initially) and <ð> (medially and finally), and these are normally expected to replace the English spelling in Anglicisms. There are, however, very few examples of words with an original <th> in the *Dictionary of European Anglicisms*, but *þriller* (< E *thriller*) can be taken as an example.

Icelandic makes use of an accent mark on vowels to represent a sound quality different from the unmarked vowels. Thus the letters <a> and <á> normally represent two distinctive sounds, and the same is true of other such pairs. The <á> and <ó> stand for diphthongs, as well as the letter <æ>, but <í> and <ú> represent the front and back high vowels respectively. These letters are normally used in Anglicisms in accordance with Icelandic pronunciation, e.g. in *dóp* (< E *dope*), *sánd* (< E *sound*), *stæll* (< E *style*), *húkka* (< E *hook*), *fíla* (< E *feel*), etc.

Compared to English, there is a different and usually more regular connection between pronunciation and spelling in Icelandic. As a consequence, Anglicisms often become quite unrecognizable from the English original in their written form, even in cases where the process of adaptation has not led to extensive changes in the phonological form.

5.3 Morphology

5.3.1 Introduction

Unlike English, Icelandic is a highly inflected language. The greatest difference is in the nominals, both nouns and adjectives, which are inflected for gender, number, and case. Furthermore, adjectives have distinct forms in definite and indefinite noun phrases, as well as an inflection for comparison. English, on the other hand, only differentiates number in nouns and comparison in adjectives. In the verbal conjugation, there is less difference between the languages, though it is still considerable. Icelandic verbs are inflected for person and number, in both the present and the past, and there is a fully inflected subjunctive in both tenses as well. Each verb, thus, has many more forms than in English. The Icelandic inflectional system is therefore rich with respect to the number of categories displayed in it. In addition, there is a number of inflectional patterns within each word class, so that nouns, for example, fall in various inflectional classes, and the same is true for the other major word classes.

Most Anglicisms adapt to the Icelandic inflectional system, to a greater or a lesser extent. How thoroughly they are integrated differs somewhat, the integration varying both for classes of words, and for individual words within them. In the latter case, there can be various reasons for one word not being as well adapted as another, such as the fact that the word is recently borrowed and has therefore not been fully integrated. The adaptability of words also differs, depending on how closely they resemble the native vocabulary. Furthermore, the usage of a word can be limited to a particular context where only one word form is needed, and there was therefore no need for the whole paradigm to emerge.

The main rule is that Anglicisms belong to the same word class as the corresponding word in English, but there are also instances of lexical borrowings which are derived from a different part of speech, such as the noun *skvísa* originating from the English verb *squeeze*, and the adjective *bí* from the English prefix *bi-*, the latter, however, used as an adjective in English slang (Beale 1989). No examples are attested of the active usage of inflectional endings borrowed from English. A few words have been borrowed with the plural ending, but in such cases the ending has been reinterpreted as a part of the stem, e.g. in *síls* (< E *sill*), *klips* (< E *clip*), and *kornfleks* (< E *cornflakes*), as clearly seen from their declensional forms, notably a plural form like *sílsar*.

5.3.2 Nouns

About three-quarters of the Anglicisms in Icelandic attested in the *Dictionary of European Anglicisms* material are nouns. A considerable part of these, almost 15 per cent, are not inflected at all. They are, for the most part, recent loans which are poorly adapted, phonologically as well as morphologically, and usually of limited distribution, as regards linguistic context, style, and register. The greater part of nouns, on the other hand, acquire gender and are declined, at least to some extent. This finding agrees with results from earlier studies of the morphological adaptation of English borrowings in modern Icelandic (Eiríksson 1975).

The attribution of gender is probably the most interesting aspect of the morphological adaptation of English nouns in Icelandic, being an example of borrowing from a language without the category of grammatical gender into one where all nouns must be marked for one of the three distinctive genders: masculine, feminine, and neuter. Apart from being interesting in itself, the gender acquired plays the main role in deciding the declension of the Anglicisms.

The Dictionary of European Anglicisms data show how nouns which do acquire gender at all are divided between the three subcategories. The results of Eiríkson (1975) are given in comparison. The *DEA* has 37 per cent M (42 per cent), 11 per cent F (6 per cent), and 52 per cent N (52 per cent). The results are more or less the same, the neuters counting for more than half of the nouns, and masculines also being numerous, whereas there are comparatively few feminines. A small number of nouns are attested in more than one gender, probably indicating that the process of morphological adaptation has yet to be completed; variation of the kind is, however, also known in a few native words, usually with a dialectal distribution of the competing forms.

An interesting question is what features of the nouns play a part in the attribution of gender, and, especially, whether the semantic or the formal characteristics are the more decisive. A closer look at the Anglicisms in question seems to reveal that the formal features play the main role, even though the meaning is of some importance as well. It has also been suggested that the neuter is the unmarked gender in Icelandic, one of the arguments being that borrowed nouns acquire neuter in the absence of special semantic or formal features marking them as either masculine or feminine (Svavarsdóttir 1993), and these results do not contradict that suggestion.

Semantic factors mainly determine the gender attribution of nouns denoting humans, in which case the grammatical gender normally agrees with sex, as in *pæja* (< E *sweetie-pie*) and *skvísa* (< E *squeeze*), both used for girls and treated as feminine, and *gæi* (< E *guy*) and *bítill* (< E *Beatle*), which denote young males and are accordingly masculine. There is, however, no direct or necessary connection between natural and grammatical gender, either in the Anglicisms or in the native vocabulary, and there are individual words where the two do not completely agree, such as the feminine *blók* (< E *bloke*) used almost exclusively for males, and various masculines that can just as well refer to females as males, like *mormóni* (< E *mormon*), *stílisti* (< E *stylist*), *lúser* (< E *loser*); nouns that connect persons to their job, beliefs, activities, etc., like those just mentioned, are usually masculine in

Icelandic. Furthermore, some neuter nouns do, in fact, refer to people, for example *frík* (< E *freak*), *snobb* (< E *snob*), etc. In addition to the natural gender, a semantic factor that should be mentioned is the impact of native words from the same semantic field as the Anglicisms, which can act as models in the attribution of grammatical gender.

The formal features that seem to have the greatest influence in gender attribution are the word-final sounds or sound sequences, and the syllable structure can apparently matter in some cases. A resemblance to native or well integrated loan suffixes is a crucial factor. All words which end in *-a*, *-ette*, *-sin(e)*, and *-tion* and most words ending in *-ing* become feminine in Icelandic: *kamera* (< E *camera*), *disketta* (< E *diskette*), *límósína* (< E *limousine*), *sessjón* (< E *session*), *klíring* (< E *clearing*). By contrast, words ending in *-er* and *-or*, such as *master* and *monitor*, are treated as masculine. Other endings characteristic of words adapted as masculines are for example *-ism*, *-ist*, *-al*, *-phone*, as in *lobbíismi* (< E *lobbyism*), *aðventisti* (< E *Adventist*), *metall* (< E *metal*), *heddfónn* (< E *headphone*), etc. A few native suffixes appear in words of more than one gender, such as *-ing*, which is very productive in the feminine but also appears in masculines. This variation is carried over to Anglicisms, where we find masculines like *fætingur* (< E *fighting*) and *fílingur* (< E *feeling*) beside the more common feminine nouns of this type, and the latter actually has an alternative feminine form. Monosyllables of all genders are found among native words, but Anglicisms of that type are normally treated as neuter. Feminines are extremely few and most of them are either older borrowings, often via Danish, e.g. *dokk* (< E *dock*) and *vist* (< E *whist*), where the mediating language might have influenced the gender, or they are homonymous with a native feminine word or bear a very strong resemblance to one, e.g. *mús* (E *mouse* (comput.)) and *blók* (cf. *bók* 'book'). Many of the masculine monosyllables, on the other hand, have a common formal feature, i.e. they end in the consonants *-s* or *-r*, e.g. *djass* (< E *jazz*), *beis* (< E *base*), *boss* (< E *boss*), *gír* (< E *gear*), *bar* (< E *bar*), which are, in turn, infrequent in the neuter; and many of the exceptions can be explained on the basis of semantic features.

The gender acquired is crucial in deciding how the Anglicisms are declined for case and number, as nouns of the three different genders in Icelandic follow different declensional patterns. Furthermore, words within each gender belong to various inflectional classes. Traditionally masculine and feminine nouns are divided into six classes each and neuters into two, but in fact there are almost thirty different paradigms for nouns and even more if irregularities in individual nouns are taken into consideration. In practice, only a small number of the declensional classes are open to borrowings. All neuter Anglicisms are assigned to the same declension, and the masculines are divided between two classes, one strong and another weak, and, in fact, the plural is the same for both, with the nominative ending *-ar*. The weak masculines acquire the ending *-i* in their basic singular form, for example *basi* (< E *base*), *túristi* (< E *tourist*), *hamborgari* (< E *hamburger*), whereas the strong either get no ending or one of the consonantal endings *-ur*, *-l*, or *-n*, as in *blús* (< E *blues*), *póker* (< E *poker*), *tvistur* (< E *twist*), *stæll* (< E *style*), *heddfónn* (< E *headphone*). The greater part of the feminines get a weak declension with the basic form ending *-a* and the nominative plural ending -*ur*, for example *filma* (< E *film*), *pósa* (< E *pose*). Some adopt a strong declension, showing greater variation in declension than any of the other groups of words, partly conditioned by different suffixes or suffix-like endings. The variation mainly appears in the plural endings; feminines in -*sjón* form the plural by the ending -*ir*: *aksjón* (< E *action*); words ending in -*ing* take -*ar*: *dílingar* (< E *dealings*); and those ending in -*k*, both monosyllabic and disyllabic, take -*ur* in the genitive singular as well as in the plural, if that is used at all, e.g. *blók* (< E *bloke*), *grafík* (< E *graphic*), etc.

In sum, nouns of English origin obtain gender on the basis of semantic and formal factors. The gender, together with some formal characteristics, conditions the declension, which varies less in these words than in the native vocabulary, the majority of Anglicisms following only four of about thirty possible declensional paradigms, even though a small number of strong feminines shows more variation.

5.3.3 *Adjectives*

Adjectives have a very rich inflection in Icelandic, which is, however, comparatively regular, as adjectives are not split into so many different inflectional classes as the other major word classes are. In the comparison, however, there is more variation in form. Furthermore, a number of native adjectives are undeclinable.

Adjectives account for almost 8 per cent of the Anglicisms in the Icelandic part of the *Dictionary of European Anglicisms*. In spite of the comparatively simple and regular inflectional system of adjectives, the greatest part of these do not inflect at all, though some of them can take part in comparison by the means of the adverbs *meira* (comp.) and *mest* (sup.), the Icelandic counterparts of English *more* and *most*. The few adjectives that are inflected are almost entirely words that have been adapted by means of adding Icelandic formatives to the stem, or by substituting an original English formative by a native one, as in *húkktur* or *húkkaður* (< E *hooked*), *akústískur* (< E *acoustic*), *topplaus* (< E *topless*), etc. These facts agree with the results of earlier research (Eiríksson 1975).

It is not clear why the adjectives behave in this way, as a morphological adaptation to the inflectional system is the rule in other inflected word classes (cf. ss. 5.3.2 and 5.3.5). Some points can be mentioned as a possible explanation, although none is entirely satisfactory. First, a small class of indeclinable native adjectives exists, so there is a precedent within the language. Those adjectives do, however, have certain formal characteristics that are usually not present in the Anglicisms. Second, many of the borrowed adjectives have a limited distribution, being used mainly in predicative position, some of them not appearing at all as attributes. In a native word, this means that not all forms of the paradigm are needed, but they still agree with the subject in gender and number, in contrast to most of the Anglicisms. Third, many of the adjectives in question have only been used for a short period of time, and have not been properly adapted phonologically, graphemically, or morphologically. In addition, some have a limited distribution with respect to register and style, belonging mainly or exclusively to colloquial speech or even slang. This is, on the other hand, also true of many Anglicisms from other word classes that have still been adapted to a greater or a lesser extent.

5.3.4 Adverbs

Adverbs are not numerous in the *Dictionary of European Anglicisms* material and none of them is inflected. This should not come as a surprise, as adverbial inflection in Icelandic is restricted to the comparison and only a part of native adverbs manifest that inflection.

5.3.5 Verbs

An inflectional adaptation of borrowed verbs seems to be a prerequisite for their usage in Icelandic, and conjugational endings are supplied in the process of borrowing, no matter how well or little the words have been adapted phonologically. In many cases it is, no doubt, only a question of adding the normal infinitive ending, *-a*, but the use of other forms does not appear to raise any problems either. It should be noted, however, that whereas there is a great variation in the conjugation of native verbs which are divided into a number of conjugational classes, weak and strong, all the Anglicisms follow the same pattern, i.e. they all enter the most regular class of weak verbs. This means that they all form their past tense with the suffix *-aði* and the past participle with *-aður*, and the endings for person and number, in present as well as past tense, are the same for all.

5.3.6 Derivation

A number of Anglicisms have been borrowed with an English suffix, and some of these sound sequences clearly act as formal factors in the assignment of gender and declension to nouns (cf. s. 5.3.2). Some suffixes are homonymous with native ones, as is the case with *-ing*, while others are already present in Icelandic in older borrowings from Danish or German, e.g. *-isti*, *-ína*, on which the morphological adaptation of the Anglicisms can be modelled. There are, on the other hand, no signs of them becoming productive in word formation in Icelandic, with the exception of some of the earlier introduced suffixes, like *-isti*, which can hardly be counted as specifically English.

In the course of adaptation, English suffixes are sometimes replaced by the corresponding Icelandic ones. This especially happens in agent nouns and others, where the English *-er* is replaced by *-ari*, e.g. *plottari* (< E *plotter*), *hamborgari* (< E *hamburger*), often leading to the existence of two competing forms for the word, e.g. *djóker* and *djókari* (< E *joker*), *dimmer* and *dimmari* (< E *dimmer*). In other cases the *-ari* has been added as part of the adaptation process, apparently only for assigning the word to a particular gender and declensional class, e.g. *sixpensari* (< E *sixpence*).

The suffix *-ari* is extremely productive in Icelandic, especially in forming agent nouns, and it is particularily prominent in word formation in colloquial language and slang (Jónsson 1984; Sigmundsson 1984), registers that many of the Anglicisms belong to. Because of its productivity it is often impossible to determine whether a particular word containing the suffix is an adaptation of a corresponding English noun or was derived from an Anglicism in Icelandic. This is true of e.g.

boxari, which can either come straight from the English *boxer* or be derived in Icelandic from the borrowed verb *boxa* (< E *box*). In other cases English has no corresponding noun so the Icelandic word is bound to be a new formation, e.g. *rokkari* and *pönkari* 'person connected to rock/punk music'. The same problem of determining the origin can arise in connection with feminines ending in *-ing*, as such a suffix is productive in Icelandic. A word like *fíling* could, therefore, either derive from the English *feeling* or be derived by a word-formation process in Icelandic from the verb *fíla* (< E *feel*).

As clearly shown by the examples above, Anglicisms can easily become the basis of derivational processes in Icelandic as stems, even though none of the borrowed suffixes has become productive. This is, of course, especially true of the better adapted and more frequent words, and is by no means restricted to nouns. Adjectives derived from nouns or verbs are common, e.g. *dópaður* 'intoxicated'< *dópa (sig)* (v.), *poppaður* 'with the characteristics of or related to pop music' < *popp* (n.), etc., as are also verbs derived from nouns, usually by the mere addition of the infinitive ending, e.g. *búsa* 'drink (much) alcohol' < *bús* (< E *booze*), *snobba* 'acting as a snob' < *snobb* (< E *snob*), etc. A derived verb of this sort that also shows how an English plural ending has been reinterpreted as a part of the stem is *tipsa* < *tips* (cf. E *tip*). Some of the adjectives mentioned correspond to English past participle forms, and they raise the same problem of determining whether there is a question of mere adaptation, the English *-ed* simply being replaced by the Icelandic suffix *-aður*, or proper word formation, as discussed above.

Finally, two processes of word formation and, at the same time, means of assimilation of Anglicisms to the Icelandic morphological system should be mentioned. One of them concerns certain abbreviations or acronyms that are interpreted as normal words in Icelandic on the basis of their pronunciation, resulting in homonyms, or, if we like, new borrowed meanings to pre-existing native words. Examples of this are the English abbreviation *GMC* 'a type of car', rendered as *gemsi* [cemsi], the Icelandic pronunciation of the abbreviation being [cɛ: ɛm: sjɛ:], and *PC* 'personal computer', rendered as *pési* [pʰjɛ:si] from the pronunciation of the abbreviation [pʰjɛ: sjɛ:]. Both already exist as native words, though with totally different meanings, usually referring to boys or young animals. The other process is a particular kind of clipping, well known in the native vocabulary, especially in nicknames. It appears especially in words deriving from proper nouns, such as *makki* 'a type of personal computer' from *Macintosh*, *letti* and *plimmi*, both referring to special brands of cars from the brand names *Chevrolet* and *Plymouth*.

5.3.7 *Compounds and combining forms*

Compounds among the Anglicisms are usually hybrids. Just like the derivatives, they are of various origin, three main types being detectable. First, one part of an English compound is frequently replaced by the corresponding Icelandic word. This is especially common in words ending in *-man* and *-woman*, replaced by *-maður* and *-kona* respectively, such as *kamerumaður* (< E *cameraman*), *séntilmaður*

(< E *gentleman*), *bisnesskona* (< E *business woman*); note, however, that this applies only to words referring to persons, as the substitution does not take place in words like *walkman*. Examples of similar substitutions are *súpermarkaður* (< E *supermarket*), *gírkassi* (< E *gearbox*), etc., and with the first part of the word replaced *íshokkí* (< E *ice hockey*), *góðtemplari* (< E *Good Templar*), etc. Second, an extra word part has been added to a simplex, apparently only as a matter of formal adaptation to Icelandic, as this second part does not change the meaning of the word, although it is decisive for its inflection. In many cases, the first part is also used by itself as a synonym, the choice between the two probably depending on the context. Examples of such compounds are *slædsmynd* (< E *slide(s)*), *bleiserjakki* (< E *blazer*), etc. Third, new compounds are being formed in Icelandic where one or even more of the components are of English origin, such as *skrifstofublók* 'office employee', *poppþáttur* 'a program with popular music', *tölvubransi* 'computer business', etc. This, of course, is the most frequent type, and the great majority of such words are not displayed in the *Dictionary of European Anglicisms* material.

Finally, there are examples of English compounds having been shortened in the borrowing process, i.e. formally the Anglicisms only consist of parts of the compound words whereas the meaning corresponds to the whole. This has happened in words such as *smóking* (< E *smoking jacket*), *steisjón* (< E *station wagon*), *meik* (n.; < E *make-up*), etc.

5.3.8 Calques

The influence of English on the lexical level extends beyond direct loans and hybrids. Loan translations, in which both parts of a compound are formally Icelandic though directly modelled on an English word, are even more common. This is especially true for the more formal registers of the language, where words of this type are easily accepted though direct borrowings are not. Examples of loan-translations are *lyklaborð* (< E *keyboard*), *fegrunarblundur* (< E *beauty sleep*).

In the material, there are also examples of semantic loans. In some cases there is a close formal resemblance between the words in both languages, as in *mús* 'computer device' (E *mouse*), *biti* (E *bit*), etc., and they can even be homophonous, like *band*, existing in Icelandic in the meaning 'string, yarn, ties, etc.' and then adding the meaning 'group of musicians' borrowed from the English word. A formal similarity is, however, not a necessary prerequisite for the meaning to be borrowed as can be seen from words like *skjár*, an old word for window, which borrowed a new meaning 'screen or monitor' from English, or *líknarbelgur* 'caul' adding the meaning of 'airbag'. In the same way the adjective *svalur* has added the extra meaning of 'excellent' borrowed from American slang. Just as with the loan translations, the borrowed meaning is often more easily accepted than an Anglicism. Both calques and semantic loans are, in fact, used in officially suggested neologisms, and loan translation is very characteristic of the vocabulary collected in dictionaries of new words, most of them being terminological works in various fields of science and technology.

5.4 Meaning

The meaning of Anglicisms in Icelandic and their semantic relationship to the English etymons has never been studied systematically. A brief look at the *Dictionary of European Anglicisms* material gives some idea of the subject, but the following account should be regarded as preliminary.

In many cases, an Anglicism does not have exactly the same meaning as the corresponding English word, even though there is bound to be some relationship between them. For the sake of convenience, the majority of Anglicisms can be divided roughly into three categories with respect to their semantic connection to the original, though there are no clear-cut boundaries between them.

The first category consists of words, typically nouns, deriving from English terms with a clear and unambiguous denotative meaning, which is usually transferred directly to Icelandic. A more or less complete semantic equivalence of this sort is especially typical in technical terms from various fields and other specialized vocabulary, for example in words that denote persons connected to the fields, as well as words denoting activities, tools, materials, methods, etc. To mention just a few examples, Anglicisms such as *frílansari* (< E *freelance(r)*), *góðtemplari* (< E *Good Templar*), *badminton*, *golf*, *vist* (< E *whist*), *radar*, *sónar* (< E *sonar*), *asdik (tæki)* (< E *asdik*), *tweed*, *viskí* (< E *whisky*), *faxa* (v.; < E *fax*), etc., have approximately the same meaning as the English originals. Equivalence in meaning is presumably also more common in borrowed compounds than in simplex words, as suggested by *bakkgrándtónlist* (< E *background music*), *bananasplitt* (< E *banana split*), *kreditkort* (< E *credit card*), *poppkorn* (< E *popcorn*), for example. Many of the compound Anglicisms are hybrids (cf. s. 5.3.7), and loan translations are usually based on compound words to which they are semantically equivalent.

The second category is Anglicisms that derive from polysemous English words. Frequently, only one or two of the meanings have been borrowed, resulting in Anglicisms with a narrower and more specific meaning than that of the corresponding English word. The semantic equivalence can, however, be just as great as in words from the first category, e.g. *gæd* (< E *guide*), which is only used for people leading a group of tourists and for guidebooks in Icelandic, *startari* (< E *starter*), which only refers to the device for starting the engine of a motor vehicle, *hol* (< E *hall*), only denoting a space or passage near the entrance of a house or apartment. Normally, the most common and general meaning of words from the basic vocabulary of English already has an equivalent in a native Icelandic word and consequently this is seldom transferred. As a result, we frequently have an Anglicism with a restricted and often specialized meaning in Icelandic deriving from a much more general English word. The fact can be illustrated by *tissjú* (< E *tissue*), which only has the meaning 'paper handkerchief' in Icelandic, the verb *svissa* (< E *switch*), which is mainly used about igniting the engine of a car or other vehicles, *húdd* (< E *hood*), which only refers to the bonnet of a motor vehicle, *flass* (< E *flash*), which only means 'flashlight', *flís* (< E *fleece*) which only denotes a special kind of synthetic material, and the verb *tvista* (< E *twist*), which only means to 'dance the twist' in Icelandic.

The third category consists of Anglicisms that have developed new meanings in Icelandic, different from any of the English ones, either as the only meaning of the word, or, more often, beside others. It should be noted, however, that the sense in question is frequently specialized and may be present in the English word, though not listed in general dictionaries. Many of the additional meanings in the *Dictionary of European Anglicisms* material are connected with registers such as nautical language and slang, and the words are, no doubt, often borrowed directly from the same register. For instance, the adjective *straight* is used in Icelandic for '(in a period of) not using drugs or alcohol', which is not listed in *COD*, though it exists in English slang (Beale 1989). A new or additional meaning of an Anglicism in Icelandic is normally the result of a slight modification, often due to the usage of the word in a specific Icelandic context. An example of this is *blokk* (< E *block*), one of its meanings being 'a solid hewn piece of frozen fish', most common in the compound *fiskblokk*, where the connection to fish is specific for the Icelandic word. Another example is *keis* (< E *case*), which means 'superstructure over the engine-room of a trawler' in Icelandic. In both cases the word has developed a more specific denotation than that of the English original. Another common word that has undergone similar development is *sjoppa* (< E *shop*), which refers to a special kind of store, selling candy, tobacco, etc., frequently with long opening hours. Sometimes, there is a more complicated semantic relationship between an Anglicism and the corresponding English word, and in many such cases it is difficult to determine exactly how the meaning of the Anglicism has developed. This is for example the case in the verb *teika* (< E *take*), which refers to an activity or play of youngsters where they grab the back bumper of a car to let it drag them on icy streets. Other examples are the nouns *skvísa* and *pæja*, both denoting a girl. They are presumed to derive from the English words *squeeze* and *pie*, even though neither of them has exactly the same meaning as the Anglicisms. The latter is usually considered to be derived from the compound *sweetie-pie*, used as an address in English slang (Beale 1989).

Many Anglicisms have various connotations, some of them deriving from the English words, others developed in Icelandic or in mediating languages. The word *sjoppa*, mentioned above, added the connotation of an unrespectable place, especially a bar or restaurant with dubious reputation, and *fés* (< E *face*) is only used as a derogatory term. The latter is borrowed via Danish where it has similar connotations.

Finally, there are numerous instances of semantic loans. The English and Icelandic pairs in question are already connected in some way, normally semantically, and sometimes there is also a formal resemblance between them, often due to shared Germanic etymology. The word *mús* (E *mouse*) has already been mentioned as an example of this (cf. s. 5.3.8), and there is also a slight formal resemblance between the Icelandic *stjarna* and the corresponding English word *star*, from which it borrows the meaning 'movie star'. The words *hýr* and *ódýr*, on the other hand, bear no formal resemblance to the semantically corresponding English words, *gay* and *cheap*, but this does not prevent them from borrowing the meanings 'homosexual' and 'poor, contemptible' respectively. There are other cases of a formal resemblance between an Anglicism and an existing native word, where there is, however, no semantic relationship, as in *fax*, with the original native meaning 'mane (of a horse)' and the borrowed meaning '(a copy produced by) facsimile transmission'. Such instances should be considered as homonomy of a native word and a formally identical Anglicism rather than semantic loans.

5.5 Usage

No detailed analysis of the usage and stylistic value of Anglicisms in Icelandic has been carried out, so the following discussion is bound to be somewhat speculative. Furthermore, the fact that the majority of Anglicisms are only attested in speech makes statements on their age and stylistic value in the *Dictionary of European Anglicisms* material a difficult and time-consuming task, and, consequently, their evaluation is more subjective than would have been the case if a number of written citations could have been consulted. However, the material clearly reveals various characteristics of the usage of Anglicisms and certain conclusions can be drawn with satisfactory accuracy.

It is clear that many Anglicisms are restricted to the spoken language, especially the colloquial register, slang, and youth language, and they are rarely found in writing. Anglicisms are also more prominent in some domains than in others, i.e. in certain subjects within technology and science such as aviation and computer science, and in various fields connected to daily life and entertainment, for example words on food and clothing, vocabulary on music, especially popular music, etc. It should also be added that some of the Anglicisms are generation-bound, notably those that are colloquial or slangy, or connected to semantic fields subject to changes of fashion, like clothing and popular music.

Synonyms made up of an Anglicism and an Icelandic neologism are frequent. Their distribution with respect to register and style tends to be predictable, the Anglicism being used colloquially or in informal situations, while the neologism is preferred for more formal purposes, especially in writing and in formal speech, as in lectures. However, in many cases an Icelandic term is the only one used, in informal as well as in more formal situations, for example terms in computer technology like *stýrikerfi* 'operating system', *lyklaborð* 'keyboard', *skjár* 'monitor'.

As already mentioned, Anglicisms frequently belong to the colloquial language and slang, and such words tend to become outdated in a relatively short period of time. Words which were quite common ten or twenty years ago are hardly used by the younger generation and will, therefore, soon become obsolete. This is common, especially within the fields of clothing, cosmetics, music, and entertainment, and some of the Anglicisms attested in these fields are already historical, such as *svagger* 'a loose coat', *sivjot* 'Cheviot', *tvist* 'twist', not to mention even older words like *city dress* or *tústep* 'twostep'. Other more general words that are widely used and stylistically neutral are more likely to become a permanent and integrated part of the Icelandic vocabulary, also because such words often become more thoroughly adapted to the language system, if only by their frequent usage. Anglicisms from various domains can be mentioned as examples, such as *jass*, *djass* 'jazz', *júdó* 'judo', *bridds* 'bridge', and *golf*.

5.6 Forms of linguistic borrowing and their categorization

Various forms of lexical borrowing from English are attested in the Icelandic material, as shown in previous chapters. They include direct loanwords, or Anglicisms, where both form and meaning are borrowed, loan translations, or calques, where an Icelandic neologism is modelled on an English word, usually a compound, borrowing both its structure and meaning, various forms of hybrids where the form is only partially borrowed together with the meaning, and semantic loans where a borrowed meaning is added to a previously existing native word, thus expanding its reference. In addition, neologisms with no direct formal connection to English are being formed from native stems and affixes to render new terms and concepts, often introduced from Anglo-American sources. These include compounds and derivations as well as the attribution of new meanings to already existing words, sometimes even by reviving archaic words by adding a new meaning to them.

No research on the proportional impact of these methods in increasing the vocabulary of Icelandic has yet been carried out. It can, however, be asserted with considerable certainty that only a minority of direct loans in Icelandic are fully accepted in all registers of the language, even though they are attested in colloquial speech and other informal language use (cf. s. 5.5). By contrast, neologisms, loan translations as well as new words formed by native word-formation processes are usually considered acceptable under all circumstances. Special language glossaries and terminologies from various fields published in recent years abound with neologisms of various types, while direct loans are few. In cases where both a direct loanword and a synonymous neologism exist, their distribution is along the same lines, usually such that the Anglicism can be expected in informal language use, notably in colloquial speech, whereas the neologism is preferred in writing and in formal situations. This also accounts for the fact that examples of some Anglicisms, even the more common ones, are extremely hard to find in written sources.

This state of affairs can, no doubt, be traced to the puristic language attitude which is not only the main characteristic of the official language policy, but also has wide general support in the speech community. Such attitude has a long history in Iceland (cf. s. 5.1.4), resulting in general requirements for the formation of neologisms when new concepts, products, etc. are introduced, as well as in a long tradition of forming new words by native means. As a consequence, there has been more emphasis on the formation of neologisms than on the adaptation of loanwords, many of which do not have a standardized written form even if they are relatively common and not among the less accepted ones. There are, at the moment, no signs that the puristic attitude is retreating, even though opinions on details of the language policy differ.

5.7 The future of Anglicisms

The future of Anglicisms in Icelandic is of course very difficult to predict. It depends on two opposing forces: a constantly increasing influence from the Anglo-American world through television programmes, films, computer games, the Internet, etc. on the one hand, and, on the other, a widely accepted language policy of purism and a long tradition of the formation of neologisms by native means. There are no signs of the English impact decreasing in the near future, and it is, in fact, likely to become even more intensive. This influence will inevitably leave some traces in the language, though we do not know at this moment how extensive they will be. That depends mainly on the question whether the balance between the two forces can be kept.

As mentioned above, many Icelandic children already have considerable knowledge of English when they start formal language learning. Therefore, it is not likely that English replacing Danish as the first foreign language taught at school will have much influence on the extension of Anglicisms, and other factors will, no doubt, play a greater part.

Most people use English to some extent in their daily lives, at least passively, but a great many also use it more actively, reading manuals, magazines, and books, watching television and going to movies, using their computer, etc. The majority of films and a great part of foreign television programmes shown in Iceland are in English. The language policy makes an Icelandic translation, usually in the form of subtitles, obligatory for all officially displayed material, as well as for videotapes sold or rented to the general public. There is, however, a lot of material in English, for example videotapes that are purchased from abroad, much of the text displayed on computer monitors as well as the necessary commands the user has to give, printed manuals and various other texts, and in the last few years a new and influential medium has been introduced with a wide access to the Internet.

As long as the Icelandic language policy of keeping the language system intact and the vocabulary as free from foreign influences as possible has sufficient support, both from the authorities, e.g. in the form of financial contributions, and even more importantly from the general public, it acts as a barrier to a wide acceptance of Anglicisms and thus counterbalances the external influence of English. There are, at the moment, no clear signs of a change in this attitude.

5.8 Research

There has been little research on Anglicisms, and on lexical borrowing in modern Icelandic in general (cf. the *Annotated Bibliography of European Anglicisms*). More energy has been spent on loanwords from a historical point of view (e.g. Eiríksson 1981; Halldórsson 1970), and on general descriptions of the language situation, both historically and with respect to the modern language (e.g. Vikør 1995). Much of the literature on loanwords and other foreign influence is speculative and very often connected to discussions on language policy and purism. There are three main topics of research:

1. Anglo-American loanwords in regard to their adaptation in modern Icelandic (e.g. Eiríksson 1975, 1987; Kress 1966*a*, 1966*b*, 1970);
2. sociocultural as well as linguistic analyses of Anglo-American influences on Icelandic vocabulary, syntax, phonology, and morphology, especially from a purist point of view (e.g. Árnason 1989; Halldórsson 1962, 1979; Jónsson 1987, 1997; Jónsson 1978);
3. analyses of the characteristics of Icelandic colloquial speech and slang, especially on the lexical level (e.g. Groenke 1966, 1975; Jones 1964; Sigmundsson 1984). An important work in this category is the dictionary of slang first published in 1982 (Árnason, Sigmundsson, and Thorsson 1982) and now being updated.

5.9 Bibliography

ÁRNASON, KRISTJÁN (1989), 'Ensk-amerísk áhrif á íslenskt mál' (English-American Influence on the Icelandic Language), *Málfregnir*, 4: 3–9.

ÁRNASON, MÖRÐUR, SIGMUNDSSON, SVAVAR, and THORSSON, ÖRNÓLFUR (1982), *Orðabók um slangur, slettur, bannorð og annað utangarðsmál* (A Dictionary of Slang) (Reykjavík: Svart á hvítu).

BEALE, PAUL (ed.) (1989), *A Concise Dictionary of Slang and Unconventional English*, from *A Dictionary of Slang and Unconventional English* by Eric Partridge (New York: Macmillan Publishing Company).

BLÖNDAL, SIGFÚS (1920–4), *Íslensk–dönsk orðabók* (Icelandic–Danish Dictionary) (Reykjavík).

BÖÐVARSSON, ÁRNI (ed.) (1963), *Íslenzk orðabók handa skólum og almenningi* (A General Icelandic Dictionary) (Reykjavík: Bókaútgáfa Menningarsjóðs), 2nd enlarged edn. 1983; 3rd edn. (on CD) 2000.

BRIEM, HALLDÓR (1875), *Kennslubók í enskri tungu: Vasabók fyrir vesturfara og aðra er eiga viðskipti við Englendinga, eða læra vilja ensku* (A Textbook in the English Language: A Pocketbook for Emigrants and Others that have Business with Englishmen, or Want to Learn English) (Akureyri).

EIRÍKSSON, EYVINDUR (1975), 'Beyging nokkurra enskra tökuorða í nútímaíslensku' (The Inflection of a Few English Loanwords in Modern Icelandic), *Mímir, blað félags stúdenta í íslenskum fræðum* 23: 55–71.

——(1981), 'Burgeisar, ribbaldar, barúnar og allt það hafurtask', in *Afmæliskveðja til Halldórs Halldórssonar* (Reykjavík: Íslenska málfræðifélagið), 85–96.

——(1982), 'English Loanwords in Icelandic: Aspects of Morphology', In R. Filipovic (ed.), *The English Element in European Languages*, vol. ii (Zagreb: Institute of Linguistics, University of Zagreb), 266–300.

GÍSLASON, KONRÁÐ (1851), *Dönsk orðabók með íslenzkum þýðingum* (A Danish Dictionary with Icelandic Translations) (Copenhagen).

GÍSLASON, ODDUR V. (1863), *Leiðarvísir í enskri tungu* (A Manual of the English Language) (Reykjavík).

GROENKE, ULRICH (1966), 'On Standard, Substandard, and Slang in Icelandic', *Scandinavian Studies*, 38: 217–30.

—— (1975), 'Sletta and Götumál: On Slangy Borrowings in Icelandic', in Karl-Hampus Dahlstedt (ed.), *The Nordic Languages and Modern Linguistics*, vol. ii (Stockholm: Almqvist & Wiksell International), 475–85.

HALLDÓRSSON, HALLDÓR (1962), 'Kring språkliga nybildningar i nutida isländska' (On Linguistic Innovation in Modern Icelandic), *Scripta Islandica*, 13: 3–24.

—— (1970), 'Determining the Lending Language', in Hreinn Benediktsson (ed.), *The Nordic Languages and Modern Linguistics*, Proceedings of the International Conference of Nordic and General Linguistics, University of Iceland, Reykjavík, 1969 (Reykjavík: Vísindafélag Íslendinga), 365–77.

—— (1979), 'Icelandic Purism and its History', *Word*, 30: 76–86.

JONES, OSCAR F. (1964), 'Some Icelandic *Götumál* Expressions', *Scandinavian Studies*, 36: 59–64.

JÓNSSON, BALDUR (1987), 'Íslensk orðmyndun' (Icelandic Word Formation), *Andvari*, Nýr flokkur 29: 88–102.

—— (1997), 'Zur formalen Anpassung von Fremdwörtern im Isländischen', *Skandinavistik*, 27 (1): 15–23.

JÓNSSON, JÓN HILMAR (1978), 'Zur Sprachpolitik und Sprachpflege in Island', *Muttersprache*, 88: 353–62.

JÓNSSON, SIGURÐUR (1984), 'Af hassistum og kontóristum', *Íslenskt mál og almenn málfræði*, 6: 155–65.

KRESS, BRUNO (1966a), 'Anglo-Amerikanisch und Isländisch', *Nordeuropa: Jahrbuch für nordische Studien*, 1: 9–22.

—— (1966b), 'Anglo-Amerikanismen im Isländischen', in *Festschrift Walter Baetke, dargebracht zu seinem 80. Geburtstag am 28. März 1964.* (Weimar: Hermann Böhlaus Nachfolger), 210–14.

—— (1970), 'Zur Einpassung anglo-amerikanischer Wörter in das Isländische', in *Proceedings of the Sixth International Congress of Phonetic Sciences Prague 1967* (Prague), 507–9.

ODDSSON, GUNNLAUGUR (1819), *Ordabók sem inniheldr flest fágiæt, framandi og vandskilinn ord, er verda fyrir i dønskum bókum* (A Dictionary that Contains Most Rare, Foreign and Difficult Words Encountered in Danish Books) (Copenhagen). (2nd edn. *Orðfræðirit fyrri alda*, vol. i (Reykjavík: Orðabók Háskólans, 1991).

ÓLAFSSON, JÓN (1882), *English Made Easy: Enskunámsbók handa byrjöndum* (An English Textbook for Beginners) (Reykjavík).

—— (1888), *Vesturfara-túlkur* (An Emigrant's Interpreter) (Reykjavík: Bókaverzlun Sigfúsar Eymundssonar).

ÓSKARSSON, VETURLIÐI (1997), 'Tæk orð og miður tæk í Blöndalsorðabók' (Acceptable and Less Acceptable Words in Blöndal's Dictionary), *Orð og tunga*, 3: 25–34.

SIGMUNDSSON, SVAVAR (1984), 'Slang på Island' (Slang in Iceland), in K. Ringgaard and Viggo Sørensen (eds), *The Nordic Languages and Modern Linguistics 5*, Proceedings of the Fifth International Conference of Nordic Languages and Modern Linguistics in Århus 26/6–1/7 1983 (Århus), 369–73.

SVAVARSDÓTTIR, ÁSTA (1993), *Beygingakerfi nafnorða í nútímaíslensku* (The Inflectional System of Nouns in Modern Icelandic), Málfræðirannsóknir 5 (Reykjavík: Málvísindastofnun Háskóla Íslands).

VIKØR, LARS S. (1995), *The Nordic Languages: Their Status and Interrelations* (Oslo: Novus Press).

ZOËGA, GEIR (1896), *Ensk–íslenzk orðabók* (English–Icelandic Dictionary) (Reykjavík: Sigurður Kristjánsson). (Reprinted several times.)

——(1904), *Íslenzk–ensk orðabók* (Icelandic–English Dictionary) (Reykjavík: Sigurður Kristjánsson). (Reprinted twice.)

6

FRENCH

John Humbley

6.1 History of language contact: historical and sociocultural factors

6.1.1 Chronology of intensive influence

French and English history have been intertwined since the Norman Conquest in 1066, a fact patently mirrored in the vocabulary of both languages. Until modern times, however, the overwhelmingly dominant influence was that of French on English. By contrast, English influence on French began very gradually, when a small number of Anglo-Saxon seafaring terms were borrowed, the most noteworthy being the points of the compass (*nord*, *sud*, *est*, *ouest*) and *boat*, adapted as *bateau*. Before the eighteenth century, English words found in French texts were almost exclusively foreignisms. The philosophers of the Age of Enlightenment looked to England for philosophy and constitutional reform, and Voltaire's stay in England helped to confirm the influence of English, which, for the first time, became the major purveyor of loanwords, supplanting Italian (Mackenzie 1939).

The history of intensive contact can be roughly split into five periods:

1. In the eighteenth century lasting influence was achieved in the political sphere (various British institutions serving as models or counter-models for the revolutionary period), in that of fashion, when *anglomanie* became a watchword, with borrowing frequent in the fields of clothing, drinks, and sports such as horse-racing. English novels were translated, resulting in the first instances of semantic borrowings (Humbley 1986); British science and medicine also influenced French (the vocabulary of the circulation of blood, for example), though native developments (Lavoisier) were much to the forefront (see Brunot 1932).

2. In the nineteenth century, industrial development led by Great Britain brought in its wake many terms of, for instance, steelmaking, clothmaking, and railway technology, which were incorporated into the special languages concerned, though often with considerable modification.

3. The latter part of the nineteenth century saw a second period of *anglomanie*, with new sports such as tennis (remodelled from French origins), football, and, in the early part of the twentieth century, basketball and new forms of swimming (Gritti 1985). Fashion was again to the forefront in borrowings, and tourism, dominated by the British and later the Americans, purveyed its own vocabulary.

4. The early part of the twentieth century, in particular the period between the two world wars, saw the emergence of AmE as a source of loans in such fields as jazz and dancing, cinema and motor cars.

5. After 1945, the influence of English on French was notably scaled up. Although American military presence in France was very limited in duration, the psychological impact was great, and the 'Atlantic alliance' carried with it considerable linguistic impact, including the military domain, which was surprisingly receptive to English borrowing. This was also the period when France opened up to the outside world and became a major trading partner, increasing contact with a world dominated by American methods of commerce, marketing, and computer and communications technology. Pop culture also came onto the scene, though French remains to this day the dominant language of pop music produced in France. The post-1945 period was also that of an organized reaction to indiscriminate borrowing, and the setting up of various institutions or services designed to promote French vocabulary especially in technical sectors.

6.1.2 Origins of influence

French research into Anglicisms has never been intent on establishing whether British or American English provided the source, and the various dictionaries of Anglicisms published in the early 1980s include words of English-language origin from all over the world. As French lexicography is particularly preoccupied with early attestations of new words, it is often possible to trace the origins of individual borrowings through such large-scale dictionaries as the *Trésor de la langue française* or the *Grand Robert*. Many words of Asian and African origins were borrowed directly into French without English mediation, or through Portuguese or Arabic transmission.

6.1.3 Types of influence

In French, English influence is almost exclusively lexical, and influence on other levels of language (spelling, pronunciation, morphology, syntax) is predominantly exerted through multiple lexical borrowings (Deroy 1956: 21). The types of integration are illustrated in s. 6.6.

English influence in French takes two main forms, which can be generally characterized as Anglo-Saxon borrowings and Latinate borrowings. The Anglo-Saxon borrowings stand out in French and pose many problems of assimilation, even for long-established and frequently used words. Latinate borrowings are particularly common, as English has such a large vocabulary of French and Latin origin (often Latin transmitted through French), which is often used in technical and scientific fields. This means that for computer technology, for example, the majority of borrowings pass unnoticed, as direct adaptation of these Latinate forms is unproblematic for French. Anglo-Norman borrowings into medieval English which are more thoroughly assimilated to English phonology can pose problems of integration into French, as witnessed by the difficulties encountered in rendering words such as *management*.

In the *Dictionary of European Anglicisms* it was decided to concentrate on the Anglo-Saxon element in Anglicisms, which has the advantage of eliminating many problematic cases (which was the source for which: *telephone* or *téléphone*, *phonograph* or *phonographe*?). The elimination of many Latinate Anglicisms in French from the *Dictionary*, however, gives a rather unbalanced picture of the place of English borrowings in French. On the one hand, this vocabulary is also where many of the semantic loans take place, some deliberate, but many unconscious, resulting in often criticized polysemy (*réaliser*, *contrôler*, *délai* can all be used with English as well as French meanings). On the other hand, English can often use Latinate forms in a way unknown in French, especially in clippings. Thus, such loans as *pétrodollar* can be criticized as being contrary to French morphology.

This aspect of influence also concerns the other Romance languages, but in the perspective of a pan-European study, a certain homogenization is imperative, even if certain language-specific phenomena are lost in the process.

6.1.4 *Chronology of purist phases*

Few French linguists would accept the long-established practice of searching for native equivalents of foreign words as purism, though an exception could well be made for some of the more extreme movements. There is a long history of such resistance to foreign influence, best illustrated in the Renaissance, when the Pléiade poets took up the defence (and 'illustration') of French against the dominant Italian model. English influence was criticized from the eighteenth century on: *anglomanie* was a critical term designed to stigmatize not only linguistic influence but other behaviour as well.

France has a long history of language planning, going back to the Edict of Villers-Cotterêts of 1539, making French the only language of law and government. Corpus planning for the general language, of a purely persuasive nature, was delegated to the Académie française, founded in 1634/5, and for special languages to the sister Académie des sciences.

In the nineteenth and early twentieth centuries, the French never had any one body dedicated to translating the vocabulary of football or the railway; while a majority of terms were adapted over the years, some retained their English forms for many decades, and, in some cases, up to the present. In general, the popular sports such as football were Gallicized more quickly than the more aristocratic sports such as tennis or, even more so, golf.

The main thrust to replace English borrowings with French equivalents has always been in scientific and technical terminology, though many of the words concerned were on the way to being incorporated into everyday French. Thus the Académie française created a Commission de la terminologie technique française moderne in 1933, a forerunner of the many committees launched after the Second World War. One such committee was founded by the Académie des sciences (1952), but the trend was to associations, which were thought to work faster; the first of these, the Comité d'études des termes techniques français (founded in 1954), is still active. Official recognition came in 1966 in the shape of the Haut Comité pour la défense et l'expansion de la langue, which was directly attached to the Prime Minister's office. This organization, which has changed names and certain attributes over the years, has been responsible for language and terminology policy in France, and coordinated the works of such associations as AFTERM and FRANTERM, as well as the Conseil international de la langue française, an association which continues its terminological field.

The Haut Comité and its successors were also responsible for the organization of what came to be known as the *commissions ministérielles de terminologie*. These bodies were set up from 1970 on in a number of public administrations (*ministères*) with the brief of eliminating Anglicisms from their own writings and the areas of their jurisdiction. Their competence was defined in a 1975 law, making the official terms mandatory in certain circumstances. After twenty-odd years of work, the commissions had produced over 2,000 official French terms, mostly, though not exclusively, replacing English terms either already in use or potentially borrowable (Humbley 1997).

In 1991 a new law, popularly known as the Loi Toubon after the then Minister of Culture, sought to strengthen the 1975 law, but the Constitutional Court declared invalid the part of the law that required private individuals or firms to use official terminology as being contrary to the constitutionally guaranteed freedom of speech (Thody 1995). Consequently, a reorganization took place in 1996 entailing a greater degree of cooperation with the Académie française so as to encourage the public to use the terms thus adopted. The official terms are still mandatory for government bodies and government officials, though no longer for private persons or for firms. Thus the code *ban* in the *Dictionary of European Anglicisms* refers to Anglicisms deprecated by the commissions, though since 1992 no obligation to avoid them is imposed on the general public.

There have been a number of studies with a view to evaluating the efficiency of the action of the *commissions ministérielles de terminologie* by such linguists as D. Becherel (1981), J.-P. Goudailler (1982, 1986), and B. de Bessé (1990), and the GEPE group in Strasbourg devoted two conferences to the subject (1982, 1988), but it was only in 1993 that the Délégation générale de la langue française, the successor to the Haut Comité, organized a conference presenting the results of a series of studies made on the work of a representative cross-section of the commissions. The results are mixed. Humbley (1988*a*), in the GEPE group, compared the reception of computer vocabulary in French and German specialist publications and found that the official terms were very largely adopted, where German generally had direct loans. In more recent studies (RINT 1994) a note of caution is sounded, as some official terms are widely known, though not necessarily also used by specialists; even where the official terms are effectively adopted, some observers lament, many new loans are coming in all the time, making the job of replacement a Sisyphean task.

French attitudes to Anglicisms and the official policy of their replacement are somewhat unique in post-war Europe. In countries where previous authoritarian governments had gone in for purist language-cleansing, most forms of corpus planning were viewed with dismay, and French policy often dismissed as retrograde (cf. Müller 1975; Nüssler 1979). The Romance countries, on the other hand, have been more sympathetic, and an international network of Latin-based terminology is actively promoting the creation of neologisms, with the French playing a prominent role. Several factors can be suggested to explain why the French have largely embraced this form of policy. One is that language planning in itself is part of French history; another is the fact that French was the leading international language until the nineteenth century, and remains an international linguistic factor with an influence well beyond what the modest number of native French speakers in the world would suggest. The idea was long current that giving French the scientific and technical terms it needed was a means of catching up in the race against English dominance. A third reason is the example of language planning in Quebec, where French was effectively threatened by English in particular in economic and professional circles; the use of terminology planning in regaining ground for French speakers was applied to the rather different situation in France.

6.1.5 Regional differences

In French-speaking countries, the major geographical differences concerning the use of Anglicisms are between Europe and North America, and these can be very great. By comparison, the differences between the Anglicisms adopted in francophone countries in Europe are quite modest. Certain Anglicisms concerned with tourism are more common in Switzerland (*tea room*, for example), but the main variation is the greater openness to Anglicisms shown by the Belgians, who sometimes adopt direct loans when the French prefer an adaptation (compare *LP* in Belgium with *microsillon* in France); the Belgian pronunciation can also be closer to the English (in *square*, for example). This is especially the case where the *commissions ministérielles* are concerned: *software* and *byte* are more commonly used even in formal situations in Belgium, but no longer in France.

Perhaps because France is a centralized country from many points of view, there seem to be few or no regional differences in the use of Anglicisms.

6.1.6 Stylistic differences

As with most neologisms, Anglicisms have come into the mainstream of the language from the periphery, e.g. from technical language, which has long been a major vector of loans, and many words remain confined to this special usage. Due to the efforts of the *commissions ministérielles*, however, technical French may well prefer the official replacement term in formal situations, such as in publications, whereas the direct loan may still be used as a familiar variant. Stylistic variation *within* language registers can thus be important.

The colloquial use of English loanwords is rather more recent, though it goes back at least to the beginning of the twentieth century with such borrowings as *because* (or *bicoz*) and the adjunction of *-man* to French elements (*faucheman* 'for someone without any money'). Popular French has often been quick to transform English loans to bring them into line with slang forms (*ticket* thus becoming *ticson*). There is no doubt that the colloquial use of English has been increasing in recent years, though its prominence in 'journalese' (both articles and advertising) does not necessarily reflect as wide a usage in other spheres. The use of English words is often a case of code-switching rather than borrowing (e.g. the use of *himself* in articles), and English is often used facetiously in plays on words.

6.1.7 Innovation and obsolescence

Although there have been several studies of the frequency of English loanwords in various corpora, there do not seem to have been any long-term studies made on the reception and elimination of Anglicisms in French in general. One study (Humbley 1974) of new Anglicisms in newspapers in 1959 and 1969 showed many new words in the latter period, but also the loss of many from the first. Forgue (1988) found one English borrowing per 170 words in *Le Monde* in 1977. He also found that the most recent borrowings were the least frequent.

6.1.8 Mediating languages

The number of Anglicisms taken into French via another language seems to be negligible. Sometimes the origin of a word can be attributed to two different sources, one of them English. This is the case of *bunker*, probably borrowed via German, but sometimes the pronunciation shows English influence, and the case of *krach*, used for a stock market crash, where German and English origin is possible. Generally, then, influence from English was direct, and no intermediary was necessary.

6.1.9 English in education

English has for long been the most widely taught foreign language in schools, though, before the post-war period, relatively few French people learnt any foreign language at all. Since the end of the Second World War, the percentage of schoolchildren learning English as their first foreign language has been rising steadily, now to some 90 per cent. Those who do not take English as their first language almost invariably do as their second language; this means that virtually all who have gone through the school system have at least four years of English study behind them. Since language teaching was introduced in primary schools in the 1990s, English has further consolidated its position (*Monde de l'éducation* 1996).

For some years certain radio programmes such as France Musique or France Culture have broadcast interviews in English without any translation, on the assumption that the listeners will be able to follow (Stuart 1985).

The effect of school English on borrowings has changed the pronunciation of English words adopted in written form (the vast majority). In the inter-war years the cigarette *High Life* was pronounced [iglif], and the first element of the recent loan *sweatshirt* is pronounced [swit] in accordance with the general pronunciation of <ea> in English.

The degree of knowledge of English among the younger generation in France, though probably not up to the standard of northern Europe, increases the use of English in code-switching situations. Gesner (1997) reports French teenagers regularly using a sounded -*s* for the plural of English borrowings, a new development indeed.

6.2 Pronunciation and Spelling

6.2.1 Pronunciation

The pronunciation of English words in French poses many problems and considerable variation may be heard between speakers. Current Anglicisms, however, usually have an accepted pronunciation, possibly with one or two variants, and this includes Anglicisms that may be restricted to special domains.

The pronunciation of Anglicisms depends on their origin: words of Latin or assimilated origins are pronounced as French words would be, including such pseudo-learned forms as *laser* [lazɛr]. Anglicisms deriving from Anglo-Norman borrowings present a particular problem: their connection with French is obvious, but they are just a little too different to be given an ordinary French pronunciation, so for words like *management* there is often some fudging. Anglo-Saxon words are generally pronounced with French vowels and an approximation to English consonants, except for /θ, ð/, though the exact pronunciation depends on the familiarity of the word and its origin (written or spoken).

One of the major differences between French and English pronunciation is in lexical stress: the stressed syllable of an English borrowing does not receive any more prominence than the other syllable(s), and there is no reduction of unstressed syllables. Since this pattern is completely regular it explains why there are no stress marks indicated for French items in the *Dictionary of European Anglicisms*. English speakers typically perceive French speakers as stressing the final syllable of a word.

Other differences are often attributable to the absence of lexical stress, so reduced vowels are usually rendered as full vowels, *jodhpurs* thus pronounced [jɔdpyʀ].

As far as individual sounds in Anglicisms are concerned, the following remarks should be made:

1. Initial unvoiced stops /p, t, k/ are not aspirated.
2. The English graphemes <j> /dʒ/ and <ch> /tʃ/ are usually pronounced as in English in new loans, and often as in French /ʒ, ʃ/ in older loans.

3. /ŋ/ was often pronounced [ng] in the immediate post-war period (Martinet and Walter 1973), but is now almost universally pronounced as in English, occupying as it does an 'empty space' in the French phonemic system (Walter 1983).
4. <th> is never pronounced [θ] or [ð], [s] and [z] being the most popular substitutes.
5. French being an r-full language, postvocalic [r] is normally pronounced in all positions.
6. French makes no distinction between /iː/ and /ɪ/, both pronounced [i], or between /ʊ/ and /uː/, both pronounced [u].
7. English vowels tend to be attributed to the 'nearest' French equivalent, though what is 'nearest' depends partly on convention. Thus [æ] is usually rendered by [a], /ɑː/ by [aʀ]. /ʌ/ is usually pronounced [œ], a pronunciation which may have influenced the pronunciation of early Anglicisms in other languages mediated by French.

The pronunciation of individual Anglicisms has changed considerably over the years. Thus *club* was pronounced with [y] in the nineteenth century, but its modern pronunciation is [œ] which is felt to be closer to English. *Baby* was pronounced (and written) *bébé*, but the spelling pronunciation of *baby* (a small whisky) is probably an inter-war years reborrowing.

6.2.2 Graphemic integration

As historians of the French language have often noted, the former French tendency to adapt English loans to French orthographical traditions (*riding coat* spelt *redingote*; *bowling green* spelt *boulingrin*) was considerably reduced as from the end of the eighteenth century. Words borrowed later tend to retain their English spelling, though with some exceptions.

Anglicisms of Latin or French provenance (in principle not included in the *Dictionary of European Anglicisms*) are generally given their French form (e.g. *compileur* for *compiler*).

The *commissions ministérielles* have proposed a number of adapted spellings, which have to some extent been adopted. This is the case for *bug* in computer terminology, written as *bogue*, especially in derivations such as *déboguer*. The plurals of words in *-y* vary between *-ys* and *-ies*.

6.3 Morphology

6.3.1 Introduction

Almost 80 per cent of the Anglicisms listed in Rey-Debove and Gagnon (1980) are nouns; over 85 per cent are used both as nouns and adjectives. Only 8 per cent are adjectives used exclusively as such, and under 5 per cent are verbs.

French plurals are generally marked by *-s*, as in English, though with obligatory attribution to masculine or feminine gender. Adjectives are inflected for number and gender, verbs for person, number, tense, and mood. Stages on the way to integration include hesitation as to the proper gender for nouns and inflexion for verbs.

6.3.2 Nouns

Gender. An Anglicism must have a gender attributed to it, though it is possible to use forms, such as the plural, where gender is not marked; this seems to be a strategy used by speakers and especially writers not sure of which gender to choose. The criteria used for determining gender are fairly similar to those used in German, but, as in German, the order of applying the criteria is not fixed. Gender allocation can be based on:

(a) phonology and graphemics: words ending in a consonant are usually masculine in the French of France (*le job*), according to the graphemic criterion, but feminine in Quebec French (*la job*), according to phonetic criteria;

(b) morphology: certain suffixes determine gender, for example words ending in *-er, -ing, -ment* are masculine;

(c) meaning: natural gender is preferred for persons (*la first lady*); a hyponym may be given the gender of its superordinate (*la day-school*, because of *l'école* (f.));

(d) unmarked gender: masculine is very much the unmarked gender in French, and most Anglicisms are attributed to this class, unless there is a cogent reason against it. This tendency seems to be growing; words like *happy end* tended to be feminine (seen as an equivalent of *la fin*), but are now overwhelmingly masculine.

Number. The plural in the majority of cases causes no conflict between English and French plural forms, as *-s* is the dominant plural in both languages. The only cases posing problems concern minor or irregular plural forms in English. Thus, the *-es* plural may or may not be followed in French, so *lunchs, sandwichs* are regular. The recent spelling reform brought in by the Conseil supérieur de la langue française (Rectifications de l'orthographe) recommends this plural form for Anglicisms as for other borrowings. On the other hand, increasing competence in English favours keeping the English plural as a mark of education. The same applies to the compounds in *-man*, which now tend to be in *-men*, despite the fact that many have been coined in French such as *perchman, câbleman*, and have no English model. The feminine form (*-woman*) is even more of an embarrassment. In French, other parts of speech used as nouns take an unmarked plural; in consequence, *check-up* or *by-pass* are usually also written without a plural *s*.

6.3.3 Adjectives

Adjectives of Anglo-Saxon origin are generally not inflected for number and gender, with the partial exception of adjectives which have the same form as nouns. The noun *black*, for example, can be pluralized as *les blacks*, and on occasion as an adjective (*les fêtes blacks*), whereas one never finds a plural form of pure adjectives such as *cool*. No feminine inflexions are attested.

More adjectives were borrowed in recent times, but they are limited to 'youth culture': *black*, *cheap*, *clean*, *cool*, *hard*, *heavy*, *high*, *hot* being typical examples.

6.3.4 Adverbs

No examples of Anglicisms in *-ly* or hybrid adjectives plus *-ment* have been attested.

6.3.5 Verbs

There has been some speculation as to whether some borrowings in *-ing* were motivated by the desire to avoid conjugating a borrowed verb, so *faire un rerecording* to avoid **rerecorder* (Trescases 1983: 98). This resistance may now be weakening, and one finds instances of borrowed verbs with awkward features: *to log in* is regularly rendered by enthusiasts as *se loguer*. Phrasal verbs pose a problem of adaptation, and, if borrowed at all, lose their 'particule'.

In all cases, the conjugation chosen is the first (*-er* verbs), the only class which is still fully productive in French. Some Anglicisms have been in French for a considerable period: *boycotter*, *handicap(p)er* are regularly used, though it is difficult to determine whether the verb was borrowed directly or whether it was derived from the noun. Participles are most uncommon; *bodybuildé* is one rare example.

6.3.6 Derivation (selection)

Gender specification. French personal nouns have a variety of feminine forms, many of which entail adding an *-e* to the masculine form. This does not seem to be applied to English-borrowed personal nouns at all. Sometimes specifically feminine forms are borrowed into French such as *sportswomen*, now obsolete, as is *sportsman*.

Agent nouns. The *-er* morpheme in English is historically equivalent to French *-eur*, and this explains some hesitation between the two forms. Thus the two forms *sprinter* and *sprinteur*, a nineteenth-century loan, are still common. The morpheme represents not only personal agents, but also instruments. In French, this function is shared with the feminine form *-euse*, and some (Quemada 1978) suggest that *-eur* forms have become more common because of the influence of the prestigious *-er* form. Certain Latin-based Anglicisms have been assimilated by use of the *-eur* suffix (*encoder → encodeur*).

-man was so often borrowed in sports and technical lexis that it has limited productivity in French (*taximan*) and is the source of a series of pseudo-Anglicisms (Thody 1995: 268–9).

Denominal verbs. Verbs such as *boycotter*, *tester* are currently used in French, though, as mentioned, it is often difficult to determine whether these verbs are borrowed or derived. Certain verbs that do not exist in English, such as *badger*, from *badge* (an ID card) prove that French can form a verb from a noun borrowed from English.

New adjectives. The only large category of new adjectives derived in French from Anglicisms is that of proper nouns having no particular adjectival form in English. Thus *Hollywood* used attributively is transformed into *hollywoo-dien*.

Deadjectival nouns. Nouns formed from adjectives are not numerous among French Anglicisms. Some may be more common than the corresponding adjective, such as *fitness* (*fit* is practically unknown in French).

Deverbal nouns. As already mentioned, French has a large number of deverbal nouns ending in *-ing*. Most were borrowed from English directly, but some were actually created in French. One series often cited is that relating to places (*camping*, *dancing*, *parking* . . .), though these are more likely to be truncated froms of English compounds. This does not seem to be the case with such words as *footing*, *listing*, *couponning*, which do not correspond to an English-language model. Semantically, the French *-age* suffix has similarities to *-ing*, and is sometimes used as a substitute (*listage* instead of *listing*). Deverbals from verbs of English origin are usually of the *-age* type (*boycotter* → *boycottage*).

6.3.7 Compounds and combining forms

French orthography tends to separate compound words which are generally written as one word in English. Thus *cowboy* is very often written *cow-boy*. It can be speculated that separating the elements makes it easier for the French speaker with limited English competence to understand the word.

French tends to rely more on derivation than composition, so the number of compounds using English elements is not large.

6.3.8 Calques (loan translations)—see also s. 6.6 below

The ease with which the Germanic languages calque English noun compounds finds no echo in the Romance languages. Compounding is generally less developed in French, and the order of elements is the opposite of English: head + modifier, with or without preposition. Nevertheless, English compound nouns regularly serve as models for French adaptations: *frogman* is thus rendered as *homme-grenouille*. Often a preposition is required: *image de marque* for *brand image*, *groupe de pression* for *pressure group*; also, the modifier may take the form of an adjective: *navette spatiale* for *space shuttle*. Sometimes calques have produced types of constructions not previously attested within a particular semantic range. Thus *haut-parleur*, modelled on *loudspeaker*, innovated in as much as the pattern adj+N+*eur* had not been previously used to name instruments.

The number of calques, especially in technical terminology, is particularly large, but is generally not recognized as being of English origin, and thus goes largely unnoticed. The degree of fidelity of a calque is also variable, as Bäcker (1975) pointed out. *Gratte-ciel* renders the two components of *skyscraper*, but substitutes a typically French syntactic structure. Loan creations often occur, in particular in the work of the *commissions ministérielles* (*ordinateur* for *com-puter*).

The use of combining forms taken from an English model is particularly common in scientific and technical French (for example *aquaplane*), but these forms are usually beyond the scope of the *Dictionary of European Anglicisms*.

6.4 Meaning

How borrowing affects the meaning of loanwords. Anglicisms in French show a narrowing of the semantic range as compared with that of the etymons and their meaning can change after borrowing, a development which may have nothing to do with the semantics of the English word.

Semantic specialization. When a word is borrowed, only one sense is taken over. Thus *happening* was borrowed only as improvised art form, and its multimedia developments, and not in the other, often more usual meanings available in English. This specialized meaning is sometimes exploited metaphorically in the press as a synonym for disorder, a specific French post-integrative development. Multiple borrowings have the effect of adding extra meanings, so that in some admittedly exceptional cases, the Anglicism finishes up by having nearly the same semantic range as in the original language. The case of *film* is instructive from this point of view. First used in a compound term for a thin layer of some substance in early cinema terminology (French already had *pellicule*, which is still used), it came to be used for the result, the filmed work. In the 1960s, a metaphorical sense, probably also borrowed from English, of a 'film of liquid', was added. The verb form *filmer* also echoes the English meaning (from the point of view of the person who uses the camera). However, some differences remain: in French an added meaning of the sequence of events (*le film des événements*) does not occur in English.

As in other languages, certain earlier borrowings cease to be used (*break* for a type of horsedrawn carriage, now used for an estate car) so that the semantic range is usually fairly different from English. One exception is technical terminology, which generally keeps exactly the original meaning (*kelvin* is the same in French as in English), as this is one major motivation for borrowing. Differences can occur here too, especially in post-integrative developments, so that, for example *marketing* in French is only partially equivalent to the English etymon.

Post-integrative development. Once a word is borrowed into a language, it takes on its own life and may develop without regard to its original meaning. Thus *box* was borrowed as part of riding and racing terminology in the sense of a horse's cubicle in a stable, and was later used for a cubicle in a dormitory or a partitioned-off table in a restaurant; its slang form *boxon* is used as a brothel, today in a jocular meaning of great disorder. At the same time, there are multiple borrowings (the *box* in courts of law) and truncation of compounds (*box* from *boxcalf*), so that the Anglicism may end up with a range of meanings very different from that of its English etymon.

The generalizations made for semantic evolutions of Anglicisms in German also hold true for French.

(a) The range of meanings is reduced. Thus *set* has two meanings in the *Petit Robert* as against twenty-four in the *COD*; *ticket* has five meanings in the *Petit Robert* (three of which are post-integrative developments) and seven in the *COD*.

(b) Individual meanings are further narrowed; thus, *lunch* is used only for a buffet meal.

(c) The range of an English item may be extended because of new meanings. Thus *gadget* is, or rather was, used in French not only for concrete objects but also for actions. For *lunch*, a widening has taken place as well as a narrowing as the meal can be taken at any time of the day.

(d) The specificity of the meaning is reduced by its application to a wider range of referents. For example, *ticket* is used for a social security attestation, specific to France, and thereafter metaphorically as a lucky charm.

It can be argued that extreme post-integrative semantic developments are becoming rarer as English increasingly takes on the status of a second language in France. The greatest divergence occurs in older loans (such as *box*), though this is often corrected by subsequent multiple loans.

6.5 Usage

Despite much interest in the English influence on French, there have been relatively few sociolinguistic or stylistic studies. Most have been of lexicological or lexicographical orientation, starting from Bonnaffé's (1920) dictionary and Behrens's (1927) study. Dictionaries are best known, two of which attain the highest standards of language description (Höfler 1982; Rey-Debove and Gagnon 1980); these reference works give valuable information on pronunciation, morphology, and semantics. These dictionaries are either of historical nature (Höfler 1982) or they contain suggestions of how to avoid Anglicisms (Rey-Debove and Gagnon 1980). Sociological studies include that of A. Cartier (1977), who adopts a Labovian methodology and indicates feminine preference for Anglicisms. Research into the adoption of official terminology has also been mentioned.

As in other languages, Anglicisms in French are particularly frequent in technical sectors on the one hand and colloquial, informal, and journalistic contexts on the other. Contrary to other languages the effect of the *commissions ministérielles* has been to popularize official equivalents at the expense of direct loans as technical terminologies become better known to the general public, as happened when the micro-computer left specialist usage to come into the home and the office.

6.6 Forms of linguistic borrowing and their categorization

The forms that borrowings can take are the same in French as in other languages; there are direct loans, which may be integrated to varying degrees, there are replacements of loans using forms of translation, and there are loans without direct models, so-called pseudo-loans. The perception of the integration of loans may differ from that of other language communities. Thus, even long-term Anglicisms in French are often felt to be somehow 'not French'.

1. *Borrowing*

   (*a*) Totally unadapted and not felt to be part of French (quotation words, code-switching, foreignisms), e.g. *himself*, *Bloody Mary*;
   (*b*) words still looking foreign in form or unadapted, e.g. *badge*, wording ending in *-ing*;
   (*c*) fully integrated loans, e.g. *film*.

The process of integration takes place at different rates according to the level of language considered. Thus it is possible for a word such as *sandwich* to be poorly integrated graphemically and morphologically (hesitation as to the plural) but well integrated in its semantic field. By contrast, in *tour opérateur* both elements are adapted to existing French units, but the term is unintegrated as to the modifier+modified order.

The official and unofficial means of avoiding direct loans entail using the resources already available in French:

2. *Replacement*

   (*a*) Translation of each element, reflecting the English morphological and semantic structure as closely as possible, e.g. *pôle-position*.
   (*b*) Free translation, either of both or all elements or close translation in part, loose translation of others, often preferred to conform with the structure of French, e.g. *courrier électronique* for *e-mail*.
   (*c*) Creation, a formally independent equivalent created to render the English model, e.g. *pontage* for *bypass*.
   (*d*) Semantic loan, an existing French word taking over a meaning of a foreign partial equivalent, e.g. *colombe* 'dove' to render a supporter of the peace movement.

3. *Pseudo-loans*

Several rather different phenomena are subsumed under the name of pseudo-loans.

   (*a*) Creations using English elements, but without an English model. This normally only happens when the elements are already in use in the language, such as *recordman* in French (for 'record-holder'). In sports many words were created with *-man* as a second element (*tennisman, racingman*).
   (*b*) Truncated or augmented loans: this is the case of *camping* 'camping area', *dancing* 'dance hall', *parking* 'parking station', which have often been borrowed in this form into other languages. It is also the case of more integrated compounds such as *pullover*, commonly clipped in French (though not in English) to *pull*. First elements may also be dropped: *lifting* for *facelift(ing)*, or middle elements (*and* from *gin and tonic* known in French as *gin tonic*). Sometimes more than one element will be dropped:

for example *basket* 'basketball shoe'. In some cases, the French form may have an element not present in the English canonical form; thus *pin's* is borrowed from *pin*, with *'s* used not only to make the word look more English, as is often the case in advertising, but also to avoid an embarrassing homophone (Bizet 1992).

(*c*) Semantic extensions, where an Anglicism is used with a meaning not attested in English (*footing*, in the sense of 'jogging').

The categories of replacements can be illustrated with French examples, distinguishing between successful and unsuccessful attempts:

A *Translations*

1. Successful, retaining the order of elements

semiconductor < *semiconducteur, microwave* < *micro-ondes, halftime* < *mi-temps, acid-party* < *acide partie*

1. Successful, modifying the order of elements

brainwashing < *lavage de cerveau, flying saucer* < *soucoupe volante, hard disk* < *disque dur, time is money* < *le temps est l'argent*

1. Successful, modifying the order or elements, introducing prepositions

blood bank < *banque du sang, cable television* < *télévision par câble*

1. Successful, modifying the order or elements, using an adjective to replace the modifying noun

body language < *langage corporel, culture shock* < *choc culturel*

2. Coexisting

missing link = *chaînon manquant, on line* = *en ligne*

3. Failures

football > (*balle au pied*), *basketball* > (*balle au panier*), *hot dog* > (*chien chaud*)

B *Renderings*

1. Successful

mountain bike < *vélo tous terrains, VTT, night club* < *boîte de nuit, orienteering* < *course d'orientation*

2. Coexisting

notebook = *ordinateur bloc-notes, indoor* = *en salle, double blind* = *double insu, brain drain* = *fuite des cerveaux, hovercraft* = *aéroglisseur*

3. Failures

cash and carry > (*payer-prendre, prendre payer*), *airbag* > (*sac gonflable*)

C *Creations*

1. Successful

LP, long-playing record < *microsillon, pacemaker* < *stimulateur cardiaque, computer* < *ordinateur, breeder* < *surgénérateur*

2. Coexisting

leasing = cession-bail, brain-storming = remue-méninges, cash flow = marge brute d'autofinancement, mailing = publipostage

3. Failures

playback > présonorisation, bulldozer > boutoir, (face)lifting > lissage, design > stylique, bucking > cabrade

D *Semantic loans*

1. Successful

mouse < souris, bottleneck < goulot d'étranglement, to feed < alimenter (en données), butterfly < papillon, Iron Curtain < rideau de fer

2. Coexisting

lattice (maths) *= treillis*

3. Failures

speckle > chatoiement, hit parade > palmarès

Several of the above-mentioned creations or adaptations may well have come about under English influence, but often reliable evidence is lacking to prove that an English model was indeed present. For this reason Höfler (1982) excluded all indirect loans from his dictionary of Anglicisms. As it is uncertain what constitutes an indirect loan from English, no statistics can be undertaken to determine the proportion of direct to indirect loans. Rey-Debove and Gagnon (1984) give a large majority of direct borrowings, corroborating Görlach's hunch for German. On the other hand, in such a specialized vocabulary as micro-computer technology, Humbley (1988) found a large majority of indirect loans, on the proviso that the vocabulary is taken to be globally inspired from AmE.

French can thus be characterized as less open to direct English borrowing than the northern European language communities. A fair number of the replacements suggested either officially or unofficially have in fact been adopted, sometimes to the exclusion of the Anglicism, but most often alongside it. On the other hand, there is a long tradition of borrowing from English and a certain resistance to using new words even of French origin in a formal situation; all this means that Anglicisms have considerable vitality, greatly enhanced by the prestige of American, indeed international English.

6.7 The future of Anglicisms

If an extrapolation is made of the trends of the last fifty years, some cautious prognostications can be made. P. Trescases (1979, 1983) in the late 1970s and mid-1980s showed a slowing down in the rate of new Anglicisms in both new word dictionaries and general language dictionaries. He notes, for example, a 40 per cent drop in the percentage of Anglicisms among the new words introduced into two comparable dictionaries from 1971 and 1980 (Trescases 1983: 99).

Although is is difficult to forecast how French will react to intensified contact with English, it is possible that differences from other European languages, especially those of northern Europe, will gradually diminish. With more and more French people learning and actually using English especially through the new media, it may be expected that the sort of interference that goes with bilingualism should become more current. However, France is one of the few European countries where the challenge of English through the Internet is being met, at both official levels, as through the *Service-France-Langue* language aid service, and informally, as French equivalents of English words are thought out and debated. French is also the only language other than English to play an important role in international relations (*UNO*, *UNESCO*, etc.), in international standardization bodies (*ISO*, *ICE*), and above all in the European Union. Awareness of this role in France in particular may well incite French speakers to be particularly careful as to its use. Whatever the development, it is likely that French will continue to be very much an exception as regards Anglicisms in the European context.

6.8 Research

Research into Anglicisms in French goes back to the inter-war years, generally carried out in the framework of French-language lexical research, rather than that of English scholars.

Research has concentrated on the following topics:

(*a*) corpus-related research often based on issues of papers and journals;
(*b*) items from special vocabularies (pop music, sports, advertising, computer technology);
(*c*) studies of the reception of official vocabulary designed to replace direct Anglicisms;
(*d*) compilation of dictionaries of Anglicisms;
(*e*) analysis of Anglicisms in dictionaries;
(*f*) historical studies of influence of various languages on French and Anglicisms and their contribution to the evolution of French in general;
(*g*) sociolinguistic studies.

6.9 Bibliography

BÄCKER, NOTBURGA (1975), *Probleme des inneren Lehnguts dargestellt an den Anglizismen der französischen Sportsprache* (Tübingen: Gunter Narr).

BECHEREL, DANIÈLE (1981), 'A propos des solutions de remplacement des anglicismes', *La Linguistique*, 17 (2): 119–31.

BEHRENS, DIETRICH (1927), *Über englisches Sprachgut im Französischen*, Giessener Beiträge 4 (Gießen: University).

BESSE, BRUNO DE (1990), 'L'État terminologue: Peut mieux faire', *Traduction et terminologie*, 1: 87–100.

Bizet, Ange (1992), 'Étude de néologie: Création d'un nouveau modèle lexical en français: pin's', *La Banque des mots*, 44: 39–44.

Bonnaffé, Édouard (1920), *Dictionnaire étymologique et historique des anglicismes* (Paris: Delagrave).

Braun, P. (ed.) (1979). *Fremdwort-Diskussion* (Munich: Fink, UTB 797).

Brunot, Ferdinand (1932), *Histoire de la langue française des origines à 1900*, vol. vi, parts 1 and 2 (Paris: A. Colin).

Butterworth, Joan (1980), 'Attitudes to Franglais in Orléans 1969', in P. H. Nelde (ed.), *Sprachkontakt und Sprachkonflikt* (Wiesbaden), 125–30.

Cartier, Alice (1977), 'Connaissance et usage d'anglicismes par les Français de Paris', *La Linguistique*, 13 (2): 55–84.

Deroy, Louis (1956), *L'Emprunt linguistique* (Paris: Les Belles Lettres).

Doppagne, Albert, and Lenoble-Pinson, Michèle (1982), *Le Français à la sauce anglaise: Lexique des termes anglais et américains relevés en une année dans un grand quotidien bruxellois* (Brussels: Commission française de la culture de l'agglomération bruxelloise).

Dubois, Jean, et al. (1960), 'Le Mouvement général du vocabulaire français de 1949 à 1960 d'après un dictionnaire d'usage', *Le Français moderne*, 28: 86–106, 196–211.

Étiemble, René (1964), *Parlez-vous franglais?* (Paris: Gallimard).

Feyry, Monique (1972), 'Les Mots anglais dans les dictionnaires de langue française', *La Banque des mots*, 3: 17–34.

Filipović, Rudolf (1977), 'Primary and Secondary Adaptation of Loanwords', *Wiener Slavistisches Jahrbuch*, 23: 116–25.

Forgue, Guy-Jean (1988), 'Le "Franglais" dans Le Monde: Essai d'analyse quantifiée de contenu (année 1977)', *Actes du II° colloque du G.E.P.E.*, Strasbourg *1986*, 64–75.

Gebhardt, Karl (1975), 'Gallizismen im Englischen, Anglizismen im Französischen: Ein statistischer Vergleich', *Zeitschrift für Romanische Philologie*, 91: 292–309.

Gesner, Edward (1997), 'Les Anglicismes en français de France: Éléments de morpho-syntaxe ou le *parlez-vous franglais?* d' Étiemble revu, corrigé et supergénialement augmenté', in Lapierre, Oore, and Runte (eds.), *Mélanges linguistiques offerts à Rostivlar Kocourek* (Paris), 327–33.

Goudailler, Jean-Pierre (1982), 'Sprache und Macht: Wie ein Gesetz in Frankreich die Sprache reinigen will', *Dialect*, 6: 28–37.

——(1986), 'Pour ou contre la langue: Vingt ans de planification linguistique en France', *Dilbilim* (Revue du Département de français de la Faculté des lettres de l'Université d'Istanbul), 7: 101–16.

Gritti, Jules (1985), 'Vocabulaire des sports, les anglicismes', in Martin Antoine (ed.), *Histoire de la langue française 1880–1914* (Paris), 175–91.

Guiraud, Pierre (1965), *Les Mots étrangers: Que sais-je?* (Paris: PUF, no. 1166).

Hausmann, Franz Josef (1986), 'The Influence of the English Language on French', in Viereck and Bald 1986: 79–105.

Höfler, Manfred (1982), *Dictionnaire des anglicismes* (Paris: Larousse).

Humbley, John (1974), 'L'Influence anglo-saxonne dans la presse Française 1959–1969', unpub. Ph.D. thesis (Paris).

——(1986), 'Les Anglicismes dans le dictionnaire critique et dans le supplément', in *Autour de Féraud: La Lexicographie en France de 1762 à 1835. Actes du Colloque international du Groupe d'études en histoire de la langue française, École normale supérieure de jeunes filles* (Paris), 147–55.

——(1987), 'L'Emprunt sémantique dans la terminologie de l'informatique', *META* 32: 321–5.

HUMBLEY, JOHN (1988a), 'La Traduction dans la terminologie informatique en français et en allemand', in *Actes du II° colloque du Groupe d'études sur le plurilinguisme européen* (*Strasbourg 1986*), 6–14.

——(1988b), 'Comment le français et l'allemand aménagent la terminologie de l'informatique', *Banque des mots* (numéro spécial CTN) (CILF), 85–148.

——(1990), 'Semantic Convergence of English Borrowings in Western European Languages', in R. Filipović and M. Bratanić (eds.), *Languages in Contact: Proceedings of the Symposium 16.1 of the 12th International Congress of Anthropological and Ethnological Sciences, Zagreb* (Zagreb: University of Zagreb, Institute of Linguistics), 82–7.

——(1997), 'Language and Terminology Planning in National, Monolingual Environments, with Special Emphasis on the Francophone Experience', in Budin Wright, *Handbook of Terminology Management*, vol. i (Amsterdam: Benjamins), 261–77.

——and BIEDERMANN-PASQUES, LISELOTTE (1995), 'Réception de mots anglais dans les journaux français: Proposition d'harmonisation graphique des mots d'emprunt anglais', *Langue française*, 108: 57–65.

IMBS, PAUL, and QUEMADA, BERNARD (1971–94), *Trésor de la langue française: Dictionnaire de la langue du XIXe et du XXe siècle (1789–1960)* (Paris: CNRS, Gallimard).

LAURIAN, ANNE-MARIE (1985), 'Vocabulaire des techniques', in Martin Antoine (ed.), *Histoire de la langue française*, 157–73.

MACKENZIE, FRASER (1939), *Les Relations de l'Angleterre et de la France d'après le vocabulaire*, i: *Les Infiltrations de la langue et de l'esprit anglais: Anglicismes français;* ii: *Les Infiltrations de la langue et de l'esprit français en Angleterre: Gallicismes anglais* (Paris: Droz).

MARTINET, ANDRÉ, and WALTER, HENRIETTE (1973), *Dictionnaire de la prononciation française dans son usage réel* (Paris: France-Expansion).

MÜLLER, BODO (1975), *Das Französische der Gegenwart* (Heidelberg: Winter).

——(1983), 'Phonologie und Purismus' (1975), repr. in Franz Josef Hausmann (ed.), *Die französische Sprache von heute* (Darmstadt: Wissenschaftliche Buchgesellschaft), 337–44.

NÜSSLER, OTTO (1979), 'Das Sprachreinigungsgesetz', in Braun 1979: 186–98.

PERGNIER, MAURICE (1989), *Les Anglicismes, danger ou enrichissement pour la langue française?*, Collection Linguistique Nouvelle (Paris: Presses Universitaires de France).

PICONE, MICHAEL DAVID (1988), 'De l'anglicisme et de la dynamique de la langue française', D.Phil. thesis (Lille: Atelier national de reproduction des thèses, Université de Lille; also available on microfiche).

——(1996), *Anglicisms, Neologisms and Dynamic French* (Amsterdam: Benjamins).

QUEMADA, BERNARD (1978), 'Technique et langage', in E. Gille (ed.), *Histoire des techniques* (Paris: Pléiade), 1146–240.

RETMAN, ROMAN (1978), 'L'Adaptation phonétique des emprunts à l'anglais en français', *La Linguistique*, 14 (1): 111–24.

REY-DEBOVE, JOSETTE (1987), 'Effet des anglicismes lexicaux sur le système du français', *Cahiers de lexicologie*, 51: 257–65.

——and GAGNON, GILBERTE (1980), *Dictionnaire des anglicismes: Les Mots anglais et américains en français* (Paris: Robert).

RINT (Réseau international de néologie et de terminologie) (1994), *Terminologie nouvelles*, 12 (Implantation des termes officiels: Actes du séminaire, Rouen, décembre 1993) (Brussels).

ROBERT, PAUL, and REY, ALAIN (1987), *Le Grand Robert de la langue française*, 2nd edn. 6 vols. (Paris: Le Robert).

——— and REY-DEBOVE, JOSETTE (eds.) (1988), *Le Petit Robert I* (Paris: Le Robert).

SCHÜTZ, ARMIM (1968), *Die sprachliche Aufnahme und stilistische Wirkung des Anglizismus im Französischen, aufgezeigt an der Reklamesprache (1962–1964)* (Meisenheim am Glan: Hain).

STUART, MALCOLM (1985), 'Langage musical et langue étrangère: Incursions de l'anglais parlé sur les ondes de France-Musique', *Actes du Colloque du G.E.P.E., Strasbourg 1984*, 161–7.

SURRIDGE, MARY (1984), 'Le Genre grammatical des emprunts anglais en français: La Perspective historique', *Canadian Journal of Linguistics*, 29: 58–72.

THODY, PHILIP (1995), *Le Franglais. Forbidden English. Forbidden American. Law, Politics and Language in Contemporary France. A Study in Loanwords and National Identity* (London: Athlone).

TRESCASES, PIERRE (1979), 'Les Anglo-américanismes du *Petit Larousse illustré*, 1979', *French Review*, 53: 68–74.

——(1983), 'Aspects du mouvement d'emprunt à l'anglais reflétés par trois dictionnaires de néologismes', *Cahiers de lexicologie*, 42: 86–101.

TRUCHOT, CLAUDE (1994), 'La France, l'anglais, le français et l'Europe', *Sociolinguistica*, 8: 15–25.

VIERECK, KARIN (1980), *Englisches Wortgut, seine Häufigkeit und Integration in der österreichischen und bundesdeutschen Pressesprache* (Frankfurt am Main: Peter Lang).

VIERECK, WOLFGANG, and BALD, WOLF-DIETRICH (eds.) (1986), *English in Contact with Other Languages: Studies in Honour of Broder Carstensen on the Occasion of his 60th Birthday* (Budapest: Akadémiai Kiadó).

WALTER, HENRIETTE (1983), 'La Nasale vélaire /ŋ/: Un phonème du français?', *Langue française*, 60: 14–29.

WEXLER, PETER (1955), *La Formation du vocabulaire des chemins de fer en France 1778–1842* (Geneva: Droz).

7

SPANISH

Félix Rodríguez González

7.1 History of language contact

7.1.1 Chronology of intensive influences

The history of cultural exchanges between Spain and other countries is well reflected in the traces of foreign terms borrowed into Spanish. For a long time throughout the Middle Ages, Arabic was—after Latin—the main foreign element, providing Spanish with more than 4,000 words. From the fifteenth to the seventeenth centuries, and most particularly during the Renaissance, Spain imported many 'learned' words, especially from Italian; in the eighteenth century, with the advent of the Bourbon dynasty, French gained the upper hand, and its influence continued through the nineteenth century up until modern times; in the nineteenth century, coinciding with the emergence of Britain as a world power, English began to exert a significant influence on Spanish as it did on other European languages, and this influence increased as time went on, with English replacing French as the main source of foreign loans.

Before the eighteenth century, English loanwords were very scarce. They were imported in small numbers, generally through French mediation. The names of the cardinal points (*norte*, *sud*—a variant of *sur*—*este*, and *oeste*) were probably the first English loans in Spanish, being attested between 1431 and 1607. The seventeenth century gave us *dogo* (< *dog*) and the eighteenth *puritano*, *bote* (< *boat*), *ponche* (< *punch*), and *ron* (< *rum*). All these words are now completely assimilated and no longer recognized as English except by etymologists.

Taking into account the most relevant Anglo-Spanish cultural and language contacts, the following main stages of lexical borrowing can be distinguished:

1. In the eighteenth century, and even more so in the first half of the nineteenth century, English literature and social and cultural life in Britain made their first impact on Spanish intellectuals. In the second half of the eighteenth century English was first taught at some schools, the first English grammar and the first bilingual dictionary were published in Spain, and the first translations from English into Spanish were made by well-known literary figures such as Cadalso, Jovellanos, and Moratín. There were also personal contacts with British culture through other men of letters like Blanco White, Espronceda, and Duque de Rivas, who emigrated to England after 1814 as political exiles fleeing the absolutist regime of Fernando VII.[1]

2. In the nineteenth century, especially in the last quarter, English influence intensified as a result of the technological developments of the Industrial Revolution, giving rise to designations in various fields such as transport and clothmaking. Of even greater lexical import were the borrowings related to social life: the late nineteenth and early twentieth centuries saw the first important wave of Anglicisms in many domains such as music, dance, drinks, clothing, breeds of dogs, motor cars, and especially sports. During this period, people started to practise or to hear about sports disciplines such as football, golf, polo, tennis, horse-racing, boxing, and hockey and became familiar with some of the English terminology. Spanish society remained relatively open to English influences, until the Civil War (1936–9) when the country experienced a period of linguistic chauvinism and political isolationism which lasted until the early 1950s during the first stage of Franco's dictatorship.

3. After 1950 the impact of English became massive. The first sign of the break with political isolationalism was the establishment of American military bases in Rota and Torrejón de Ardoz (Madrid) in the early 1950s; this was the first physical contact with the so-called 'American way of life'. In the 1960s, contact was widened under a technocratic cabinet; this was reflected in increasing tourism which now reached its peak and was given its own ministry. Spanish coasts became the favourite sites for British tourists, some of whom decided to settle permanently on the Costa Blanca, Ibiza, and Costa del Sol in particular. The British Isles, and especially London, also became the most popular place for 'modern' young Spaniards to visit.

In the 1970s, with dictatorship lingering on, the more radical and politically conscious youth were attracted by the North American underground movement which made an imprint on Spanish marginal literature (comics, *fanzines*, etc.). Two of their basic themes, drugs and music (especially rock), became important sources of inspiration and of new words (cf. Rodríguez 1989: 153–5). The oral media (TV and FM radio programmes) and journalism (humour magazines, and general news magazines such as *Cambio 16*) contributed to this development.

The 1970s and especially the 1980s saw the emergence of new technical fields such as computers, and the 1990s brought the Internet, with growing numbers of

---

[1] In reference to them, 'Anglicisms' appeared in various publications—the Spanish word *anglicismo* 'Anglicism' itself is attested as early as 1848 (cf. Fernández García 1970: 25), and in an earlier form, *anglismo*, existed from 1784 (cf. Lorenzo 1996: 13).

users and its characteristically Anglicized jargon. Moreover, media coverage of sports (aerobics, windsurfing, baseball, golf, etc.) increased in popularity; much of their jargon is English.

Therefore, the importance of Anglicisms, as a source of new words in present-day Spanish, is easy to understand. According to the account of Mighetto (1991: 181), 2.7 per cent of the lexis used in the *El País* journal is of foreign provenance. If we consider that more than half of the foreign terms are of English origin, Anglicisms form some 2 per cent of the overall vocabulary of journalism. Another investigation, relating to the oral usage of native educated people from Madrid, revealed 291 Anglicisms out of a total 16,897 items, which represents 1.73 per cent of the lexis (Quilis 1984: 413).

7.1.2 *Origins of influence*

Although one can assume for Spanish a general decline of BrE influence after 1945 and an increasing dominance of AmE, as in other languages (cf. Busse and Görlach in this volume), the identity of the forms and the borrowing of many Americanisms through the mediation of BrE make it impossible to differentiate between Briticisms and American words. However, some terms have a distinctively British or American cultural reference. Thus, *porridge*, *cottage*, *bed and breakfast*, *cricket*, *Beatle* can be counted as 'foreignisms' used with a predominantly British reference (sometimes defined more specifically as *xenismos* in Spanish linguistic jargon), and in the early part of the twentieth century soccer terminology (*gol*, *corner*, *penalty*) was introduced from Britain. Similarly, after the Second World War Anglicisms have a particularly American stamp in the domains of technology and youth subcultures: for example *motel*, *hippie*, *freak*, *flower power*, *grunge*, and *reality show*.

Occasionally, two or more near synonyms of different origin were borrowed at different stages, such as the early BrE form *jersey* and the later and prestigious AmE *sweater* (more frequently in its adapted form *suéter*).

7.1.3 *Types of influence*

English contact with Spanish can influence all levels of language. It is most visible in spelling, pronunciation, morphology, and lexis, and is hardly notable in semantics (cf. s. 7.3.8), pragmatics, and syntax.

Takeovers in the domain of syntax (for example in the non-Spanish use of prepositions and verbal forms) will not be examined here, but grammarians agree that they are the most 'harmful' to a language. Moreover, there is an unconscious tendency, notably in translation from English, to make use of constructions which are especially frequent in English (e.g. forming adverbs in -*mente*, such as *básicamente* from *basically*) neglecting the native counterparts (such as *en el fondo*). This phenomenon, known as 'frequency Anglicisms', has been studied in detail by Vázquez-Ayora (1977).

In the last few decades, the influence of English on Spanish has invaded unexpected terrains, such as typography. Among the innovations are the frequent capitalization of initials in titles and headings, and the occasional use of the slash to indicate a disjunctive, *y/o* from E *and/o* (Lorenzo 1988), and some symbols: & for the copulative conjunction *y* 'and', and logographic ♥, for *(yo) amo* '(I) love' (Rodríguez and Lillo 1997).

A comprehensive study of English influences in Spanish should also take into account paralinguistic elements and other non-verbal signs, such as the use of the index and middle finger to mark the V of 'victory', the thumb and index finger to form a circle, etc. (Lorenzo 1995: 174).

7.1.4 Chronology of purist phases

The adoption of foreign terms in Spanish, and in particular the influx of loans from English, has traditionally met with resistance from linguists and lexicographers as well as from social and political institutions. The criticism levelled against Anglicisms (and also acronyms) is basically founded in their exotic nature.

Foreign terms should be considered not only from a purely linguistic perspective but also from a social angle. They are bound to introduce special connotations related to the idiosyncrasy of their speakers and the political position of the donor country. Thus Anglicisms evoke the hegemony of Anglo-Saxon countries, especially the United States, in the international community, and this may trigger markedly purist (nationalist) attitudes. The massive impact of foreign languages, formerly of French and later of English, has indeed led to various strong purist and nationalist phases which can be correlated with some of the periods mentioned above.

1 (*a*) Prior to the eighteenth century, Latin was a prestigious model which contributed to the formation of a standard Spanish language and its renovation. There were reactions against the misuse and overuse of loanwords, but not against 'necessary' new words or expressions. Given the close genetic relations to the mother tongue, Latin loanwords were not perceived as really 'foreign'.

   The first strong feeling against foreign elements was felt towards the avalanche of French loanwords in the eighteenth century. France, and in particular its capital Paris, became the favourite place to visit for the affluent of the time. But that century also saw the beginning of concern for the purity of the national language among men of letters, who objected to the excessive number of Gallicisms, which were thought to corrupt the language. These views led to the foundation of the Real Academia Española (1713), which received strong official support and quickly published its first dictionary, the so-called *Diccionario de autoridades* (1726–39). This criticism was puristic, rather than nationalistic and chauvinistic, even though a war of independence was declared against the French troops and a French—and therefore foreign—dynasty (the Bourbons). Throughout the nineteenth century this influence was a normal pattern and when Anglicisms first appeared they were not identified as such, because they were mostly mediated by French: in consequence, words such as *biftec*, *dandy*, and *tilbury* were considered Gallicisms.

2 (*a*) Dictatorial regimes tend to be particularly hostile to the use of foreign words. In 1927, under the dictatorship of Primo de Rivera, foreign signs were

banned so that a famous Barcelonian cabaret, the *Royal Concert*, came to be called *Real Concierto*. Years later, after the Civil War and up until 1950, the Home Ministry of the Franco regime issued regulations against the use of foreign words, especially in the field of sports. As a result, a good number fell into disuse: *encuentro* replaced *match*, *defensa* replaced *back*, and *locutor* replaced *speaker*, but the attempt was not successful in the case of *cóctel* (*combinado*), *sandwich* (*emparedado*), *record* (*marca*), and *football* (*balompié*).

3 (*a*) The regime eased its strictures in the age of the modernization after the 1960s. But the unexpected influx of foreign terms which followed was felt to be a heavy burden by certain language-conscious people. As a result, new purist tendencies arose among academics and men of letters, who exaggeratedly referred to Spain as a colony of the United States. The articles by Salvador de Madariaga (1962) and Alfaro's dictionary (published in Spain in 1964) are the best exponents of this view. More moderate views were held by other prominent academics such as Lapesa, Lorenzo, and Seco, reflected in more liberal policies towards the inclusion of foreignisms in some dictionaries.

7.1.5 *Regional differences*

The intensity of English influence in this century was more strongly felt first in the Latin American countries which, to a greater extent, have been subject to economic and political dependence on the USA (Mexico, the Antilles, and Central America), than in other countries including the more distant Spain. Thus, in Puerto Rico, the Dominican Republic, Panama, Guatemala, Costa Rica, and Mexico—countries close to the USA—the English term *folder* is used, whereas the more remote areas of Venezuela, Paraguay, Uruguay, Argentina, and Spain employ the native equivalent *carpeta* (cf. Marrone 1974). However, distance is not the only factor. Nationalistic and chauvinistic attitudes are also relevant, as is illustrated by the example of Cuba where the number of Anglicisms is still considerably smaller than elsewhere in the region.

On the other hand, the intensive cultural contacts in modern times diminish distances to such an extent that the old Bloomfieldian dichotomy between cultural and intimate borrowings has lost part of its validity. In this light, one should not be surprised if further research came to reveal that the large body of English terms found in present-day Peninsular Spanish does not differ significantly from that found in countries of the southern hemisphere such as Argentina or Chile.

Despite this increasing levelling some peculiarities survive, especially in the case of words mediated by French. Given the proximity and the intensity of cultural contacts between Spain and France, French-influenced variants tend to prevail in Peninsular Spanish; e.g. *partenaire*, *dopage*, and *cognac* are more often used than English *partner*, *doping*, and *brandy*. The same is true for calques; thus, whereas French has been the model for the Peninsular Spanish terms *ordenador* (< *ordinateur* 'computer'), *horas punta* (< *heures de pointe*), *papel higiénico* (< *papier hygiénique* 'toilet paper'), *Asuntos exteriores* (< *Affaires étrangères*), English has been the model for the equivalent South American expressions *computador* (< *com-*

puter), horas pico (< *peak hours), papel toilette* (< *toilet paper), Relaciones exteriores* (< *Foreign Relations*), etc. (cf. Haensch 1995: 244).

7.1.6 Stylistic differences

The majority of Anglicisms have, from the beginning, occurred in technical registers, especially in writing. The range of technical fields is wide: Anglicisms are found in science as well as in popular jargons of sports and leisure activities. There are also borrowings with a more colloquial and unconventional flavour from many fields, most frequently in journalese (including political columns and the underground press) and in youth language, from where they may seep through into the general language. The reasons for their use are both denotative or referential and connotative or expressive. Some users, particularly journalists, employ nonce borrowings for stylistic reasons—in cases of code-switching, or with a clear humorous intention. Nonce expressions, because of their idiolectal and ad hoc nature, are subject to criticism, disqualifying them for an entry in dictionaries (cf. Rodríguez 1996*b*).

7.1.7 Innovation and obsolescence

In his study of Anglicisms from the period between 1891 and 1936, Fernández García (1970) includes 816 entries, to which many unlemmatized derivatives could be added. Alfaro's oft-quoted dictionary of Spanish includes about 1,200, but he does not discriminate between terms from South American and Peninsular Spanish, the latter being poorly represented.

More interesting are the statistical accounts provided by dictionaries of foreign words which allow us to weigh the relative influence of English in regard to other foreign influences. Pérez Rioja's (1990) study of the Spanish language in the 1920s provides valuable statistics for what is considered to be the first important stage in the history of English borrowings. He records 162 Anglicisms against 125 Gallicisms, which seems to show that a shift to English had already occurred in some fields, notably sports. These figures are revealing since it has been traditionally assumed that Spanish did not start borrowing more English than French terms until the 1950s (cf. Pratt 1980: 51; Haensch 1995: 243).

In the second half of this century, the dominance of English is well established. Alzugaray's (1988) *Diccionario de extranjerismos* lists 2,400 terms, of which 1,301 (that is, 54 per cent) are borrowed from English, vs. 667 (27.8 per cent) from French, and well ahead of Latin (4.3 per cent), a ratio which is particularly significant given the Romance character of the Spanish language. A recent account by Gómez Tarrego (1992) lists 633 foreign terms, of which 389 are Anglicisms (Gómez Capuz 1994: 468), which raises the percentage of English loans to 61.4 per cent.

A fairly exhaustive recent dictionary by Rodríguez and Lillo, the *Nuevo diccionario de anglicismos* of 1997, although restricted to terms in present-day use or in the second half of the century, far exceeds these figures. It lists more than 2,800 entries, including certain morphological variants and derivatives as well as loans which have lost their Englishness.

With time, words become obsolete; thus, a check of Fernández García's data shows us that of 816 Anglicisms, 315 (38.6 per cent) are no longer current. Some items have been reborrowed with different or added meanings: *baby*, *cutter*, *stick*, *leggins*, *meeting*, *mister*, *sandwich*, or they have reappeared as fashionable equivalents such as *basketball* and *volleyball*, which had long been replaced by native terms (*baloncesto* and *balonvolea* respectively).

7.1.8 Mediating languages

In the past a good number of terms whose ultimate etymon is English were borrowed into Spanish through the mediation of a neighbouring language. It was through French that Spanish imported *biftec/bistec* (< *beefsteak*), *confort* (< *comfort*), *lugre* (via French *lougre* < *lugger*) *redingote* (< *riding coat*) and *vagón* (< *wagon*). In the majority of cases, the accent, shifted from the first to other syllables, as well as graphemic and morphological adaptation betray French mediation. In other items, the English look of the word (cf. *footing*, *smoking*, still co-occurring along with *fútin* and *esmoquin* and transmitted through French) makes this recognition more difficult.

Morphological similarity of two languages can cause ambivalence, variation, or faulty etymological interpretations. Thus *bunker* is a Germanism when used in the political field and an Anglicism in golf terminology; *kindergarten* is a Germanism also handed down as an Anglicism in the form *kindergarden*; *handball*, known now through its calque *balonmano*, is regarded by many as an Anglicism, although it came from German *Handball* (Lorenzo 1996), and the same is true with *rimmel* 'mascara' which is derived from the name of the nineteenth-century German cosmetologist Eugen Rimmel (Rodríguez 1996*a*).

Moving towards the Romance languages, Latin is also morphologically similar to Spanish, which disguises the English origin of *vídeo*, *multinacional*, *veredicto* (cf. Pratt 1980: 145). As neo-Latin internationalisms they are usually not included in dictionaries of Anglicisms.

7.1.9 English in education

The notable increase of English loanwords after 1950 was also connected with the introduction and spread of English in Spanish education, both at secondary schools and at university level. In the 1950s, English was taught as an optional first foreign language in secondary schools to no more than 5 per cent of the students, whereas those who studied French exceeded 90 per cent (cf. Lorenzo 1996: 17). Today the situation is reversed: English has rapidly pushed French into a modest second place. At the universities 'English Philology', introduced in the curriculum in 1953, has become the 'queen' of foreign philologies. Besides, English is widely taught in language schools and by private tutors, supported by a general belief that unfamiliarity with this language is a sign of functional analphabetism in today's world which hinders the accessibility of certain posts.

7.2 Pronunciation and spelling

7.2.1 Pronunciation

The pronunciation of English loans is highly variable; it depends on the age of the loan, its degree of linguistic and social integration, the channel of transmission (oral/written), and some sociolinguistic variables such as the age and education of the users. Most important, however, are the differences in the phonological system of the two languages and the articulation of some individual sounds. Thus, the fricatives / ʃ, dʒ, ʒ/, the bilabial fricative /v/, the final velar /ŋ/, and initial /h/ do not occur in Spanish. Some are rendered systematically in Spanish with small or hardly any phonetic change: the opposition /z/ vs. /s/ is neutralized, the [z] being devoiced as in *jazz* [jas]; the <v> is pronounced [b], as in *vip* [bip], the final velar /ŋ/ is usually pronounced /n/, as in *footing* [fútin] and *smoking* [esmokin]; and initial /h/ always shifts to /x/, sometimes reflected in the spelling (*jobi, joldin*, etc.).

The pronunciation of the sibilant /ʃ/ varies between /ʃ/ and /s/ in *minishort* [miniʃór or minisór], and between /ʃ/ and /tʃ/ sometimes reflected in spelling (*sheriff/chérif, show/chou*). The initial affricate /dʒ/ is pronounced with a semiconsonant fricative /j/, in *judo* [júdo] and optionally [j], [dʒ] in *jazz* [dʒas, jas], *jumbo* [dʒumbo, jombo], *disjockey* (disdʒokei, disjoki]. Occasionally there is a /j/ ~ /x/ alternation, as in *mánager* [mánajer, manáxer], *jeans* [jins, xeans], the /x/ phoneme being an obvious spelling pronunciation in speakers unfamiliar with English.

There are also phonotactic restrictions in Spanish such as in clusters with initial [s-] (*sl-, sm-, sp-, st-*). This presents a problem for language teaching but it does not affect the borrowing process. The solution is generally the insertion of a prothetic /e/ ([estand, estandar], etc.), the preservation of the English pronunciation being usually regarded as a sign of affectation.

Some consonants in Spanish do not occur in final position: /b, d, f, g, m, p, t/. Variation is hardly noticeable when the consonant remains voiced (*m* in *boom* [bum, bun], but it shows when it is devoiced. This is particularly evident in inflexion or suffixation. English *pub* gives Spanish plural *pubes* (as used in the *ABC* journal, by analogy with *clubes*) and the derivative *pafeto*, and two variants are derived from English *speed*: *espídico* and *espitoso* (following a process analogous to *Madrid* [madríd, madrít] in the pair *madridista* and *matritense*).

Consonant clusters are sometimes simplified: *compact* [kómpak], *gangster* [gánster], *minishort* [minisór]; the reduction may depend on various factors related to style (informal or hypercorrected) and the education and profession of the speaker. Here variation is also reflected in the derivational process: *standard* [estándard, estándar] → *estandardización/estandarización*; *flash* [flaʃ/flas] → *flashear/flasear*, etc.

Another source of variation is the combination [wa-], in which [w] is pronounced in three different ways, namely as [w], *walkie-talkie* [wokitóki/wokitáki], the cultivated variant; as [g], humorous *gualquitalqui* [gualki tálki]; or as [b], systematically pronounced that way in *water* [báter], sometimes written with phonetic spelling *váter*. In *water-polo* most people pronounce [wa-] in order to avoid confusion with *water* [báter] 'toilet'.

The disagreement between pronunciation and spelling in English leads to variation in some Anglicisms. Thus, English <ce>, <ci>, and <z> are pronounced with a sibilant, and in Spanish sometimes with an interdental (*city* [siti], *la City—el Intercity* [θiti], *iceberg* [aisberg/iθebérg], *magazine* [magasin, magaθíne]).

Greater variation is found with letters representing vowels and vowel combinations. Some are pronounced close to English: (*funky* [fanki], *bacon* [beikon], *off-side* [ofsaid]), others follow the Spanish system (*yuppy* [jupi], *eye-liner* [ejeliner], *close-up* [kloseup]). There is also some variation: *punk* [punk, pank], *punky* [punki, panki], *bacon* [beikon, bakon, beikon], *gay* is pronounced [gai] and [gei].

The most striking variation is found in borrowings which contain [ʌ]. This phoneme, which does not exist in Spanish, seems to be perceived differently by individual speakers. Also, the <u> suggests [u] for Spanish speakers. Not surprisingly, four different spellings are attested for [ʌ]:

<o>: *broshing* (< *brushing*), *yonqui* (< *junkie*)
<u>: *punqui/punki* (< *punk*)
<a>: *namberguan* (< *number one*), *fanqui* (< *funky*)
<e>: *nember guán* (< *number one*)

In a few examples, the Spanish choice is clearly determined by the need to avoid a homonymic clash. Thus in *yonqui*, <a> which would have been the most natural option, was avoided because of the previous existence of *yanqui* 'North American'. In golf *putting* [putin] or [patin] contrasts with the derivative verb 'to strike a golf ball gently' which is *potear* in SAm Spanish and *patear* in European Spanish, which avoid the embarrassing homonymy with the word *putear* ('to be a nuisance', from *puta* 'whore'). The choice of the phonological variant is often sociolinguistically motivated: the pronunciation closer to English is found in more cultivated speakers ([panks] [pankis]), and the popular un-English variant—[punks], [punkis]—is based on the written form.

This explanation is simplified: we should also consider the age, the channel, subject matter, and the education and socioeconomic status of the speaker and of the addressee. Thus, one can understand why many TV adverts are pronounced according to Spanish usage, like *close-up* [kloseup], since they are addressed to the general public, including many people from the working class. By contrast, in the world of fashion and music, we often hear the pronunciation [fanqui], the form also attested in a magazine read by the young, and found in the slang term *jipifanqui* (Ramoncín 1989).

The word *bacon* is also illuminating from a sociolinguistic point of view: it is normally pronounced [beikon] among cultivated speakers, which contrasts with *beicon* [bakon] heard from some working-class housewives shopping in the market. The same is true of the spelling. I have found *bacon* on the menu of some fairly refined restaurants, but the 'Boutique del jamón' on the Explanada of Alicante advertises it as *beicón*.

The time factor may cut across social and educational distinctions. Many early loans were borrowed from written English, their pronunciation being Spanish:

spray [esprái], *picú* (from *pick-up*), *radar* [radár], *flirt* [flirt]. By contrast, more recent loanwords are from spoken English; they include *girl* [gel], *pick up* [pikap] 'a kind of truck', *play* [plei] (in *playback*, *playboy*, etc.). Recent borrowings tend to preserve the English spelling and pronunciation as a result of the growing familiarity with English.

As for word stress, there are relatively few differences, although some terms show some deviation or variation, e.g. *radar*, *bacon*, *pick up*, *bungalow*, *drugstore*.

7.2.2 *Graphemic integration*

Although there are notable differences in the graphemic system of English and Spanish, the English spelling is readily accepted especially in early loans. The foreignness of Anglicisms results from the existence of unusual letters (<k> and <w>) and letter combinations (<sh, wh, chr, oa, ou>), including doubled vowel graphemes (<oo, ee>) and consonants (<bb, nn> etc.). In due course, many loans were adapted to Spanish rules, as shown by the substitution of <c> for <k> and <v, g> for <w> and the simplification of combinations. Recently, there has also been a tendency to retain the spelling. As a result of these conditioning factors, both from a synchronic and diachronic perspective, there are many cases in which the English spelling and its Spanish adaptation have coexisted for a long time: <folklore/folclore>; <smoking/esmoquin>; <water/váter>; <boomerang/bumerán>.

The choice of a particular variant is not made randomly; various stylistic, semantic, and sociolinguistic factors can be distinguished.

Graphemic/morphophonological adaptation is linked with popular and informal usage, and with the slang of certain sociolects and technolects. By contrast, the English term is preserved in the formal and literary language, as can be illustrated by <bungalow/bungaló>, <flash/flas>, <joint/yoin>, <junkie/yonqui>, <office/ofis>, <travelling/travelín> (in the film jargon) and <whisky/güisqui>.

At times, style, and register differentiation is linked with a change of meaning which is usually associated with the adapted Spanish term, whereas the English spelling retains the original meaning, e.g.: <K.O.> 'knocked out', in boxing/<cao> 'flustered' = Spanish *aturdido*, <sheriff> 'a US official'/<chérif> 'boss', <speech> 'speech' = Spanish *discurso*/<espich(e)> 'lecture', fam. = Spanish *perorata*, *rollo*, <baby> 'child' / <babi> 'pinafore', a school term.

Occasionally, this pattern of semantic differentiation is reversed so that an Anglicism adapted in the past with a specialized meaning has recently been reintroduced with the original English spelling and a new meaning which is more in accordance with English usage; e.g. *legui* (military jargon)/*legging* (women's clothes), *mitin* (politics)/*meeting* (athletics), *estique* (sculpture)/*stick* (golf, cosmetics, publicity). It seems as if the spelling difference of these Anglicisms is used to disambiguate the meaning (cf. English *discreet* and *discrete*, *human* and *humane*).

The stylistic differences associated with mere spelling adaptations are highlighted in modern journalism: a newspaper distinguishes two major classes of information known as news (that is, basically informative), and comment (basically interpretative). The first is in a more formal style, and foreign terms are preserved in their original form. The second, which encompasses sections which are humorous, is more informal and thus receptive to colloquialisms and phonetic spellings. This is a striking phenomenon which can be noticed in the columns of well-known journalists. The informal style and the satirical or iconoclastic tone lead to experiments with new forms such as *biuti* and *biutiful* (< E *beautiful people*), *esquésch* (*sketch*), *joldin* (*holding*). These adapted forms start as ideolectal spellings, but occasionally they get established in the language, as illustrated by *biuti* which has won popularity among journalists.

Another level of sylistic variation contrasts the headline and the body of the text (occasionally the marked or more unusual form is used in the headline).

Sometimes semantic differentiation correlates with graphemic variation as in <football/fútbol>. During the last world soccer championship there were frequent references in the press to *fútbol* 'soccer', as opposed to *football*, understood as 'American football'.

Finally, not all graphemic variation is a product of graphic and phonetic adaptations of the original form. Sometimes the writer hypercorrects, as when *establishment* and *Foreign Office* are sometimes spelt <stablishment> and <Foreing Office>. Likewise, *candy* (in *azúcar candy*) is mistaken as English and accordingly spelt with final *-y*. Similarly, Spanish *vermu(t)* and its French source *vermout* are sometimes replaced by English *vermouth*.

7.3 Morphology

7.3.1 Introduction

The majority of Anglicisms in Spanish are nouns. As they become integrated they can pose problems in the assignment of gender and number. Verbs and adjectives, which show less capacity for inflection, are found less frequently.

7.3.2 Nouns

Gender. The assignment of gender is very simple for Anglicisms with animate reference, for which natural sex is decisive (e.g. *una starlet* = Spanish *pequeña estrella*, F; *una disc jockey* = Spanish *pinchadiscos*, M/F), but the situation is much more complicated with inanimate referents. There are cases in which the choice depends on phonology and morphology (words ending in *-er* and *-ing* and mono-syllables ending in consonants are mainly masculine) but usually the allocation is based on semantic criteria.

However, these can conflict at times, which leads to some fluctuation because of the complex nature of the associative process involved. The underlying concept and the importance of analogy is established by synonyms and illustrated by the use of alternative articles to distinguish meanings, as in *el speed* (= 'narcótico, estupefaciente' = E 'drug', 'narcotic'), *la speed* ('droga')/*el cannabis* (= 'narcótico, estupefaciente')/*la cannabis* ('droga'), *el American way of life* (= 'modo, estilo')/*la American way of life* (= 'manera, forma'), *el sex-shop* (= 'comercio')/*la sex-shop*

(= 'tienda'), *los girl-strips* ('cómics')/*las girl-strips* ('historietas'), *la gang* (= 'banda, pandilla')/*el gang* (= 'grupo'), *el action painting* (= 'estilo, expresionismo abstracto, arte, etc.')/*la action painting* (= 'acción, pintura, . . .').

Sometimes the fluctuation is found in Anglicisms as a consequence of different Spanish words considered synonyms/equivalents. Thus the *-ing* form, which is almost invariably associated with the masculine paradigm (*el jogging*, *el surfing*, etc.), is variable in *el action painting* (~ 'estilo, expresionismo abstracto, arte')/*la action painting* (~ 'acción, pintura'). The importance and the conflicting nature of such associations explains why fluctuations in the assignment of gender pass unnoticed and may be taken as journalistic licences.

On a diachronic level, we notice a shift of gender from the feminine to the masculine, which is the unmarked term, despite the strong associations with feminine concepts (*el party* 'fiesta', *el gang* 'pandilla', *el speed* 'droga', etc.). By contrast, we have a very singular case in (*el*) *jet set* which in the 1970s was the only form and now has given way to the feminine, probably by association with (*la*) *jet society*.

Number. Most Anglicisms end in a consonant (*pin*, *scaner* or *escáner*, *slogan* or *eslogan*) and, because of their strange or exotic morphology, form the plural in three different ways: by simply taking over *-s* (*pins*, *escáners*, *slogans*) or its allomorph *-es* (*pines*, *escáneres*, *eslóganes*, *faxes*), and using a zero morph (*los pin*, *los fax*). The majority retain the English plural, fewer are used with zero inflexion, and fewer still with Spanish *-es*. There is a correlation, then, between forms of the plural and the degree of integration. Thus, *los faxes* can be interpreted as more integrated than *los fax*.

The stylebooks of the newspapers are not always uniform. *El País* recommends adaptations to the native system for Anglicisms such as *eslogan* (*eslóganes*), etc. in marked contrast with *slogans*, etc. which is the form consistently used in *El Mundo*, *Diario 16*, etc. On the face of it this is surprising because the latter follow a more popular line, addressing a less cultivated readership.

A particular case of variation in the plural, especially at the graphematic level, is the series of Anglicisms ending in *-y*. In *hippy* or *penalty*, the plural is formed as in English: *hippies*, *penalties*, despite the common pronunciation [xipis] and [penaltis], thus establishing an unusual problem of disagreement between spelling and pronunciation. Halfway between this form and the adapted *hipis* (or *jipis*) and *penaltis* are the hypercorrect spellings *hippys* and *penaltyes*. The formation of un-English plural in *-yes*, *-ys*, as well as *-s* in *-man* (in *gagmans*), possibly indicates that the writer is unfamiliar with English and belongs to a lower class (unless the Anglicism is fully established like *clergymans*, in which case the plural in *-men* might sound pretentious or bookish).

7.3.3 Adjectives

Adjectives in predicative position are not particularly frequent among Spanish Anglicisms (*está missing*, *está groggy*, *es muy in*, *está muy out*, *es muy heavy*). The same function and condition applies to participles (*estar flipado* < (to be) *flipped out*). Their capacity to form comparatives and superlatives is still more limited, but results do not sound odd except in derivatives such as *campísimo* or *esnobísimo*.

More common are attributive adjectives forming part of compounds or compound phrases: *periodista freelance, fiesta acid, música acid, cremas after-shave, discoteca after-hours, cultura underground*. Likewise, it is quite common to find nouns used in restrictive apposition and therefore fulfilling the same adjectival function (*personalidad borderline, equipo high-tech, zanahorias baby, cultura pulp*). Occasionally the noun forming part of a compound group is dropped and thus the adjective acquires a nominal function which is non-existent in English: *una (motocicleta) custom*; *full* (hand), in poker.

7.3.4 Adverbs

Adverbial -*ly* is never attested in Spanish loans— although in two instances the corresponding Spanish -*mente* is found: *windsurfisticamente* and *gangsterilmente*— but there are some adverbs (*yes, of course*) and adverbial expressions (trabajar *full time, fifty-fifty, in person, on line*), in addition to the humorous pseudo-Anglicism *by the face* (= *por la cara*) 'cheekily'.

7.3.5 Verbs

The number of borrowed verbs is limited: *chequear* (< *to check* 'to examine'), *driblar* (< *to dribble*), *dropar* (< *to drop*, in golf), *esnifar* (< *to sniff*), *flipar* (< *to flip* (*out*)), *linkar* (< *to make a link*), *topar* (< *to top*, in golf); some of these may have been reinforced by the almost simultaneous—if not previous—existence of a borrowed noun (*chequeo, dribbling, flipe*). That the verb is derived from a noun is clear in other cases such as *boicotear* (= *hacer un boicot* 'to boycott'), *chatear* (*mantener un chat* 'to hold a chat', on the Internet), *espitar* (= *coger speed* [espit] 'to get high', in drugs), *esprintar* (= *hacer un sprint* 'to make a sprint'), *faxear* (= *enviar un fax* 'to send a fax'), *flirtear* (= *mantener un flirt* 'to flirt'), *liderar* (= *actuar como líder* 'to act as a leader'), *testar* (= *someter a un test* 'to put to a test'), *zapear* (= *hacer zapping* 'to zap a TV spot'), and this seems to be the general pattern.

The verbal morphemes -*ar* and -*ear* (both of the first conjugation) are almost evenly represented]. Items ending in -*ear* usually have a colloquial tinge and an iterative meaning, and this semantic conditioning may account for the few cases of vacillation found in the use of the two morphemes. I found a single doublet in Peninsular Spanish: the rare *zapar* and *zapinear* along with the now successful *zapear*.[2]

The derivational process becomes morphologically obvious with the suffix -*iz* (*ar*) (= English -*ize*), as in *estandarizar* (= *convertir en standard* 'to make standard' or 'turn into a standard'), *sponsorizar* (= *hacer de sponsor* 'to sponsor or act as a sponsor'), although this pattern is not very productive.

---

[2] In comparison with Peninsular Spanish usage, other morphological variants are attested in some areas of Latin America: e.g. *parquear* in Colombia (Haensch 1995: 234) vs. Sp *aparcar* 'to park', *ensnifar* and *chutiar* in Puerto Rico vs. Sp *esnifar* 'to sniff' and *chutar* 'to shoot'.

Homonymy results from the conflation of some Anglicized forms with native words such as *espitar* which also means 'to tap, broach', *testar* also 'to make one's will', and *zapar* also 'to sap, mine'; this conflict may be the reason for the restricted usage of such terms. In *zapear* ('scare away') the distinctive form may have contributed to the acceptance of the term.

7.3.6 Derivation

Gender specification. Spanish personal nouns usually indicate feminine gender by means of *-a* (*profesor, -a; señor, -a*). Loanwords, however, express gender only by means of a determiner, most often the article (*un/una babysitter, los/las fans, los/las groupies*). In addition to this marking, there are some pairs contrasting natural gender (*un mister/una miss, un lord/una lady, un boy/una girl*); in some cases the meaning denotatively or contextually differs from English. Such lexemes are used to form dyadic sets of compounds (*milord/milady, un cowboy/una cowgirl, un playboy/una playgirl*); the most common is *-man/-woman* (*bluesman/blueswoman, recordman/recordwoman, superman/superwoman, showman/showwoman*), the use of which has produced a few pseudo-Anglicisms.

For sociocultural reasons, there is a trend to associate certain concepts with the masculine: *boss, dandy, disc jockey, hooligan, jockey, referee, yonqui*; this gender is particularly frequent with nouns formed with the suffix *-er*: *biker, broker, crooner, docker, killer, handicapper, headhunter, lover, ranger, rocker, speaker, squatter*. There are also some nouns ending in *-man* which lack a feminine equivalent (*barman, cameraman, chairman*). Substantival Anglicisms restricted to the feminine are rare (e.g. *majorette, nurse*).

Agent nouns. English expresses agency predominantly by *-er* and *-man*, which have left a clear mark on Spanish morphology. As a nominal suffix, *-er* does not exist in Spanish but a great number of English words in *-er* have been taken over unchanged. Most are deverbals with an animate and personal reference (*catcher, hacker, latin lover, dealer, manager, leader/líder, sprinter*) but there are also derivatives which refer to inanimate objects (*scanner, tester, thriller*). Spanish has a similar suffix *-ero* and occasionally there is vacillation in the use of the English and the Spanish morphemes, *-er/-ero* (*biker/bikero, raper/rapero, rocker/rockero* and *reporter* [and, now very rare, *reportero*]), *-ero* being a clear sign of integration. There are also Spanish creations with no equivalent in English such as *choppero* (< *chopper*), *comixero* (< *comix*), *clinero* (< *kleenex*), *funero* (< *fun* 'funboard'), *sandwichera/sangüichera* (< *sandwich*), and *ticketero* (< *ticket*). Some Spanish *-ero* formations are also used as adjectives.

In addition to *-ero*, *-ista* stands out as a productive agential suffix in Spanish which contrasts with the scarcity of *-ist* formations in English. Save for *chartista* (< *chartist*), all Spanish derivatives in *-ista* have been formed natively and have unisomorphic equivalents in English: e.g. *bluesista, clubista, folklorista*, and the sports terms *basquetista, beisbolista, crolista, surfista, tenista, waterpolista, windsurfista*, some of which may have been coined by analogy with the old and well-known *futbolista* and the general term *deportista* 'sportsman'.

Other suffixes include Spanish *-ador* (*bateador* (< *bate* 'bat'), *bisneador* (< *business*), *boxeador* (< *boxear* 'to box'), *noqueador* (< *noquear* 'to knock out'), and English *-man* (*barman, cameraman, clubman, funkman, gagman, jazz-man, showman, soulman, supermán*) and *-ie* (*folkie, groupie, junkie, trekkie, walkie-talkie*).

Some Anglicisms show vacillation in the use of derivational suffixes, or play with the different connotations; thus, in addition to pairs in *-er/-ero*, the following alternants are attested: *surfer/surfista, beisbolero/beisbolista, bestsellero/bestseller-ista, bluesero/bluesista/bluesman, soulman/soulero, folkie/folkero, windsurfista/wind-surfeta*.

Denominal verbs. As explained under s. 7.3.5 it cannot in all cases be established whether denominal verbs were borrowed or derived from an earlier loanword in Spanish (*chequear*).

New adjectives. In general, adjectives are rarely borrowed. Two adjectives such as *cool* and *groovy* (both 'excellent') are infrequently attested in the youth press; *hot* is also used in figurative meanings ('exciting'). Two others were recorded in the past and are now marked as archaic (*fashionable, shocking*). Among the special-ized terms, *daltonian* has given rise to the adapted forms *daltoniano* and *daltónico*.

This scarcity of adjective forms directly borrowed from English contrasts with the number of adjectival forms derived from borrowed nouns. To render English n. + n. compounds Spanish requires a denominal adjective for the modifying element. Examples of this 'anisomorphism' (cf. Pratt 1980) are the Spanish coinages *aeróbico* (< *aerobics*), *bítico* (< *bit*), *clownesco* (< *clown*), *crupal, cruposo* (< *croup*), *espídico/espitoso* (< *speed*), *grungeriano* (< *grunge*), *hipioso* (< *hippie*), *popero* (< *pop*).

A novelty in the Spanish language is the recurrent use of adjectives ending in the English suffix *-y/-ie*. Apart from isolated *groovy* and the restricted attribution of the noun *baby* (*zanahorias baby, lechugas baby*), derivatives such as *punky, punqui* (< *punk*), *poppy* (< *pop*), and *grungy* (< *grunge*), most probably coined in imitation of the noun *hippy* (or *hippie*), are found in the subcultures of pop music and youth.

De-adjectival nouns. The few adjectives borrowed from English do not permit derivations. *Fitness* has been adopted directly but the adjective *fit* is not recorded in Spanish.

7.3.7 Compounds and combining forms

In Spanish there are a number of Anglicized words of a composite structure, most of which have been borrowed directly from English; therefore their existence does not entail the previous use or later adoption of their constituent lexemes. Thus, *brain trust, brain drain, duty-free, feedback, hat-trick, cowboy*, and *disk jockey* occur in Spanish, although none of the elements is ever found by itself. However, the recurring presence of a word as part of a compound may eventually lead to its adoption. A good case in point is the adjective *hot* recently attested in the press, which was preceded by an extensive lexical family of borrowed compounds such as *hot dog, hot jazz, hotline, hot pants*, and *hot money*. Also *lover* is occasionally found in Spanish; here *latin lover* has undoubtedly paved its way. Similarly, *bike* and *biker* owe much of their use to the popularity of the *mountain bike* in the 1980s. In none of these cases is the favoured monolexematic borrowing the result of an ellipsis, in contrast with the pattern explained in s. 7.6.3*b*.

When a loanword enters Spanish, it is freely used in combination with native elements to form hybrid compounds such as *cremas after-shave, lechugas baby*. In other cases, however, the hybrid character may be the result of a partial translation of an English expression, as in *fiesta acid* (ecstasy) (< *acid party*), *música acid* (< *acid music*), *mercado bull* (< *bull market*), *cazadora bomber* (< *bomber jacket*); note the non-English sequence of the constituents.

The familiarization with English patterns of word formation sometimes leads Spanish speakers to coin compound English-looking expressions independent of the donor language. The frequency of *showman* in Spanish accounts for the fairly frequent use of *showwoman*, which contrasts with English, where that term is very rare and not recorded in dictionaries. There are cases where users have gone still further by creating terms which do not exist at all, such as *recordman/recordwoman* mentioned above, or *sexy boy* for a male stripper.

The same happens with the use of some affixes and combining forms like *mini-* and *micro-*, as in *minishort*, much more frequently used in Spanish, and *minipull* and *micropull* (from *pullover*), which are unattested in English.

7.3.8 Calques (loan translations, cf. s. 7.6 below)

The phenomena of calquing and of semantic Anglicisms are less conspicuous, at least from a morphological and graphemic point of view, but have long drawn the attention of researchers (Bookless, Pratt), especially those interested in translation (Lorenzo, Santoyo). However, the fact that the foreign origin of calques is not self-evident, not known to the general public, and soon forgotten, explains the fact that there is comparatively little general interest in the phenomenon. In the absence of any comprehensive study in Spanish, it would be difficult to compare figures of borrowings and calques; impressionistically we can formulate some trends and contrastive patterns at some levels of analysis.

First, it seems that contemporary Spanish is, and has always been, more open to borrowings than to calquing; this impression is confirmed by looking at all dictionaries of Anglicisms and foreign terms. In this respect the situation is not very different from other languages subject to massive English influence like, for example, German.

But a closer look shows that the number of Anglicisms exceeds that of translations only as far as semantic calquing is concerned. With regard to the calques proper such as *rascacielos* from *skyscraper*, or *mantener un perfil bajo* from *to keep a low profile* the trend is the opposite: there are more calques than borrowings, and this for a similar reason. For speakers of a Romance language like Spanish, it is difficult to memorize a complex structure or morphology; thus following a principle of least effort they are prompted to switch to a Spanish code. If the Spanish equivalent is semantically transparent and comprehensible, the takeover is assured. There have been many changes from borrowing to calquing in the course of time which meet such conditions (*delantero centro* from *centre-forward*, *platillo volante* from *flying saucer*, and more recently, *pago por visión* from *pay per view*).

When borrowings resist replacement by a native item, it is usually because of their shortness (*football* vs. *balompié*, *cash flow* vs. *flujo de caja*, *e-mail* vs. *correo electrónico*) or difficulties of translatability (compare *jet set/jet society* with the awkward or non-existent *juego/serie/sociedad/grupo de personas que cogen el avión a reacción*). No doubt the previous occurrence of at least one constituent (*jet* and *set* in *jet set*, *show* in *reality show*) or as a bound part of a compound (*ball* in *football*, and later in *volleyball* or *voleibol*) facilitates their adoption and permanence. The last example illustrates the power of analogy and the economic principle since the Anglicism is gaining ground again after it had been successfully replaced by *balonvolea* in the past.

Often the two patterns coexist. This situation can continue for a time and give rise to stylistic or sociolinguistic nuances, but much more often the calque is not preceded by an Anglicism (*libre comercio* from *free trade*, *sexo en grupo* from *group sex*, *sexo seguro* from *safe sex*). Sometimes the fact that the equivalence of two terms is based on translation cannot be established beyond doubt; thus it is difficult to determine whether Sp *goma*, an informal term for *condón*, was first employed independently or as a semantic calque on E *rubber*, and the same is true for E *tax-free* and Sp *libre de tasas*.

7.4 Meaning

Only one sense is retained in each borrowing process so that there is usually an obvious difference between the range of meanings of polysemous English words and the senses taken over by Spanish. *Party* is known in Spanish only as 'social gathering', and *rap* as a technical term for 'a style of rock'; both are far behind the six meanings recorded in the *COD* for each. Differences are still more conspicuous when one compares different grammatical categories or functions. *Overall* was borrowed as a special kind of 'trousers', but not in its more general sense as an adjective or adverb. Such differences are greater in the general or basic everyday vocabulary than in technical nomenclatures where there is a special need for unambiguous reference.

In addition, an individual meaning may be significantly altered in the receiving language during or after the borrowing process. The meaning or reference may be more restricted in Spanish: *back-up* 'support' is only used in relation to computers, *rally* is only used with reference to a competition of vehicles (especially cars), *strip* does not refer simply to nudity but to a special kind of it, i.e. 'strip-tease'. *Meeting/ mitin* is only applicable to a special kind of meeting, notably a political one, a use which contrasts with E '(political) rally'.

Alternatively, the range of the English meaning may be extended, giving rise to a (semantic) pseudo-Anglicism, as mentioned above. This may occur

1. through metonymic extension: *baby*, usually spelt *babi*, is also used for 'a child's pinafore', and *burger* is most frequently used as a 'burger shop';
2. through figurative or metaphoric extension: *zapping* for switching from one thing to another (in English its obsolete use is restricted to TV programmes);

3. through ellipsis, a common pattern which accounts for *smoking* for 'smoking jacket', *top* for 'top model', etc.

The latter examples are instances of semantic changes which developed after the loanword was established in the receiving language. Occasionally, there are also extensions of the English meanings which can be thus considered from the first appearance of the loan, as a result of some kind of misunderstanding or error in interpreting the foreign term. Thus *footing* was first used in Spanish as a folk etymology, by association with *foot*, a well-known constituent of the term *football*. A similar process took place in *crack*, which was mistaken for *crash* to refer to the 'financial crash' of 1929 probably because of its onomatopoeic associations. *Bungalow* 'a one-storeyed house' developed to refer to a new Spanish concept in modern housing, the type known as town house or semi-detached house (cf. Sp. *chalet adosado*).

7.5 Usage

There has not been any comprehensive sociolinguistic and stylistic analysis of Spanish Anglicisms to date. Such an account is also difficult to give in a field where vocabulary changes at great speed and is highly variable among users. However, a look at the large body of data handled in the *Dictionary of European Anglicisms* collection and the *Nuevo diccionario de anglicismos* allows us to catch a glimpse of the factors and problems involved.

To begin with, there are no fixed rules in the use of Anglicisms and native terms. The varying use of Anglicisms depends on many sociolinguistic factors which have to do with the status of the user, the means or channel of communication, the subject matter, etc. More technically and following Halliday's terminology, we can distinguish two major types of factors: those linked to the language *use*, or register, and those linked to the language *user* who belongs to a specific group of speakers reflected in his or her sociolect (age, education, and socioeconomic status).

Very often these factors coincide in favouring a particular usage. In effect, most Anglicisms are used in a special and restricted field, and this explains their greater use in the written language. Also, generally speaking, the use of Anglicisms is linked to the level of education of the speakers or writers, and therefore many have a learned character.

Clear examples of the influence of these factors, especially of the first type, are *thriller* and *film*. *Film* (or its adapted form *filme*) is the usual term in the specialized written language whereas its corresponding Spanish term, *película*, is favoured in speech. The learned and specialized character of the English term accounts for the double forms found in derivatives and compounds, in agreement with two well-differentiated registers: *película* is the basis of colloquial *peliculón* and *peliculero*; of *film*, the formal variant, the series *filmar*, *fílmico*, *filmografía* and *filmología*, *filmoteca*, *filmina*, *microfilm*.

These register distinctions do not always follow the same direction; Anglicisms are sensitive to different aspects of communication. For example, the dimension of formality is independent of technicality, as is illustrated by terms such as *eyeliner* and *marketing*. *Eyeliner*, pronounced the Spanish way [ejeliner], is the general term used in the speech of beauticians, while more educated speakers who are not so familiar with the trade might use the Spanish equivalent (*lápiz*) *perfilador de ojos*, especially in the written language. Likewise, *marketing* is a more established term both in the publicity field and in the general language; however, some journalists use *mercadotecnia* when trying to provide the text with a literary flavour.

One can also find instances of the contrary trend: a professional group may prefer a Spanish term so as to achieve a higher register. Thus, *barman* was borrowed in the 1960s at the time of the first waves of foreign tourism and took root, but in present-day publicity jargon and in the colloquial language it is giving way to its superordinate term, *camarero*, often accompanied by a qualifier (*camarero para barra, camarero de barra*).

The use of Anglicisms also correlates with age. In several fields, like modern music, sports, drugs, etc., Anglicisms are more frequently used among the young, as illustrated by the example of *basket* cited above. This is easy to understand if we take into account the recent introduction of English in school curricula, and the link of many English terms with new technical innovations and social and cultural phenomena. We also know how ready young people are to accept new fashions and everything that smacks of modernity. In consequence, the young are largely responsible for the growing use of Anglicisms in slang and colloquial language.

Some Spanish and English equivalents stay in the language, and will continue to do, because of their specialized uses, as in the semantic differences between E *sandwich* and Sp *bocadillo*, and E *bacon* and Sp *panceta* or *tocino*. In such cases the users have to decide which term to choose according to the context. In other cases, the two terms occur within a single text; they may even alternate, when the author (speaker but generally writer) aims at stylistic or elegant variation. There are many examples of this principle in the media, such as: *jeans/tejanos, basket/baloncesto, sponsor/patrocinador*, and *rating/calificación* (cf. Rodríguez 1996*b*).

7.6 Forms of linguistic borrowing and their categorization

1. *Borrowing*
   (*a*) Totally unadapted and not felt to be part of Spanish (quotations, code-switching, foreignisms);
   (*b*) words still looking foreign or unadapted (= *Fremdwörter*, aliens): *boy-scout, disc-jockey, thriller*;
   (*c*) fully integrated items (= *Lehnwörter*, denizens): *bar, líder, motel*.

2. *Replacement*

   A *Translation*
   1. Successful

goalkeeper < *guardameta, brainwashing* < *lavado de cerebros, flying saucer* < *platillo volante, skyscraper* < *rascacielos, non-aligned* < *no alineado, black box* < *caja negra*;

2. Coexisting
basketball = *baloncesto, Big Brother* = *Hermano Mayor, fútbol* (from *foot-ball*) = *balompié, hard rock* = *rock duro, public relations* = *relaciones públicas*;

3. Failures
password > *palabra de paso, water polo* > *polo acuático*;

B *Renderings*

1. Successful
bodyguard < *guardaespaldas, Iron Curtain* < *el telón de acero, self-made man* < *hombre hecho a sí mismo;*

2. Coexisting
marketing = *mercadotecnia, barman* = *camarero de barra, brainstorming* = *tormenta de ideas, best-seller* = *éxito de ventas, corner* = *saque de esquina, recordman* = *plusmarquista*;

3. Failures
sex shop > *tienda erótica*

C *Creation*

1. Successful
babysitter < *canguro, bungee jumping* < *puenting, go-slow* < *huelga de celo*;

2. Coexisting
body-building = *culturismo, jeans* = *vaqueros, tejanos, joint* = *porro, password* = *contraseña, raider* = *tiburón* (in finance), *tie-break* = *muerte súbita*;

3. Failures
cóctail > *combinado, hardware* > *soporte físico, sandwich* > *emparedado*;

D *Semantic loans*

1. Successful
addict < *adicto* (to drugs), *butterfly* < *mariposa* (in swimming), *centre* < *centrar* (in soccer), *mouse* < *ratón* (in computers);

2. Coexisting
trip = *viaje, tripar* = *viajar*;

3. Failures
boy scout > *explorador*.

3. *Pseudo-loans*

(*a*) Lexical pseudo-loans
Sp *recordman/-woman* instead of *record-holder*, *footing* instead of *jogging*;

(*b*) Morphological pseudo-loans
biuty from *beautiful* (people), *pull* in *minipull* from *pullover*) through compounds (Sp *happy end* from *happy ending*) to phrases and phraseologisms

(Sp *gin tonic* from *gin and tonic*) and to blends of Spanish and English elements (Sp *sillón-ball*);

(*c*) Semantic pseudo-loans

where the Anglicism develops a meaning in Sp that is absent from E: Sp *slip* 'briefs, (under-)pants', *clergyman* 'clergyman suit, clerical collar'.

7.7 The future of Anglicisms

Taking stock of the impact of Anglicisms in Spanish and of their future perspectives implies making an assessment first of the acceptability of loans and of the different types and mechanisms which operate in their introduction and use. Anglicisms are unevenly represented in the different domains and they respond to various conditioning factors, a fact which should always be borne in mind when approaching the oft-mentioned problem of the erosion of the language.

If we accept as valid the simplified and loose distinction between necessary and unnecessary loans, it seems logical to approve of the former and predict that borrowing will continue in the general language. As to stylistic borrowings we should consider some as necessary in so far as they are specialized or provide certain stylistic possibilities which make them attractive to their users, fulfilling functions similar to slang and vogue terms. The problem lies in those words which, prompted by humour and a search of prestige, sound a bit too much, ridiculous or silly. Such words do not tend to be permanent, however.

As for technical terminology, there is an ever increasing transfer to the general language. According to some lexicographic accounts, there are at least one million words in the English scientific vocabulary (well ahead of the 700,000 words contained in the Merriam-Webster file as reported by Allen Walker Read and quoted by Landau 1989: 17), and if the ultraspecialized computer language and the expanding stock of acronyms were taken into account, the number would well exceed that figure. And it is in these specialized fields that the impact of English is most strongly felt, and will continue to be as long as American political, cultural, and technological hegemony remains. It is true that this makes the reader often feel helpless, that there are certain dangers for our language, and that therefore some policies of terminological normalization are necessary and welcome. But it is also true that in the global village growing intercommunication of people favours the consolidation of a lingua franca, particularly in science and technology where there is a pragmatic trend to search for universal terms. In this perspective, Anglicisms are an unavoidable language resource to which we have to get accustomed. The search for a proper and convenient balance rather than an entrenched linguistic purism should be the logical result.

With increasing literacy and a greater diffusion of English as a second language, it is difficult to foresee a diminution of Anglicisms. In journalistic language in particular, many of these will come and go, but only a comparatively small fraction will seep into the general language and into everyday speech. A further increase in the number of Anglicisms is to be expected, together with the invasion of new spheres of life, especially in the written language, whereas speech is expected to remain more stable and resistant to change in keeping with its lower register, its more natural style, and a certain resistance of many speakers to employ a lexicon which appears to be alien to our linguistic system, and therefore conspicuous and not easy to integrate.

7.8 Research

Spanish Anglicisms have been the focus of research for Spanish Anglicists and foreign Hispanists since the 1950s, and especially in the 1970s, when Anglicisms began to take deep roots in our language. Considering such a small span of time, the full list of published titles (in the *Annotated Bibliography of European Anglicisms*) looks impressive, especially when contrasted with the information available for other European languages. Research has concentrated on the following topics:

(a) the phonological, morphological, stylistic, and typological analysis of Anglicisms;
(b) the compilation of items current in special vocabularies (sports, drugs, computers, economy, medicine) as well as in the colloquial language;
(c) the compilation of dictionaries of Anglicisms and dictionaries of foreign terms;
(d) corpus-related analysis based on particular newspapers (*Blanco y Negro, El País, La Vanguardia*, etc.);
(e) a small and insufficient number of investigations exploring sociolinguistic issues related to usage, correctness, and social attitudes.

7.9 Bibliography

The list includes the titles mentioned in the chapter and a selection of the most relevant works not quoted. For full evidence the *Annotated Bibliography of European Anglicisms* should be consulted where more important titles are accompanied by short annotations.

ALFARO, RICARDO J. (1970), *Diccionario de anglicismos*, 3rd edn. (Madrid: Gredos). (2nd edn. 1964; 1st pub. Panamá, 1950.)
ALZUGARAY AGUIRRE, JUAN-JOSÉ (1985), *Diccionario de extranjerismos* (Madrid: Dossat).
FERNÁNDEZ GARCÍA, ANTONIO (1970), *Anglicismos en el español* (Oviedo: Gráficas Lux).
GÓMEZ CAPUZ, (1994), review of Gómez Tarrego, *El buen uso de las palabras*, *Anuario de Lingüística Hispánica*, 10: 462–70.
GÓMEZ TARREGO, LEONARDO (1992), *El buen uso de las palabras* (Madrid: Arco Libros).
HAENSCH, GÜNTHER (1995), 'Anglicismos y galicismos en el español de Colombia', in Klaus Zimmermann (ed.), *Lenguas en contacto en Hispanoamérica: Nuevos enfoques* (Vervuert: Hispanoamericana), 217–51.

LANDAU, SIDNEY I. (1989), *Dictionaries: The Art and Craft of Lexicography*, 2nd edn. (Cambridge: Cambridge University Press). (1st edn. 1984, by Charles Scribner's Sons.)

LAPESA, RAFAEL (1966), 'Kahlahtayood: Madariaga ha puesto el dedo en la llaga', *Revista de Occidente*, 4 (36): 373–80.

LORENZO EMILIO (1955), 'El anglicismo en la España de hoy', *Arbor*, 119: 262–74. (Repr. (1980) in *El español de hoy, lengua en ebullición* (Madrid: Gredos), 96–121.)

—— (1988), '¿Inútil y/o superfluo?', *ABC* (Madrid) 17 June: 3.

—— (1995), 'Anglicismos', in M. Seco and G. Salvador (eds.), *La lengua española, hoy* (Madrid: Fundación Juan March), 165–74.

—— (1996), *Anglicismos hispánicos* (Madrid: Gredos).

MADARIAGA, SALVADOR DE (1962), 'El español, colonia lingüística del inglés', *Cuadernos del Congreso por la libertad de la cultura* (Paris), 59: 45–9.

—— (1966), '¿Vamos a Kahlahtayood?', *Revista Occidente*, 4 (36): 365–73.

MARRONE, NILA (1974), 'Investigación sobre variaciones léxicas en el mundo hispano', *Bilingual Review*, I: 152–58.

MIGHETTO, DAVID (1991), 'Las palabras-cita y los libros de estilo', *Moderna Språk*, 82/2: 180–5.

PÉREZ RIOJA, JOSÉ ANTONIO (1990), *La España de los años veinte en el lenguaje* (Madrid: Asociación de Escritores y Artistas Españoles).

PRATT, CHRIS (1980), *El anglicismo en el español contemporáneo* (Madrid: Gredos).

QUILIS, ANTONIO (1984), 'Anglicismos en el español de Madrid', in *Athlon: Satura grammatica in honorem Francisci R. Adrados* (Madrid: Gredos), 413–23.

RAMONCÍN [José Ramón Martínez Márquez] (1989), *El tocho cheli: Diccionario de jergas, germanías y jerigonzas* (Madrid: Ediciones Temas de Hoy).

RODRÍGUEZ GONZÁLEZ, FÉLIX (1989), 'Lenguaje y contracultura juvenil: Anatomía de una generación', in Félix Rodríguez González (ed.), *Comunicación y lenguaje juvenil* (Madrid: Fundamentos), 135–66.

—— (1996*a*), 'Lexicografía de los anglicismos en español contemporáneo: A propósito del proyecto *Nuevo diccionario de anglicismos*', in Christian Schmitt and Wolfgang Schweickhard (eds.), *Die iberoromanischen Sprachen aus interkultureller Sicht: Akten der gleichnamigen Sektion des Bonner Hispanistentages. Bonn, 2–4 März 1995* (Bonn: Romanischer Verlag), 300–14.

—— 1996*b*, 'Functions of Anglicisms in Contemporary Spanish', *Cahiers de lexicologie*, 1(68): 107–28.

—— and LILLO BUADES, ANTONIO (1997), *Nuevo diccionario de anglicismos* (Madrid: Gredos).

SANTOYO, JULIO-CÉSAR (1988), 'Los calcos como forma de traducción', in *Problemas de la traducción* (Madrid: Fundación Alfonso X El Sabio), 91–7.

VÁZQUEZ-AYORA, GERARDO (1977), 'Anglicismos de frequencia', in *Introducción a la traductología: Curso básico de traducción* (Washington: Georgetown University Press), 102–40.

8

ITALIAN

Virginia Pulcini

8.1 History of language contact

8.1.1 Chronology of intensive influences
(Cartago 1994; Durante 1981; Zolli 1991)

The earliest records of linguistic contact between Britain and the Italian peninsula date back to the thirteenth century, in the form of occasional exchanges between merchants and diplomats. These exchanges introduced a few commercial English terms (the very first being *sterlino*, 'pound sterling'). Later, in the fifteenth and sixteenth centuries, words relating to British social and political life appear, with instances of international political jargon recorded in the writings of Venetian ambassadors to England (e.g. *alto tradimento* 'high treason'). The first Italian–English dictionary, John Florio's *A Worlde of Wordes*, was published in England in 1611 and was addressed to English learners of Italian.

However, it was not until the eighteenth century that the influence of the English language and lifestyle became permanent and noteworthy in Italy. Several Italian–English dictionaries were printed in both countries, and English grammars for Italian learners of English became available. Various English literary works were translated, although in many cases these were made through already existing French translations. The term 'anglomania' was used to describe a fashion which was characterized by a fascination with English culture (Graf 1911), a phenomenon which previously had spread more intensely in France. The majority of loanwords of that period belonged to the fields of politics, navigation, and fashion.

In the nineteenth century cultural exchanges between Britain and Italy intensified. The number of Anglicisms also increased considerably, mostly with French acting as an intermediary. English loanwords of this period were now often borrowed without any adaptation, a practice which differed from the preceding centuries. The number of words relating to politics and fashion increased, as did terms relating to means of transport and communication and, most of all, to a large number of sporting disciplines.

Up to the first half of the twentieth century the most widely known and most influential foreign language in Italy was French, but from 1945 English took over. The massive penetration of Anglo-American culture in many key domains, such as science, technology, and the mass media, was shared with most other Western European countries.

8.1.2 Origins of influence

BrE prevailed as a model in Italian education up to a few decades ago but more recently the demand for AmE has increased. While in the ELT world the linguistic and cultural weight attributed to one or the other variety has reached a fair balance, AmE has become the strongest linguistic donor of loanwords to Italian.

The provenance of a minority of the loanwords can be established on cultural grounds, i.e. their relation to facts and events of British or American society (e.g. *cowboy* from North America, *tweed* from Great Britain) or on the basis of spelling (USA: *disk*, *program*, *center*; GB *disc*, *programme*, *centre*).

8.1.3 Types of influence

(Berruto 1987; Dardano 1986; Durante 1981)

The majority of English loanwords are nouns, and noun phrases. There are some adjectives, usually in unadapted forms, and a few verbs with Italian endings. Integration and adaptation are not necessarily linked: there are English words in Italian which display no morphological adaptation (e.g. *film*, *bar*), which are nevertheless widely used and no longer marked as English in dictionaries nor generally considered foreign. Conversely, there are fully adapted words whose use is quite restricted.

The adoption of English words containing grapheme or sound combinations alien to the Italian morphophonological rules has been regarded as an important innovation in contemporary Italian. Other remarkable linguistic phenomena— mostly ascribable to the influence of English—are found in recent developments of lexis and word formation, such as the increased use of prefixes and suffixes, compounds and abbreviations. In the area of syntax, English short sentence patterns have prompted similar patterns in Italian, especially in advertising; in film dubbing, there has been an increased use of discourse markers such as *Bene* ('Well'), *Prego* ('Please'), and the typically American *Wow* has become an Italian expression.

By contrast, the adoption of so-called 'Anglo-Latinisms', i.e. adapted Anglicisms containing Latin or Greek morphemes, has never been regarded as a source of disturbance for Italian because they do not conflict phonologically or morphologically with the rules of the language. Even in the periods of great opposition to foreignisms, 'Anglo-Latinisms' have been readily accepted.

8.1.4 Chronology of purist phases

(Dardano 1986; Raffaelli 1983; Pulcini 1997)

Several historical periods in Italy have witnessed various forms of purism. Throughout the nineteenth century writers and poets found inspiration in the archaic language of the fourteenth and sixteenth centuries and abhorred any form of linguistic innovation, including 'barbarisms' and scientific words. On the other hand, Romantic authors (Giacomo Leopardi is an outstanding member of the movement) stressed the importance of foreign languages and literatures, and the adoption of foreign words to denote new ideas or concepts. However, the nineteenth century was dominated by the search for national identity, achieved with the unification of Italy in 1861, and a strong effort to define a national language, which excluded interference from foreign languages and even dialects.

Such purist concerns were transformed by the Fascist regime into a xenophobic campaign which imposed the abolition of foreign words, such as names of towns, public houses, public signs, and advertisements. A special commission of the *Regia Accademia d'Italia* was committed to policing the purity of the Italian language and providing substitutes for foreign words, especially in the fields of commerce and industry. Violations were punished with fines and even imprisonment. In spite of these legislative measures, many Anglicisms resisted substitution. Although the linguists of the period did not agree with a kind of purism based on nationalistic or racist principles, they disapproved of the excessive 'hospitality' extended to foreign terms, on the grounds of structural incompatibility. Migliorini, who founded 'Neo-Purism' in 1942, did not deny the historical dimension of language and its need to renew itself through contacts and exchanges with other languages. He was in favour of words which could be adapted and structurally harmonized to Italian, but objected to 'barbarisms'.

As Dardano (1986) explains, the spread of English in Italy after the Second World War was favoured by the particular sociolinguistic situation of the country. First, a reaction against the purist policy of the Fascist regime brought about a more tolerant attitude towards linguistic innovation. Secondly, the interference of foreign languages was no longer seen as a drawback for the national language: in fact, the knowledge of standard Italian has been growing steadily (today it is spoken by about 90 per cent of the population), as the use of dialects has rapidly decreased, because of the growth of literacy and the unifying impact of the mass media.

Most Italian linguists today refuse to make a stand against the presence of Anglicisms. They generally prefer to describe, rather than prescribe. The spread of English in Italy is considered as a historical event, which no academy should attempt to control by linguistic imposition from above. It is generally agreed that English has become the most influential language because the American culture is the most vital, creative, and interactive in modern western societies (Beccaria 1988). For this reason, Italian has been defined as a 'democratic language', open to neological borrowing from other languages, as opposed to 'introvert languages' like Icelandic, French, and Spanish.

Purist complaints are still heard today, in the form of letters from readers and word-watchers to the press, directed against the flood of Anglicisms which has penetrated Italian in the past decades. The terms 'Itangliano' and 'Italiese' are used derogatorily to denote spoken or written styles which contain many Anglicisms. These are often regarded as a form of 'exhibitionism' (e.g. in journalism and youth speech), or criticized because they comprise wrong translations and faulty shifts in meaning (e.g. in film dubbing). Sometimes academic voices also join in the chorus of protest; the linguist Castellani (1987) called the phenomenon a 'morbus anglicus'.

8.1.5 Regional differences

The presence of local dialects in the different regions of the Italian peninsula determines divergencies in the pronunciation of standard Italian itself. In the pronunciation of Anglicisms regional differences are also remarkable. Since the treatment of Anglicisms in Italian dialects has been insufficiently researched so far, we can only mention some characteristic tendencies. For example, the word *club* still retains a French pronunciation /klœb/ in the areas close to France (the northwest), especially with older speakers, but elsewhere it is pronounced /klɛb, klab/. The addition of a final syllable with gemination of the final consonant is characteristic of central and southern Italy: e.g. /klɛb, klabbe, fɪlmə, fɪlme, rɔkkə, rɔkke/. (Italian communities in the United States and Australia are here excluded, because the close-contact conditions have resulted in quite different patterns of interference and borrowing.)

8.1.6 Stylistic differences
(Dardano 1986)

In the eighteenth and nineteenth centuries Anglicisms were mainly Anglo-Latinisms, always adapted to the structures of Italian; they were confined to special domains and exclusively used by the upper classes, i.e. by aristocrats and intellectuals.

Through the agency of the action of mass communication in the present century Anglicisms have become accessible to the general public and have spread in the colloquial register, especially in the language of young people (pop music) and in the media (advertising, the press). Technical Anglicisms are used in particular by restricted groups of people: managers in business and administration, and, to a lesser extent, industrial managers and journalists. Anglicisms are also often used by speakers or writers as instances of 'code-switching' to create stylistic effects. Anglicized Italian, in fact, seems to enjoy high prestige (even higher than literary Italian, according to Sanga 1981).

8.1.7 Innovation and obsolescence
(Rando 1969, 1973, 1987, Klajn 1972; Moss 1992)

Several counts of the number of Anglicisms in present-day Italian have been made. The overall incidence of unadapted English loanwords seems to range from 1 per cent to 1.4 per cent of the entire lexicon (that is between 1,500 and 2,000 of about 150,000 words). This percentage has been confirmed by Zingarelli's dictionary (1996, on CD-ROM) which contains 1,888 unadapted Anglicisms out of 134,000 entries (1.4 per cent); note that words like *film* and *sport* are not classified as Anglicisms by this dictionary.

If we turn back to the nineteenth century, we find a first record of about twenty unadapted Anglicisms out of about 4,100 entries recorded in Fanfani and Arlìa's dictionary (1877). Subsequently, a much higher number of English words was recorded in Panzini's *Dizionario moderno* (first edition in 1905, tenth edition in 1963). The proportion of Anglicisms in this dictionary according to Rando (1969) shows a rise from 8.5 per cent (1923) to over 11 per cent (1963). This count, however, included unadapted and adapted Anglicisms, derived forms, and different types of calques of English words and phrases. The number of Anglicisms contained in Rando's dictionary of Anglicisms (1987)—the only one available for Italian— amounts to 2,300 entries. This dictionary, however, includes a heterogeneous selection of unadapted and adapted loans, and calques, as well as encyclopedic information on institutions, trademarks, geographical names, and archaic, popular, and dialectal variants. A comparison between different counts is therefore seriously restricted by non-comparable criteria of inclusion.

There is a general consensus that frequency counts carried out on specifically selected corpora and in special domains may be more revealing: for example 30 per cent of business and commercial terms in Italian are Anglicisms (Pasquarelli and Palmieri 1987). Many glossaries of neologisms, usually based on newspaper collections and often addressed to a non-specialist market, provide lists of new foreign words, mostly English. Lurati (1995), for instance, has about 600 Anglicisms (out of 3,000 neologisms) found in various newspapers in the 1980s. The intake of Anglicisms in the 1990s seems to have been even greater.

Anglicisms denoting means of transport, games, dances, and instruments reflecting transient fashions have gone out of use, although many of them are still found in dictionaries of contemporary Italian. Because of legislative measures in the 1930s and 1940s, many Anglicisms, especially sports terms, were replaced by Italian equivalents. Purist campaigns were, however, not always successful. An interesting episode is quoted by Raffaelli (1983): a competition promoted by a metropolitan daily newspaper in 1932 asked for substitutes for foreign loanwords (among them, fifteen Anglicisms); this move effected the disappearance of one (*five o'clock 'tè*'), the maintenance of six (*jazz, smoking, tight, bar, klacson/clacson, film*), and the survival of the rest alongside Italian substitutes (*copyright, dancing, raid, flirt, golf, record, sandwich, taxi*).

The terms related to the popular game of football have undergone progressive Italianization, unlike those connected to other more 'elitist' sports such as tennis and golf. The name of the game itself has been almost completely replaced by Italian *calcio* (literally 'kick'), as has *goalkeeper* by *portiere* and *foul* by *fallo*. Some terms still coexist (*goal/rete, corner/angolo*), yet others have resisted substitution (*dribbling, pressing*).

Virginia Pulcini

8.1.8 *Mediating languages*
(Klajn 1972)

Throughout the centuries Italian has borrowed words from many 'exotic' languages, among them French, German, Spanish, and English (Scotti Morgana
1981; Marello 1996). The French language dominated linguistically and culturally
in Italy and elsewhere in Europe up to the mid-twentieth century and, as we have
seen, it acted as a 'go-between' for English loans in Italian up to a few decades ago.
This situation has drastically changed in the second half of the century, owing to
more intense, direct exchanges between English and Italian, and partly as a result
of French legislation directed against Anglicisms.

The mediation of French is evident in many aspects of early loanwords, such as
the spellings of *poney* and *rallye* (now *pony* and *rally*) and in derived forms
(*stripteaseuse*, *linciaggio* 'lynching'). In many cases it is impossible to decide
whether a word came from French or English, because of the similarity and the
historical links between them: for example, words of ambiguous and neoclassical
provenance (*cellophane*, *pamphlet*), French loans integrated in English (*cinema*),
old Anglicisms in French (*redingote*), homographs (*chance*, *exploit*), and words
which Italian has received from both sources (*choc* and *shock*; *confort* and *comfort*). The pronunciation of English loanwords tends to adhere to a French model
in the older generations, whereas the reverse is typical of younger speakers (who
tend to Anglicize French loans).

8.1.9 *English in education*
(Pulcini 1997)

The first university chairs of English in Italy were created in 1918. Since then
English has gradually expanded in Italian education, and in the 1960s French gave
way to English as the most widely taught foreign language in schools. It is now
studied by 60 per cent of students, followed by French (35 per cent), German (5 per
cent), and Spanish (1 per cent). The drastic drop of French (from 90 per cent in the
1950s) caused a difficult situation in Italian schools, with the suppression of
teaching posts for French. This was partly solved by the introduction of two
foreign languages in some middle schools. The request for English is strong also
in elementary schools, where a foreign language was made obligatory in 1990.

8.2 Pronunciation and spelling

8.2.1 *Pronunciation*
(Klajn 1972; Pulcini 1990)

Anglicisms borrowed in past centuries were adapted to Italian structures graphically, phonetically, and morphologically. Early borrowings were imported mainly
through written sources and spoken English was little known. Recent times have
witnessed a reverse tendency: loanwords are now increasingly borrowed close to

their native form and through oral sources, and Italians' competence in English has greatly increased.

Today, then, Anglicisms tend to be pronounced according to the English model. However, the divergence of the English and Italian sound systems and the irregularity of the spelling–pronunciation correspondence in English are the source of minor phonetic adjustments, and adapted or hypercorrected pronunciations. The most important differences between the Italian and the English consonant systems are outlined in Table 8.1.

Consonant phonemes which are unique either to English or to Italian are indicated in bold; those which have an equivalent in the other language are in roman type.

The following are typical Italian deviations in the pronunciation of English loanwords:

1. underdifferentiation of vowel contrasts: /iː, ɪ/ → /i/; / ʌ, ɑː/ → /a/; /uː, ʊ/ → /u /;
2. closer realization of some vowel phonemes: /æ/ → / ε, e/; / ɔ /; / ɔː/ → /o/;
3. substitution of central vowels with closer equivalents: *flirt* (/flɜːt/ → /flɛrt/), or the French pronunciation /(flœrt/);
4. simplification of certain diphthongs, especially the central ones: *baby* /'beibi/ → /bebi/; *show* /ʃəʊ / → /ʃo/; *goal* / gol / gəʊl/ → / gɔl/

Table 8.1. Consonant phonemes

English	Italian
p	p
b	b
t	t
d	d
k	k
f	g
v	f
θ	v
ð	s
s	z
z	ʃ
ʃ	**ts**
ʒ	**dz**
h	tʃ
tʃ	dʒ
dʒ	m
m	n
n	**ɲ**
ŋ	l
l	**ʎ**
r	r
w	w
j	j

5. replacement of fricatives /θ, ð / with /t, d/;
6. realization of the grapheme <r> as a dental trill (Italian is *r*-full);
7. *h*-dropping;
8. pronunciation of final <- ng> as /ŋg/ instead of /ŋ/;
9. initial <s> followed by voiced consonant is voiced: /smɔg/ → /zmɔg/;
10. simplification of consonant clusters, especially in connected speech (/'stændəd/ → /'standar/);
11. as a form of hypercorrection, stress placement in initial position (/self kən'trəʊl/ → /self 'kɔntrɔl/);
12. strong pronunciation of weak syllables (*mister* → /'mister/);
13. other minor differences are the mispronunciation of syllabic consonants (*jam-session* → dʒɛm sɛʃon), deviant allophonic realizations (e.g. Italian has only clear [l]); and the pronunciation of double consonant graphemes, as geminates.

Apart from the age of the loans, other sociolinguistic variables in the pronunciation of loanwords are generational and class differences in speakers. Older pronunciations may be brought closer to the source model: *jazz* has both the older /dʒɛts/ and the recent pronunciation /dʒæz/.

Latin words such as *junior* still retain the classic pronunciation (/'junjɔr/) but the English model /'dʒu:njə/) has rapidly spread (this variant is sometimes stigmatized).

8.2.2 Graphemic integration

(Upward and Pulcini 1996)

The Italian alphabet has twenty-one letters. The graphemes <j, k, w, x, y>, existed in Latin (apart from <w>) but became totally or partially disused in Italian. Today the number of words containing non-Italian graphemes has increased, as well as words beginning with <h>, and these are usually loanwords. Foreign graphemes have become fashionable in Christian names (e.g. *Tony*, *Mery*, the latter often spelt with <e>). The grapheme <k> is used in advertising for its supposed visual and acoustic impact.

The input of English loanwords has introduced a few distributional features, such as words ending in a consonant or consonant clusters (most Italian words end in a vowel) and words containing unusual consonant clusters (<ngst> in *gangster*). Graphemic integration of Anglicisms is not a noticeable phenomenon in Italian and when it occurs it is usually influenced by pronunciation. It may affect the whole spelling of the word or only part of it, as is shown in the following examples: *jungle* → *giungla*, but also *jungla*, *goal* → *gol*, *nylon* → *nailon*, but also *nylon*, *roastbeef* → *rosbif*, *rosbiffe*, but also *roastbeef*, and *folklore* → *folclore*, but also *folklore*. Other instances of graphic assimilation are confined to uneducated uses or varieties of Italian spoken by Italian communities overseas (in America and Australia): e.g. *job* → *giobba*, *shoeshine* → *sciuscià*. Integration can also be restricted to derivates as in *clown*, but *claunesco*, *Shakespeare*, but *scespiriano*.

8.3 Morphology

(Klajn 1972; Dardano 1986)

8.3.1 Introduction

Italian inflects for gender (masculine and feminine) and number (singular and plural) in nouns, pronouns, adjectives, and articles, and for person, number, gender, tense, and mood in verbs. Adapted and derived loans are treated as Italian in form and follow its rules for gender and number specification. Formal adaptation is rare today, except for verbs.

8.3.2 Nouns

Grammatical gender is attributed to loanwords on the basis of:

1. natural gender, if possible;
2. formal features; for instance, Anglicisms in -ion and -ty are feminine because they correspond to It -ione and -tà;
3. the gender of the closest native semantic equivalent;
4. gender preference: in Italian the masculine is the unmarked gender, in that it also indicates 'common' gender (inclusive of masculine and feminine); if the three criteria above are not applicable, masculine gender is therefore likely to be attributed to the loanword.

These rules are not without exceptions. Over time, words with multiple equivalents in Italian have changed gender: *film* was initially feminine but became masculine, *suspense* is feminine but is occasionally treated as masculine, *pigiama* is masculine in spite of its typically feminine ending because of the influence of French (*le pyjama*).

Adapted Anglicisms take Italian plural endings. Unadapted Anglicisms do usually not take any plural inflection; however, the English -s is often found in spoken and written uses, especially in journalism, and in words which are more frequently used in the plural, e.g. *hippies*. This phenomenon is partly due to inadequate guidance in dictionaries and grammars on the morphological treatment of Anglicisms; on the other hand, it may be interpreted as a form of hypercorrection on the part of users who have gradually become more competent in English.

The use of the masculine article before nouns beginning with <h> and <w> poses a morphological problem. Usage varies between the Italian article *l'* and *lo* before <h>, depending on whether it is silent (*l'hotel*) or not (*lo humour*); before the semiconsonant /w/ the article *il* is almost always preferred to *l'* (*il whisky*), even though, by rule *l'* should precede this semiconsonant.

8.3.3 Adjectives

Italian has borrowed very few English adjectives. Unadapted loans can be used predicatively and attributively. They are more easily inserted in Italian discourse in predicative position, following the noun according to the Italian 'head-modifier' pattern (*sexy girl* → *ragazza sexy*; *funky music* → *musica funky*; *part-time job* → *lavoro part-time*). Some English nouns can be used as adjectives (*snob* = 'snobbish').

8.3.4 Adverbs

A few unadapted adjectives can be used adverbially, without any morphological change (*to work part-time* → *lavorare part-time*). There has been no borrowing of English adverbs *per se* into Italian.

8.3.5 Verbs

The Italian verbal system is characterized by complex endings for mood, tense, person, gender, and number specification. Verbal Anglicisms must necessarily be adapted in Italian: typically they are assigned to the most common verb conjugation, which ends in *-are* (thus, *boicottare*, *filmare*, *stoppare*, etc.).

8.3.6 Derivation

Gender specification. Gender specification in nouns is signalled by the preceding article (*il manager*, M; *la manager*, F). If further clarification is needed, especially for female reference, hybrid compounds are created (e.g. *la donna manager*). Otherwise gender-specific terms are borrowed (*businessman/businesswoman*).

    Agent nouns. The English ending *-er* denoting agent nouns appears in very common Anglicisms (*leader*, *designer*, *mixer*, *freezer*); therefore it is widely recognized as a morpheme although alien to Italian.

    Denominal verbs. Verbs are derived from nouns with the addition of the infinitive inflexion *-are*.

    New adjectives. New adjectives are derived from integrated English borrowings without apparent restrictions, such as *sportivo* from English *sport* and *clownesco* from *clown*.

    Deadjectival nouns. Some adjectives are borrowed and used as nouns in Italian, e.g. *big* (with the sense of 'important person'), *topless* (topless dress or swim suit). This phenomenon is linked to that of the reduction of the right-hand element of a compound, as *cross-country skiing* is reduced to *cross-country*.

8.3.7 Compounds and combining forms

Compounding is a very productive word-formation process in English. As a consequence, a great number of Anglicisms in Italian belong to the class of compounds. The order of the elements of English compounds (*determinans+determinatum*) violates the syntagmatic order of Italian which usually places the modifying element on the right of the modified one. However, because of the influence of English and of Germanic languages in general, a reversed order has become familiar in Italian as well, as appears in various calques reproducing the English structure (*gentleman* → *gentiluomo*). Orthographically, Italian tends to use the hyphen more frequently than does English, although usage in English is very variable.

Another characteristic of the integration of compound Anglicisms is the reduction of the right-hand element which gives *night* from *night club*, *boxer* from *boxer shorts*, and *beach volley* from *beach volleyball*. The truncation is based on the interpretation of the compounds on a Romance model; thus, the wrongly supposed modifying element is eliminated. In other cases, the compound is normally abbreviated in the same way as it would be in English, e.g. *scout* for *boy scout*, *jeans* for *blue jeans*.

Hybrid compounds are coined with English elements such as *-centre -shop*, and *-store*, as well as Latin or Greek combining forms, although the latter are not considered in the *Dictionary of European Anglicisms*.

8.3.8 Calques (loan translations)

(Bombi 1989–90)

Calques are frequently and easily coined in Italian if the technical terms contain Latin or Greek elements (*microwave* → *microonde*). By contrast, words tend to maintain their unadapted form when they are difficult to translate, as is the case with compounds containing a preposition or adverb (*by-pass*, *turnover*, *top-down*, *bottom-up*), items which would require a long, less economic paraphrase in Italian.

We can distinguish between structural and semantic calques, the former reproducing the form of the foreign item (completely or partially), the latter reproducing only its meaning, which is added to an indigenous item (semantic loans). Some calques faithfully translate the English model (*high society* → *alta società*). In most cases Italian calques reverse the order of the English components, either with juxtaposition of the elements (*electric chair* → *sedia elettrica*) or with the second element in the form of a prepositional phrase (*head hunter* → *cacciatore di teste*). Another classification distinguishes *calco omonimico*—calques which, apart from semantic equivalence, also have a formal resemblance with the English word because of common etymology (e.g. *public relations* → *pubbliche relazioni*) and *calco sinonimico*—calques which display little formal affinity with the foreign source (e.g. *Iron Curtain* → *cortina di ferro*).

Hybrids or semi-calques have only part of the word translated or are freely rendered in the receiving language, with the other part left unchanged (*American football* → *football americano*). This pattern is common with words having Latin or Greek affixes (*antifreeze* → *antigelo*).

The similarity between the many Latinate words in English and Italian makes it often difficult to distinguish between calques and adaptations, as in the case of *anglicanismo* (*Anglicanism*) or between calques and semantic loans, as in *impatto* (*impact*). Indeed, some are borderline cases or fall in the category of internationalisms (that is, words which are widespread in European languages, and which cannot be attributed unambiguously to an English origin).

8.4 Meaning
(Dardano 1986; Pulcini 1995)

The semantic aspect of language contact is a complex phenomenon because it involves referential, connotative, contextual, and sociocultural components of meaning. New words are created or borrowed because of the need to name new things and concepts (or rename old ones); this explains why most neologisms are nouns.

Loanwords belonging to technical terminologies tend to be monosemic, i.e. each denotes a single referent so that it can be shared internationally by scientists working in the same field (*big bang theory* → *teoria del big bang*) or across different disciplines (*feedback*, used in physics, psychology, etc.). It must be observed, however, that technical terms can be used outside their specialized contexts, in which case they may be attributed a metaphorical sense.

As a rule, the meaning of loanwords is restricted. For example, *dry* is used in Italian only with reference to a drink, with the meaning of 'not sweet', whereas in English *dry* has a much wider range of referents and contexts of use.

A 'luxury loan' is a word which is introduced to rename an already existing item or concept in the receiving language; in this case a semantic conflict arises between the competing terms. The English word may replace the Italian equivalent (*baby-sitter* has pushed out the old-fashioned *bambinaia*; *body-building* sounds more attractive than *culturismo*), coexist with it (*goal* with *rete* in football terminology) or be used in separate registers (e.g. *meeting* denotes a formal managerial style; while *riunione* is neutral). The English word may also acquire connotations that it did not possess in the donor language, e.g. *shopping* has a more frivolous tone than Italian *spese* or *compere*; *know-how* has sophisticated overtones that are absent in English.

Finally, the original meaning of the loanword may be changed, especially through metonymic modifications, as in the case of the word *flipper* which in English denotes one of the two wing-shaped mechanisms for hitting the balls in a pinball machine, whereas in Italian *flipper* is the name of the machine and of the game itself. Another example is *spot*, which in English has a wide range of meanings, but not the one it has in Italian, which is 'television commercial'.

8.5 Usage

The impact of English in relation to sociolinguistic and stylistic variables has received only impressionistic treatment so far. Existing research, newspaper corpora, and *Dictionary of European Anglicisms* data have shown that a great proportion of Anglicisms tend to be 'technical', i.e. restricted to scientific and technical fields of usage. Another conspicuous group of Anglicisms is found mainly in mass communication and youth language, being linked to various cultural expressions of modern society.

8.6 Forms of linguistic borrowing and their categorization

Borrowings are normally divided into two broad categories: loanwords and calques. Loanwords maintain the original English form (unadapted loans) or are modified according to the orthographic and morphological rules of Italian (adapted loans); a certain degree of phonological assimilation is always present, even when the pronunciation is very close to the native model. Calques reproduce the foreign word (its form and meaning or only its meaning) with Italian elements, along three degrees of resemblance with the original (translation, rendition, and creation). Within these broad categorizations, more refined distinctions can be drawn:

1. *Loanwords*

   (*a*) totally unadapted and not felt to be part of Italian (quotation words, code-switching, foreignisms): *bed and breakfast, boat people, squatter, penny*;
   (*b*) unadapted or partially adapted loans, still looking foreign in form but felt to be integrated in the language: *airbag, babysitter, scooter*;
   (*c*) fully adapted and integrated items: *flanella, scellino, dribblare, dollaro*.

2. *Calques*

   (*a*) translation, reflecting the form of the English words as closely as the structure of the receiving language permits. In many cases, only part of the foreign word is translated (*semi-calque*) (for examples cf. group A 1–3 below);
   (*b*) rendition (*calco parziale*), translating only part of the foreign item and providing looser equivalents for others (cf. group B below);
   (*c*) creation (*calco libero*), a formally independent equivalent whose coinage was prompted by the foreign word (cf. group C below);
   (*d*) semantic loan (*calco semantico*), an existing Italian word taking one meaning of the foreign (partial) equivalent (cf. group C below).

3. *Pseudo-loans*

The coinage of pseudo-loans is prompted partly by a limited competence in English and by the creative desire to coin an English-looking word for stylistic purposes. The following types of pseudo-loans can be distinguished:

   (*a*) lexical pseudo-loans, i.e. combinations of English lexical items and/or Latin prefixes to form a word which does not exist in English, e.g. *recordman* ('record-holder'), *autostop* ('hitch-hiking'), *autogol* ('own goal'), *beauty-case* ('make-up bag');
   (*b*) morphological pseudo-loans, i.e. reduction of a compound or elision of an element in the English expression, e.g. *happy end* (*happy ending*), *trench* (*trench coat*), *smoking* (*smoking jacket*), *gin tonic* (*gin and tonic*);
   (*c*) semantic pseudo-loans, i.e. attribution of a new meaning to an already existing English word, e.g. *footing* ('jogging'), *speaker* ('newsreader'), *slip* ('panties'), *stage* ('short training course').

The categories 2 (*a–d*) can be illustrated with Italian specimens, distinguishing between successful borrowings, coexisting items, and those which have not been accepted.

A *Translations*

1. Successful

handball < *pallamano*, honeymoon < *luna di miele, skyscraper* < *grattacielo, brainwashing* < *lavaggio del cervello, cyberspace* < *ciberspazio, black box* < *scatola nera, credit card* < *carta di credito, birth control* < *controllo delle nascite, no man's land* < *terra di nessuno, public relations* < *pubbliche relazioni*

2. Coexisting

basket(ball) = *pallacanestro, hi-fi* = *alta fedelta, on-line* = *in linea, full-time* = *tempo pieno, hard rock* = *rock duro*

3. Failures

cornflakes > *fiocchi di grano, beat generation* > *generazione beat*

B *Renderings*

1. Successful

aftershave < *dopobarba, airline* < *compagnia aerea, checkpoint* < *posto di controllo, crossword* < *parole crociate, trademark* < *marchio di fabbrica, blank verse* < *verso sciolto, space shuttle* < *navetta spaziale, brain drain* < *fuga dei cervelli, cable television* < *televisione via cavo, centre-half* < *centromediano*

2. Coexisting

hard disk = *disco fisso, copyright* = *diritti d'autore, by night* = *di notte*

3. Failures

baby boom > *boom delle nascite*

C *Creations*

1. Successful

pipeline < *oleodotto, waterpolo* < *pallanuoto, cash flow* < *autofinanziamento, fringe benefit* < *beneficio accessorio*

2. Coexisting

bookmaker = *allibratore, bungee jumping* = *salto con l'elastico*

3. Failures

cameraman > *operatore televisio*

D *Semantic loans*

1. Successful

backhand < *rovescio*

2. Coexisting

3. Failures

stuntman > *cascatore*, *check-in* > *accettazione*

8.7 The future of Anglicisms

(Simone 1988; Beccaria 1988)

Many Italian linguists have tried to outline possible linguistic scenarios for the future. There is widespread agreement that English will be the language of international communication and Italians' competence in English will keep improving. English has also provided a conspicuous lexical store of scientific and technological terminology which will presumably continue to develop. As far as the input of Anglicisms is concerned, some linguists have signalled a maximum peak in the 1980s and stability since then. It is unlikely that legislation will be introduced to control the spread of English in Italy, as has happened in France. The growing number of Anglicisms recorded in Italian dictionaries seems to be too low to cause noticeable changes in Italian. By contrast, some linguists foresee dramatic changes for the English language itself owing to the development of native and non-native national varieties of English.

8.8 Research

(Moss 1992)

Substantial information about the input of English lexis to Italian is contained in books on the history of the Italian language. Specific studies of the influence of English on Italian exist, though they are not very numerous. The types of research which have been published in Italian can be summarized as follows:

1. articles addressed to specialists concentrating on formal features, synchronic development, and dating of Anglicisms;
2. dictionary-type collections of neologisms and Anglicisms, generally based on newspaper corpora and often addressed to a non-specialist readership;
3. studies on the lexes of special fields (economics, politics and culture, advertising, sports, etc.).

8.9 Bibliography

BECCARIA, GIAN LUIGI (1988), *Italiano antico e nuovo* (Milan: Garzanti).

BERRUTO, GAETANO (1987), *Sociolinguistica dell'Italiano contemporaneo* (Rome: La Nuova Italia Scientifica).

BOMBI, RAFFAELLA (1989–90), 'Calchi sintagmatici, sintematici e semantici sull'inglese in italiano', *Incontri linguistici*, 13: 97–149.

BOMBI, RAFFAELLA (1991), 'Di alcuni falsi anglicismi nell'italiano contemporaneo', *Incontri linguistici*, 14: 87–96.

CARTAGO, GABRIELLA (1994), 'L'apporto inglese', in L. Serianni and P. Trifone (eds.), *Storia della lingua italiana*, iii, Le altre lingue (Turin: Einaudi), 721–50.

CASTELLANI, ARRIGO (1987), 'Morbus Anglicus', *Studi linguistici italiani*, 10: 137–53.

CORTELAZZO, MANLIO, and CARDINALE, UGO (1989), *Dizionario di parole nuove, 1964–1987* (Turin: Loescher).

DARDANO, MAURIZIO (1986), 'The Influence of English on Italian', in Wolfgang Viereck and Wolf-Dietrich Bald (eds.), *English in Contact with Other Languages* (Budapest: Akadémiai Kiadó), 231–52.

DURANTE, MARCELLO (1981), *Dal latino all'italiano moderno* (Bologna: Zanichelli).

FANFANI, PIETRO, and ARLìA, CESARE (1877), *Lessico della Corrotta Italianità* (Milan: Libreria d'Educazione e d'Istruzione di Paolo Carrara).

FLORIO, JOHN (1611), *Queen Anna's New Worlde of Wordes* (London: A. Hatfield for Edw. Blount; facs. Menston (EL 105)).

GRAF, ARTURO (1911), *L'anglomania e l'influsso inglese in Italia nel secolo XVIII* (Turin: Loescher).

KLAJN, IVAN (1972), *Influssi inglesi nella lingua italiana* (Florence: Leo S. Olschki Editore).

LURATI, OTTAVIO (1995), *3.000 parole nuove: La neologia degli anni 80–90* (Bologna: Zanichelli).

MARELLO, CARLA (1996), *Le parole dell'italiano: Lessico e dizionari* (Florence: La Nuova Italia).

MIGLIORINI, BRUNO (1991), *Storia della lingua italiana*, (Florence: Sansoni). (1st pub. 1937.)

MINI, GUIDO (1994), *Parole senza frontiere: Dizionario delle parole straniere in uso nella lingua italiana* (Bologna: Zanichelli). (1st edn.: *L'italiano integrato, l'apporto di voci straniere nel nostro linguaggio* (Padua: La Galiverna, 1990).)

MOSS, HOWARD (1992), 'The Incidence of Anglicisms in Modern Italian: Considerations on its Overall Effect on the Language', *The Italianist: Journal of the Department of Italian Studies* (University of Reading), 129–36.

PANZINI, ALFREDO (1963), *Dizionario Moderno*, 10th edn. (1st edn. 1905) (Milan: Hoepli).

PASQUARELLI, GIANNI, and PALMIERI, GERMANO (1987), *Parole d'oggi: Guida ai termini economici e d'uso corrente* (Rome: Buffetti).

PULCINI, VIRGINIA (1990), *Introduzione alla pronuncia inglese* (Alessandria: Edizioni dell'Orso).

——(1994), 'The English Language in Italy', *English Today*, 10 (4): 49–52.

——(1995), 'Some New English Words in Italian', *Textus: English Studies in Italy*, 8: 267–80.

——(1997), 'Attitudes toward the Spread of English in Italy', *World Englishes*, 16: 77–85.

RAFFAELLI, SERGIO (1983), *Le parole proibite: Purismo di Stato e regolamentazione della pubblicità in Italia (1812–1945)* (Bologna: Il Mulino).

RANDO, GAETANO (1969), 'Anglicismi nel "Dizionario Moderno" dalla quarta alla decima edizione (1923–63)', *Lingua Nostra*, 30: 107–12.

——(1973), 'Influssi inglesi nel lessico contemporaneo', *Lingua Nostra*, 34: 111–20.

——(1987), *Dizionario di anglicismi nell'italiano postunitario* (Florence: Leo S. Olschki Editore).

SANGA, GLAUCO (1981), 'Les Dynamiques linguistiques de la société italienne (1861–1980)', *Languages*, 61: 93–115.

SCOTTI MORGANA, SILVIA (1981), *Le parole nuove* (Bologna: Zanichelli).

SIMONE, RAFFAELE (1988), 'Che lingua parleremo nel Duemila?', in Maystock, *Il linguaggio spiegato da una bambina* (Florence: La Nuova Italia), 187–205.

UPWARD, CHRISTOPHER, and PULCINI, VIRGINIA (1996), 'Italian Spelling and How it Treats English Loanwords', *Journal of the Simplified Spelling Society*, 20: 19–24.

ZINGARELLI, NICOLA (1996), *Lo Zingarelli in CD-ROM: Vocabolario della lingua italiana* (Bologna: Zanichelli).

ZOLLI, PAOLO (1991), *Le parole straniere*, 2nd edn. (Bologna: Zanichelli). (1st pub. 1976.)

9

ROMANIAN

Ilinca Constantinescu, Victoria Popovici,
and Ariadna Ştefănescu

9.1 History of language contact: historical and sociocultural factors

9.1.1 Chronology of influences

(Mociorniţă 1983; Chiţoran 1986)

Historians and researchers interested in earlier periods of culture and civilization (Iorga, Botez, Grimm, Cernovodeanu, and Demeny, in Romania, and Tappe, Hope, and Deletant, in Britain) have found evidence of cultural and economic relations between Britain and Romania from the sixteenth century on. Occasional earlier contacts were analysed by A. Trofin (1975) in his unpublished Ph.D. thesis and in a number of articles.

Compared to West European languages, the influence of English in Romanian came quite late, mainly, no doubt, because of geographical distance. Major influence on Romanian vocabulary started in the second half of the nineteenth century when economic and cultural contacts intensified. Moreover, the first English borrowings were not direct but were mediated by other languages, primarily French, but also by German, Russian, and Italian. This impact is only briefly mentioned in treatises on the history of literary language.

The earliest discussions of English etymologies are found in works of a general character dealing with neologisms and terminologies, or in works concerned with correctness. Some foreignisms (both British and American) such as *baseball*, *cent*, *Derby race*, *dollar*, *earl*, *gallon*, *lady*, *sir*, *sport*, *tennis*, *tory*, *whig* are found in Diaconovici's encyclopedic dictionary (1898–1904) and, occasionally, in other lexicographic works published around the turn of the century. A minor source of influence was that many Romanians emigrated from Transylvania and the Banat to America between the 1880s and the First World War; some returned to their native villages, others encouraged their families to join them in the USA (Hartular 1996).

In the twentieth century several factors contributed to bridging the distance between Romania and Britain, and between Romania and the USA. The development of various branches of industries upon West European models, many of them of British origin, brought English technological methods to the attention of specialists in oil drilling, mining, steel production, shipbuilding, weaving, etc. In 1916, Romania joined the Triple Entente countries in their fight against the Central Powers. Queen Maria, the wife of Ferdinand I (who was king from 1914 to 1927), a strong and charming personality, was a grandchild of Queen Victoria, born in England.

9.1.2 Origins of influence

University professors of the inter-war years who spoke English were either visiting specialists whose native tongue was English, or a few Romanians who had graduated from British (rarely American) universities. Young intellectuals when given the possibility to study abroad traditionally chose France, Germany, and Italy.

In the second half of the twentieth century the influence of English grew steadily in spite of the purist attitude which was favoured for political reasons. One may interpret the interest in Anglo-American culture and civilization as a spontaneous form of opposition to Communist indoctrination.

In Romanian schools the British variant was favoured in the teaching of English for many years. The influence of AmE first exerted itself through films, then records, and recently through television and audio and video cassettes.

Since the downfall of the totalitarian regime in December 1989, there has been a substantial influx of Anglicisms in all fields of activity. Some linguists have reacted against the exaggerated use of Anglicisms especially in journalese (Stoichiţoiu-Ichim 1993, 1996).

9.1.3 Types of influence

The direct English influence on Romanian was discussed in scholarly articles in the 1960s (Bujeniţă 1966; Trofin 1967). Cultural history will prove that many Anglicisms entered the language long before their presence was noted in general dictionaries. For instance, the words *aut* (E *out*) and *ofsaid* (E *offside*) in sports terminology seem to be earlier than the 1950s, the information given in dictionaries (cf. *Dicţionarul limbii române* (*DLR*)), since football matches were played in Cluj as early as the 1890s and soon spread to other towns. The same is true for other fields dominated by English terms.

The most comprehensive list of English borrowings in Romanian is given by Ciobanu (1996), which has some 1,400 words and a few phrases. If we add to these all the entries in the *Dicţionar de neologisme* (*DN3*) (Marcu and Maneca 1978), in which English is mentioned as a possible direct or indirect source, and all the words discussed in various language studies over the last three decades, it becomes clear that the number of Anglicisms exceeds by far the number of entries marked as Romanian in the *Dictionary of European Anglicisms*.

As Chiţoran (1986) has pointed out, the dominant trend in the vocabulary of modern Romanian is the growing number of neologisms of Romance origin; this fact is significant for the assessment of the impact of English on Romanian since many English scientific words are themselves made up of Latin elements. These easily fit into the existing Romanian patterns and are therefore not felt as 'foreign'.

9.1.4 *Chronology of purist phases*
(Iordan 1956; Munteanu and Ţâra 1983; Chiţoran 1986)

In spite of its Latin ancestry, the language spoken by the people in Dacia at the beginning of the Christian era had no written form; thus Old Slavic became the written language of the Church, of official correspondence, and of secular documents; the earliest surviving Romanian texts (of the sixteenth century) made use of the Cyrillic alphabet (and phonetic spelling).

Although the 'Roman extraction' of Romanians had been claimed by some seventeenth-century scholars (the chroniclers), awareness of the Latin character of the language acquired a programmatic form as late as in the second half of the eighteenth century. It is connected with the Romanian illuminists (the Transylvanian School) who advocated the deliberate 're-Latinization' of the vocabulary through replacing part of the non-Romance lexis with coinages from Latin etymons and the use of the Latin instead of the Cyrillic alphabet.

The Latin alphabet was adopted by the Academic Society in the 1860s; the orthography recommended was etymological. However, no important writer of the time followed the recommendations. Twenty years later, in 1881, the Romanian Academy tried to impose what the linguist Sextil Puşcaiu called a 'pseudo-etymological' spelling. This was formally in use until 1953, when the newly established Academy of the Communist regime issued an orthographic reform imposing the phonemic spelling.

The comprehensive normative dictionary of 1982, *Dicţionarul ortografic, ortoepic şi morfologic al limbii române* (*DOOM*), was also built on the phonemic principle. The latest orthographic reform (1993) makes minor concessions to the 'pseudo-etymological' spelling without affecting English loanwords.

The powerful English influence, a twentieth-century phenomenon, affected the vocabulary, semantics, and, to a smaller degree, syntax. The purist attitude favoured under the Communist regime was never strict; it fluctuated in intensity according to specific interests. From personal experience and evidence provided by elderly colleagues it appears that the 1950s was the period most intensely marked by xenophobia. Cosmopolitanism was deprecated in any of its manifestations, linguistic or otherwise. Nothing coming from the capitalist world was to be accepted uncritically. By contrast, influence from the socialist countries, first and foremost from Russia, was looked upon as beneficial and hailed by the pro-Communist activists.

When Romania began to assume an air of independence within the socialist bloc in the 1970s the search for Russian models was gradually discarded, and more and more English words found their way into technical terminologies and the standard language. Translations of scientific and literary writings greatly enriched the Romanian vocabulary. At the end of the twentieth century we may speak of an unprecedented English influence which manifested itself at the beginning mainly via French and is now succeeded by a direct English influence exerted mainly through second language teaching and the mass media, and supported by fashion and prestige. Purist voices speak of an 'invasion' of Anglicisms and an 'Anglicization' of the language. However, most linguists have a moderate attitude, and purist protests or warnings are voiced mainly through newspaper articles.

Present-day linguists are convinced that Romanian has a capacity to regulate the penetration and ultimate integration of foreign elements. Therefore there is no open war against Anglicisms similar to the rejection and replacement of Slavicisms in the late eighteenth and early nineteenth centuries. Romanian normative linguists never went so far as to rule out the use of Anglicisms by law. In conclusion, the English influence has developed largely free of any philologic bias and purist constraints.

9.1.5 Regional differences

There has been no research devoted to geographical variation in the distribution of Anglicisms in Romania. We assume that there are no marked regional differences. However, certain terminologies relating to specific activities are probably better known to a larger number of speakers in those areas where that activity is carried out. On the other hand, the mass media, both written and oral, have contributed permanently to the propagation of Anglicisms over the entire territory.

Given the emigration to the USA mentioned above, it might be expected that in the Banat and Transylvania the number of non-technical borrowings from everyday speech would be greater as a consequence of family relations with Americans of Romanian descent. However, this must remain a hypothesis since the necessary sociolinguistic studies are still lacking.

Concerning research on Anglicisms in the Romanian language spoken in the Republic of Moldova, no article or book has come to our attention so far. The *Scurt dicţionar etimologic al limbii moldoveneşti* (Raevski and Gabinski 1987), covering some 15,000 words, registers a few English borrowings—perfectly integrated—such as *meci* 'match', *set*, *sport*, *tenis*.

9.1.6 Stylistic differences

Stylistic aspects of Anglicisms have occasionally been mentioned (Bantaş 1977; Stoichiţoiu 1986; Avram 1997) but no special research has been devoted to them so far. The listing of Romanian Anglicisms in the *Dictionary of European Anglicisms* is comprehensive enough to illustrate that the technical and colloquial registers are most affected. The number of archaic and obsolescent loans is small—not surprisingly if we consider that direct English influence was sporadic up to the inter-war period, and has grown in intensity and scope only since the 1960s.

The change in the status of a word from highly specialized to common technical term and then to its acceptance in the standard language very often depends on the concept designated. Words such as *boiler*, *buldozer*, *fax*, *feribot*, *pager*, *scaner*, and *video* are no longer felt as alien or highly technical. The word *brocăr* (*broker*) attested in Romanian from the end of the nineteenth century was reborrowed as *broker* in the 1990s after a period of obsolescence extending over four decades of socialist economy. Certain terms like *bypass* (and the derived verb *a bypasa*), *brainstorming*, *feedback*, *interfaţă* (*interface*), *input*, and *output* become technical metaphors when used outside the specific domains in which they originated.

Satirical writings (especially as found in newspapers) often make use of jocular coinages based on Anglicisms. These strike the user through their novelty or expressivity. A verb like *a drinkui* 'to drink' may also suggest 'to indulge in drinking' by association with *a benchetui* ('to indulge in a big party' from *banchet*). Other Anglicisms are used for euphemistic reasons: *gay* (with its jocular adaptation *ghei*), *condom*, *girl*, and *gipsy* have been taken over by journalese from youth language or colloquial speech.

Romanian integrates verbs of English origin normally in the first conjugation in -*a* (cf. s.9.3.5). All the Romanian verbs of English origin which belong to the fourth conjugation ending in -*i* are felt to be jocular (*mitingi*, *joggingi*). Another grammatical change with stylistic jocular impact is the creation of the feminine *fană* [fanə] for the masculine noun *fan*.

By adding Romanian suffixes (rich in connotations) to loanwords one obtains new words marked stylistically (e.g. *sponsoragiu* 'male sponsor' [+ pejorative]; *sponsorică* 'female sponsor' [+ diminutive] [+ derogatory]; *sponsorărie* 'sponsorship' [+ pejorative] because of its possible association with *sforărie* 'dishonest scheming'. For expressive effects, English lexemes are sometimes combined with Romanian ones, as in *tarabman* 'man selling at a market stall', *Andagate* (modelled on *Watergate*) 'unlawful surveillance by the Secret Service on the Anda Terrace'.

The use of what we may call 'luxury' or 'superfluous Anglicisms' like *planning*, *promotion*, *staff*, *standing*, and *listing* is motivated from the speaker's point of view by the prestige of an English term (and as therefore beneficial to an enterprise, say trading activities), or as proof of multilingual competence (as some newsmen seem to believe).

There also seems to be a vogue for code-switching, by which English words and phrases are employed to adorn the speech or the writing in order to impress the addressee. In written texts, they are often marked graphically by using different typefaces or inverted commas (Pârlog 1971). Code-switching is quite frequent in headings and titles, advertising leaflets, and on signboards of commercial companies.

Variants of Anglicisms tend to be stylistically differentiated. The recommended standard Romanian forms are *blue jeans*, *chewing gum*, *sandviş*, *video*, *whisky*, and not *blugi*, *ciungă*, *senvici*, *vidou*, *vizichi*, which can have jocular connotations. In addition, some of the 'uneducated' variants like *geacă* < E *jacket* and *bişniţă* < E *business* exhibit semantic specialization. *Superman* belongs to journalese, whereas the calque *supraom* (which translates the German *Übermensch* or the French *surhomme*) is used in philosophical language.

English borrowings penetrated into all the functional styles of Romanian (even into modern and postmodern poetic language). Anglicisms have contributed to the formation of some technical languages as those of sports and computer language, or at least to their enrichment. Moreover, many of the Anglicisms trigger specific stylistic connotations and semantic specializations whenever they establish synonymic relations with other Romanian words.

9.1.7 Innovation and obsolescence

There are no statistical accounts of how many Anglicisms there were in any specific period of Romanian. Bantaş (1982) refers to 'the nearly 4000 words, derivatives, compounds and phrases' that should be considered. One may infer that this number includes archaic and obsolescent borrowings. Evidence preceding the early twentieth century as found in dictionaries is not conclusive since most lexicographers of the time registered a limited number of neologisms and, anyway, favoured Romanian ones.

Since the 1970s more and more Anglicisms have found their way into dictionaries, whether works of a general nature such as *Dicţionarul explicativ al limbii române* (*DEX1* and *DEX2*), dictionaries of neologisms (*DN3*), or recordings of new words (Dimitrescu 1982, 1997: *Dicţionar de cuvinte recente* (*DCR1* and *DCR2*)), and indeed specialized dictionaries restricted to individual domains (e.g. computer science, finance and trade, marketing, sports, and medicine).

No diachronic evaluation of the English element in Romanian has been made so far, but we find in various studies data about either losses of Anglicisms (replaced by a calque, as in *fundaş* for the football player formerly called *bek* < E *back*) or new borrowings that are synonyms for existent Romanian words (*trainer/antrenor*, *court/teren*, *team/echipă*, *trend/curent*).

That the English element in Romanian is increasing has been demonstrated by Manolescu (1990) who compared the number of Anglicisms listed in a segment of *DEX1* and its *Supliment* (1988) with the corresponding segments in two general dictionaries published half a century ago.

Technical terminologies contain a great number of terms of English origin. Even in a work of a general character such as *Lexiconul tehnic român* (*LTR1, 2*), attesting mid-twentieth-century technical usage, the number of English borrowings is considerable. There are no statistical counts of these borrowings. From a linguistic point of view, this lexicon has shortcomings in that it gives no hint to pronunciation and only occasionally mentions grammatical features, such as the plural of nouns.

An obvious development in the last decade is the re-Anglicization of the pronunciation and the spelling of some earlier borrowings (see ss. 9.2.1 and 9.2.2).

9.1.8 Mediating languages

In the past, Anglicisms were often not borrowed straight from English but were transmitted via another language. French was the most important mediating language handing on words like *beefsteak*, *budget*, *jury*, *riding coat*, and *wagon* which are now fully adapted as *biftec*, *buget*, *juriu*, *redingotă*, and *vagon*. There are Anglicisms with several spelling and pronunciation variants which attest that the word entered Romanian via French and again straight from English: *bluf* [blœf], *flirt* [flœt], *joule* [ʒul] were taken from French, while *bluf* [blaf], [flirt / flə:t], *joule* [dʒul] are variants borrowed directly. German also served as a transmitter of English terms. The English words *coke(s)* and *drops* entered Romanian via German and have become *cocs* and *drops(uri)*. A few English words entered Romanian via Russian, e.g. *conveier* and *screper* from E *conveyer* and *scraper*.

The theory of *multiple etymology* put forward by Graur in 1950 was developed and refined by Th. Hristea, Al. Rosetti, Iorgu Iordan, Ion Coteanu, Marius Sala, and other linguists in successive articles and studies (see Hristea 1968: 103–8; Coteanu and Sala 1987). The Romanian vocabulary underwent many foreign influences, some of which exerted themselves simultaneously, converging on the same results. A word borrowed from two or more different sources almost at the same period is considered a word of multiple etymology. The first attestations of many neologisms in Romanian are undocumented, and this has given additional weight to the theory of multiple etymology in the great dictionaries of the last half of the century.

In consequence, many words such as *campus*, *compost*, *manager*, *memorial*, *modul*, *monorai*, *optimiza*, *pachebot*, *placebo*, *prospecta*, *stagflaţie*, *stress*, and *video* are presented in dictionaries as coming from several mediating languages (French, Italian, German, and English) without any differentiation between these and the original language. Most of these are coined from Latin and Greek elements, and are therefore not 'felt' as 'English'. Florica Dimitrescu (1995: 257) counted the borrowed Roman neologisms coined in French and English respectively, using the lexical inventory of *DCR* (Dimitrescu 1982) as the basis of her statistics. According to her count, 19.3 per cent of the Romance neologisms borrowed by Romanian are of French and 12.3 per cent are of English origin. The figures reflect the borrowing trends of the period 1960–80.

Sometimes lexicographic works mark the last etymologic link and not the original source. It is therefore difficult to make statistical estimates of the English element on the basis of the dictionaries. For instance in *DEX2* some of the words mentioned above appear as borrowings from French (*biftec*, *buget*, *juriu*, *redingotă*, *vagon*, with no reference to English); German (*cocs*, *drops*, with no reference to English); and English/Russian (*conveier*, *screper*).

9.1.9 English in education

As a result of the growing and diversifying interest of Romanians in the English-speaking world (in the fields of literature, politics, technologies, sports, films, etc.), English studies were introduced in the university curriculum: in 1917, Ioan Botez of the University of Jassy, who held a doctor's degree from University College London, started the teaching of English literature in Romania. In 1925, his professorship was changed into a Chair of English Language and Literature. Petre Grimm initiated a seminar in English studies at the University of Cluj in 1921. Several years later, in 1936, a Chair of English was inaugurated also in Bucharest.

As elsewhere in Europe, teaching focused on British English in the first period. The teaching of English in schools has been optional and in competition with other widely spoken European languages: mainly French and German. In the 1950s Russian became an obligatory part of the curriculum in all secondary schools. There was a greater number of teachers of French and of German than of English. All this made English less available even if desired. The situation gradually changed in the next decades, so that towards the end of the 1980s English was coming close to French statistically.

9.2 Pronunciation and spelling

The pronunciation of Anglicisms in Romanian is a complex problem. It has attracted the attention of at least two categories of linguists: those who write normative or prescriptive works and those who are interested in describing the facts as a case of language contact without trying to influence usage.

Being familiar with a phonetic (phonemic) spelling system, Romanians are often puzzled when confronted with the less predictable sound–letter relationships of English. To solve the problem without violating Romanian equivalences two strategies are possible: retaining the English spelling, but reading the words in a Romanian way, or rendering the English pronunciation as closely as permitted by the phonemic inventory of Romanian (i.e. transphonemization). Neither of these solutions was adopted with consistency. English borrowings in Romanian reveal a variety of compromises between the two strategies. Vacillation in the treatment of Anglicisms has resulted not only in diachronic variation (as a sign of gradual integration) but also in synchronic variants. It seems that the greater the number of 'connoisseurs', the longer the borrowings maintain their alien peculiarities.

Words coined in English from Latin or Greek elements are never pronounced in Romanian according to English patterns, but are assimilated, by analogy, to well-established phonetic models in keeping with the specific letter–sound correspondences of Romanian.

9.2.1 Pronunciation

(Ciobanu 1983, 1991; Chiţoran, Augerot, and Pârlog [n.d.]; Chiţoran 1986)

When discussing English borrowings and the spoken form they acquire in Romanian, one should start from the structural differences between the sound systems of the two languages in order to account for the transphonemization process.

These differences have been analysed by a number of phoneticians (V. Ştefănescu Drăgăneşti, A. Tătaru, A. Hartular, G. Ciobanu) who have published their conclusions in academic journals or in publications devoted exclusively to English studies. The series of publications that materialized (from 1971 to 1978) in what is referred to as *RECAP* (Chiţoran, Augerot, and Pârlog n.d.) is also worth mentioning.

9.2.1.1 Vowel systems

There are seven vowels in Romanian and twelve monophthong vowel phonemes in English. Whereas in English vowels are [±long] depending on the value they have for the feature [±tense], all Romanian vowels are [−long] and [+tense]. According to Vasiliu (1965), the main distinctive oppositions in the Romanian vowel system are [±front], [±central], [±open], [±close].

With the exception of [ɨ], each Romanian vowel corresponds to two English vowels within the same 'phonetic space', i.e.:

Romanian [i] ~ E [iː] and [ɪ]
Romanian [e] ~ E [e] and [æ]
Romanian [a] ~ E [ʌ] and [ɑː]
Romanian [u] ~ E [uː] and [ʊ]
Romanian [o] ~ E [ɔ] and [ɔː]
Romanian [ə] ~ E [ɜː] and [ə]

9.2.1.2 Diphthongs

In spite of a number of qualitative differences (regarding their nuclei or the articulation of their final glides) there are Romanian diphthongs close enough to the English to identify loanwords:

[ej] for E [eɪ] in [plejboj]
[aj] for E [aɪ] in [dizajn]
[aw] for E [aʊ] and [oj] for E [ɔɪ]—in [kawboj]
[ow] for E [əʊ] in [ʃow]

An interesting recent development is that diphthongs occurring in Anglicisms are no longer reduced when situated in medial position (E *game*, *ghem* [gem] now replaced by [gejm]), nor are they decomposed into two vocalic elements according to a distributional constraint specific to Romanian for interconsonantal position (E *safe* [se-if] > [sejf]; the diphthongized form tends to replace also the older variant [sef]).

The centring English diphthongs [ɪə, ɛə, ʊə] are all monophthongized in the borrowed words, because there are no equivalents in Romanian (*clearing* = *cliring* [kliriŋg], *fairplay* = [ferplej], E *tourism* = *turism* [turism]).

9.2.1.3 Consonant systems

The consonant inventories of English and Romanian are similar, both in the number of phonemes and in their phonetic realizations. Transfer from one system to the other is therefore relatively straightforward.

Stops and most fricatives pose no problem with the exception of interdental fricatives [Φ, ð]; they are replaced by [t] or [s] (*fathom* [fatom]; *thriller* [srilər/trilər]). [r] is rendered in Romanian by a corresponding rolled alveolar liquid, pronounced also in final and preconsonantal positions. BrE [l] is also easily adapted to Romanian pronunciation, although phonetic details may differ. Velarization in final or preconsonantal position is rarer and its syllabic function in certain contexts is blocked: Romanian phonotactics require a vowel to be appended to word-final [l] preceded by a consonant (as in English *dribble*, Romanian *dribla* [dribla]).

The semivowels [j, w] are fairly similar in the two languages. When [w] is represented in writing by <w>, this is often pronounced as [v] (by analogy with German words).

Distributional characteristics of sounds in the two languages differ particularly with respect to the nature of consonant clusters (Chițoran, Augerot, and Pârlog n.d.; Chițoran 1986). Such differences require either some modifications in the nature or position of sounds in order to comply with Romanian patterns, or the introduction of new clusters. As yet the number of English loanwords containing such specific clusters is too small to allow regular patterns to be discerned.

9.2.1.4 Stress

A great number of English borrowings are monosyllabic, and therefore pose no problem. In the corpus considered by Ciobanu (1983) they represented 25 per cent of the total. Because accent is mobile in Romanian, there is a readiness in the speakers to accept new accentual patterns. According to Ciobanu, some 50 per cent of the Anglicisms are taken over with their English stress pattern whether their pronunciation is indicated in various Romanian dictionaries or not.

9.2.2 Graphemic integration

Some English loanwords have developed integrated graphemic forms, others are still used with their original spelling. Recent borrowings maintain their form even if breaking Romanian spelling rules. Moreover, older borrowings, integrated a few decades ago, are now re-Anglicized in spite of recommendations found in dictionaries and articles on correctness. Consequently many orthographic variants are in use.

Fully integrated Anglicisms are written and pronounced alike by all speakers, in keeping with Romanian orthoepic rules: *baril, hol, lider, meci, miting, șut*, etc.

Words like *aisberg, bobslei, bodicec, futbol, gem, golgeter, *hailaif* (now a deviant variant), *ofsaid, scheci, scuter, snec, șoc*, etc. are pronounced (approximately) like their etymons, *iceberg, bobsleigh, bodycheck, football, jam, goalgetter, highlife, offside, sketch, scooter, snack, shock*. Many of them have variants, either deviant or obsolete.

Romanian uses diacritical marks with the following letters <ș> [ʃ], <ț> [ts], <ă> [ə]—and <â; î> [ɨ] which does not, however, occur in English loanwords. The letters <k>, <w>, and <y> are found mainly in foreign words (see below).

The sound values of Romanian letters result in the following regular adaptations:

1. Romanian <ș> renders the E <sh> in any position: *finiș* < E *finish*; *flaș* < E *flash*; *șampon* < E *shampoo*; *șut* < E *shoot*; *șerif* < E *sheriff*; *șiling* < E

shilling; *şoc* < E *shock*; *şort* < E *shorts*. But note retention of <sh> in: *shetland*, *shop*, *shopping*, *show*, *T-Shirt*.

2. Romanian <ţ> renders E <ds>: *henţ* < *hands*

3. <ă> at the end of a noun is the grammatical morpheme indicating feminine singular. Therefore the *-ă* of some Anglicisms is a sign of morphological integration: *draglină* from *dragline*; *gigă* from E *gig*; *nursă* from *nurse*; *padelă* from *paddle*; *ială* from *yale*; *pasă* from *pass*, etc.

4. Romanian <c> renders E <k> or <ck> in any position, as in *brec* from *break*, *coca* from *coke*, *cnocaut* from *knockout*, *folclor* from *folklore*, *padoc* from *paddock*. By contrast, <(c)k> is retained in *folk*, *know how*, *o.k.*, *snack(s)-uri*, *sticksuri*.

5. Romanian <v> sometimes renders English <w> by analogy with its value in German words. Substitution: *bovindou* from *bow window*; *tramvai* from *tramway*; *sandviş* from *sandwich*; in *clovn* from E *clown* the grapheme was transliterated ignoring its phonetic value. Coexistence: *whisky* vs. *vizichi* (non-standard variant). Retention: *chewing gum*, *far west*, *week end*, *western*.

6. Romanian <u> renders English <w>, possibly influenced by the pronunciation (spelling integration). Thus substitution (as in *ciungă*, considered a deviant variant of *chewing gum*), *bovindou* from *bow window*, *interviu* from *interview*) vs. retention (*clown*—a variant used but not accepted by the normative works).

7. Romanian <i> renders English <y>, thus substitution (*derbi* from *derby*, *iard* from *yard*, *penalti* from *penalty*) vs. coexistence (*bebi/baby*, *iac/yac*, *iaht/yacht*, *iahting/yachting*, *iahtman/yachtman*, *ială/yală* from *yale (lock)*) and (retention *yankeu* from *yankee*, *yearling*, *yeoman*, *yes-man*, etc.).

There is a tendency to re-Anglicize many of the words in which English <y> was in the past replaced by <i>. In journalese we find *derby*, *penalty*, *baby*, etc. more and more frequently, showing a preference for <y>, especially in final position.

Other cases of graphematic integration:

8. Romanian <h> renders English <ch>. Coexistence: *iaht* (the standard form)/*yacht*, *iahting/yachting*, *iahtman/yachtman*.

9. Deletion of <e> inside the word in order to avoid its being pronounced: *forhand*, *forpic*.

10. Deletion of any letter or any group of letters that lack phonetic value: *bobslei* from *bobsleigh*, *bodigard* from *bodyguard*.

11. Double consonants. Reduction: *budincă* from *pudding*, *dolar*, *dres*, *dribling*, *foxterier*, *galon*, *ofsaid* (< E *offside*), *presing*, *scaner*, *schif* (< E *skiff*), *tobogan*, etc. Retention: *flipper*, *jogging*, *lobby*, *setter*, *terrier*, etc. Re-Anglicizing: *jaz*, now *jazz*.

12. Romanian <che> renders the English <ke> or <cke> groups. Substitution: *baschet*, *chec*, *marcher*, *pachebot* (*packet boat*), *pocher*, *scheci* (*sketch*), etc. Coexistence: *jocheu/jockey*. Retention: *cracker*, *yankeu* from *yankee*.

13. Romanian <chi> renders the English <ki>, <key>, or <ky> groups. Substitution: *moleschin, parching, schif, smoching, vizichi* 'whisky' (facetious variant).
14. Romanian <ghe> renders the English <ge> [ge] group: *golgheter* from *goal getter*.
15. Romanian <ghi> renders the English <gi> [gi] group. Coexistence: *yoghin/ yogin* from *yogi*.
16. Romanian <ci> or <ce> renders the English <(t)ch(i)>, <ch(a)>, or the <(t)che> group. Substitution: *cengi* (slang variant) from *change, bodicec* from *bodycheck, dispecer* from *dispatcher, meci* from *match, scheci* from *sketch*. Retention: *chip* [tʃip] used in computer science (homograph of Rm *chip* [kʹip] 'face'), *scotch* from E *Scotch Tape, thatcherism*.
17. Romanian <ge> or <gi> renders the English <j> or <g> [dʒ]. Substitution: *geacă* or *giacă* (corrupt form) from *jacket, cengi moni* (corrupt form) from *change money, gem* from *jam, gigă* from *jig*. Retention: *jokey, jogging, joint, judo*.

It is worth mentioning that some of the examples under 'Coexistence' and 'Retention' are semantically justified. They are commercial names, names of breeds, derivatives from proper names (cf. *thatcherism*), names of exotic sports (cf. *judo, yoga*), foreignisms relating to Anglo-American realities (cf. *yankeu, yeoman, western*), etc.

Often the hyphen links inflexions to neologisms whose original form has not changed, as in *singles-ul* (singular) and *singles-uri* (plural), *slang-ul, design-ul, workshop-uri*, etc.

A diachronic analysis reveals several stages of graphematic integration. *Derby* was spelt *derby* in 1937 and *derbi* in 1958, *dribling* was the form in 1921 and *dribbling* in 1937, *forehand* in 1939 and *forhand* in 1958, *knock out* in 1934, *knock-auta* in 1937, and *cnocauta* in 1958.

Romanian has still many vacillations of spelling, sometimes conflicting with forms recommended in dictionaries and normative works.

9.3 Morphology

9.3.1 Introduction

Romanian inflects for case, number (and gender) in nouns, adjectives, pronouns, and articles, and for person, number, tense, and mood (by means of specific morphemes) in verbs.

The main difficulties of Romanian morphology in comparison to other Romance languages lie in the positioning of the definite article after the noun and the existence of three genders. Loanwords are integrated into the Romanian morphological system over a variable period of time; this period is nowadays short for Latin and neo-Latin loanwords, because equivalent paradigms exist. In the case of Anglicisms this period is longer. Some Anglicisms are uninflected; in others, gender attribution and the addition of plural morpheme and the definite article to the noun can be difficult (*show* with the definite article *show-ul* 'the show', pl. *show-uri*; *rocker*, pl. *rocker-i* 1970, *rockeri* 1990s).

9.3.2 Nouns

(Băncilă/Chiţoran 1976, 1982; Pârlog 1983; Avram 1997)

The majority of English loanwords in Romanian are nouns. Their integration presents problems in four respects:

(*a*) *Gender*. There are three genders in Romanian. Of these the neuter (which some authors call *ambigen*) does not have its own paradigm, but uses a combination of the masculine paradigm in the singular and the feminine in the plural (Table 9.1)

Gender allocation is semantically predictable: for animate nouns, grammatical gender generally corresponds to the natural gender. Inanimate nouns, especially neologisms, are often neuter, but there are also many cases of inanimate nouns integrated into the masculine or feminine paradigms. Approximately 70 per cent of all Romanian Anglicisms are neuter, 21 per cent masculine, and only 6 per cent feminine; this result is not surprising, considering the much higher frequency of Anglicisms with inanimate reference. Gender attribution is well illustrated by *-er* words: *dispecer*, *designer*, *punker*, *rocker*, *spicher* are masculine (because they name people); by contrast, *mixer* (the tool), *pager*, *scan(n)er* and *sveter* are neuter.

In cases where animateness is not decisive, the choice depends on:

1. analogies with indigenous synonyms: *hot dog* M after *cârnat* 'sausage'; *Jonathan* (*freckle*) > *ionatan* N (after *măr* 'apple').
2. (in compounds) the gender of the second element: *sex-simbol*, *top-model* are neuter (after *simbol*, *model*), although they designate females. In these cases syntactic difficulties appear: *top-model* can appear in the singular in some

Table 9.1.

Gender	Sing.	Plural	Example
Masc.	cons.	-i [ⁱ]	*pom/pomi* 'tree'
	-e	-i [ⁱ]	*câine/câini* 'dog'
	-i [j]	-i [j]	*ardei/ardei* 'red pepper'
Fem.	-ă [ə]	-e	*casă/case* 'house'
	-e	-i [ⁱ]	*mare/mări* 'sea'
	-ă [ə]	-i [ⁱ]	*gară/gări* 'station'
	-a [a]	-le	*stea/stele* 'star'
	vocal	-uri [urⁱ]	*mătase/mătăsuri* 'silk'
Neuter	cons / -u [w]	-uri [urⁱ]	*loc/locuri* 'place'
			birou/birouri 'desk'
	cons	-e	*scaun/scaune* 'chair'

contexts with a masculine adjective (according to its grammatical neuter gender) or with a feminine, according to its natural gender.

3. phonetic analogies: *pijama* F (via French, but with a change in gender from French M) after the model of feminines ending in *-a*.

With some recent loanwords the gender has not yet been fixed. The identity of M = N in the singular, and F = N in the plural leads to some oscillation between M and N (sg. *pampers*, pl. *pamperşi* (M)/*pampersuri* (N)), or F and N (*party*, pl. *partyuri*, sg. *o party* (F) or *un party* (N); *un story* (N)/*o story* (F), but with the postposed definite article only N: *story-ul*).

(*b*) *Number* (Avram 1975). Romanian denotes singular and plural by means of specific inflections (the most frequent combinations are listed in Table 9.1). The use of *-i* for the plural M (less often F) actually indicates the palatalization of the previous consonant or consonant group; in the case of these plurals Romanian has an allomorph for the 'stem-morpheme', specifically for the plural: *copac* [kopak] 'tree', pl. *copaci* [kopatʃⁱ]; *bărbat* [bərbat] 'man', pl. *bărbaţi* [bərbatsⁱ].

Most masculine Anglicisms are inflected on *-i* showing typical Romanian palatalization: *bos(s)* [=E], pl. *boşi* [boʃⁱ]; *bodigard* [=E], pl. *bodygarzi*, [bodigarzⁱ]; *steward* [=E], pl. *stewarzi* [stjuarzⁱ]; *box* (a variant on *boxer* 'dog'), pl. *bocşi* [bokʃⁱ], *rapper*, pl. *rapperi* [repərⁱ]; *outsider* [awtsajder], pl. *outsideri* [awtsajderⁱ].

Masculine nouns on *-man* often show the characteristics of written transmission: they retain *-man* in the singular and *-men* in the plural. The age of the loanwords and their register generally determine their degree of integration. Old or frequent words are adapted: **wattman*, a pseudo-Anglicism from French, gave *vatman*, pl. *vatmani* [vatman̲ⁱ]; and *barman*, pl. *barmani* [ba̲rmañⁱ]. More recent loanwords which are also restricted (at least in the beginning) to 'high' registers are recognizable by their double plural: *businessman*, pl. *businessmeni*; *gag man* > *gagman*, pl. *gagmeni*; **tenisman* (pseudo-Anglicism), pl. *tenismeni*. Masculine nouns which in the singular end in *-y* tend to remain unchanged, according to the Romanian model found in *ardei*: *cow-boy*, *dandy*, *disk jockey*, *penny*, *playboy*, all have Ø plural. For *hippy* (variant sg. *hipi*) the plural is usually *hipi*—but *Hippy* is also quoted as the noun with several plural forms.

Nouns classified as feminines normally have the typical inflexions added: E *stewardess* > *stewardesă* [stjuarde̲sə], pl. *stewardese* [stjuardese]; *pyjamas* > *pijama* [piʒama̲], pl. *pijamale* [piʒama̲le]. In cases of incomplete adaptation the plural can remain unchanged (*lady*, pl. *lady*) or the inflection is supplied from other classes (*miss*, pl. *miss-uri*, although *-uri* is neuter; the hyphen generally denotes incomplete adaptation).

Neuter nouns, as already shown under gender, are pluralized in *-uri* or *-e*, *-uri* being preferred for neologisms: *hall* > *hol*, pl. *holuri*; *job*, pl. *joburi*; *lift* 'elevator', pl. *lifturi*; *offside* > *ofsaid*, pl. *ofsaiduri*; *punch* 'drink' > *punci*, pl. *punciuri*; *safe* > *seif*, pl. *seifuri*; less frequent words, especially those not adapted graphically, have *-uri* hyphenated: *remake*, pl. *remake-uri*; *show*, *show-uri*.

It seems that *-e* is preferred for neuters ending in *-r*: *mixer*, pl. *mixere*; *pager*, pl. *pagere*; *sweater* > *sveter*, pl. *svetere*; *monitor*, pl. *monitoare* (with regular alternation *-o-/-oa-*). After other consonants, the choice of the plural inflection is analogous: *Jonathan* (*freckle*) > *ionatan*, pl. *ionatane* after *măr*, pl. *mere*.

Romanian has no plural in *-s*. Therefore, *-s* in masculine and neuter nouns indicates incomplete adaptation: *skinhead*, pl. *skinheads* M, *(Negro) spiritual* 'religious folksong', pl. *(Negro) spirituals* N. Plural *-s* tends to be replaced by the normal plural: *hot dog* [=E], pl. *hot dogs* [=E], recently also *hot dogi* [hɔtdodʒʲ]; *hippy*, pl. *hipis*, *hippies* [=E], but also *hipişi* [hipiʃʲ].

A certain number of English plurals were perceived as singulars: *drops* 'sweet' > *drops* sg., pl. *dropsuri*; *sticks* sg. 'salty biscuit' > pl. *sticksuri*. New singulars like *sticks* have been created; this is also true for *jeans* (M sg.) with the more frequent plural *jeanşi* (cf. *bos(s)*, pl. *boşi*); *comics* (N sg.), pl. *comicsuri*. Another possibility is the creation of a new Romanian sg. through backformation as in *shorts* > *şort*, pl. *şorturi* (N).

(*c*) *Case*. Gender-specific inflections are added as in native words; however, if the noun is considered foreign, the inflexion is hyphenated: *boss*, genitive *boss-ului*.

(*d*) *Definite article*. The definite article is placed after the noun with which it forms a common body. Adapted Anglicisms add the definite article without any restrictions: *managerul*, pl. *managerii* M, *stewardesa*, pl. *stewardesele* F, *computer-ul*, pl. *computerele* N. The selection of an article is restricted in some cases probably for phonetic reasons: *un/o story* (indefinite article M/F) but only *story-ul* (definite article M = N).

9.3.3 Adjectives

Romanian has taken relatively few adjectives from English. These remain generally uninflected: examples are *live*, *non(-)stop*, *sexy*, *shocking* (a small class of uninflected native adjectives exists). Adjectives used attributively normally follow the noun (*o rochie sexy*, 'a sexy dress'). Unchanged adjectives can also be used predicatively (*rochia ei e sexy*, 'her dress is sexy'). English nouns used attributively are also sometimes added to Romanian nouns (*comportament fair-play*, *acordul stand-by*).

9.3.4 Adverbs

Romanian adverbs are formally identical with adjectives. No English loanwords in *-ly* are attested.

9.3.5 Verbs

Romanian differentiates between four conjugations (following the Latin *-āre*, *-ēre*, *-ĕre*, *-īre* classes), of which the first (Rm *-a* with two subgroups) and the fourth (Rm *-i*, *-î*, with different subgroups) are productive. Verbs of English origin are almost entirely integrated into the first conjugation, infixing *-ez(-)* in the indicative and the subjunctive as in *to dope* > *a dopa*, *eu dopez*; *to mix* > *a mixa*, *eu mixez*; *to shoot* > *a şuta*, *eu şutez*.

9.3.6 Derivation

(Avram 1997)

Gender specification. It is obligatory in Romanian to mark the feminine forms of personal nouns, most often by the suffix *-ă* (*student: studentă*), corresponding to adjectives (*bun: bună*) and adjectival participles (*văzut: văzută*). This usually also applies to Anglicisms (*dispecer: dispeceră; lider: lideră; snob: snoabă; sprinter: sprinteră; handicapat: handicapată*).

A second suffix *-iţă* is especially frequent in colloquial language (*barman: bărmăniţă; disk jockey: disk jockeiţă; spicher: spicheriţă; vatman: vătmăniţă*; for some words both feminine forms coexist (*barmană/bărmăniţă*).

Diminutives. The addition of the frequently used diminutive suffix *-aş* indicates that an Anglicism is old and adapted: *dollar > dolar → dolăraş; poker > pocher → pocheraş; reporter* (via Fr/Ge) → *reporteraş*.

Agent nouns. Denominal agent nouns are commonly derived by *-ist*: *monotype* > Romanian *monotip → monotipist; hard* (= *hardware*) → *hardist; soft* (= *software*) → *softist; bridge → bridgist; rugby, rugbi → rugbist*. The suffix *-ar* [ar], normally used for native denominal agent nouns, is less frequent in Anglicisms; it is found most often in adoptions from colloquial Romanian: English *snack > snack → snecar*; English *business > bişniţă → bişniţar*.

Unstressed *-er* as in *rocker* is untypical for Romanian. Stress on *-er* indicates an adoption from or via French, as in > *docher* from English *docker*. Unstressed *-er* in names for technical instruments appears adapted as *-or*, influenced by the Romanian suffix *-or* (used initially in French loanwords): E *digitizer > digitizor* [didʒitizor]; *economizer > economizor* [ekonomizor].

Deverbal nouns. The normal procedure in Romanian, which also applies to Anglicisms, is the addition of a feminine ending in *-re*, cf. E *randomize > randomiza → randomizare* ('distribution of data by random process').

Denominal verbs. Most recent denominal verbs are integrated into the first conjugation (ending in *-a*): *bodycheck > bodicec → bodiceca; bodyguard > bodygard → bodygarda*. With this type of derivation, it is sometimes difficult to tell whether the verb is formed in Romanian or borrowed: *sprint > sprinta*. The suffix *-iza* is also used frequently: *sponsor → sponsoriza*. To select the fourth conjugation in recent words can indicate an ironic intention: *meeting > miting → a mitingi; business > bişniţă → bişniţar → bişniţări*.

New adjectives. These are formed by adding the suffix *-esc* (*gangster → gangsteresc*) with the variant *-icesc* (*reporter → reportericesc*), *-istic* (*fotbal → fotbalistic; rugby, rugbi → rugbistic*).

The very few adjectives that are borrowed from English have not derived any deadjectival nouns. Theoretically they can be used as nouns without a suffix added.

9.3.7 Compounds and combining forms

Word compounding in Romanian is less important than derivation; native compounds normally have the order *determinatum + determinans*: *floarea-soarelui* 'sunflower'. The reverse sequence of English has apparently started to influence

Romanian word structure, especially within company names (*Student-Club*, *Nord-Hotel*) which has given rise to hybrid compounds as in *-gate*: *Andagate* (see s. 9.1.6), *Safi-gate* 'scandal about the Safi bank' (both rare and facetious).

9.3.8 Calques

As a consequence of native word structure, among the various types of calques the number of renditions exceeds by far the number of loan translations (see s.9.6):

renditions: *creier electronic* (rendering 'electronic brain'), *laborator de limbă* ('language laboratory'), *navă spaţială* ('spaceship'), *politică de mare putere* ('big power politics'), *rachete de croazieră* ('cruise missiles'), *sfârşit de săptămână* ('weekend'), *universitate deschisă* ('open university'), as against

loan translation: *cercetare şi dezvoltare* ('research and development'), *numără-toare inversă* ('count down').

9.4 Meaning

The loanwords most likely to retain their original meaning are technical terms, *henry*, *laser* (phys.), *hogback* (geol.) or *Dixie* (jazz), and monosemous words, such as *motel*, *pulover*, *skinhead*, *tramvai*.

Narrowing of meaning(s) is found in *baril* (from *barrel*) which is used only in relation to crude oil; *drink* means only 'strong drink' (a case of apheresis); *event* is used in Romanian only in relation to sports contests (mainly horse races), etc.

By contrast, an *extension of meaning* is found in *bar* which has acquired the meanings 'night club', 'bar room', 'hotel bar', 'pub', 'drink cabinet'. A case apart in the process of meaning extension is that of 'false friends'.

Tricky resemblances occur especially in the case of words of Romance and Latin descent. Most of the mistranslations ridiculed some thirty years ago are now in wide circulation (and some accepted as new meanings in recent Romanian diction-aries). Thus, *aplicaţie* borrowed the English meaning of 'formal request', *audienţă* acquired the English meaning of 'assembled listeners, spectators at an event, performance, concert etc.', *contacta* (v.) 'get into communication with a person', *departament* 'a branch of study and its administration at a university, school etc.', *oportunitate* 'favourable occasion', *rezoluţie* 'firmness', *realiza* 'to understand', and *suport* 'help or countenance'. The most comprehensive description of English and Romanian deceptive cognates is by Iarovici and Mihăilă (1970, 1979). Their contrastive dictionary is a systematic classification of English–Romanian equiva-lences based on the analysis of distinctive semantic features. Of the two subgroups, completely deceptive and partly deceptive cognates, the latter favours semantic loans as a consequence of frequent mistranslations. This problem made Romanian teachers of English devise 'cautioning works' devoted to this aspect (cf. Bantaş and Rădulescu 1967).

Pleonastic combinations are frequent in journalese and in speech: *pâine tost*, *bord de conducere*, *minge de baseball*, *femeie vamp*, *mijloace mass-media*, *thriller îngrozitor* (*pâine* 'bread', *de conducere* 'leading', *minge* 'ball', *femeie* 'woman', *mijloace* 'means', *îngrozitor* 'terrifying'). This unsurprising semantic accident occurs mainly with fashionable neologisms.

Hybrid phrases containing an Anglicism like *din start, a dribla pe cineva, a prinde în ofsaid, a fi out, a se purtala fi fair-play, a şunta pe cineva, a bypassa pe cineva, a face fifty-fifty, a fi full, a fi groggy, a fi dizzy, a fi tip-top*, etc. prove the integration of the Anglicism in the receiving language. Many of these phrases were originally used in sports or technical languages. Their double character—native and neological—marks them stylistically. They tend to be restricted to colloquial Romanian.

Elaboration of the semantic paradigm of an Anglicism. Often the acceptance of a term into a foreign language engenders the partial completion of its lexical field. For example, Romanian has first accepted *human rights* and later *animal rights, politically correct* and then *religiously correct, superman* and *superstar*, and afterwards *superworker, superleader, superwoman*. Usually the connections between the items of a lexical field are attributable formally to the lexical item which all the members of the field share and to a certain ideology or a cultural movement.

Clichés. English is now also making an important contribution in disseminating clichés or catch phrases (used both in their original form and translated): *angry young men* translated as *tineri furioşi, far from the madding crowd* as *departe de lumea dezlănţuită, last but not least* as *ultimul dar nu cel din urmă, looking back in anger* as *privind înapoi cu mânie*, and *vanity fair* as *bâlciul deşertăciunilor*.

9.5 Usage

The social, cultural, and pragmatic factors that influence Romanian usage are very similar to those in other parts of Europe. The speech of young, educated persons living in urban areas contains more Anglicisms than that of elderly inhabitants with less schooling who live in rural communities. Journalese and to a certain extent also standard Romanian are characterized by a great number of phonetically and morphologically unadapted Anglicisms, called by some researchers 'luxury' or 'futile' borrowings (Stoichiţoiu 1993).

Romanian has been considered a 'hospitable' language. It also needs to fill some terminological gaps, and is thus ready to accept foreignisms. It is a language spoken by a society in transition, facing new realities such as market economy, technological updating, and changes in cultural outlook. It is thus not surprising that the most immediate reflection of new realities is found in specialized terminologies, in journalese, and in youth language.

In computer science Anglicisms are being felt as a necessity. They result in what is jocularly called *româneză* (a blend of *român(ă)* + *(engl)eză* 'Romanian + English', the Romanian equivalent of *franglais*)—a jargon in which the neologism is preferred to the native word (e.g. *enter, field, mouse, level, user, print* instead of their translations). There is a pragmatic need for precision, which favours the use of the English term. The language of computer technology abounds in fashionable neologisms or calques such as *hacker* or *pirat, cyberspace* or *ciberspaţiu, net* or *reţea*, *virus*, *realitate virtuală*, *utilizator*. Moreover, if we survey its evolution at the level of spoken technical slang used by engineers and then examine the language of the technical magazines or the language of advertisements, we discover that the rate of foreignisms does not decrease. At the same time the linguistic phenomenon of adaptation is at work. Often Romanian has a certain difficulty in rendering the English verbs: thus *to click* was first rendered by *a da/face (un) click*, and afterwards the derivative *a clicăi*; for the English *to print*, Romanian coined the verbal phrases *a da/face/scoate un print* which are now competing with the verbal derivative *a printa*; for *to enter*, Romanian coined the phrase *a da (un) enter* and for *to zoom*, *a da/face (un) zoom*. In general the tendency is to prefer the verbal phrase with the verbs *a da* and *a face* instead of the verbal derivative which often has a facetious or slangy connotation.

New foreign cultural models and visible imports come with their own terminology: from *fast food* to *pay TV* and *video*, from *teleshopping* to *NGO*, from *hot line* to *business administration*, from *body building* to *exit poll*, *melting pot*, and *politically correct*. Romanian society speaks about 'integration into European standards', 'entering European structures', 'Euro-optimism' and 'Euro-scepticism', etc. In this context and linguistic register, the adaptation of Anglicisms is not a priority—it is even avoided by some users. The original form of the word is seen as a guarantee of conceptual accuracy and as a sign of the internationalization of the Romanian vocabulary. Not all of the unadapted neologisms are felt as 'strikingly foreign'. In many cases the English form is preserved unchanged because it is considered technically necessary, fashionable, or international. There is, then, nowadays a readiness of speakers for the *tale quale* acceptance of Anglicisms. The rejection of newly entered Anglicisms is perceived as a manifestation of self-isolation or of cultural provincialism.

Less evident is the situation regarding the jargon of drug addicts. The social phenomenon itself is of recent date, its hidden and underground nature hinder the overt spread of drug-related terms, and for the same reason the lexis is difficult to study.

A noticeable development during the last decades has been the parallel influence of English and French (sometimes in favour of the former, especially among the young). A number of doublets (or even triplets) are registered. So, we have *cherie* (from French) and *darling/baby/honey*; *şic* and *tip-top*; *au revoir* and *(bye-)bye!*; *alo!* (starting a telephone conversation) and *hello* (starting a conversation *hic et hoc*); *imprimantă* and *printer*; *ordinator*, *computer*, and *calculator* (probably from French) which, though inappropriate for naming a computer, is nevertheless frequently used. Also compare *miniordinator* and *minicalculator* in comparison with *minicomputer*. In children's talk we hear the interjections *uau!* (probably *wow!* frequent in cartoons) and *oh, non!* [o:non] (jocular) (from French *oh, non!*).

Young employees use *O.K., boss!* (alongside the hybrid *O.K., şefu'!*) and pleonastic and hybrid formulas such as *O.K., s-a făcut!*, *O.K., e-n regulă!*, and the hybrid *totul e O.K.* ('everything is OK'). The frequent use of *O.K.* resulted in the jocular derivative noun *O.K.-ist* 'a highly conformist person'.

English influence may be traced also in the names of companies, restaurants, snack bars, shops, boutiques, sports clubs (e.g. *Sporting Club Bucureşti*, *AdTech*

(= *Advanced Technology*), *Cybernet, Romteam Solutions, Romus Industries, Ana Electronic, General Store, Fan Club, Beauty Salon, Saloon, Hermes City, Refreshing Icecream, O.K. Dolly*, and many more). Borrowing American/British terms for specific cultural items is looked upon as a good omen.

Besides synonymic richness (sometimes approaching the brink of inflation (see s.9.1.6) mutations are noticeable also in semantics. An important role is played by 'false friends' (see s.9.4); the frequency of such words increases through taking over meanings from their English equivalents. Age, profession, and other social factors influence the attitude of speakers to semantic borrowing. Knowledge of English is indeed important in that it enhances awareness of semantic pitfalls.

The jocular English-like pronunciation of the Romanian words *complicaţie, instalaţie, combinaţie* is to be found in colloquial/familiar speech, in youth language, in journalese or satirical literature (as *complicheişăn, instaleişăn, combineişăn*). The noun *asculteităr* was coined for 'a person spying on a telephone conversation' (Avram 1997). In the last century a similar reaction served to ridicule the exaggerated uses of French borrowings.

In conclusion, at the end of the twentieth century, traditional Romanian Francophilia is rivalled by an unprecedented Anglophilia.

9.6 Forms of linguistic borrowing and their categorization

(Hristea 1968; Bantaş 1977; Avram 1997)

The influence of English has been mediated through educated people or at least people who have a certain knowledge of English. This has resulted in a slow-down of the adaptation process. Many Anglicisms retain their 'strikingly foreign' form even in the normative works on the Romanian language. The evolution from the stage of unadapted neologisms, through that of incompletely adapted words, to that of totally adapted items is a partially controlled, diachronic process. This does not depend solely on the longevity of the word and on the linguistic channel through which it entered, but also on a number of social, pragmatic, and historical parameters.

I. *Borrowing*

(*a*) Totally unadapted and not felt to be a part of Romanian.

Quotation words: *to be or not to be, time is money*, with the antonymic variant *money is time, put a smile on your face it's so nice to be happy* (refrain sung at social manifestations of protest in 1990), *touch the screen*, the hippy slogan *make love not war*, etc.

Code-switching: *take it easy, what's so funny, no comment, yes, sir!, Oh, God!, gentleman's agreement*, forms of address such as *baby, honey, darling, boss*; *Dirty Nasty* (nickname of the tennis player Ilie Năstase, taken over from foreign press and accepted both by the admirers and non-admirers of the sports star), *condom, anti-baby pill*. By contrast, *board, building, challenge, establishment, overdose, pen-friend, pet, pub*, and *scholarship* are considered snobbisms and unnecessary neologisms.

(*b*) Words still looking foreign in form.

A clear-cut distinction between 1 (*a*) and 1 (*b*) is difficult to draw because we are dealing with Anglicisms (almost) unadapted in pronunciation and grammar. The criteria of frequency, modernity, and necessity of the Anglicism, or its status as a term of a scientific discipline determined the assignment of the following English neologisms to 1 (*b*). We interpret this level as being less fluctuating than level 1 (*a*) and not so much influenced by the pragmatic factors of communication.

Names of radio/TV programmes or of columns in newspapers, magazines: *drive-time*, *flash informativ*, *show biz*, *top-show*, probably hybrid coinages, *Bingo Europa*, *Robingo*, *Teleeurobingo*, etc.

Recent terms from social sciences, philosophy, the arts, and the media: many of these neologisms are graphically marked and are accompanied by definitions, explanations, paraphrases, and even by suggested equivalences. The untranslatable character is often mentioned as in the case of *corporate world*, *exit poll*, *melting pot*, *privacy*, *serendipity* (which has a Romanian adaptation—*serendipitate*). Even Anglicisms which could be easily integrated as calques, such as *challenge*, *go-between*, *leftism*, *politically correct* (and, by analogy, *religiously correct*), are preferred in their English form because the terms have already been taken over by the Romanian lexis. A replacement of these Anglicisms by calques would be perceived as a loss of accuracy. Other examples include *animal rights*, *baby-sitter*, *baby-sitting*, *big-bang*, *board*, *body-guard*, *boom*, *dealer*, *empowerment*, *full-time*, *gender blind*, *hands on*, *item*, *job*, *joint*, *know how*, *neutral*, *part-time job*, *peace maker*, *projections*, *public relations*, *self made man*, *sexism*, *superleader*, *superwoman*, *think tank*, *yes-man*, and the hybrid phrase *salon de joburi*.

Technical terms from different scientific fields, especially from computer technology: *briefing*, *consulting*, *e-mail*, *feedback*, *hacker*, *input*, *monitoriza* (v.) (< English *monitor*), *network*, *on-line*, *output*, *update/updata* (which is morphologically and phonetically adapted), etc.

Abbreviations preserved as in the donor language: *GMT*, *HC*, *IBM*, *k.d.*, *k.o.*, *LP*, *NATO*, *PC*, *SF*, *UFO*, *UK*, *USA*, *WTA*, *WWW*, etc.

Anglicisms specific to Anglo-American culture: *afro-american*, *black*, *far west*, *gospel*, *laburist*, *lord*, *melting-pot*, *mylady*, *negro*, *porridge*, *pudding*, *reaganism*, *saloon*, *sir*, *thatcherism*, *tomahawk*, *tory*, *yankeu*, *yard*, *yeomen*, etc. Some of these are 'neologisms' almost a century old in Romanian, while others are very recent. There is only slight adaptation of these neologisms which can be accounted for semantically.

Relatively new names of restaurants and foods: *Fast Food*, *McDonald's* (from which the adjective *mcdonaldizat* was derived), *McDrive*, *pub*, *Spring Time*, *big mac*, *cheeseburger*, *donuts*, *Flinstone snack*, *hamburger*, *hot dog* (and the unrecommended variant *hodog*), *lollipop*, *mc chicken*, (*pâine*) *tost*, *pizza snack*, *sticksuri*, etc.

(*c*) Fully integrated items.

In this category we find the oldest English lexical influences. They are phonetically, grammatically, and morphologically adapted neologisms with variants and derivatives. Many are no longer felt as Anglicisms or have lost the status of 'travelling words' (cf s. 9.5).

A slang and derogatory variant of *business* is *bişniţă*, the basis of the following pejorative derivatives: *bişniţar* ('businessman'), *bişniţări*, *bişniţăreală*, *bişniţăr(a)ie*; *geacă* (1970s) (from *jacket*) has the variants *jakă*, *jacă* which are not admitted by literary Romanian; *docar* (from *dog cart*); *miciman* (from *midshipman*), both early twentieth century; *sandviş*, *sandvici* both accepted by literary Romanian, with the variants *senviş*, *senvici* (end of the nineteenth century) (from *sandwich*), and with the diminutives *sandvişuleţ*, *sandvişel*; *blue jeanse, jeanse, jeanşi, blugi* (1970s); the last variant gave, through backformation, the singular *blug*; *chewing gum*, which is the form listed by the normative works, competes with the slang and corrupt form *ciungă*. Compare from the mid-twentieth century *trening* (*training*); *tenişi*, plural noun (from *tennis shoes*); *şipşandru* (the term may be older) (from *ship chandler*), etc.

Anglicisms adapted for morphological reasons include *jocheu, troleu, yankeu* (from *jockey, trolley, yankee*) where [-i/-j] could be mistaken for the Romanian plural morpheme *-i*.

Phonetic spellings (approximating to the pronunciation of the English etymon): *bodicec, bodiceca* (v.), *cliring, futbol, ghem, golgheter, henţ, lider, meci, miting, nailon, pasă, scuter, snec, şoc, şut*, etc. contrast with Anglicisms adapted through spelling pronunciation: *antidumping* is pronounced [antid**u**mpiŋg], *filibuster* [filib**u**ster]. Besides, there are items with several pronunciations: *gentleman* and *dancing* retain the English pronunciation (also the one accepted by literary Romanian), and a facetious pronunciation spelling ([dʒentleman] and [dantʃiŋg]). For *gentleman* there is a third pronunciation with epenthetic [-e-], [dʒenteleman], considered wrong but justified by the fact that the consonant cluster [-ntlm-] is unusual and difficult for Romanian speakers. The same applies to *camping, fan, scanner* which have a spelling pronunciation besides the English one, *treiler* is the variant corresponding to the spoken form of the etymon; *safe* [saf**e**] and *safeu* [saf**e**w] are variants that came into Romanian through French, *seif* pronounced either [se**i**f] as recommended by the literary norm, or [sejf] are forms with different degrees of adaptation which correspond to direct English influence.

Other Anglicisms such as *bluf, flirt, joule, pointer, rummy* have two pronunciation variants: an English and a French one, which prove that the word was simultaneously borrowed straight from English and mediated by French. *Sprint* and *start* retain the English spelling and pronunciation and by analogy with German words developed the hypercorrect variants *şprint*, *ştart* with [ʃp], [ʃt].

The factors that favour complete integration of an Anglicism in Romanian are the age and frequency of the lexical item, the phonetic and morphologic adaptation, the phonemic spelling, spelling pronunciation, and finally normative consensus. Divergence from the etymon, semantic changes, and the formation of derivatives are all indicators of adaptation.

2. Replacement

(a) Translations and semi-calques

  1. Successful

     brainwashing < *spălarea creierelor*, *cyberspace* < *ciberspaţiu*, *directory* < *director* (in computer terminology), *half* < *mijlocaş*, *interface* < *interfaţă*, *partnership* < *parteneriat*, *screening* < *ecranare*, *self-service* < *autoservire*, *human rights* < *drepturile omului*, *black box* < *cutie neagră*, *Cold War* < *război rece*, *first lady* < *prima doamnă*, *flying saucer* < *farfurie zburătoare*, *Iron Curtain* < *cortina de fier*

2. Coexisting
craker = *spărgător*, *overdose* = *supradoză*, *printer* = *imprimantă*, *superman* = *supraom*, *chewing gum* = *gumă de mestecat*, *hot line* = *linie fierbinte*, *public relations* = *relaţii cu publicul*, *sales promotion* = *promovarea vânzărilor*, *sandwich man* = *om sandviş*, *second hand* = *della mâna a doua*

3. Failures
boxer > *pumnaci*, *chip* > *pastilă*, *mouse* > *şoricel*

(*b*) Renderings, translating only part of the foreign item and providing looser equivalents for other parts

1. Successful
air conditioning < *aer condiţionat*, *skinhead* < *capete rase*, *skyscraper* < *zgârie-nori*, *homepage* < *pagină de prezentare*

2. Coexisting
corner = *lovitură de colţ*, *network* = *reţea*, *şort* = *pantaloni scurţi*, *workshop* = *atelier de lucru*, *exchange office* = *casă de schimb (valutar)* / *oficiu de schimb (valutar)*, *five o'clock tea* = *ceaiul de la ora cinci*, *no comment* = *fără (alte) comentarii*

3. Unsuccessful
skating > *patinaj pe rotile*

(*c*) Creation: a formally independent equivalent whose coinage was prompted by the foreign item

1. Successful
footing < *joc de picioare*

2. Coexisting
in press = *în curs de apariţie*, *input* = *intrare*, *output* = *ieşire*, *summit* = *întâlnire la nivel înalt*

(*d*) Semantic loan: an existing Romanian item taking over one meaning of the English partial equivalent

1. Successful
aplica (v.) (added the English meaning of 'to request'), *formal* (received the English meaning of 'ceremonial'), *memorial* (added the English meaning of 'object, institution established in memory of a person or an event'), *modul* (received the English meaning of an 'independent unit of a spacecraft'), *naş* (added the English meaning of 'head of Mafia'), *zebră* (took over the English meaning 'striped pedestrian crossing'), etc. (cf. s.9.4).

3. *Pseudo-loans* (English-looking items which do not exist in English)

Lexical pseudo-loans combining English morphemes into new linguistic units that do not exist in the donor language.
At first Romanian borrowed *golaveraj* and *setaveraj* from French. The ending

-*averaj*, originally from the English *average*, was interpreted as an element of derivation. In sports language it then sparked off other words such as: *coşaveraj, ghemaveraj, meciaveraj, punctaveraj, tuşaveraj*. Other pseudo-Anglicisms are: *cupman, daviscupman* (variant *Davis-cupman*), *electrobuz* (regionally also *firobuz*), *recordman* M, *recordmenă* F, *tenisman* M (with *tenismenă*, and *tenis-woman* as alternative for the F gender), *vatman*. Although looking like an Anglicism, *handbal* was taken from German—the game being a German creation (Hristea 1974, 1975*a*).

9.7 The future of Anglicisms

With the development of the electronic media and their recent spread to all parts of the world one may foresee that English influence will become a lasting reality. Political openness towards Western Europe and integration into various international organizations (political, economic, military, etc.) make English a requirement in many fields of activity as an efficient means of communication. Lexical borrowing will be a natural consequence, but how many words will be adapted in the long run is hard to predict, as are the consequences for Romanian grammar and phonology.

9.8 Research

Although the influence of English on Romanian has steadily grown since 1945, up to the 1960s this fact was tacitly overlooked. Dictionaries were slow to reflect the situation. In the 1940s few lexicographic works were published. In the following decade, general dictionaries (e.g. *Dicţionarul limbii române moderne*, 1958) registered only fully current and integrated Anglicisms. English loanwords used in technical terminologies, some retaining their original spelling, are to be found in that period only in *LTR*—but no indication is given with respect to their pronunciation.

In the 1960s the two editions of *DN1, DN2* (1961, 1966) acknowledged not only the existence of an increasing number of Anglicisms, but also their variants, giving their pronunciation and a brief morphological description.

The first articles devoted exclusively to English borrowings discussed maritime terminology (Bujeniţă 1966) and sports terminology (Trofin 1967). Since the 1970s, various aspects of English influence on Romanian have preoccupied a growing number of linguists (see the *Annotated Bibliography of European Anglicisms*). Research has focused on the following aspects:

- use and misuse of Anglicisms;
- the status of English borrowings in special vocabularies (sports, navigation, medicine);
- corpus-related analysis based on newspapers and journals;
- phonological adaptation;

- morphological adaptation;
- general description of the complexity of the process;
- compilation of a dictionary of Anglicisms;
- mediating languages (French in the first place) and international vocabulary of English origin.

The coverage of Anglicisms in various dictionaries, or in subsequent editions of an individual dictionary, has not yet been properly analysed. Even so, it is easy to see that the number of words of English extraction is on the increase in *DN3* and *DEX2*.

9.9 Bibliography

AVRAM, MIOARA (1975), 'Desinenţe pentru cuvinte străine în limba română contemporană' (Endings of Foreign Words in Contemporary Romanian), *Studii şi cercetări lingvistice*, 26: 319–24.

——(1997), *Anglicismele în limba română actuală* (Anglicisms in Contemporary Romanian), Conference delivered at the Romanian Academy, 13 Feb. (Bucharest: Editura Academiei).

BANTAŞ, ANDREI (1977), 'A Bird's Eye-View of English Influences upon the Romanian Lexis', *Studia Anglica Posnaniensia*, 9: 119–33.

——(1982), 'Aspects of Applied Semantics: For Modernizing Bilingual Dictionaries', *Revue roumaine de linguistique*, 27: 219–26.

——and RĂDULESCU, MIHAI (1967), '"Capcanele" *vocabularului englez*' ('Pitfalls' of the English Vocabulary) (Bucharest: Editura Ştiinţifică).

BĂNCILĂ, FLORICA, and CHIŢORAN, DUMITRU (1976), 'Remarks on the Morphological Adaptation of English Loanwords in Romanian', *Analele Universităţii Bucureşti*: *Filologie*, 25: 35–44.

—— ——(1982), 'The English Element in Contemporary Romanian', in R. Filipović (ed.), *The English Element in European Languages*, vol. ii (Zagreb: University of Zagreb), 378–420.

BĂNCIULESCU, VICTOR (1984), *Limbajul sportiv*: *o investigaţie sentimentală* (Sports Language: A Sentimental Investigation) (Bucharest: Editura Sport-Turism).

BUJENIŢĂ, M. (1966), 'Din terminologia nautică românească. II: Termeni marinăreşti de origine engleză' (Romanian Maritime Language. II: Maritime Terms of English Origin), *Limba română*, 15: 83–91.

CHIŢORAN, DUMITRU (1986), 'The English Element in Romanian: A Case Study in Linguistic Borrowing', in W. Viereck and W.-D. Bald (eds.), *English in Contact with Other Languages. Studies in Honour of Broder Carstensen on the Occasion of his 60th Birthday* (Budapest: Akadémiai Kiadó), 287–307.

——AUGEROT, JAMES E., and PÂRLOG, HORTENSIA (eds.) (n.d.), *The Sounds of English and Romanian RECAP* (Bucharest: Bucharest University Press).

CIOBANU, GEORGETA (1983), 'Adaptarea fonetică a cuvintelor româneşti de origine engleză' (The Phonetic Adaptation of Romanian Words of English Origin), unpub. D.Phil. thesis (Bucharest University).

——(1990), 'The English Element in Romanian: The Phonetic Level', in Rudolf Filipović and M. Bratanić (eds.), *Proceedings of the Symposium 16.1 'Languages in Contact'* (Zagreb: University), 358–63.

—— (1996), *Anglicisme în limba română* (Anglicisms in the Romanian Language) (Timişoara: Editura Amphora).

COTEANU, ION (1994*a*), 'Manager, Managerial, Management', *Opinia naţională*, 41: 2.

—— (1994*b*), 'Feriţi-vă de fausse-friends' (Beware of False Friends), *Opinia naţională*, 48: 2.

—— and SALA, MARIUS (1987), *Etimologia şi limba română* (Etymology and the Romanian Language) (Bucharest: Editura Academiei Republicii Socialiste România).

DIACONOVICI, C. (1989–94), *Enciclopedia română*, 3 vols. (Sibiu: Editura şi tiparul lui W. Krafft).

Dicţionarul explicativ al limbii române (An Explanatory Dictionary of the Romanian Language) (1975) (Bucharest: Institutul de Lingvistică din Bucureşti, Editura Academiei Republicii Socialiste România) (*DEX1*; *Supliment* (1988)).

—— (1996), 2nd edn. (Bucharest: Institutul de Lingvistică 'Iorgu Iordan', Univers Enciclopedic) (*DEX2*).

Dicţionarul limbii române (Dictionary of the Romanian Language) (1913–2000), 14 vols. (Bucharest: Academia Română. Librăriile Socec. şi C. Sfetea/Monitorul Oficial şi Imprimeriile Statului/Editura Academiei) (*DA/DLR*).

Dicţionarul limbii române moderne (Dictionary of Modern Romanian) (1958) (Bucharest: Institutul de Lingvistică din Bucureşti, Editura Academiei Republicii Populare Române).

Dicţionarul ortografic, ortoepic şi morfologic al limbii române (An Orthographical, Orthoepical and Morphological Dictionary of the Romanian Language) (1982) (Bucharest: Institutul de Lingvistică al Universităţii Bucureşti, Editura Academiei Republicii Socialiste România) (*DOOM*).

DIMITRESCU, FLORICA (1982), *Dicţionar de cuvinte recente* (Dictionary of Recent Words) (Bucharest: Editura Albatros) (*DCR*); (2nd edn. Bucharest: Logos, 1997) (*DCR2*).

—— (1995), *Dinamica lexicului românesc* (The Dynamics of Romanian Lexis) (Cluj-Napoca: Editura Clusium-Logos).

DUMITRIU, GETA (1987), 'English Studies at the University of Bucharest', *Analele Universităţii Bucureşti: Limbi şi literaturi străine*, 36: 61–75.

GRAUR, AL. (1937), *Neologismele* (Neologisms) (Bucharest: MO, Imprimeria Naţională).

—— (1950), 'Etimologia multiplă' (Multiple Etymology), *Studii şi cercetări lingvistice*, 1: 22–34.

—— (1978), *Dicţionar de cuvinte călătoare* (Dictionary of Travelling Words) (Bucharest: Editura Albatros).

GRUIŢĂ, MARIANA (1974), 'Adaptarea cuvintelor de origine engleză la sistemul fonetic şi ortografic al limbii române actuale' (The Adaptation of Words of English Origin to the Phonetic and Orthographic System of Present-Day Romanian), *Limbă şi Literatură*, 19: 51–7.

HARTULAR, ANCA (1996), *Merem la America* (We are Going to America) (Bucharest: Editura Fundaţiei Culturale Române).

HRISTEA, THEODOR (1968), *Probleme de etimologie* (Problems of Etymology) (Bucharest: Editura Ştiinţifică).

—— (1974), 'Pseudoanglicisme de provenienţă franceză în limba română' (Pseudo-Anglicisms of French Origin in Romanian), *Limba Română*, 23: 61–71.

—— (1975*a*), 'Un nou element de compunere: -*averaj*' (A New Element of Composition: -*averaj*), *Studii şi cercetări lingvistice*, 26: 375–9.

—— (1975*b*), 'Calcul internaţional' (The International Calque), *Studii şi cercetări lingvistice*, 26: 499–504.

IAROVICI, EDITH and MIHĂILĂ RODICA (1970), 'Introduction to a Contrastive Analysis of the English and Romanian Vocabularies', *Analele Universităţii Bucureşti: Limbi germanice*, 19: 23–37.

IAROVICI, EDITH and MIHĂILĂ RODICA (1979), *Lexicul de bază al limbii engleze: Dicţionar contrastiv* (Lexicon of Basic English: A Contrastive Dictionary) (Bucharest: Editura Ştiinţifică şi enciclopedică).

IORDAN, IORGU (1956), *Limba română contemporană* (Contemporary Romanian) (Bucharest: Editura Ministerului Învăţământului).

Lexiconul tehnic român (1949–1956), 7 vols. + 1 vol. index (Bucharest: Editura Tehnică) (*LTR1*).

MANOLESCU, ZOIA (1990), 'Proportions of the English Element in Contemporary Romanian', in R. Filipović and M. Bratanić (eds.), *Proceedings of the Symposium 16.1 'Languages in Contact'* (Zagreb: University), 120–5.

MARCU, FLORIN, and MANECA, CONSTANT (1961, 1966, 1978), *Dicţionar de neologisme* (Dictionary of Neologisms) (Bucharest: Editura Academiei) (*DN1, DN2, DN3*).

MOCIORNIŢĂ, MARIA (1980), 'Momente premergătoare semnificative pentru instituirea învăţământului universitar de limbă engleză' (Important Moments in the History of Teaching English at the University), in *Momente din istoria învăţământului limbilor străine la Universitatea Bucureşti* (Bucharest: Universitatea din Bucureşti), 83–8.

——(1983), 'Romanian-English Cultural Relations in the 16th and the 17th Centuries', in Ioan Aurel Preda (ed.), *English Literature and Civilization: The Renaissance and the Restoration Period* (Bucharest: Editura Didactică şi Pedagogică), 188–92, 211–13.

MUNTEANU, ŞTEFAN, and ŢÂRA, VASILE D. (1983), *Istoria limbii române literare* (History of the Romanian Literary Language) (Bucharest: Editura Didactică şi Pedagogică).

PÂRLOG, HORTENSIA (1971), 'Termeni de origine engleză în publicistica română contemporană' (Terms of English Origin in Present-Day Romanian Periodicals), *Analele Universtăţii Timişoara*, 9: 55–68.

——(1983). 'English Loanwords in Romanian', in *Sajavaara, 241–53.

PUŞCARIU, SEXTIL (1976), 'Influenţe culturale' (Cultural Influences), in Sextil Puşcariu, *Limba română*, i: *Privire generală* (Bucharest: Editura Minerva), 370–415.

RĂDULEŢ, REMUS (ed.) (1957–66), *Lexiconul tehnic român (Elaborare nouă)*, 18 vols. (Bucharest: Editura Tehnică) (*LTR2*).

RAEVSKI, N., and GABINSKI, M. (eds.) (1987), *Scurt dicţionar etimologic al limbii moldoveneşti* (A Short Etymological Dictionary of the Moldavian Language) (Kishinev: Redacţia principală a enciclopediei sovietice moldoveneşti).

REY-DEBOVE, JOSETTE, and GANGNON, GILBERT (1988), *Dictionnaire des anglicismes: Les Mots anglais et américains en français* (Paris: Les Usuels du Robert).

STOICHIŢOIU, ADRIANA (1986), 'A Functional Approach to the Study of Recent English Borrowings in Romanian', *Analele Universităţii Bucureşti: Limba şi literatura română*, 35: 84–92.

——(1993), 'Anglomania: O formă de snobism lingvistic' (Anglomania: A Form of Linguistic Snobbism), *Comunicările 'Hyperion'*, 2: 270–80.

——(1996), 'Observaţii privind influenţa engleză în limbajul publicistic actual (I; II)' (Notes Regarding the English Influence on Contemporary Journalese), *Limba şi literatura română*, 2: 37–46; 3/4: 25–34.

TROFIN, AUREL (1967), 'Observaţii cu privire la adaptarea terminologiei de origine engleză în limba română' (Notes Regarding the Adaptation of Terminology of English Origin in Romanian), *Studia Universitatis Babeş-Bolyai: Series Philologia*, 2: 125–30.

——(1975), 'Istoria anglisticii româneşti: Privire specială asupra predării limbii engleze în România' (History of English Studies: Research on the Teaching of English in Romania), unpub. D.Phil. thesis (Cluj-Napoca).

VASILIU, EMANUEL (1965), *Fonologia limbii române* (The Phonology of the Romanian Language) (Bucharest: Editura ştiinţifică).

10

RUSSIAN

Tamara Maximova

10.1 History of language contact

10.1.1 Chronology of intensive influences
(Frone 1968; Aristova 1980; Krysin 1968)

After isolated early instances of loanwords, the infiltration of English words into the Russian language progressed in the age of Peter I (seventeenth/eighteenth centuries). Most Anglicisms were used alongside their Dutch equivalents as they belonged to nautical terminology shared by the two languages. During this period Russian linguists avoided using the term 'Anglicisms', preferring to use 'Germanisms' or 'western-Europeanisms' instead. The existence of parallel terminological systems in Russian may also have resulted from English influence on the form of the common Germanic words (*shkval/skval, shtandart/standart, shtorm/ storm*, etc.) in the eighteenth century, when about 300 words were borrowed by Russian. These were not only shipbuilding and nautical terms but also included items like *rost-bif, puding, rom*, and *éntuziazm*, many of which belong to the domain of 'social life'.

The Anglicisms of the nineteenth century pertain to various domains in which the Russians had an interest: English science, technology, social sciences, agriculture, and education. Lexical borrowing from English was one of the consequences of the Industrial Revolution. English words and phrases entered the literary style and spread in the speech of the aristocracy. Some words were borrowed in their phonological shape: *dzhentl'men, kottedzh, kolledzh, glaĭder*; others preserved their foreign spelling (here given in transliteration): *vulgar, kloun*.

The second half of the nineteenth century and the beginning of the twentieth century saw the growing influx of direct borrowings from English. This was due to the strengthening of English–Russian contacts before the First World War, and the well-known Anglomania of the middle class and the aristocracy, as well as purely literary influence through the translations of English or American novels and poetry. Some noted authors very popular in Russia included Kipling, Longfellow, Whitman, and Byron. The development of capitalism and the revolutionary movement also added to the growth of the borrowed word stock relating to social and political terminology: *boĭkot*, *lokaut*, *tred-yunion*, etc.

At the end of the nineteenth century and at the beginning of the twentieth century a great number of sports terms were adopted, at first as foreignisms: *beĭsbol*, *boks*, *futbol*, *laun-tennis*, *match*, *rekord*, *start*, *trek*, etc. In addition, the names of dances and some other new concepts of everyday life, such as designations for music, drinks, and breeds of dogs, appeared in Russian. The use of some words in their English form was restricted to written genres in journalism, scientific registers, and business.

The twentieth century is characterized by several subsequent waves of borrowing, especially after the Second World War. In the late 1960s not only British but also American English words massively penetrated into Russian during the period of general 'liberalization' of political, economic, scientific, and cultural relationships between the East and the West. New borrowings relate to social, political and economic domains (*impichment*, *menedzher*, *daĭdzhest*, *praĭmeriz*); culture and arts (*big-bit*, *khéppening*); sports (*sërfing*, *karting*, *spidveĭ*); transport (*laĭner*, *boing* 'aeroplane', *aérobus*); food and drink (*chipsy*, *kreker*, *sherri*, *dzhus*, *krast*); clothes and fabrics (*tvid*, *bleĭzer*, *orlon*), and various fields such as emotions and greetings, normally in the form of interjections (*gud baĭ*, *o'keĭ*).

Researchers have identified a considerable influx of English borrowings between the 1960s and the 1980s with negative connotations as in *striptiz*, *supermen* (*supermeny* is used for a team of students), and *smog* (as in *spiritual smog*).

The same period is characterized by heavy borrowing of youth slang. The first of such Anglicisms were recorded in the speech of the senior grade pupils of specialized English schools and students of philological faculties. The use of foreign words apparently enhanced the prestige of the speakers. Much of this lexis is, of course, ephemeral: many fashionable words introduced for stylistic reasons went out of use in the 1980s; some were replaced by native slang terms.

The 1980s and 1990s were characterized by a new wave of English vocabulary as a consequence of Russia's transition to the market economy. The domains affected in previous decades are being enriched, in particular music, sports, e.g.: *fén*, *khit*, *klip*, *sheĭping* (E *fan*, *hit*, *clip*, *shaping* 'women's sport to create a good shape (appearance)'). However, the majority of neologisms are clearly found in the areas of economy, technology, business, trade, and advertising, as illustrated by *kholding*, *distrib'yutor*, *diler*, *dzhobber* (E *holding*, *distributor*, *dealer*, *jobber*).

10.1.2 Origins of influence

The term 'English' here stands for borrowings from both Great Britain and the USA. It is almost impossible to distinguish between British and American variants because very often the words do not differ in form and many Americanisms were originally transmitted through British English.

10.1.3 Types of influence

All levels of language—pronunciation, spelling, morphology, derivation, syntax, lexis—are affected by the process of borrowing; vocabulary is of the greatest interest because of its variability and complexity (see details in s. 10.6).

The degree of influence on spelling, pronunciation, morphology, and word formation depends on the number of borrowings, the degree of their assimilation in the receiving language, and the attitudes of the language community.

10.1.4 Chronology of purist phases

(Krysin 1968; Sorokin 1968)

Attitudes towards borrowing belong to one of the two opposing types. The first is represented by purist movements aimed at restricting the intake of foreign words. The main drawback of purist attitudes is that they ignore the historical development of the language. While admitting old borrowings which have already been accepted in the language, purists tend to oppose new foreignisms. By contrast, the second kind of attitude considers loanwords to be inevitable and indeed an enrichment of the vocabulary.

The reaction of Russian society towards the impact of foreign languages varied over time. The formation and development of the Russian literary language of the seventeenth century was unique in that no other language was felt to threaten its existence. The basis for the new literary language was Old Russian enriched by words from Church Slavonic and from European languages. The quick adaptation of foreign words reflected an underlying confidence in the literary language. The first signs of purism appeared in the seventeenth century, in the epoch of Peter I, when West European loans were mainly of Greek and Latin origin, since these were the international languages of European science in the Middle Ages. Even representatives of purist attitudes were moderate and used loanwords themselves. The period was short-lived: it neither led to the eradication of foreign words nor brought the borrowing process to a stop.

The second half of the eighteenth century saw a long period of purism and strong resistance to foreign words. It was connected with the final standardization of the Russian literary language achieved by the great scientist and linguist M. V. Lomonosov. During this time the reaction of well-educated people towards foreign words was negative; it was echoed in the works of the great Lomonosov, whom A. Pushkin called 'the first Russian university'. His views on borrowings were shared by such distinguished writers and linguists as A. Sumarokov, I. Krylov, G. Derzhavin, and A. Radishchev. Their linguistic ideas were realized not only in their own works, but also in their contributions to the first academic Slavonic and Russian dictionary in six volumes (1789–94), in which only 2 per cent of all the headwords are foreign. The rest of the earlier borrowings were replaced by Russian synonyms or translations. Of all the loanwords adopted during the eighteenth century, 52 per cent were borrowed in the first three decades, 27 per cent between 1740 and 1760, and only 21 per cent in the period 1770 to 1790.

The end of the eighteenth century and the first two decades of the nineteenth century mark the next period of clearly purist impulse in Russian. The concept of the purity of the Russian language can be traced in the works of scholars such as A. Shishkov, N. Gnedich, N. Grech, and the strongest opponent of the new foreign words, V. Dal'. However, even he included about 750 borrowed words in his dictionary. Dal' understood that in many cases it was impossible to suggest a suitable substitute for a foreign word or term.

Since 1840 purism has not been nationalistic: it is more academic in nature. Recent purist attitudes were mainly the result of a general stylistic reform of Russian and to some extent reflected the general political reaction. The debate has centred on the expediency and limits of foreign borrowings. Most purists thought that words already borrowed should be retained in Russian, but new ones should be ousted because speakers misused them and thus spoiled the Russian language. Some linguists suggested that loanwords should be replaced by Russian equivalents (*tozhdeslovy*); their suggestions were not followed in practice.

In Russia the nineteenth century is famous for lexicography: various dictionaries of foreign words were published. They were intended as guides on how to replace foreign words by Russian equivalents and to avoid further influence of foreign languages on Russian.

Purism continued in the twentieth century too. V. Lenin was the first in Soviet Russia to warn against 'spoiling' the Russian language with foreign words. The post-war period (1940s–1950s) was a time of even more active purism through the political regime's language policy; its general ideological tendency was to eliminate servility to the West. As a result of this policy, there was an attempt to purge loanwords in the domains of sport. For instance, instead of *golkiper* (E *goalkeeper*) the word *vratar'* came into being and *traktornaya lopata* (E 'tractor shovel') was used instead of *skreper* (E *scraper*). However, this policy largely failed: it did not stop the process of borrowing in Russian, which nevertheless began to lag behind in time compared to both Western and some Eastern European countries.

Many Russian linguists have favoured purist tendencies, calling the intake of Anglicisms into Russian unnecessary, and claiming it contributes to informational bankruptcy and misrepresentation of facts and sense. However, there is general consent that the elimination of foreign words is unlikely to produce a desirable effect. The problem of foreign influence demands a discreet and unbiased attitude as there is no use in struggling against 'alien' words while the international contacts exist.

10.1.5 Regional differences

There do not seem to be any purely regional differences in Russian as far as Anglicisms are concerned. The differences that exist are mainly educational, and related to urban vs. rural speech, with Moscow (probably) having the greatest influx of English words. However, in the absence of reliable scholarly investigations such statements cannot be more than hunches.

10.1.6 Stylistic differences

Anglicisms in Russian are generally stylistically marked. Loanwords prevail in technical and colloquial registers of language belonging to specialist areas, for example, industry, computer technology, and sports, or to youth speech and journalese. Colloquialisms, which are frequent in present-day Russian, do not seem to become permanent loans: rather, they are employed ephemerally by writers for some special stylistic effect, and then fade from fashion.

10.1.7 Innovation and obsolescence
(Gorbachevich 1984; Shanskiĭ 1972)

There have not been many linguistic analyses of the growth of Anglicisms in Russian. Gorbachevich (1984) compiled valuable data on the number of Anglicisms borrowed by Russian from the beginning of the sixteenth century up to the 1980s; these are shown in Table 10.1. The figures show convincingly an ever-growing English contribution to Russian. The 1980s and 1990s in particular have witnessed an intensive growth of Anglicisms. The latest items are, of course, not registered in dictionaries; they appear in journalese or in youth language, and it is uncertain whether they will be fully integrated into the Russian lexical system.

Some Anglicisms have become obsolete for one or more of the following reasons:

1. the objects or concepts they designated have become obsolete (as happened to materials like *boston*, dances like *fokstrot*, *blyuz*, or clothes like *dzhemper* (from *jumper*, obsolete in Russian);
2. the loanwords were replaced by calques, such as *blyuming* (E *blooming*) by *prokatnyĭ stan* (E *blooming train*), *infaĭting* (E *infighting*) by *blizhniĭ boĭ* (E *close combat*);
3. they were replaced by another loanword, such as *kembrik* (E *cambric*) by *batist*, *kondom* (E *condom*) by *prezervativ* (E *preservative*).

An obsolete Anglicism sometimes reappears in Russian or the same word is reborrowed with another meaning, as happened to E *golf* 'cardigan', E *tandem* 'a group of two people united by something', E *clip* 'a short span of a film or video'.

Table 10.1.

Period	No. of E loans	% of all Anglicisms
1500–1700	52	2.2
1701–1800	287	12.1
1801–1900	714	30.2
1901–80	1314	55.5
	2367	100

10.1.8 Mediating languages

Some Anglicisms found their way into Russian via French, German, or Dutch. In some cases it was Russian through which other languages borrowed English words. Examples of Anglicisms borrowed into Russian through:

> French: *ésse* (E *essay*, Fr *essai*); *flanel* (E *flannel*, Fr *flanelle*); *bobina* (E *bobbin*, Fr *bobine*); *boksër* (E *boxer*, Fr *boxeur*); *drenazh* (E *drainage*, Fr *drainage*); *budzhet* (E *budget*, Fr *budget*); *zhyuri* (E *jury*, Fr *jury*);
> German: *keks* (E *cake*, Ge *Keks*); *koks* (E *coke*, Ge *Koks*); *kompost* (E *compost*, Ge *Kompost*); *kroket* (E *croquet*, Ge *Krocket*); **bankir* (Fr *banquier*, Ge *Bankier*);
> Dutch: *yakhta; boss, brendi.*

On the other hand, Anglicisms were handed on to other languages via Russian, such as *dispetcher* to Ge *Dispatcher*, Rm *dispecer*, Po *dyspeczer*, Al *dispeçer* etc.; *khokkeĭ* to Bg *khokeĭ; kombaĭn* to Ge *Kombine*, Rm *combinaĭ*, Bg *kombaĭn*, Al *kombajnë* etc.; *skreper* to Rm *screper*, Bg *skreper*; and *snaĭper* to Po *snajper*.

10.1.9 English in education

In Soviet Russia, German was the most common foreign language taught in schools. After the Second World War English began to compete with German and French, and has long overtaken them.

In the 1960s, many specialized schools were opened in Moscow and other large cities, since English was considered to be prestigious and fashionable. The number of English speakers has been growing at a constant rate. Professionals began to attend English language courses, realizing it was necessary for their careers. The new style of life recently established in Russia has created unprecedented opportunities for using English and thus there are new motivations for language learning. The many bilinguals who are transmitters of new Anglicisms contribute to their rapid acceptance and quick integration into the Russian lexis.

10.2 Pronunciation and spelling

10.2.1 Pronunciation

(Timofeeva 1985; Aristova 1980; Vasil'ev 1980)

English words undergo different types of change when they are adapted to Russian phonology: these processes have not been fully investigated. The degree of integration of each loan depends on a number of linguistic and extralinguistic factors such as the age of the loan, its popularity, the path of borrowing (through written or acoustic channels), the age of the language users, and their knowledge of English.

English and Russian are from different language families, and their phonological systems and the articulation of individual sounds differ considerably. Table 10.2 illustrates these differences: English phonemes not found in Russian are italicized whereas phonemes peculiar to Russian are in bold type. There are also the following phonotactic differences: stops and fricatives are regularly devoiced at the end of Russian words, a rule extended to loanwords. Also note regressive voice assimilation in cases like *futbol* [fudbol], *ketgut* [k'ɛdgut].

Every consonant in Russian pronunciation is either palatalized (if followed by the front vowels /i/, /e/) or non-palatalized (before back vowels /a/, /o/, /u/, /y/ =<bɪ>; consonants in English loanwords are treated accordingly, cf. *regbi* / r'egb'i/, *lider* /l'id'er/. Some words of English origin retain the non-Russian sequence of [e] preceded by the non-palatalized sound: *demping* (*dumping*), *kokteĭl'* (*cocktail*), *test* (*test*), etc. The new tendency to use the phoneme [ε] instead of [e] shows that the previous consonant is not palatalized (hard).

Table 10.2. A conspectus of English and Russian phonological correspondences

Consonants		Honophthongs	
English	Russian	English	Russian
b	b, **b**′	iː, i	i
p	p, **p**′		
t	t, **t**′	e	ε
d	d, **d**′	aː	a
k	k, **k**′	ɔː, ɔ	ɔ
g	g, **g**′	uː, u	u
m	m, **m**′	ʌ	—
n	n, **n**′	ə	ə
f	f, **f**′	ə	—
v	v, **v**′	æ	—
s	s, **s**′	[There are no diphthongs in Russian.]	
z	z, **z**′		
ʃ	ʃ		
dʒ	—		
tʃ	tʃ		
j	j		
l	ļ, **l**′		
r	r, **r**′		
h	—		
—	x, **x**′		
θ	—		
ð	—		
w	—		

Most English loans retain their original stress, but note a few examples where the stress is on the last syllable: *batterflyaĭ, khuligan, striptiz*. The morphemes *-bol, -men, -izm, -ist*, are stressed as in *voleĭbol, biznesmen, bikheviorizm, futbolist*.

From the point of view of articulation standard Russian has a different [r] from English, it lacks the aspirated stops (p, t, k), does not differentiate between /n/ and /ŋ/ etc. All these peculiarities are important for language teaching but irrelevant for the borrowing process.

The pronunciation of English loans may be based on spelling if they were borrowed from written English: *klub*, *kutter*, *kar*, *laun tennis*; or words which are very similar to an existing Russian word were identified with their Russian equivalents, as in *bobbi* [o], *disk* [i].

Note that [ei] has been interpreted in Russian in various ways. Some equivalents are: [e] in *lẹdi*, *bẹbi*; [é] in *lẹ́di*, *bẹ́bi*; [eĭ] in *leĭdi*, *beĭbi*, *peĭdzher*, *tineĭdzher*, *sheĭping*; or [éĭ] in *peĭdzher*, *tinéĭdzher*, *shéĭping*, etc. whereas [æ] is either [e, é] or [a] (all three are found in variant pronunciations of *kidnapping*).

Long vowels have been replaced by short counterparts in Russian: English *masterclass* → Russian *masterklass*; and other non-Russian diphthongs became monophthongized (English *holding* → Russian *kholding*) or replaced by an intra-morphemic vowel sequence (English *file* → Russian *faĭl*).

A few specific English consonants have more than one possible substitute in Russian: /h/—/x/, /g/; /w/—/v/, /u/; /ð/—/d/, /z/; /θ/—/t/, /s/, /f/; non-Russian [ŋ] is represented by the sound combination [ng]; and word-final [z] is not always devoiced; in a few cases (*brothers* → *braderz/braders*) this is reflected in spelling.

Note that [l] followed by a consonant may have two interpretations in Russian: [l], [lʹ] → *folk*, *folʹk*; and that words adopted via French and German retain their non-English pronunciation: *koks* for *coke*, *keks* for *cake*, *byudzhet* for *budget*, and *bifshteks* for *beefsteak*.

With more English words penetrating into the language, words borrowed from written sources come to be pronounced closer to the English model: this has happened to [ladi] > [ledi/leĭdi] *lady*; [dandi] > [dendi] *dandy*, but some English words have remained unadapted in Russian: *dzhaz* from *jazz*, *triller* from *thriller*, *zhokeĭ* from *jockey*.

However, since the phonological type of borrowing from acoustic sources is more frequent today, the latest borrowings tend to render the English pronunciation quite closely: *késh*, *kreĭzi*, *éggkhéd*, *bobsleĭ*, *imidzh-meĭker*.

10.2.2 Graphemic integration

Since Russian and English use different alphabetical systems, a number of modifications were necessary. The foreignness of English loanwords can be felt from untypical combinations of letters (*ng*, *ew*, *wr*) and from the sounds they signify in a non-Russian way.

There are two ways of converting English loanwords into Russian orthography: orthographical (letter-for-letter correspondence) and phonological; commonly English loanwords in Russian are transliterated in a letter-for-letter correspondence. Here and in the *Dictionary of European Anglicisms* the Russian Cyrillic orthography has been transliterated into the Roman alphabet for the benefit of the English-speaking reader. The system of transliteration adopted here is the one given in the *Concise Oxford Dictionary*.

In the case of orthographic borrowing, the English spelling is largely retained so that the correlation between a Russian borrowing and its English etymon is felt: E *cross* = *kross*, but note slight differences in E *laser*— *lazer*, E *pudding*—*puding*.

The most important changes undergone by English loans on the level of spelling in Russian are as follows:

<x> is replaced by <ks>, <gz>; <th> by <d, t, z, v, f>; <w> by <v, u>
Silent consonants are either transliterated or omitted: E *talk*—<tok>, E *arm-wrestling*—<armrestling>, E *performance*—<perfo(r)mans>; silent <e> is always dropped: E *rave*—<reĭv>.
Duplicated consonant graphemes are mostly retained: *boss*, E *summit*—<sammit>; but sometimes a single letter is used: E *office*—<ofis>, E *offset*—<ofset>, E *pudding*—<puding>.
The spelling of compound words is far from being standardized; three different solutions are found: unhyphenated (E *notebook*—<noutbuk>, E *bodyguard*—<bodigard>), hyphenated (E *talk show*—<tok-shou>, E *body-art*—<bodi-art>), and separated (E *horror fan*—<khoror fén>, E *disk jockey*—<disk zhokeĭ>). Some have alternative forms: E *big band*—<big bend, big-bend>, E *showman*—<shou men, shoumen>.

10.3 Morphology

10.3.1 Introduction

Russian nouns, pronouns, and adjectives are inflected for case, gender, and number; verbs for person, number, tense, aspect, and mood. Borrowed words must be morphologically integrated to become part of the lexical system.

10.3.2 Nouns

(Aristova 1980; Shanski 1972; Avilova 1967)

Gender is one of the obligatory categories for Russian. Nouns ending in consonants (with Ø inflexion in nom. sg.) are M, e.g. *trener, sandvich, seĭf*. This applies also to English plural forms like *bifshteks, turneps*. Nouns ending in *-a* (*-ya*) are F, e.g. *aérobika, guttapercha* and those ending in *-o*, (*-e*) are N, e.g. *dzyudo, bungalo*. Uninflected nouns with the non-Russian endings *-i, -u* in nom. sg. are always N, e.g. *khobbi, zyuri, shou, interv'yu*. Natural or semantic gender is only found with uninflected nouns denoting persons or certain animals, e.g. *zhokeĭ, dendi* are M; *ledi, miss* are F; *poni* M, *kolli* F (= modelled on the fem. appelative *sobaka* 'dog') (membership of a set by analogy with existent Rs words).

Words ending in *-ics, -ion, -y* are adapted to Russian *-ika, -iya* and are, in consequence, F: *bionika* F from *bionics, aérobika* F from *aerobics*. This follows the pattern adopted with words taken from Latin (cf. *émansipatsiya* F from

La *emancipatio*). The transfer of English consonantal stems into Russian vocalic *a*-stems of the feminine gender is rare but possible: *orbita* F from *orbit*, *pul'pa* F from *pulp*, *draga* F from *drag*. The pattern is typical only of old, fully adapted loans.

English has made a very small contribution to the stock of nouns without specifically marked feminine forms. In modern Russian for words such as *instruktor*, *professor*, *lider* ('leader'), *staĭer* ('distance runner'), *trener* ('trainer') the masculine form can also be used for feminine without any morphological modification.

Some Anglicisms are not morphologically integrated, and remain as foreignisms: e.g. *penni* (E *penny*), *cherri-brendi* (E *cherry-brandy*). They are uninflected for case but display gender and number attribution in syntactic agreement with pronouns and adjectives. Normally they are N if they denote inanimate objects but some are M if the objects are living beings: *malen'kiĭ poni* M 'a little pony', but *moë penni* N 'my penny', etc.

Case. All integrated nouns are inflected according to native patterns of case, number, and gender distinction in Russian.

Plurals in Russian are mostly formed by adding *-i/-y* to the base form: *pleĭer* M sg.—*pleĭery* pl.; *spinning* M sg.—*spinningi* pl. Native speakers do not differentiate between simple and derived stems as in *orbita* and *tanker* and give endings in the plural without changing the borrowed stem; *orbity*, *tankery*.

In general, words tend to be borrowed as unanalysed wholes, their internal structure being opaque to the borrower. Russian speakers are therefore often not aware of the meaning of the English plural morpheme *-s*; this can lead to double plural marking through the addition of a Russian inflection to an English plural; as in *pampersy*, *dzhinsy*, *chipsy*. Occasionally we observe the loss of the original plural ending *-s* and its replacement by the native one: *pikuli* (E *pickles*). All these are used only in the plural. In some cases the original *-s* serves in Russian as a marker of the masculine gender: *keks* M sg.— *keksy* pl., *rel's* M sg.—*rel'sy* pl. (E *rail*).

10.3.3 Adjectives

As a rule, English adjectives are not borrowed in their base forms (except for a few recent colloquialisms such as *kreĭzi*, *groggi*). Adjectives are given special suffixes, as well as being marked for gender (*-ov/-n + -yĭ/-sk + -iĭ*) (M), *-aya* (F), *-oe* (N)/ -M, *-a* (F), *-o* (N). Short forms follow the Russian pattern, cf. *Neper—Neperovo (chislo)*.

10.3.4 Adverbs

No English adverb in *-ly* is found in Russian, possibly because there is an awareness that *-ly* is a morpheme.

10.3.5 Verbs

English verbs are borrowed into Russian as nominal roots which must then be suffixed (see s. 10.3.6.3). English participles are not borrowed into Russian.

10.3.6 Derivation (selection)

Gender specification. The system of suffixation for indicating M and F gender is highly developed in Russian. Russian personal nouns indicate the F form mainly by adding specific suffixes such as *-ka*, *-sha*, which are transferred to loanwords *tennisist—tennisistka*, *kombaĭnër—kombaĭnërsha*. Very seldom gender-specific nouns are borrowed from English as in *styuard—styuardessa*.

Agent nouns. Since both English and Russian have the suffix *-er*, it is often not possible to distinguish derivations formed in Russian from items taken over from English (*boksër*, *kutter*). The same holds true for *-ist* formations (except for obvious non-English coinages like *tennisist* and *futbolist*). Agent nouns with *-man* form a closed class and are borrowed in their entirety: *barmen*, *biznesmen*, *blyuzmen*. The bound morpheme *-man* is not used productively in Russian to form words from native roots.

Denominal verbs. All English verbs borrowed into Russian are denominal. The denominalizing suffixes are: *-ova-t'*, cf. *blefovat'*, *mitingovat'*, *parkovat'*;*-irovat'*, cf. *boksirovat'*, *finishirovat'*, *lobbirovat'*; and *-izirova-t'*, cf. *komp'yuterizirovat'*, *standartizirovat'*, *monopolizirovat'*.

New adjectives (see s. 10.3.3) are formed with the following suffixes: *-n-yĭ*, cf. *lazernyĭ*, *khokkeĭnyĭ*; *-sk-iĭ*, cf. *dzhentel'menskiĭ*, *khuliganskiĭ*; and *-ov-yĭ*, cf. *dzhazovyĭ*, *kempingovyĭ*.

Deadjectival nouns. Since adjectives are commonly not borrowed by Russian in their English base form, but undergo some structural adaptation, only a few of them permit further derivation: *variabel'nost'*, *eksklyuzivnost'*, *seksapil'nost'*.

10.3.7 Compounds and combining forms

Compounding is productive in both English and Russian, but the types of word formation do not coincide. It is obvious that English has made a great contribution to the new type of 'abutted compounds' (without a linking vowel) in Russian, because the derivation of new adjectives (to form traditional Russian adj.+n. combinations) was not sufficient. The borrowing of words like *sport-klub* (E *sport club*), *doping-kontrol'*, *dzhazfestival'* has resulted in the morphological assimilation of this pattern and analogical derivation of compounds (loan translations and loan blends). Examples are: *gid-perevodchik* (E *guide-interpreter*) and *bortprovodnik* (E *steward*).

A tendency to use a limited number of root morphemes for new compounds has become evident recently. The most productive are *-shop*,*-shou*, as in *tok-shou*, *dog-shou*, *motor-shou*. For many of such items it is not clear whether they are independent Russian coinages or whether they represent partial translations.

10.3.8 Calques (loan translations, cf. s. 10.6 below)

Some derivatives, compound words, and word groups can be exactly translated, e.g. E *semi-conductor—poluprovodnik*, E *self-service—samoobsluzhivanie*. However, many English items that cannot be rendered closely in Russian because the morphological structures of the two languages differ, as in *teoriya vzryva* for *big bang theory*, or *khokkeĭna l'du* for *ice-hockey*. In some cases it is very difficult to prove that the Russian forms are calques, as in *chain smoker* vs. *zayadlyĭkuril'shchik*, *Indian summer* vs. *bab'e leto*.

10.4 Meaning
(Aristova 1980; Martinek 1971)

How borrowing affects the meaning of loanwords. Anglicisms becoming part of Russian undergo various changes: meanings do not always match those of the English etymon. This is not so much the case in terminology because the reference is identical.

The following types of semantic change in Anglicisms can be observed. For polysemous words only one meaning is borrowed at a time. Even though a second meaning may be added by renewed borrowing, it is hardly ever the case that the whole semantic range of a polysemous word is repeated in a recipient language. For instance, Russian took over two senses each of *bunker* for 'container' and 'reinforced shelter', *starter* for 'an automatic device', and 'a person giving the signal for a start', and *menedzher* for 'a person administrating a business' and 'a person controlling the training, affairs (sport, entertainment)'.

Having entered Russian, the loanword undergoes the process of integration in its semantic field. This inevitably leads to changes in its connotative and denotative components. As a result, an Anglicism can acquire shades of meaning not found in English, as in *vagon* 'a great quantity of sth.', or *reĭd* 'an unexpected check-up of social organizations'.

The most typical kinds of semantic change affecting English loanwords in Russian are:

1. The word is never borrowed in its entirety with all its various meanings. For example, if we take the *COD* definitions as a basis, the range of English *bar* is reduced from seven meanings to three in Russian, *wagon* from six to two.

2. An individual meaning may be narrower in Russian, acquiring specifying features that do not hold in English; *butsy* < E *boots* (only in relation to special sports shoes) or *penal'ti* < E *penalty* (in relation to sports).

3. An English word may have its meaning enlarged as a result of metaphoric or metonymic processes in Russian: *charter* (of a ship or airplane) also covers the meaning of English *voyage*; *greĭder* has been expanded to mean English 'road, way', *broĭler* denotes not only a young chicken but also the place it is raised in.

4. Sometimes, the process of borrowing may result in a considerable change in semantic range and a generalization of meaning. The Anglicism in Russian may acquire much broader denotational and connotational meanings: for

example, *ballast* in Russian has acquired two additional meanings—'extra weight, burden' and 'a useless person'.

Research carried out by V. M. Martinek (1971) confirms these observations both theoretically and statistically: 25 per cent of the monosemous loanwords do not change their semantic structure; of the polysemous words 70 per cent considerably narrow their semantic range, the remaining 30 per cent develop new meanings in Russian.

10.5 Usage

(Krysin 1995; Lomakina 1985)

Sociolinguistic variables include stylistic properties, domains of speech, frequency value, attitudes, education level, and professional backgrounds of speakers.

The majority of borrowed words are stylistically marked, as technical terms (some 50 per cent according to Lomakina 1985) or as colloquial expressions. The Anglicisms collected and analysed in the *Dictionary of European Anglicisms* confirm these findings. They tend to be:

1. terminological (from the vocabulary of science, technology, or professional jargons) and, in consequence, restricted, and only partially integrated, but generally monosemous;
2. colloquial or slang words typical of spoken use, rather frequent in youth speech and interviews. In written use they are found in journalism and advertising. The degree of their integration is often uncertain and their meanings tend to be vague.

10.6 Forms of linguistic borrowing and their categorization

(Naumova 1982; Shanskiĭ 1972)

Borrowings may be loans which retain or closely model the form of the etymon or they may be translated; also, the meaning only of a foreign word may be borrowed. Loanwords may be monomorphemic (*summit*), derivatives (*overtime, recycling*), compounds (*body-building*) or phraseological word groups (*hot line*). It is obvious that morphologically and semantically motivated and transparent words can be more or less easily rendered in Russian. But calquing is not necessarily a mechanical process rendering systematic morpheme-for-morpheme correspondences between English and Russian words. It operates with linguistic items characterized by semantic equivalence, even where their form cannot always be clearly related because of structural differences between the two languages. Thus English compounds have, as a rule, phrasal equivalents in Russian: E *microwave*—Russian *mikrovolnovaya pech'*, E *aftershave*—Russian *los'on posle brit'ya*, E *feedback*—Russian *obratnaya svyaz'*. Calques may undergo semantic adjustment, acquiring properties they may have never possessed in English, just as happens with loan-words proper.

1. Borrowings are found on a continuum which has three identifiable stages:

- totally unadapted and not (yet) part of Russian (quotation words: *who's who, no problem,* or foreignisms: *Wall Street, Cockney, derby*);
- words still looking foreign in form (aliens): *kam-bék* ('come-back'), *promoushen* ('promotion'); and
- fully integrated Anglicisms: *futbol* (*football*), *kombaĭn* (*combine*), *lider* ('leader').

Integration may be a lengthy process.

Languages have also native resources for rendering new foreign concepts, employing replacements or pseudo-loans.

2. Replacement takes four forms, all illustrated below.

- translation, which represents the morphological structure of the unit as closely as possible. Sometimes, only part of an Anglicism is translated (semi-calque) (for examples, see group A 1–3 below);
- rendering, where only part of the foreign item is translated, the rest is rendered by looser equivalents (cf. group B below);
- creation, the coinage of an independent equivalent, prompted by the foreign word (cf. group C below);
- semantic loan, where an existing Russian word borrows one meaning of the foreign partial equivalent (cf. group D below).

3. Pseudo-loans

There are a few cases of English-looking words which do not exist in English:

- lexical pseudo-loans, which are combined from English morphemes to form new items that are not found in English: *rekordsmen, krossmen*;
- morphological pseudo-loans, i.e. the shortening of different linguistic units: monomorphemic words (Russian *profi* from E *professional, kep* from E *captain*); compounds (Russian *khéppi énd* from E *happy ending*): word groups (Russian *dzhin tonik* from E *gin and tonic*);
- semantic pseudo-loans where an English word develops a meaning in Russian which does not exist in English: Russian *vagon*—'a great quantity of sth, much'; *bufer*—'a person improving relations between two other people, peacemaker', *spinning*—'a special fishing rod used for spinning'.

Replacements can be illustrated with Russian examples, distinguishing between successes and failures.

A Translations

1. Successful

self-service < samoobsluzhivanie, skyscraper < neboskrëb, workaholic < trudogolik, soap opera < myl'naya opera, Bloody Mary < krovavaya Meri, shopping centre < torgovyĭ tsentr

2. Coexisting

bodyguard = *telokhranitel'*, *blocking* = *blokirovanie*, *underground* = *podpol'nyĭ*, *black box* = *chërnyĭ yashchik*, *first class* = *pervyĭ klass*, *big business* = *bol'shoĭ biznes*, *do-it-yourself* = *sdelaĭ éto sam*

B *Renderings*

1. Successful

ice hockey < *khokeĭ na l'du*, *database* < *baza datykh*, *Parkinson's disease* < *bolezn' Parkinsona*

2. Coexisting

skinheads = *britogolovye*, *keep smiling* = *prodolzhaĭte ulybat'sya*

C *Creations*

1. Successful

cruise missile < *krylataya raketa*, *airbag* < *podushka bezopasnosti*, *big bang (theory)* < *teoriya vzryva*

2. Coexisting

native speaker = *nositel' yazyka*, *second hand* = *byvshiĭ v upotreblenii*, *mass media* = *sredstva massovoĭ informatsii*

D *Semantic loans*

1. Successful

mouse < *mysh'* (computer), *bull* < *byk* (stock exchange), *make money* < *delat' den'gi*, *bear* < *medved'* (stock exchange)

2. Coexisting

bug = *klop*

10.7 The future of Anglicisms

English is now used all over the world. It has had a considerable effect on the vocabularies of many languages including Russian. Since the nineteenth century its influence on Russian has been constantly growing, as proved by the statistical figures quoted above.

The number of Anglicisms in Russian is not particularly large in comparison to other receiving languages. However, since Russian society has now opened up to the West, a further considerable growth of English words in Russian is happening under our eyes. The access to and influence of worldwide communications—press, radio, and television—makes speakers of Russian aware of new English words, many of which will, sooner or later, penetrate into their language. Many words relating to western contemporary technology are becoming part of the vocabulary of the world's languages, including Russian.

The influence of English on the Russian language will continue to be favourable in the near future unless certain factors come to restrict the process of borrowing from English. These might be saturation because all lexical gaps have been filled, a drastic reorientation of political, economic, and cultural life, and linguistic purism, including legislative measures.

10.8 Research

Anglicisms and other foreign words in Russian have lately become a focus of research. The bibliography reflects the main problems which have been of interest to linguists. Research has been devoted to the following topics:

1. historical studies, showing the growth of the English influence;
2. the analysis of Anglicisms in corpora of newspapers and journals;
3. the investigation of items current in special vocabularies (sports, advertising, pop music, etc.);
4. the lexical and stylistic analysis of words taken from studies of types (2) and (3);
5. the analysis of Anglicisms contained in dictionaries;
6. the assimilation of Anglicisms on the level of pronunciation, morphology, etc.;
7. sociolinguistic investigations.

10.9 Bibliography

The list consists of the titles mentioned in this survey and some important works not referred to. For further reference see the *Annotated Bibliography of European Anglicisms*, where important titles are accompanied by very short annotations describing their content and quality.

ARISTOVA, B. B. (1980), 'Anglo-russkie yazykovye kontakty i zaimstvovaniya' (Anglo-Russian Linguistic Contacts and Borrowings) (16th–20th century). D.Phil. thesis (Leningrad).

AVAKOVA, A. S. (1976), 'Naimenovanie sportsmenov: Igrokov v sovremennom russkom yazyke' (Terms for Sportsmen: Players in Contemporary Russian), *Étimologicheskie issledovaniya po russkomy yazyku*, 8: 15–29.

AVILOVA, N. S. (1967), *Slova internatsional'nogo proiskhozhdeniya v russkom literaturnom yazyke novogo vremeni* (Words of International Origin in the Contemporary Russian Literary Language) (Moscow).

BELYAEVA, S. A. (1984), *Angliĭskie slova v russkom yazyke XVI–XX vv* (English Words in the Russian Language of the 16th–20th Centuries) (Vladivostok).

BOBROVA, A. V. (1982), 'Imena sushchestvitel'nye na -ing v russkom yazyke' (Nouns Ending in -ing in the Russian Language). Unpubl. D.Phil. thesis (Moscow).

BONDARENKO, I. V. (1992), *Angliĭskaya terminologiya kak predmet filologicheskogo issledovaniya* (English Terminology as the Subject of Philological Studies) (Moscow).

ELIZOVA, T. K. (1978), 'Zaimstvovanie angliĭskoĭ leksiki v russkiĭ yazyk v 60–70 gg. XX v'. (The Borrowing of English Words in the Russian Language in the 60s–70s). Unpub. D.Phil. thesis (Rostov-na-Donu).

FILIN, F. P. (ed.) (1981), *Leksika russkogo literaturnogo yazyka XIX-XX vv.* (The Vocabulary of the Russian Literary Language of the 19th–20th Centuries) (Moscow).

FRONE, G. (1968), 'Ob angliĭskikh zaimstvovaniyakh v russkom yazyke' (On English Loanwords in the Russian Language), *Russkiĭ yazyk v shkole*, 3: 76–8.

GORBACHEVICH, K. S. (1984), *Russkiĭ yazyk: Proshloe, nastoyashchee, budushchee* (The Russian Language: Past, Present, Future) (Moscow: Prosveshchenie).

KOMLEV, N. G. (1992), *Inostrannoe slovo v delovoĭrechi* (Foreign Words in Business Language) (Moscow).

KOTELOVA, N. Z., and SOROKIN, YU. S. (eds.) (1973), *Novye slova i znacheniya: Slovar'-spravochnik po materialam pressy i literatury 60-kh godov* (New Words and Meanings: Dictionary Material from Periodical and Non-periodical Literature of the 60s) (Moscow: Sovetskaya Éntsiklopediya).

KRYSIN, L. P. (1968), *Inoyazychnye zaimstvovaniya v sovremennom russkom yazyke* (Foreign Borrowings in Contemporary Russian) (Moscow).

—— (1981), *Lexika russkogo literaturnogo yazyka XIX–m. XX v.* (The Vocabulary of the Russian Literary Language of the 19th–20th Centuries) (Moscow).

—— (1995), 'Yazykovoe zaimstvovanie i vzaimodeĭstvie vnutrennikh i vneshnikh faktorov' (Linguistic Borrowing: Interrelation between Inner and Outer Factors), *Rusistika segodnya* (Institut russkogo yazyka: Russian Academy of Sciences), 1: 117–34.

LARIONOVA, E. V. (1993), 'Noveĭshie anglitsizmy v sovremennom russkom yazyke' (The Latest Anglicisms in Contemporary Russian), unpub. D.Phil. thesis (Moscow).

LOMAKINA, Z. I. (1985), *Zaimstvovanie i osvoenie russkim yazykom inoyazychnoĭ leksiki v 60–80 gg. XX v.* (Borrowing and Adaptation of Foreign Words of the 60s–80s in the Russian Language) (Kiev).

MARTINEK, V. M. (1971), 'Leksiko-semanticheskaya assimilyatsiya angliĭskikh zaimstvovaniĭ v russkom literaturnom yazyke sovetskoĭ épokhi' (Lexico-semantic Assimilation of English Borrowings in the Russian Literary Language of the Soviet Period), unpub. D.Phil. thesis (Dnepropetrovsk).

MAXIMOVA, T. V. (1996), 'The Phonetic and Morphological Assimilation of Anglicisms in Russian', *Vestnik Volgogradskogo universiteta*, 1 (2): 62–6.

—— and PELIKH, E. A. (1994), 'Angliĭskie zaimstvovaniya v russkom i drugikh evropeĭskikh yazykakh' (English Loanwords in Russian and other European Languages), in *Materialy XI nauchnoĭ konferentsii professorsko-prepodavatel'skogo sostava* (Volgograd), 356–60.

NAUMOVA, I. O. (1982), 'Frazeologicheskie kal'ki angliĭskogo proiskhozhdeniya v sovremennom russkom yazyke (na materiale publitsistiki)' (Phraseological Loan-Translations of English Origin in Contemporary Russian (from Press Material), unpub. D.Phil. thesis (Moscow).

NOVIKOV, L. A. (1963), 'O semanticheskom pereoformlenii zaimstvovannykh slov v russkom yazyke' (On Semantic Changes of Loanwords in the Russian Language), *Russkiĭ yazyk v shkole*, 3: 5–10.

PANOV, M. V. (ed.) (1968), *Leksika sovremennogo russkogo literaturnogo yazyka: Russkiĭ yazyk i sovetskoe obshchestvo. Sotsiologo-lingvisticheskoe issledovanie* (The Vocabulary of the Contemporary Russian Literary Language: The Russian Language and the Soviet Society. Sociolinguistic Studies) (Moscow).

SEN'KO, E. V. (1980), *Novoe v leksike sovremennogo russkogo literaturnogo yazyka* (New Words in the Vocabulary of the Contemporary Russian Literary Language) (Leningrad).

SHANSKIĬ, N. M. (1972), *Leksikologiya sovremennogo russkogo yazyka* (Lexicology of Contemporary Russian) (Moscow).

SOROKIN, Y. S. (1968), *Razvitie slovarnogo sostava russkogo literaturnogo yazyka (30e–90e gody XIX v)* (The Development of the Word Stock of the Russian Literary Language) (Moscow).

TIMOFEEVA, G. G. (1985), 'Fonetiko-orfograficheskoe osvoenie novykh zaimstvovannykh slov' (Phonetic and Spelling Adaptation of New Loanwords), unpub. D.Phil. thesis (Leningrad).

VASIL'EV, V. A. (1980), *Fonetika angliĭskogo yazyka* (Phonetics of English) (Moscow).

WARD, D. (1986), 'The English Contribution to Russian', in W. Viereck and W.-D. Bald (eds.), *English in Contact with Other Languages* (Budapest: Akadémiai Kiadó), 307–32.

11

POLISH

Elżbieta Mańczak-Wohlfeld

11.1 History of language contact

11.1.1 Chronology of intensive influences

The ties between Poland and England have never been as close as those with its neighbouring countries, or with France and Italy, and these closer connections have obviously determined the process of borrowing. Generally speaking, Poland's political relations were dependent on close allies, but it also had some cultural contact with England, going back to the fifteenth and sixteenth centuries when the first Poles went to England to study. In the same period some Scottish exiles started to settle in Poland and actors' troupes and representatives of other professions from Britain began to come to the country.

The early eighteenth century saw the beginning of the development of trade between Poland and England with the signing of a trade treaty in 1706 in Gdańsk (Danzig). In the same period, an influential Polish aristocratic family, the Czartoryskis, wanted to forge official relations with Britain. As a consequence, after 1759 an English political party became established in Poland, led by the last Polish king—Stanisław August Poniatowski—and Adam Kazimierz Czartoryski. Just before the partition of Poland there were some attempts to reconstruct both Polish government and Parliament after the English model. Unfortunately, these attempts came to nothing because Poland lost its independence. Although many Poles thought England might support them in their struggle for independence, these hopes turned out to be illusory. In the course of partition (1773–1918) many of the richest members of the Polish society continued to go to England to study. After the failure of the so-called November Insurrection in 1831 the Polish exiled government was established in London. In turn, during the January uprising of 1863, owing to Polish intervention, an English ship was sent by the British government to Poland to help the insurgents.

On the whole, the Poles treated Britain and the British in a friendly way; they admired its industrialization, the social developments, and the organization of cooperatives, although they objected to some aspects of English policy directed against Polish interests. In 1822–3, the first English magazine *Pustelnik z ulicy Pikadilly* (*The Hermit from Piccadilly Street*) appeared. It was devoted to the description of British life and institutions. At that time a number of English literary works were translated into Polish, for example those of Pope, Gray, Johnson, Scott, and Byron. Simultaneously, Shakespeare's plays in Polish were staged all over Poland. In the course of the nineteenth century English was gradually becoming more and more popular among the aristocracy, in part replacing the predominance of French. Towards the end of the nineteenth century the first reports about Britain began to appear in the Polish press.

Relations between Poland and the United States go back to the 1830s when Polish emigration began; this was different from later waves because the emigrants consisted of gentry and of better-educated people who left Poland after the collapse of the 1831 uprising. The first Polish settlement was in fact founded in 1854 in Texas. An even greater number emigrated after the failure of the 1863 insurrection and from the turn of the nineteenth century onwards. Most of these later emigrants were peasants who left the country because of poverty.

Polish and British/American relations began to flourish after the First World War thanks to the development of the navy, the merchant fleet, sports, and tourism. Bilateral relations reached their peak after the Second World War and still continue today (Dąbrowski 1962; Konopczyński 1947; Lipoński 1978). It should not be forgotten that after the Second World War the Polish government in exile was in London, and a large number of soldiers and officers remained in Britain. Polish emigration to Great Britain and to the USA continues to the present time; for instance, many Poles left after the introduction of martial law in Poland in 1981.

11.1.2 Origins of influence

The social contact conditions summarized above are reflected in the Polish language: the early impact of BrE and AmE on Polish is limited to so-called *cultural borrowings*, which, as Bloomfield (1933: 458) put it, 'show us what one nation has taught another'.

The process of proper borrowing from English into Polish began in the course of the eighteenth century. According to Kasprzycka (1971) a contemporary geographical dictionary included five entries of English origin: **bord* denoting 'a ship' and four other Anglicisms still in use: *jacht* 'yacht', *kecz* 'ketch', *kutter* 'cutter', *sloop* 'sloop'.

In the first great Polish dictionary (an equivalent of Johnson's *Dictionary*), written by Linde at the very beginning of the nineteenth century, fourteen clearly English loans are mentioned: *flanela* 'flannel', *foksal* 'Vauxhall', *frak* 'frock', *galon* 'gallon', *golf* 'golf', *klub* 'club', *kwakier* 'Quaker', *mada* 'mud', *muchair* 'mohair', *piknik* 'picnic', *poncz* 'punch', *porter*, and *rum*—all still used—and one ephemeral: *pikier* 'picker' (Mańczak-Wohlfeld 1987a). At that time, two other English lexical items were known to speakers of Polish, namely *bill* and *budżet* 'budget').

We observe a gradual increase of English borrowings in Polish, which is in agreement with the general European tendency. In the first Polish lexicon of foreign words from the middle of the nineteenth century about 100 Anglicisms are included. Only a few of them constitute such ephemeral words as: *baard* < E *board* 'a kind of vessel used for transport' or *flip* 'a drink made of beer, vodka, and sugar' or *boll* 'measure of capacity of grain equal to 218.147 litres' (Mańczak-Wohlfeld 1994b).

The twentieth century saw a steady increase of Anglicisms, but it was not before the second half of the twentieth century that the impact of English became dramatic. Fisiak found over 700 English loans, and in his 1986 article he mentioned over 1,000 attested by 1985. My findings in 1994 show about 1,600 documented Anglicisms (Mańczak-Wohlfeld 1994a) and there were over 1,700 to be found a year later, which indicates the penetration of English in recent years (*Dictionary of European Anglicisms*; Mańczak-Wohlfeld 1995).

However, my research has shown that the impact of foreign words, and in particular English lexemes, on Polish is not so extensive as is often implied. For instance, Damborský (1974: 347) claims that, in the only available Polish dictionary of frequency by Kurcz, Lewicki, Sambor, and Woronczak (1974–7), in the part devoted to journalism, three-quarters of the entries are of Polish origin and one quarter loanwords. If we analyse the language of journalism, every second lexical item is of foreign origin. However, if we take into consideration other text-types, the situation looks different; namely three Polish lexical items for each loanword. In the 1990 version of the quoted dictionary of frequency of 10,355 entries, only fifty-nine headwords are from English (forty words and nineteen derivatives). It may be claimed that the results of these calculations are not fully satisfactory as the lexicon is outdated. The authors analyse data collected in the years 1963–7. However, the above observations are supported by the examination of two more recent dictionaries: a minimum lexicon of Polish by Kurzowa and Zgółkowa (1992) consisting of 1,520 entries of the most frequently occurring words which includes only twelve English loanwords, and Markowski's (1995) dictionary of foreign words used in the mass media which contains some 1,100 words of foreign origin. As we are told in the preface to the lexicon, Markowski tried to include as many English loans as possible, and still found only 126 borrowings and 11 semantic loans, just over 10 per cent of the total foreign words included in the lexicon. The majority of loanwords are from Latin and, less frequently, from Greek. Though the influence of English on Polish is considerable, there is, then, no danger that Polish will be submerged by English, as some scholars have claimed (cf. Mańczak-Wohlfeld 1996a).

11.1.3 *Types of influence*

The influence of English on Polish is largely limited to lexis (see exceptions detailed in s. 11.6). Older borrowings are well integrated and are not even felt to be loans by Poles not knowing English: their spelling and pronunciation agree with the rules of Polish, they follow Polish grammar, and their meanings are obvious to every Pole. By contrast, recent loanwords behave differently. Their spelling tends to vary, e.g. the lexeme *business woman* is written in four different ways: <businesswoman>,

<business woman>, <busineswoman>, <bizneswoman>. Their pronunciation is based either on spelling, *nylony* [nɪlɔni], or is close to the etymon, *out* [aut]. With some new loans we observe a certain degree of hesitation about correct pronunciation, as in [kɛtʃup] vs. [kɛtʃap]. Recent borrowings conform to the rules of Polish grammar relatively easily. Since a majority of Anglicisms constitute nouns, they are assigned an appropriate gender (in most cases masculine) and are declined accordingly. There are fewer verbs, adjectives, adverbs, and interjections. Usually the meaning of Anglicisms in Polish agrees with one of the meanings of their English counterparts.

11.1.4 Chronology of purist phases

As indicated in s. 11.1.2, some attempts to eliminate the use of borrowings from different languages can be observed in Poland. As early as the end of the eighteenth century some literary people criticized the overuse of Gallicisms. However, the first grammarian to opt for the purity of Polish was Kopczyński, who in his grammar book (1817) suggested writing a dictionary consisting of Polish equivalents of loanwords. Another nineteenth-century scientist warned that due to the influence of foreign languages Polish might disappear. This purist attitude has been adopted by a number of nineteenth-century and twentieth-century scholars, including linguists (Mańczak-Wohlfeld 1995). The tendency to eliminate loans became particularly strong when Poland gained its independence in 1918 after a long period of partition. Since Poland was occupied by Russia, Prussia, and Austria, the Polish language was under the influence of Russian and German. Therefore there was a strong trend to replace Russianisms and Germanisms by Polish equivalents. This tendency was still observed after the Second World War. Nowadays scholars are only worried by supposed overuse of Anglicisms (cf. s. 11.1.2).

11.1.5 Regional differences

The impact of English is basically limited to standard Polish. Occasionally, the influence of English is restricted to individual Polish dialects, e.g. *bokietek* or *bakiet* < E *bucket* 'milk can' or *dyniarka* < E *dinner-bucket*, *nektajza* < E *necktie*, or found in the jargon of soldiers (*bren* < E *Bren gun*), sailors (*czif* < E *chief* 'the first naval officer'), or teenagers (*na ful(l)a* < E *full* 'maximum volume'), cf. Mańczak-Wohlfeld (1996*b*).

11.1.6 Stylistic differences

As in the case of other languages influenced by English, Anglicisms are found mainly in two registers, namely technical and colloquial. The first group comprises terms from fields such as sport, fashion, music, food, biology, sea words, economy, transport, computer terminology, politics, physics, chemistry, trade, medicine, military expressions, mining and metallurgy, minerals, geology, religion, arts, agriculture and gardening, tourism, electricity. Colloquialisms are fairly frequent in journalese, since journalists often quote English words that do not necessarily become part of Polish. They can also be found in youth language. They include polite words like *sorry*, indifferent lexical items, e.g. *butterfly* 'a kind of knife', and dirty words (cf. Mańczak-Wohlfeld 1966*b*).

11.1.7 Innovation and obsolescence

In the two dictionaries of the Polish language from the middle of the nineteenth century and from the beginning of the twentieth century we find a first notable occurrence of obsolete items: out of 180 English borrowings found in *The Vilnius Dictionary*, about 30 are now obsolete, such as *bording* 'a small ship' or *groat* 'an English coin = 10 copecks = 10 groshes' (Mańczak-Wohlfeld 1987*b*). In turn, in *The Warsaw Dictionary*, out of 250 Anglicisms 48 loans are ephemeral words, like *krona* ('crown') 'an English coin = 1 rouble 41 copecks' or *riot* 'a rebellion' (Mańczak-Wohlfeld 1988). More recent Anglicisms (introduced before the Second World War and after) are in most cases still used.

Nowadays we observe an interesting tendency to use original English spellings of some already assimilated loans, like *biznes > business*, *dżin > gin* (cf. s.11.6).

11.1.8 Mediating languages

Anglicisms are often borrowed straight from English, for example the afore-mentioned English loans found in some dialects; some were introduced by Polish immigrants coming back from the United States. Numerous early Anglicisms were transmitted via German (e.g. *befsztyk* < E *beefsteak*), French (e.g. *szewiot* < E *cheviot/Cheviot*), or Russian (e.g. *snajper* < E *sniper*), cf. Mańczak-Wohlfeld (1996*b*).

11.1.9 English in education

The first attempt to introduce English as a school language took place in the Knights School in Warsaw when John Lind was its director of studies (1767–72). It is interesting to note that he was in favour of teaching foreign languages through conversation as well as reading and that he was against memorizing grammar, but when he returned to England, he left no followers behind. It is most likely that he taught English from books published in France or Germany because the first English grammar book appeared in Poland as late as 1788 (Julian Antonowicz, *Gramatyka dla Polaków chcących się uczyć angielskiego*, Warsaw; cf. Mańczak-Wohlfeld 1996*c*).

Interest in learning English as a foreign language increased only at the end of the nineteenth century when English became popular mainly among the aristocracy, often replacing French. In the period between the two world wars English was fashionable among the Polish intelligentsia. Since the Second World War it has gradually entered Polish schools particularly from 1956, a development which reached its peak after the change in the political system in 1989. To be more precise, although in the period of 1945–89 Russian was the only compulsory language taught both in primary and secondary schools, English became more and more popular. It was only taught in secondary schools and occasionally at universities. However, already in the 1960s most students chose English as a second language. (There was also the possibility of attending English private courses.) The situation was radically changed in 1989 when English teacher training colleges were established, a number of English private schools were founded, and English was introduced to primary schools.

11.2 Pronunciation and spelling

11.2.1 Pronunciation

The phonological systems of English and Polish differ quantitatively and qualitatively. For example, in English twelve simple vowel phonemes are distinguished whereas in Polish there are only eight; English vowel phonemes are also characterized by quantity, while in Polish there is no such distinction; word stress is fairly free in English, whereas it usually falls on the penultimate syllable in Polish words. What follows is a list of phonological changes that take place during the process of integration.

Vowel phonemes (including diphthongs):

/i/		/'biznis/	> /biznɛs/
/ə/		/pəd ʒa:məz/	> /piʒama/
/i:/ ——→ /i/		/'tʃestəfi:ld/	> /tʃesterfilt/
/iə/		/'kliəriŋ/	> /kliriŋk/
/e/		/tʃek/	> /tʃɛk/
/æ/		/'bædmint(ə)n/	> /badmintɔn/
/ʌ/		/blʌf/	> /blɛf/
/i/ ——→ /ɛ/		/'biznis/	> /biznɛs/
/ə/		/'biznismən/	> /biznɛsmɛn/
/i:/		/'si:lskin/	> /sɛlskinɨ/
/ei/		/'bleizə/	> /blɛzɛr/
/ʌ/		/rʌgbi/	> /ragbɨ/
/æ/		/'pækais/	> /pakajs/
/o/ ——→ /a/		/frok/	> /frak/
/ə/		/'ræglən/	> /raglan/
/ʌ/		/klʌmp/	> /klɔmp/
/o/		/'bobslei/	> /bɔpslej/
/ə/ ——→ /ɔ/		/'nɔ:fək/	> /nɔrfɔlk/
/ə:/		/'əuvərˌɔ:l/	> /ɔvɛrɔl/
/əu/		/'əu'kei/	> /ɔkej/
/u/		/buk/	> /bukɔvatç /
/ʌ/ ——→ /u/		/'bʌdʒit/	> /budʒɛt/
/u:/		/bu:m/	> /bum/
/i/		/'britʃiz/	> /britʃɛsɨ/
/i:/ ——→ /i/		/'sti:lən/	> /stɨlɔn/

Also /ar/, /ɛr/, /r/, /ai/ are equivalents of vowel phonemes due to their spelling pronunciation:

/a:/—/ar/	/ˈfa:mə/	> /farmɛr/
/ə/—/ɛr/	/ˈspi:kə/	> /spikɛr/
/ə/—/ɔr/	/kɔ:t/	> /kɔrt/
/aiə/—/ajr/	/ˈnonˈaiən/	> /nɔnajrɔnka/
/ə/—/ɔl/	/ˈnɔ:fək/	> /nɔrfɔlk/.

Consonant phonemes:

/p/—/p/	/pʌzl/	> /puzlɛ/
⟩/b/	/ˈbaipa:s/	> /bajpas/
/b/—/p/		
	/skæb/	> /skɛp/
/t/ — /t/	/təust/	> /tɔast/
⟩/d/	/ˈdɔ:ltəˈniz(ə)m/	> /daltɔnism/
/d/— /t/		
	/bænd/	> /bɛnt/
/k/—/k/	/kənˈsʌltiŋ/	> /kɔsultink/
/g/	/geim/	> /gɛm/
/g/		
⟩/k/	/log/	> /lɔk/
/tʃ/	/ˈtʃa:tə(r)/	> /tʃartɛr/
/tʃ/		
⟩/ʃ/	/ˈtʃeviət/	> /ʃɛvjɔt/
/dʒ/	/dʒæz/	> /dʒɛs/
/dʒ/		
⟩/ʒ/	/piˈd ʒa:məz/	> /piʒama/
/f/—/f/	/flɜ:t/	> /flirt/
/v/—/v/	/ˈvelvit/	> /vɛlvɛt/
/s/	/ˈtæmwəθ/	> /tamwɔrsɨ/
/θ/		
⟩/t/	/ˈθrilə(r)/	> /trilɛr/
/s/	/spɔ:t/	> /spɔrt/
/s/		
⟩/ʃ/	/ˈbi:fˈsteik/	> /bɛfʃtɨk/
/z/	/zu:m/	> /zum/
/z/		
⟩/s/	/dʒi:nz/	> /dʒins/
/h/—/x/	/ˈhæpi/	> /xɛpi/
/m/—/m/	/ˈma:kit/	> /markɛt/
/n/	/net/	> /nɛt/
/n/		
⟩/ŋ/	/ˈmɔ:gəˈniz(ə)m/	> /mɔrgaŋism/
/ŋ/—/ŋk/	/səˈroŋ/	> /sarɔŋk/
/l/—/l/	/ˈliliˈpju:ʃ(ə)n/	> /liliput/

/r/—/r/	/riˈpɔːtə(r)/	> /rɛpɔrtɛr/
/f/	/ˈskwotə(r)/	> /skvatɛr/
/w/—/v/	/ˈwelɪŋt(ə)n/	> /vɛliŋktɔn/
/w/	/wiːkˈend/	> /wikɛnt/
/j/ /j/	/ˈjʌpi/	> /japi/

and syllabic /l/, /n/, e.g.

| | /ˈbætldres/ | > /bɛtɛldrɛs/ |
| | /ˈstetsn/ | > /stɛtsɔn/ |

On the basis of the above list it may be concluded that in the process of borrowing, English vowel phonemes are simplified in Polish, whereas English consonant phonemes are rendered in Polish in a more complex way. Finally, it is worth noting that out of 1,700 loans, 250 preserve their English pronunciation, which means that English phonemes are identified by Polish 'equivalents', e.g. *check*, *net*, *yuppy*, about 1,400 words are Polonized on the phonological level, e.g. *business* [biznɛs], *frock* [frak], and, in the case of about 40 items, a certain degree of hesitation is observed, e.g. *cheviot* [ʃevjɔt, tʃevjɔt], *grapefruit* [grejpfrut, grejfrut], *mackintosh* [makintɔʃ, mekintɔʃ].

11.2.2 Graphemic integration

The grapheme system of English and Polish differs to a certain extent: <x>, <q>, and <v> are only used in English, whereas Polish adds e.g. <ą, ę, ó, ł>, [ã, ẽ, u, w]. The combination and the distribution of letters are also different in the two languages. Finally, it is worth stressing that the English spelling system is less phonemic than the Polish system.

    My analysis of 1,700 Anglicisms showed that 550 items preserve the English spelling, for example *fair*, *lobby* (a tendency which increasingly affects borrowings of the 1980s and 1990s), whereas the spelling of 250 loans varies, as in *bandżo/ banjo*, *tim/team*. In the remaining 900 borrowings, the following changes are observed, which indicate various types of assimilation on the graphic level.

Consonants or groups of consonants:

c		
k	*cutter*	> *kuter*
ck	*frock*	> *frak*
c—s	*pack ice*	> *pakajs*
ch—cz	*Chartism*	> *czartyzm*
d—t	*trend*	> *trent*
g—ż	*budget*	> *budżet*
dż	*gin*	> *dżin*
gh—j	*bobsleigh*	> *bobslej*
h—ch	*hooligan*	> *chuligan*
j—dż	*jet*	> *dżet*

l —ł	*virginal*	*> wirginał*
qu —kw	*Quaker*	*> kwakier*
ph —f	*pamphlet*	*> pamflet*
rh —r	*rhumb*	*> rumb*
s —z	*quasar*	*> kwazar*
sh —sz	*shock*	*> szok*
t —c	*escalation*	*> eskalacja*
tch—cz	*Fletcher*	*> fleczer*
th ⟨ t / s	*Jonathan freckle*	*> jonatan*
	Tamworth	*> tamworsy*
v ⟨ w / f	*velvet*	*> welwet*
	Vauxhall	*> Foksal*
w —u	*clown*	*> klaun*
wl —ł	*trawl*	*> trał*
wh—w	*Whig*	*> wig*
x —ks	*maxwell*	*> makswel*
z —ż	*bulldozer*	*> buldożer*

The reduction of double consonants:

bb—b	*bubble*	*> buble*
dd—d	*paddock*	*> padok*
ff—f	*offside*	*> ofsajd*
gg—g	*bootlegger*	*> butleger*
ll—l	*bullionism*	*> bulionizm*
nn—n	*flannel*	*> flanela*
pp—p	*peppermint*	*> peperment*
rr—r	*bull terrier*	*> bulterier*
ss—s	*business*	*> biznes*
tt—t	*globetrotter*	*> globtroter*

Vowels or groups of vowels:

a ⟨ o / ej	*hall*	*> hol*
	interface	*> interfejs*
a	*backhand*	*> bekhend*
ai—e	*trainer*	*> trener*
ea	*sealskin fur*	*> selskiny*
ai—ej ⟨ aj / e	*cocktail*	*> koktajl*
	trailer	*> trejler*
	drain	*> dren*
aw—o	*lawrencium*	*> lorens*
e ⟨ a / o	*clerk*	*> klark*
	buffer	*> bufor*

ea—i	*leader*	> *lider*
ee ⟨ i	*feet*	> *fita*
ee ⟨ y	*afreet*	> *afryt*
	combiner	> *kombajner*
i ⟨ aj / e / j / y	*shirting*	> *szerting*
	broiler	> *brojler*
	bridge	> *brydż*
o—a	*out*	> *aut*
oa—o	*board*	> *bord*
oo—u	*boomerang*	> *bumerang*
	lockout	> *lokaut*
ou ⟨ au / e / u	*double*	> *debel*
	karibou	> *karibu*
ow—u	*bowline*	> *bulina*
	uppercut	> *aperkut*
u ⟨ a / e / i / w	*runner*	> *rener*
	business	> *biznes*
	guinea	> *gwinea*
y ⟨ i / j	*lynch*	> *lincz*
	boycott	> *bojkot*

The reduction of double vowels:

ee—e	*beefsteak*	> *befsztyk*
oo—o	*cook*	> *kok*

Finally, it should be added that occasionally a letter is added (e.g. E *bunker* > <bunkier> or omitted (e.g. E *acre* > <akr>).

11.3 Morphology

11.3.1 Introduction

The morphological system of each language has its own characteristics. Therefore every Anglicism first undergoes morphological analysis in order to be allocated to a given category.

11.3.2 Nouns

As with other languages, the majority of borrowings are nouns (about 1,600 out of 1,700 loans documented). They are assigned an appropriate gender on the basis of either their form or their meaning. Most are masculine, including those ending in a consonant, for example *badminton*, *kidnaping*, *kombajn*, *komiks*, *serial*, and those at least spelt with a word-final consonant, for example *blezer*, *komputer*, *spiker*.

Some nouns that end in -*y* also take the masculine gender, for example *burburry* or *caddy*, as well as those that end in -*ist* which is rendered as -*ista* in Polish, e.g. *eskapista, folklorysta*. *Collie* and *dingo* are masculine for semantic reasons, since they are associated with the Polish word *pies* 'dog', which is masculine. Nouns ending in -*a* are feminine, e.g. *gwinea, gymkhana, sekwoja*. This includes nouns to which -*a* is added, for semantic reasons, such as *girlsa, mopa*, or the suffixes -*ka*, (e.g. *dżokejka, striptizerka*), -*ówka*, (e.g. *tenisówka, treningówka*) or -*cja*, (e.g. *szerardyzacja, wirescencja*). -*a* or suffixes ending in -*a* are added for various reasons:

1. purely morphological reasons which may be exemplified by the word *mop* with its variant *mopa*;
2. the mediation of German where some of these loans are feminine, e.g. *round* > German *die Runde* > Polish *runda*;
3. semantic reasons, which is the case for e.g. *girlsa, trenerka* 'woman trainer'; *whisky* takes the feminine gender because it is associated with the Polish lexeme *wódka*.

In turn, the neuter gender is assigned to nouns ending in /i/, /y/, /o/, /u/ (*bikini, derby, party, disco, waterpolo, dżiu-dżitsu*) or that graphically end in a vowel (e.g. *yale*). Fairly infrequently, borrowings that end in a consonant are attributed the neuter gender, for example *hula-hoop*.

Case and number. The endings regular for the respective class are attached. There are some nouns without fixed gender, mainly *pluralia tantum*, e.g. *bryczesy* < *breeches, buble* < *bubbles* 'products worth nothing', *dżinsy* < *jeans, pikle* < *pickles, farmerki* 'trousers worn by farmers'. Their declension is therefore incomplete, being similar to those nouns that do not take the plural. Very few nouns are undeclined, which shows that English borrowings are relatively easily integrated into Polish grammar. In a few cases the English plural is retained, for example *gospels, marines*. As in other languages 'double plurals' are occasionally found, for example *dropsy* < E *drops, dżinsy* < E *jeans*.

11.3.3 Adjectives

Half of the adjectives (about twenty items) taken from English are well adapted and thus are inflected according to the Polish patterns, e.g. *kompatybilny* < E *compatible*. The remaining half have not been assimilated, that is, they have English forms and are not inflected, e.g. *happy*. They can only be used predicatively, unlike the integrated adjectives which occur both predicatively and attributively.

11.3.4 Adverbs and interjections

Both adverbs (ten items, including *fifty-fifty, non-stop*) and interjections (three words, e.g. *halo* < E *hallo*) are not assimilated in Polish. They are unadapted on all the linguistic levels except for pronunciation, where they do undergo phonological substitution.

11.3.5 Verbs

The majority of verbs are fully assimilated by the addition of the suffix -*ować*, as in *parkować* < *to park*, *trenować* < *to train*, and they are inflected according to the rules of Polish. Some are partly assimilated, differing from the former category by lacking complete sets of forms in Polish, e.g. *besemerować* 'to produce steel in Bessemer's converter', *jazzować*, 'to play jazz'. A few verbs are used in one form, the imperative, e.g. *play*, *stop*. Most of these verbs have their counterpart in English; only two verbs have been formed from gerunds: *dopingować* < E *doping*, *dubingować* < E *dubbing*, and two from nouns: *chuliganić* < E *hooligan*, *wistować* < E *whist* (Fisiak 1985).

11.3.6 Derivation (selection)

As regards word formation, almost all English loans are treated as morphemically simple in Polish. Derivational affixes are attached to about 300 Anglicisms (out of 1,700 analysed words), proving a high degree of assimilation; these are frequent especially for adjectives derived from nouns which are necessitated (as in other Slavic languages) by the linguistic structure (for instance, rendering English n.+n. compounds). Half of these borrowings take only one derivational affix, for example *bobslej* → adj. *bobslejowy* (< E *bobsleigh*). Half of them are followed or preceded by more than one affix, occasionally reaching a dozen or so suffixes, e.g. *koks* < *coke* 'a solid substance left after the gases have been extracted from coal' → *koksik*, diminutive of *coke*, *koksowanie* (gerund), *koksiarnia* 'coking plant', *koksownica* 'coke oven', *koksujący* (adj.), *koksowniczy* (adj.). The attachment of the suffix sometimes results in a change in the part of speech, e.g. the noun *czarter* is converted to the adjective *czarterowy* (< E *charter*). However, in most cases twenty-nine different suffixes that are added to nouns result in a change in the subclass of the same part of speech, e.g. -*ek* (*barek* < *bar* 'a small bar'), -*owanie* (*boksowanie* < *boks* 'boxing'), -*owiec* (*filmowiec* < *film* 'film-maker'). The gender of these derivatives conforms to the rules of Polish grammar. To obtain adjectives ten different suffixes may be attached to nouns, e.g. -*owy* (*brydżowy* < *brydż* 'bridge'), -*ski* (*dżentelmeński* < *dżentelmen* 'gentleman'). On the other hand, adverbs are formed from adjectives already created in Polish by the addition of the suffixes -*o* or -*ie*, e.g. adv. *komfortowo* < adj. *komfortowy* ('comfort'). As mentioned before, verbs take -*ować* or -*ić* (cf. s. 11.3.5). Infrequently, prefixes are attached to nouns and adjectives, e.g. *przedmecz* 'match played by teams of lower class', *wysportowany* 'athletic'. Also prefixes are added to verbs to indicate complete forms, e.g. *wytrenować* 'to train'.

11.3.7 Compounds and combining forms

As mentioned in s. 11.3.6 almost all English loanwords are treated as morphemically simple in Polish. There are only two exceptions, namely -*gate* and -*land*. The former morpheme is added to different Polish words to indicate a 'scandal' or an 'affair' whereas the latter when added to words used in Polish implies 'a large shop', e.g. *drewland* 'a shop selling wooden products'.

11.3.8 Calques (loan translations)

Due to the fact that Poland and English-speaking countries are not in close geographic contact there are very few calques. A few of them may serve as an illustration: E *teenager* > *nastolatek*, E *brain-washing* > *pranie mózgu*, E *summit conference* > *konferencja na szczycie*, E *skyscraper* > *drapacz chmur*.

11.4 Meaning

How borrowing affects the meaning of loanwords. According to my analysis (Mań-czak-Wohlfeld 1992), English borrowings are found in forty-five semantic fields. They are most numerous in such fields as 'sport', 'man', 'clothing', and 'music'. I presented there a detailed analysis of the semantic processes taking place in the field of 'clothing'. Since similar changes occur in the case of other English borrow-ings, I will quote my results. The retention of the original meaning occurs in thirty-six (53 per cent) out of sixty-eight Anglicisms, as in *dżinsy* (E *jeans*), *nylony* (E *nylons*), *pidżama/piżama* (E *pyjamas*).

Less frequently a change of the sense, or of one of the senses, of English borrowings occurs after their integration into Polish. This, the second largest group consisting of ten items, constitutes 15 per cent of the data.

The next group (nine lexemes: 13 per cent) is the borrowings that undergo a complete semantic change. What is preserved is their dominant feature [CLOTHING] which allows them to be kept in the discussed field, e.g. *dres* in Polish denotes 'tracksuit' whereas in English the word *dress* has three different meanings in reference to clothes.

Less frequently (six cases: 9 per cent) a transfer occurs of one sense of an English lexeme into Polish, while the second or possibly the third or fourth senses, also referring to 'clothing', do not occur in Polish, for example *frak* 'dress coat' vs. six different senses for *frock* listed in the *COD*.

The second to last group, consisting of four lexical items (6 per cent), is charac-terized by the following: in one sense the English borrowings are identical to their English counterparts, whereas in the second sense they only share the dominant feature [CLOTHING], e.g. *owerol/owerole/overol/overoll* in both languages refers to 'an outer garment worn to keep out dirt, wet, etc.' but in Polish it also denotes 'sweatshirt', whereas in English it additionally means (1) 'protective trousers, dungarees or a combination suit, worn by workmen, etc.', (2) 'close-fitting trousers worn as part of army uniform'.

The last group consists of three lexemes (4 per cent) that are characterized by the fact that the English loanwords have one sense common to their English equiva-lents and also another sense unknown in English, e.g. *blezer* (E *blazer*) meaning in both languages 'a man's plain jacket, often dark blue, not forming part of a suit' and additionally in Polish referring to 'a cardigan'.

11.5 Usage

No comprehensive study of the field has ever been conducted in Poland. Results from the *Dictionary of European Anglicisms* have only confirmed what had been known impressionistically before and is typical of other languages as well; most of the Anglicisms in Polish are either technical or colloquial.

11.6 Forms of linguistic borrowing and their categorization

The influence of English on Polish is mainly characterized by the introduction of loanwords. There are three categories of them: citations (e.g. *jilted generation*), unadapted borrowings (e.g. *hobby, science fiction*), and well-assimilated loans (e.g. *dżinsy* < E *jeans, tramwaj* < E *tramway*). The presence of hybrids and calques is far less frequent (cf. s. 11.3.7). In Polish, similarly to other languages, we find some pseudo-Anglicisms like *smoking* < E *smoking jacket, trencz* < *trench coat*, where the second element is skipped; only in one word the first element is eliminated: *slipy* < E *bathing slips*. Another category concerns semantic loans; again there are not many of them, e.g. *dieta* (*diet*) 'food in general', *konwencja* (*convention*) 'an assembly of the delegates of a political party to select candidates for office'.

The influence of English on Polish extends beyond simple loans to hybrids like *autoservice* (E *car service*), *pizza party, spaghetti western*, and calques (cf. s. 11.3.8).

Recent years have seen the following changes in the impact of English on Polish:

1. the usage of original spellings of some already assimilated loans, like *biznes* > *business, dżin* > *gin*;
2. the occasional introduction of the genitive ending *-'s* added even to Polish names, e.g. *Witek's* 'the name of a firm';
3. the aforementioned usage of English suffixes (cf. s. 11.3.7);
4. the adoption of noun+noun compounds, an hitherto unknown type in Polish, for example *fliz shop* ('tile shop'), *hurt-land* ('wholesale'), *Sobieski crown* (Sobieski = the Polish king's name) and in compounds containing no English loanwords, e.g. *auto lakiernia* ('car varnish'), *auto złom* ('car scrap');
5. the widespread preposition of adjectives, which is contrary to the Polish word order, e.g. *formalna analiza* instead of *analiza formalna* (E *formal analysis*).

11.7 The future of Anglicisms

Due to our contacts with Western Europe it is evident that the impact of English on Polish will continue to grow but there is no danger that Polish will be submerged by English, as some linguists claim.

11.8 Research

So far major research has been exclusively conducted by Fisiak and Mańczak-Wohlfeld; in addition a number of MA dissertations written in English and Polish departments all over the country deal with the problem. Recently, a project on the influence of English as a spoken language of the younger generation of well-educated Poles has been launched. Besides, some Polonists occasionally publish short articles or notes on single Anglicisms.

11.9 Bibliography

AMSZEJEWICZ, M. (1859), *Dykcjonarz zawierający wyrazy i wyrażenia z obcych języków polskiemu przyswojone, a mianowicie: . . .* (Dictionary Containing Words and Phrases Assimilated in Polish, Namely . . .). (Warsaw).

ANTONOWICZ, JULIAN (1788), *Gramatyka dla Polaków chcączych się uczyć angielskiego* (Grammar for Poles Willing to Study English) (Warsaw).

BLOOMFIELD, LEONARD (1933), *Language* (New York).

DĄBROWSKI, J (1962), *Polacy w Anglii i o Anglii* (Poles in England and on England) (Cracow).

DAMBORSKÝ. J. (1974), 'Wyrazy obce w języku polskim' (Foreign Words in the Polish Language), *Poradnik Językowy*, 7: 341–55.

FISIAK, JACEK (1961), 'Zapożyczenia angielskie w języku polskim' (English Loanwords in Polish), unpub. D.Phil. thesis (University of Łódź).

——(1985), 'A Note on the Adaptation of English Loanwords in Polish', *ITL Review of Applied Linguistics*, 67–8: 69–75.

——(1986), 'The Word-Formation of English Loanwords in Polish', in W. Viereck and W.-D. Bald (eds.), *English in Contact with Other Languages: Studies in Honour of Broder Carstensen on the Occasion of his 60th Birthday* (Budapest: Akadémiai Kiadó), 253–63.

HAUGEN, EÍNAR (1988), 'The Influence of English: A Transatlantic Perspective', *Folia Linguistica*, 22: 3–9.

JESPERSEN, OTTO (1930), *Growth and Structure of the English Language*, 6th edn. (Leipzig).

KARŁOWICZ, J., KRYŃSKI, A., and NIEDŹWIEDZKI, W. (1900–23), *Słownik języka polskiego* (Dictionary of the Polish Language), 8 vols. (Warsaw).

KASPRZYCKA, A. (1971), 'Materiały do polskiej leksykografii nautycznej XVIII w.' (Materials for Polish Nautical Lexicography from the 18th Century), *Nautologia*, 2–4: 57–70.

KNAPSKI, G. (1632), *Thesaurus Polono-Latino-Graecus* (Cracow).

KONOPCZYŃSKI, W. (1947), 'Anglia a Polska w XVIII w.' (England and Poland in the 18th Century), *Pamiętnik Biblioteki Kórnickiej*, 4: 93–129.

KOPCZYŃSKI, O. (1817), *Gramatyka języka polskiego* (Grammar of Polish) (Warsaw).

KURCZ, I. (1990), *Słownik frekwencyjny polszczyzny współczesnej* (A Frequency Dictionary of Contemporary Polish) (Krakow).

——LEWICKI, A., SAMBOR, J., and WORONCZAK, J. (1974–7), *Słownictwo współczesnego języka polskiego: Listy frekwencyjne* (Vocabulary in Contemporary Polish: Frequency Lists) (Warsaw).

KURZOWA, Z., and ZGÓŁKOWA, H. (1992), *Słownik minimum języka polskiego* (A Minimum Dictionary of Polish) (Poznań).

LIPOŃSKI, W. (1978), *Polska a Brytania 1801–1830* (Poland and Britain 1801–1830) (Poznań).

MĄCZYŃSKI, J. (1564), *Lexicon Latino-Polonicum* (Królewiec).

MAŃCZAK-WOHLFELD, ELŻBIETA (1987*a*), 'Najstarsze zapożycznenia angielskie w polszczyźnie' (The Oldest English Borrowings in Polish), *Język Polski*, 67: 25–31.

——(1987*b*), 'Efemerydy pochodzenia angielskiego w *Słowniku wileńskim*' (Ephemeral Anglicisms in the Vilnius Dictionary), *Poradnik Językowy*, 2: 100–3.

——(1988), 'Anglicyzmy w *Słowniku warszawskim*' (Anglicisms in the Warsaw Dictionary), *Język Polski*, 68: 24–9.

——(1992), *Analiza dekompozycyjna zapożyczeń angielskich w języku polskim* (Decomposition Analysis of English Borrowings in Polish) (Cracow: Wydawnictwo Uniwersytetu Jagiellońiskiego).

——(1994*a*), *Angielskie elementy leksykalne w języku polskim* (English Lexical Elements in the Polish Language) (Cracow).

——(1994*b*), 'English Loanwords in Amszejewicz's Dictionary', *Kwartalnik Neofilologiczny*, 41 (3): 251–4.

——(1995), *Tendencje rozwojowe współczesnych zapożyczeń angielskich w języku polskim* (Tendencies in the Assimilation of Contemporary English Loanwords in Polish) (Cracow).

——(1996*a*), 'The Frequency of English Loanwords in Written Polish' (*Suvremena Linguistica*) 22 (1–2): 623–8.

——(1996*b*), 'The Influence of English on the Language of Polish Teenagers', *Studia Etymologica Cracoviensia*, 1: 67–8.

——(1996*c*), 'Parę uwag o pierwszej gramatyce języka angielskiego wydanej w Polsce' (Some Remarks on the First English Grammar Published in Poland), *Języki Obce w Szkole*, 5: 395–8.

MARKOWSKI, A. (1995), *Praktyczny słownik wyrazów obcych używanych w prasie, radiu i telewizji* (A Practical Dictionary of Foreign Words Used in the Press, Radio, and Television) (Warsaw).

SAPIR, EDWARD (1921), *Language* (New York).

THOMPSON, D. (ed.) (1995), *The Concise Oxford Dictionary of Current English*, 9th edn. (Oxford: Oxford University Press).

ZDANOWICZ, A., et al. (1861), *Słownik języka polskiego* (A Dictionary of the Polish Language), 2 vols. (Vilnius).

12

CROATIAN

Rudolf Filipović

12.1 History of language contact: historical and sociocultural factors

12.1.1 Chronology of intensive influences

The infiltration of the English language on the Continent is closely connected with the so-called nineteenth-century discovery of England (Smith 1948: 44). Since then there has been a continuous linguistic relationship between English and other European languages—and Croatian is no exception.

Anglo-Croatian cultural relations, which are of long standing, showed some interesting features in the first half of the nineteenth century when the new Croatian literary language and modern Croatian literature were being created. Croatian cultural history in that period was closely related to that of Austria, Germany, Italy, and France but was not completely cut off from England. The study of this literary period has shown that English influences on the Croatian literature of that time were abundant (Filipović 1953: 92–157).

12.1.2 Origins of influence

However, the intermediary function of certain European languages should not be neglected, especially of German and French (less so of Italian): all transmitted a certain number of English words to Croatian. Although Croatia has a strong link with the USA through Croatian immigrants (about two million Croats emigrated to the USA between the end of the nineteenth century and the present day) most English borrowings are in the BrE form. Americanisms normally date from the second half of this century but many of these were mediated through BrE. This is certainly because the teaching of English in Croatia on all levels is still carried out in the BrE variant. The influence of American music and films can be noticed in the young generation, but there is no sign that AmE will replace BrE in the near future.

12.1.3 Types of influence

Language contact can influence all levels of language— spelling, pronunciation, morphology, syntax, and particularly lexis. English influence on Croatian is especially strong in the sphere of lexis. The degree of adaptation depends on various factors, especially on frequency of use.

'Internationalisms' are excluded from the *Dictionary of European Anglicisms* (which defines Anglicism by form), even if they are coined in England and exported from England as English words. The number of calques used in Croatian is relatively large (see *Dictionary of European Anglicisms*).

12.1.4 Chronology of purist phases

The tendency of Croatian language planners has been to use a native word whenever possible, and to use a foreign word only for new concepts and objects taken from a foreign culture. Croatian seldom translates foreign words; borrowed words quite often undergo adaptations and changes of various kinds. This tradition has operated for a considerable period of time and dates back to the days of P. R. Vitezović, who expressed it in purist terms in the introduction of one of his works published in 1684. He wanted to purge the Croatian language of all foreign words: languages should be free from lexical imports except those connected with indispensable cultural and material importations.

A very similar idea can be found later in J. Đurkovečki (1826). He pointed out the need to replace foreign words by native or other Slavonic ones, but came to the conclusion that Croatian had to accept certain loans just as Latin retained some Greek words. However, as soon as a native word was found a foreign word ought to be abandoned; only those which had been 'Croatized' should be kept and their number should not be too large (Đurkovečki 1826: 205).

At the end of the nineteenth century, I. Broz, another supporter of linguistic purity, advocated that the number of foreign words in Croatian should be as restricted as possible (Broz 1886: 104–67). His younger contemporary T. Maretić formulated the rule as follows: 'Do not use unnecessary foreign words, that is those for which good substitutes can be found in the vernacular' (1899: 681).

There have, however, never been any consistent attempts or any legal measures taken (as has happened for instance in France) to defend Croatian against the influx of loanwords. The struggle against foreign words and particularly against Anglicisms was carried out by linguistic purists who never had any legal support. Their activity has always been restricted to academic linguistic circles. Dictionaries of modern standard Croatian have recorded all the Anglicisms used by Croatian writers in their literary works. It was only in the last two decades, when the tendency to use them grew, that Croatian linguists went on the alert. They warned people against the danger of Anglicisms, which were considered the strongest threat to the Croatian language. Appeals were made to replace them by Croatian words or to create new words. The result of this campaign is very modest for several reasons, mainly because Anglicisms are needed in everyday communication. Thus, quite a number of loanwords have accumulated in Croatian, most as a result of a need to express new concepts connected with cultural and material developments.

12.1.5 Regional differences

In Croatia there are no discernible regional differences in the use of Anglicisms, nor between the capital Zagreb and the provinces. However, no research has been done so far to document the extent of homogeneity or possible differences.

12.1.6 Stylistic differences

In studying the stylistic aspects of the use of Anglicisms there appear to be two approaches: to distinguish registers (usually technical versus colloquial), and to examine the parallel use of loanwords and their equivalents in the borrowing language. The latter is usually characterized as an attempt to achieve variation of style (Filipović 1960: 11) by avoiding the repetition of a word in a text of limited length (examples of such pairs are *ekipa—momčad* 'team', *teatar—kazalište* 'theatre'). In Croatian literature there are more interesting uses. The use of English words in a text helps to produce a foreign atmosphere. Translators often leave some items untranslated to indicate that the action of a drama, a novel, or a short story takes place in an English-speaking country. By means of English words an author may also achieve some comic effect or a play on words. Finally, the author can use an English word instead of a long expression from Croatian to achieve economy of expression.

12.1.7 Innovation and obsolescence

There has never been an attempt to give a statistical account of how many English loanwords there are in Croatian. More innovations can be found in periods when purism was weak and when the need to express new concepts was met by borrowing English words. In the history of the Croatian language there have been periods when purism was strong and consequently the number of new Anglicisms was small (cf. s. 12.1.4). On the other hand, when purism was abandoned the borrowing of English words and expressions was more intensive and the number of Anglicisms increased (Filipović 1995b), as illustrated by the *Dictionary of Anglicisms* (Filipović 1990b), in which the number of Anglicisms has doubled compared with that found in dictionaries of foreign words published during the period of purism.

12.1.8 Mediating languages

The phonological form of some Anglicisms in Croatian can only be explained by consideration of the function of the mediating languages. For historical reasons these were mainly German and French. German mediation is for instance seen where / ʌ / and /ɜ:/ are both represented by Cr /e/: this is impossible to explain phonetically, i.e. the change of / ʌ / and /ɜ:/ to /e/ must be a consequence of extralinguistic reasons. The most likely explanation is that in early English–Croatian dictionaries and several handbooks the IPA transcription symbols / ʌ / and /ɜ:/ were represented by /ö/, used in English–German dictionaries and handbooks printed in Croatia. Since in Croatian there are no rounded vowels, German rounded vowels were changed to /e/:

English	German	Croatian
bluff [blʌf]	[blöf]	[blef]
flirt [flɜ:t]	[flört]	[flert]

This /e/ representation is also found in the Croatian Anglicisms representing English *butterfly*, *cup*, *lunch*, and *sir* [ser]. Other Anglicisms in Croatian borrowed via German, all characterized by incorrect morphological analysis, include *keks*, *koks*, and *drops*.

German as a mediating language also influenced verb morphology. In Croatian, the infinitive is formed by adding the suffix -a- and the infinitive formant -ti to the verbal stem. Under German influence the infinitive of a number of Anglicisms is formed by using the German suffix -ier- (> Cr -ir-), as in *fascin-ir-ati* and *galop-ir-ati* (German *faszinieren*, *galopieren*); -ir- can, however, also appear independently as in E *interview*—Cr *intervju-ir-a-ti*, E *kidnap*—Cr *kidnep-ir-a-ti*.

On the semantic level, too, German influenced some Anglicisms. The meaning of *bar* was extended to 'night club' under the influence of the German Anglicism *Bar* at the beginning of the century (Filipović 1986). Even more interesting is the development of the form and the meaning of the Croatian Anglicism *smoking*. It developed from the English word *smoking jacket* through ellipsis into *smoking* and changed its meaning into *black-tie* and *tuxedo* (Filipović 1971).

French, too, functioned as a mediating language for Anglicisms in Croatian, although their number is smaller; a possible example is Cr *žiri* < E *jury*. However, since German has 'French' pronunciation in *jury*, the word could, again, have been transmitted through German.

Italian may also be a mediating language but in my corpus there is no conclusive evidence.

12.1.9 English in education

English as a foreign language in Croatian general schools was first introduced in 1945; since then it has been taught in all state secondary schools. Before 1945 the only two foreign languages taught were French and German[1]. English was a

---

[1] Italian was seldom and sporadically taught in schools on the Adriatic coast of Croatia.

subject only in nautical schools and in some private schools for girls. Although quite a number of English loanwords were used in spoken and written Croatian, they were comparatively fewer than words from German and French. The great change came after the break with the Soviet Union in 1948, when the influx of Anglicisms came through several fields of British and American culture, mostly through films, TV, and popular music.

12.2 Pronunciation and spelling[2]

12.2.1 Pronunciation and phonological integration

Transphonemization, 'phoneme substitution', is the term for the adaptation on the phonological level. There are three types:

1. *Zero transphonemization* denotes the equation of English phonemes with Croatian ones: E *chief* [tʃiːf]—Cr *čif*.
2. *Compromise or partial transphonemization* is the replacement of English phonemes, for example bridging a difference in the degree of opening with vowels or in the place of articulation with consonants. The manner of articulation, however, is the same: E *spot* [spɒt]—Cr *spot*.
3. *Free transphonemization* is the replacement of English phonemes by phonemes which are not even partial articulatory equivalents: E *thriller* ['θrɪlə]—Cr *triler* [triːler].

12.2.2 Graphemic integration

There are four possibilities found in the adaptation of Anglicisms:

1. The spelling is based on the English pronunciation (E *team*—Cr *tim*).
2. The spelling is unchanged (E *bard*—Cr *bard*).
3. The spelling of an Anglicism follows partly the spelling and partly the pronunciation of the model (E *interview*—Cr *intervju* [intervjuː]).
4. The spelling is based on the pronunciation of an intermediary language (e.g. German: E *strike* [straɪk]—Ge [ʃtraɪk]—Cr *štrajk*; or French: E *jury*—Fr/Ge [dʒyːrɪ]—Cr *žiri*).

---

[2] In Filipović (1986) I suggested that the analysis of Anglicisms should be based on a pattern which begins with (1) the orthography of Anglicisms, (2) the phonology, (3) the morphology, and (4) the semantics of Anglicisms.

An important conceptual and methodological contribution to the theory of languages in contact and an innovation concerning the stages of adaptation on three levels in terms of the model, compromise replica, and replica is the distinction of primary adaptation and secondary adaptation, which helps record certain changes which remained outside the scope of the earlier theoretical and methodological framework. Primary adaptation results in a compromise replica or a replica of the model. Secondary adaptation takes place after the Anglicism has been completely integrated into the borrowing language and can change like any other native word. Primary and secondary changes take place in the adaptation of English models on the phonological, morphological, and semantic level.

12.3 Morphology

12.3.1 Introduction

Adaptation on the morphological level is termed *transmorphemization*, 'morpheme substitution'. There are three types:

1. *zero transmorphemization*: the status of the Anglicism as a free morpheme is not changed as in E *half*—Cr *half*;
2. *compromise transmorphemization*: the adoption of an E. derivative as a monomorphemic loanword, as in E *rating*—Cr *rejting* 'rating', E *stylist*—Cr *stajlist* 'stylist';
3. *complete transmorphemization*: suffix substitution as in E *box-er*—Cr *boks-ač* 'boxer', E *strik-er*—Cr *štrajk-ač* 'striker'.

12.3.2 Nouns

Gender. The citation form of a noun in English differs substantially from that in Croatian, which is directly linked with the gender of the noun. Gender in Croatian is grammatical. In the process of assigning gender to Anglicisms in Croatian the masculine tendency prevails.

E *bar* n.   >   Cr *bar* M
E *team* n.   >   Cr *tim* M

This rule does not apply to nouns denoting people where gender is regulated through sex: Cr *džentlmen* M, Cr *gerla* F. Some Anglicisms determine their gender through contamination: Cr *bola* 'bowl' F (by analogy with *zdjela* F). Loanwords are fully integrated into the inflexional system of Croatian for case and number. In a few cases the English plural form is used as a singular in Croatian, and the plural of such Anglicisms is formed according to the rule of forming plurals in Croatian by adding a plural ending; e.g. E *cake-s*—Cr sg. *keks*, pl. *keksi*.

12.3.3 Adjectives

Adjectives are borrowed either through direct transfer of a free morpheme as in E *fair*—Cr *fer*, E *fit*—Cr *fit*, E *groggy*—Cr *grogi*; or through secondary adaptation and complete transmorphemization (see below).

12.3.4 Adverbs

Adverbs in Croatian have the same form as adjectives; they are classified according to the syntactical context:

adj. E 'He is a fair player'   Cr 'On je fer igrač'
adv. E 'He played fair'   Cr 'On je igrao fer'

12.3.5 Verbs

Verbal Anglicisms are adapted to the rules of word formation in the borrowing language. In Croatian a verb is formed by means of an infinitive suffix (-a-, -ova-, -ira-) and an infinitive formant (-ti): E *start*—Cr *start-a- ti*.

Since Croatian has a kind of verbal aspect which has no equivalent in English, borrowed verbs require special treatment: in primary adaptation they either mark verbal aspect only contextually as with E *interview*—Cr *intervjuirati* (biaspectual verb). Alternatively, in secondary adaptation verbal Anglicisms may indicate aspect as it is marked in native verbs, by using prefixes and infixes. Contrast: E *bluff*—Cr *blef-ira-ti* (neutral) vs. Cr *iz-blefirati*, *od-blefirati* (perfective).

12.3.6 Derivation (selection)

Gender specification. Gender of Croatian personal nouns can be indicated by phonological form:

1. masculine nouns end in a consonant
   E *gentleman* > Cr *džentlmen*
2. feminine nouns end in -a, or -ica
   E *girl* > Cr *gerla*
   E *single* > Cr *singlica*
3. nouns ending in -o are neuter in Croatian (Cr *selo*), but English nouns ending in -o are masculine (Cr *bufalo*, *bungalo*, *polo*, all M)

Agent nouns. The English suffix -er denoting agent nouns is generally replaced in Croatian by the equivalent formant -ač.

Denominal verbs. Verbal Anglicisms are formed from nouns by using three infinitive formants -a-, -ira-, -ova-, and the infinitive suffix -ti. There are examples which show two infinitive forms: E *tank* n. → Cr *tankirati/tankati*.

New adjectives. The transfer of English adjectives into Croatian vocabulary is very limited in number; they are: *fair*, *fit*, *groggy*, etc. They have not been adapted to the Croatian adjectival system and do not express gender, number, and case. In secondary adaptation, adjectives are formed from nouns by adding one of three Croatian adjectival suffixes:

-*ski*, e.g. *bar-ski*, *film-ski*
-*ov*, e.g. *bard-ov*, *lord-ov*
-*an*, e.g. *record-an*, *standard-an*

These new adjectives are completely integrated into the Croatian system.

12.3.7 Compounds and combining forms

All integrated nouns can be used as constituent parts of compounds. There are practically no restrictions in forming compound Anglicisms since Croatian is a language which has a complete freedom in forming compounds; e.g.:

E *hi-fi* → Cr *haj-fi -linija* ('line'), *-set* ('set'), *-tehnika* ('technique'), *-uređaj* ('equipment')

12.3.8 Calques (loan translations)

A calque or loan translation is used if no free morpheme is imported from English. Foreign elements are translated, i.e. replaced by elements from the borrowing language, following the pattern of the English model; e.g. E *skyscraper*—Cr *neboder*. There have been several attempts to replace loanwords with:

    (a) native words of the borrowing language, and
    (b) loan translations or calques.

While the first group of words is rather limited, the second occurs very frequently. Croatian linguists have made quite an effort to supply Croatian native words to replace English loanwords. They have suggested replacing *computer* by *računalo*, which has been accepted, and replacing *play off* by *doigravanje*. On the other hand the suggestion to replace *hardware* by *željezarija* and *time out* by *predah* has not been accepted.

12.4 Meaning

Adaptation on the semantic level can be of five types: zero extension, restriction of meaning in number, restriction of meaning in a semantic field, expansion of meaning in number, and expansion of meaning in a semantic field.

1. *Zero extension* denotes that there is no change of meaning in the borrowing process as in E *interviewer*— Cr *intervjuer*.
2. *Restriction of meaning in number* represents a reduction from several meanings of a polysemous etymon. Thus, the three meanings of E *folklore* are reduced to one in Cr *folklor*.
3. *Restriction of meaning* in a semantic field is rare; it adds specifying components by a restriction of the reference, as in E *pantry* (2), which in Cr *pentri* refers only to a pantry on a boat.
4. *Expansion of meaning in number* means the development of new senses as in *corner* (in football), which in Croatia also came to be used for 'a corner kick' and the 'corner area'.
5. The meaning of a loanword can also be more general (less specific) than that of the etymon.

12.5 Usage

No systematic stylistic or sociolinguistic analysis has been made of the use of Anglicisms in Croatian. *Anglicisms in Croatian* (Filipović 1990*b*) and the *Diction-*

ary of Anglicisms (Filipović 1990*a*) show that Anglicisms in Croatian belong to various fields of human activities. As in other European languages, the majority of Anglicisms are technical terms (mostly written) or come from colloquial, fashionable styles (youth language, journalese, etc.) Two special cases can serve to illustrate how difficult it is to make general statements.

Band Aid. During the famine in Ethiopia special concerts were organized both in Great Britain and in the USA to support the people in Ethiopia. Soon after the first concert this English item was transferred into Croatian and adapted into Croatian forms: *band aid* and *bend ejd*. The Anglicism became so popular that new compounds were formed by analogy: *classic aid*, *jazz aid*, *sport aid*, *ferry aid*, etc. keeping the basic meaning of the first Anglicism *band aid*.

Watergate. Some Anglicisms are so well established in the receiving language that a part of them can be used in a new hybrid. The formant *-gate* was further used in English denoting a scandal: *Irangate*, *Contragate*, etc. When *-gate* was transferred into Croatian, new hybrids were formed and used in spoken Croatian: *agrogejt*, *Šajbergate*, *Fadilgate*, and *ideogate*, always denoting a kind of scandal.

12.6 Forms of linguistic borrowing and their categorization

The number of Anglicisms recorded in the *Dictionary of Anglicisms in Croatian* (Filipović 1990*b*) proves that Croatian is open to Anglicisms from various fields and that it would be interesting to compare the number of Anglicisms in the present-day Croatian with the number of Germanisms and Gallicisms in the same period. Without studying the question thoroughly, we can state that Germanisms prevailed in the period ending with the First World War (1918), that Gallicisms were much used between the two world wars (1918–45), and that Anglicisms are in a majority since the end of the Second World War (1945).

1. *Borrowing*
   (*a*) There are quite a number of examples which show that a borrowing can be completely unadapted, e.g. *body-building*.
   (*b*) Some borrowings can still look foreign in form but are integrated in the Croatian system; e.g. *frogman*.
   (*c*) Fully integrated loanwords are completely adapted to the Croatian system and their forms look like any other native word; e.g. *kamp*.

2. *Replacement*
   (*a*) Translation takes place quite often and loan translations calques are very numerous; e.g. E *Cold War*—Cr *hladni rat*.
   (*b*) Semantic loans can be divided into two groups:

   • according to the form: E *paper*—Cr *papir*;
   • according to the meaning: E: *mouse*—Cr *miš*.

3. *Pseudo-loans*

Incomplete competence in the donor language can lead to English-looking items which do not exist in English itself. These are composed of borrowed English elements, but are not themselves English expressions. They are, then, the result of secondary adaptation only (Filipović 1985).

A *Translations*

1. Successful

brainwashing < pranje mozgova
flying saucer < leteći tanjur
penalty-kick < kazneni udarac
Iron Curtain < željezno zavje
mixed double < mješani par
semi-conductor < poluvodić
time is money < vrijeme je novac

2. Coexisting

bodyguard = tjelesni čuvar
Big Brother = veliki brat

3. Failures

sweater > vesta
do-it-yourself > učini sam

B *Renderings*

1. Successful

centre-forward < centarfor
be in the same boat < biti u istom sesu
skyscraper < neboder
lose face < izgubiti obraz
matter-of-fact <činjenica

2. Coexisting

boat people = izbjeglice
keep smiling = budi nasmijan

C *Creations*

steeplechase = trke s proponama
topless = bez gornjeg dijela kupaćeg kostima
non-aligned = nesvrstan
air conditioning = klima uređjaj
black box = crna kutija u avionu

D *Semantic loans*

mouse = miš
make money = zaraditi novac
bottleneck = usko grlo
butterfly = stil leptir

Relative frequency. It is difficult to state the ratio of borrowed items and calques; judging by the *Dictionary of Anglicisms in Croatian* (Filipović 1990*b*), it seems that borrowed words are much more numerous.

Pseudo-loans are formed in three ways:

1. by composition, using two Anglicisms already integrated into the system of the borrowing language: Cr *golman* 'goalkeeper';
2. by derivation, using a suffix from the donor language (*-er*): Cr *teniser* 'tennis player'; Cr *džezer* 'jazzman, jazz musician';
3. through ellipsis: the suffix *-ing* is dropped in a few English words: Cr *hepiend* (< E *happy ending*); Cr *box meč* (< E *boxing match*); Cr *air-condition* (< E *air conditioning*).

12.7 The future of Anglicisms

The explosive increase of foreign words was particularly strong after the Second World War, partly as a reaction to the embargo imposed on their use during the war. Linguistic purism in Croatia then lessened this influx for a few decades. But soon after that period the traditional purist tendency got stronger, and the struggle for and against the use of foreign words, particularly Anglicisms, began. However, as the new modern way of life and the cultural and commercial relations between Croatia and Great Britain and the USA require a great number of Anglicisms (cf. Filipović 1995*b*), the attempt to replace Anglicisms by loan translations and Croatian words has not yet been very successful.

12.8 Research

Research on Anglicisms in Croatian and other European languages has been presented in *An Annotated Bibliography (1958–1995)* of the project 'The English Element in European Languages' (Filipović 1996a) and in *ABEA*. Four books deserve to be mentioned in particular: Filipović 1960, 1971, 1986, 1990*a* and *b*.

12.9 Bibliography

BROZ, IVAN (1886), 'Hrvatski jezik' (The Croatian Language), *Crtice iz hrvatske književnosti*, 1: 104–67.
ĐURKOVEČKI, JOŽEF (1826), *Jezičnica horvatsko-slavinska* (Croato-Slavonic Grammar) (Pešta), 200–6; (repr. 1933) in *Građa XII* (Zagreb).
FILIPOVIĆ, RUDOLF (1953), 'Anglo-Croatian Literary Relations in the 19th Century', *Slavonic Review* (London), 32: 92–102.
——(1960), *The Phonemic Analysis of English Loanwords in Croatian*, Acta Instituti Phonetici 8 (Zagreb: University of Zagreb).

FILIPOVIĆ, RUDOLF (1971), *Kontakti jezika u teoriji i praksi* (Language Contacts in Theory and Practice) (Zagreb: Školska knjiga).

—— (1985), 'Pseudoanglicisms in European Languages', in Pieper and Stickel (eds.), *Studia linguistica diachronica et synchronica* (Berlin: Mouton de Gruyter), 249–55.

—— (1986), *Teorija jezika u kontaktu* (A Theory of Languages in Contact) (Zagreb).

—— (1990a), 'Secondary Anglicisms in a Dictionary of Anglicisms in Serbo-Croatian', in *The Bell of Freedom: Essays Presented to Monica Partridge on the Occasion of her 75th Birthday* (Nottingham: Astra Press), 1–11.

—— (1990b), *Anglicizmi u hrvatskom ili srpskom: porijeklo—razvoj—značenje* (Anglicisms in Croatian or Serbian: Origin—Development—Meaning), Djela JAZU, knjiga 70 (Zagreb: Jugoslavenska akademija znanosti i umjetnosti, Školska knjiga).

—— (1995a), 'Some Problems in Compiling an Etymological Dictionary of Anglicisms', in Werner Winter (ed.), *On Languages and Language: The Presidential Addresses of the 1991 Meeting of the Societas Linguistica Europaea* (Berlin: Mouton de Gruyter), 127–43.

—— (1995b), 'Linguistic Purism versus Linguistic Borrowing in a Changing Europe', in K. Sornig, D. W. Halwachs, Ch. Penzinger, and G. Ambrosh (eds.), *Linguistics with a Human Face*, Grazer Linguistische Monographien 10 (Graz), 53–61.

—— (1996a), 'English as a Word Donor to Other Languages of Europe', in Reinhard Hartmann (ed.), *The English Language in Europe*, Europa II (Oxford: Intellect), iii. 37–46.

—— (1996b), *An Annotated Bibliography (1958–1995): The English Element in European Languages*, 4 vols. (Zagreb: Institute of Linguistics).

MARETIĆ, TOMO (1899), *Gramatika i stilistika . . .* (Grammar and Stylistics) (Zagreb).

SMITH, L. P. (1948), *Words and Idioms*, 5th edn. (London).

STRANG, BARBARA M. H. (1962), 'The Phonemic Analysis of English Loan-Words in Croatian', *Notes and Queries*, 9 (5): 190–2.

VITEZOVIĆ, PAVAO RITER (1684), *Odiljenje sigetsko* (The Siege of Siget) (Linz).

13

BULGARIAN

Nevena Alexieva

13.1 History of language contact: historical and sociocultural factors

(Danchev 1986; Maslov 1982; Videnov 1982)

13.1.1 Chronology of intensive influence

The Bulgarian language belongs to the South Slavonic group, together with Serbian, Croatian, Macedonian, and Slovenian. Old Bulgarian was the first Slavonic language for whose literary needs an original alphabet was created in the ninth century AD. In its second, simplified variant it came to be known as Cyrillic. (On its role as an assimilatory factor in borrowing see s. 13.2.1.) It was named after its creator, St Cyril, an eminent medieval European scholar, later canonized. This alphabet was subsequently taken over by the other Slavs.

Old Bulgarian, like the rest of the Slavonic languages, was inflected. However, it came repeatedly into contact with various Turkic languages. The most important early contact was with the language of the Proto-Bulgarians, who settled on the Balkan peninsula in the seventh century AD. Another important influence was Turkish, the language of the empire which dominated the Balkans from the fifteenth to the nineteenth centuries. These contacts led not only to lexical borrowing, but, far more important, to a gradual typological change: Modern Bulgarian has lost its nominal case inflexions and is now a largely analytical language, which makes it exotic among the modern Slavonic languages. This structural peculiarity has a direct bearing on borrowing—it facilitates the morphological integration of loanwords, which are predominantly nouns (see s. 13.3.2.) Greek has been another important source of lexical influence—ever since the creation of the first Bulgarian state and especially during the period of Byzantine domination (eleventh to twelfth centuries), as well as during that of Turkish domination, when Greek was the official language of Orthodox religious practice.

The post-Renaissance socioeconomic and industrial progress of Western and Central Europe gradually worked its way into the Balkans in the eighteenth century, which marked the beginning of the Bulgarian National Revival. The emerging class of merchants and manufacturers was the first social group to come into contact with the more developed European countries, and to feel the need to learn languages other than Turkish or Greek. In the early nineteenth century the patriotic spirit of the Revival contributed to the emergence of a national intelligentsia. Its members either came from the new bourgeois class, or received financial help from it, enabling them to obtain a good education abroad. The young Bulgarian intelligentsia, acquainted with the progress of European culture, came to play a major role in the Europeanization of the emerging national language. Thus, the lexical influence of the major European languages increased after the liberation from Turkish domination, when the new Bulgarian state was in need of a modern, polyfunctional language.

13.1.2 Origins of influence

One of the channels for meeting the intellectual demands for new lexis was, naturally, borrowing. It is characteristic of the Bulgarian language at the end of the nineteenth century that its Europeanization was mainly indirect—it borrowed extensively from and via Russian, a language already highly developed and also closely related to Bulgarian both linguistically and culturally.

13.1.3 Types of influence

The analysis of the Bulgarian data in the *Dictionary of European Anglicisms* has shown that Anglicisms have not affected the core of the Bulgarian lexical system. They have contributed, however, to filling lexical gaps, created as a result of new social developments: for example, items such as *reĭting* 'rating' and *imidzh* 'image' have a central position in the new vocabulary of political democracy. In the present period intensive international contacts are mainly through English, and there is daily cultural exposure of the nation to some English—via the mass media; accordingly the use of Anglicisms has become a distinguishing mark of the linguistic behaviour of predominantly young people who associate it with a fashionable lifestyle.

The influx of Anglicisms has also led to a few innovations in the phonological system of Bulgarian (see s. 13.2.1). Moreover, observations on the grammatical behaviour of current new loans have revealed interesting tendencies in Bulgarian morphology, word formation, and syntax as a result of the appearance of invariant word groups (see s. 13.3.3). Widely used modern Anglicisms have become noticeably productive in the derivation of new words and the creation of new, figurative, meanings (see s. 13.4).

13.1.4 Chronology of purist phases

Purism, understood as a concern for the purity and the aesthetic quality of the national language, has always been moderate in modern Bulgarian. The attempts of some of the leading linguists in the first decades of the twentieth century (cf. Moskov 1958) to purge an already stable literary language of 'alien' words did not have a palpable impact on language practice. These linguists only managed to influence the attitudes of educated speakers, who even today consider it their patriotic duty to profess their rather abstract concern for the purity and indigenous richness of Bulgarian and their reaction against the 'invasion' of foreign words. However, Bulgarians are rarely bothered by their presence, unless the use is excessive; frequently speakers are not even aware of them—often an indicator of thorough integration.

This conflict between negative attitudes in principle and unawareness in practice is found even in the linguistic behaviour and professional activity of the majority of contemporary Bulgarian scholars (Videnov 1982). In general they accept the inevitability of lexical borrowing, but they try to reconcile it with their puristic bias by dividing foreign words into 'aliens' and 'loanwords'. In recent decades, attention has been directed mostly to new loans, which are subjected to highly critical analyses not only in specialized journals (Andreĭchin and Stankov 1951–), but also in newspaper language columns. New loans, mostly Anglicisms, are scrutinized individually and decisions are voiced on their 'fate', the criteria being based on their 'usefulness for Bulgarian' and their 'euphony'.

13.1.5 Regional differences

In spite of the existence of regional dialects, the Bulgarian-speaking community is essentially homogeneous. The standard metropolitan variety of Bulgarian leads the way in linguistic innovation, including borrowing. My interviews with dialect speakers have confirmed this tendency. For example, they regarded *grogi* (E *groggy*) as a slang item, and not a colloquial word, that is, as a stylistically more marked word. Folk etymology is more frequent in dialect: for example, *vaterbol* is used instead of *vaterpolo* (E *water polo*), by analogy with *futbol* (E *football*) and the other, more familiar, -*ball* games.

13.1.6 Stylistic differences

Anglicisms in Bulgarian are most numerous in specialized terminologies; in this respect Bulgarian does not differ from the other European languages. The greatest influx of loans is at present observable in the vocabularies of computing, pop music, sports, drugs, and youth fashion. The other stylistic register obviously affected by borrowing from English is that of colloquial and slang usage, most typical of youth language and journalese, purposefully exploiting the emotive power of fashionable loans. Playful nonce-words and code-switches are also common. The register can be illustrated with a colloquial loan (*mŭni*, E *money*) and a modernism bordering on slang (*kilŭr*, E *killer* 'excellent'). More examples of youth slang, mostly uninflected adjectives, are analysed in s. 13.3. Stylistic differentiation (colloquial vs. neutral) can also be found in the category of specialized terms, for example in the forms of swimming and football terms *krol/kroul* from *crawl* and *fal/faul* from *foul*.

13.1.7 Innovation and obsolescence

It is interesting that only six of the early, indirect loanwords (see s. 13.1.8) have become obsolete; most other early introductions are still widely used.

The increasing popularity of English as a world language, which reflects the internationally dominant status of the United States after 1945 in particular, has resulted in a steady growth of direct importations. They belong to various thematic groups: technical and scientific terminologies, sports, music, politics, food and drink, and clothing. Therefore, successive editions of the dictionaries of foreign words in Bulgarian (*DFW*) list an ever growing number of Anglicisms—from about 130, recorded at the turn of the century, through about 600 in the 1970s, to about 1,300 in the latest editions of 1982 and 1999 (cf. about 1,600 Bulgarian entries in the *Dictionary of European Anglicisms*). The sudden rise from 600 to 1,300 can, however, partly be attributed to differences in etymological approach.

The growing knowledge of English, and, hence awareness of the spoken form, has resulted in the reborrowing of a number of words, e.g. *kovboĭ/kauboĭ* (E *cowboy*), *keks/keĭk* (E *cake*), *kolezh/kolidzh* (E *college*), *viski/uiski* (E *whisky*), *menazher/menidzhŭr* (E *manager*), *stek/steĭk* (E *steak*), etc. The first form, the older, indirect loan (s. 13.1.8), is being replaced by direct importations, often stylistically marked (fashionable) variants: *keĭk, kolidzh, steĭk*.

13.1.8 Mediating languages

Early Anglicisms were transmitted via Russian, French, and later German, often following a chain-like pattern: French/German to Russian to Bulgarian. For example, the five early loans (*biftek, byudzhet, zhuri, redingot, vagon*) transmitted via French are found among sixty-four nineteenth-century borrowings discussed in the first important study of Anglicisms in Bulgarian by Vankov (1971). The author mentions as intermediary languages also Italian, Turkish, Greek, and Romanian. Among the Anglicisms mediated through German are the misinterpreted plural forms *keks* 'cake', *koks* 'coke', and *drops* 'round sweets'.

13.1.9 English in education

After Bulgaria's national liberation in 1878 French became the second foreign language in the schools after Russian. German appeared on the scene only after 1918. Language contacts between English and Bulgarian remained limited well into the twentieth century; English was nowhere near as popular as French and German until the 1960s and was introduced into the school curriculum only after 1945; the first English-language high school was set up in Sofia in the late 1950s. Although French and German have kept their foothold in foreign language teaching up to the present, English has steadily increased its territory and prestige among both teenage and adult learners. It is generally preferred as the first foreign language in schools and universities and has come to enjoy an unprecedented popularity. ELT is no longer the only important source of access to it: British and American radio programmes are freely available to learners with sufficient proficiency.

13.2 Pronunciation and spelling

13.2.1 Pronunciation
(Danchev 1989; Tilkov 1982)

There are considerable phonemic and phonetic differences between English and Bulgarian in the system of the vowels and diphthongs and in dental and alveolar consonants. The Bulgarian sound system consists of forty-five phonemes: six vowels (V) and thirty-nine consonants (C), nearly half of which are palatalized variants of the others. The combination VV is not characteristic of Bulgarian, the preference being for a more or less even distribution of vowels and consonants (VCV, CVC). However, the vowels can combine with the only semi-vowel /j/ to form diphthongs (/aj, ej, oj/).

The Bulgarian vowels /a, o, u, i, e, ə/ are close to the Cardinal Vowel types, and are similar to those of Spanish. The vowel /ə/, which is close to English /ə/, /ʌ/, and /ɜ:/, is a characteristic feature of Bulgarian vocalism—found not only in unstressed positions, but, unlike the other Slavonic languages, also in *stressed* positions (see s. 13.2.2). (On the spelling of Bulgarian /ə/ see s. 13.2.2.) The six vowels are intermediate with respect to the oppositions short : long and broad : narrow, which means that they fall in between the approximately fourteen English short and long, lax and tense monophthongs. Thus, Bulgarian vocalism differs from that of English both quantitatively and qualitatively. This presents a problem mainly for language teaching, whereas in lexical borrowing it leads only to doublet forms.

Bulgarian vocalism is on the whole monophthongal; where the diphthongal combinations /aj, ej, oj/ occur in native words they are usually found on a morpheme boundary. Their distribution is generally limited to open syllables and interjections, but they are also unproblematical in English loans in closed syllables, as in /lajf/ from E *life* and /kejk/ from E *cake*. The same holds for the distribution of /ij/ in rendering English /i:/ as in /bijt/ (E *beat*). Borrowing from English, then, has led to phonological innovation by widening the distribution of the Bulgarian diphthongs (Danchev 1994), although this goes unnoticed by Bulgarian speakers.

The vowel /u/ behaves almost as a glide in native interjections (/au!/) and in the rendition of English /au/ as in /aut/ (E *out*), /nou-xau/ (E *know-how*), and /boulink/ (E *bowling*). Since the diphthong /ou/ is alien to the Bulgarian phonemic system, English /əu/ is found difficult by learners, and the combination /ou/ is perceived as 'foreign-sounding' in Anglicisms. Thus it has become established only in more recent loans.

Bulgarian lacks the semi-vowel /w/, which is regularly replaced by /u/, as in /uokmen/ (E *Walkman*), /tuist/ (E *twist*), and /uiski/ (older /viski/) (E *whisky*), or in older and indirect loans by /v/, /vagon/ from E *wagon* and /tramvaj/ 'tram', from E *tramway*. Especially in initial position /ui, uo/ sound alien and are felt as phonetically difficult combinations.

The comparison, whether descriptive or intuitive, between the sound structures of the two languages leads to the conclusion that Bulgarian speakers regard English as a basically diphthongal language and, accordingly, tend to treat loans containing diphthongs as Anglicisms (Danchev 1994: 103). But attitudes even to such words depend on a variety of factors, some of which are extralinguistic.

Consonants. Although a number of correlative consonants differ both in quality and distribution, the adaptation of English consonants poses fewer problems on the whole than that of vowels. While English /t, d, l, n/ are alveolar, the corresponding Bulgarian sounds are dental. Bulgarian /r/ is trilled and is pronounced in all positions in the word. As a result of these phonetic differences Bulgarian lacks affricates of the type of English /tr, dr/. The Bulgarian nasal /n/ has the allophone /ŋ/ preceding /k, g/. Since voiced consonants are devoiced in word-final position, -*ing* in loans is always pronounced as /-iŋk/ in the singular and /-iŋg-/ in the plural as in /mitiŋk/, /mitiŋgi/ 'rally' from E *meeting*).

Word accent. Bulgarian stress is dynamic, centralizing, and positionally free, that is, it can fall on any syllable; this in principle allows Anglicisms to preserve the original English stress. The dynamic character of Bulgarian stress means that accented vowels are nearly twice as prominent and slightly longer than unaccented ones. This fact creates difficulties for learners of English even at more advanced levels, leading to confusion between English short and long vowels, as in /ʃiːjp/ and /ʃip/ (E *ship*); this also affects borrowings, as in /strijptijs/ (E *striptease*), which has two alternative variants: /striptijs/, /striptis/.

The centralizing nature of Bulgarian stress means that words of three or more syllables, common in Bulgarian, usually have only one stress. In Anglicisms this changes the English pattern of rhythmic succession of stressed and unstressed syllables: such loanwords tend to be pronounced with one stress rather than with a combination of primary and secondary stresses. This also holds for borrowed compounds, which are reinterpreted as simple words, for example /puʃpul/ vs E *push-pull*. On the other hand, transparent loan compounds can have two stresses as in /supermarket/.

13.2.2 *Graphemic integration and transliteration*

Bulgarian and Russian use the Cyrillic alphabet. This means that Anglicisms are as a rule transliterated. However, there is a fashionable tendency to preserve the English spelling of some Anglicisms (*Change*, *WC*, *PC*, etc.).

The Bulgarian variant of Cyrillic has thirty letters; these render forty-five Bulgarian phonemes on a basically phonetic principle, that is in a nearly one-to-one relation: the additional fifteen phonemes are mostly palatalized variants of the basic consonants, and in writing they are handled by a combination of a basic consonant and one of the graphemes <Я, Ю, Ъо>, which phonemically stand for /ja, ju, jo/, transliterated as < ya, yu, yo>.

As Bulgarian pronunciation and spelling are very closely related they easily tend to influence one another. Whereas earlier Anglicisms (nineteenth and early twentieth-century) were borrowed mostly indirectly and/or from written sources, comparatively recent loans, especially after 1945, tend to be direct and testify to an awareness of their English pronunciation. This means that the Cyrillic transliteration of earlier loans was modelled mostly on their English or other foreign spelling, e.g. <kovboĭ> (E *cowboy*), <vagon>, from (E *wagon*).

A new loan will tend to be pronounced the way it is spelt in Bulgarian; this discourages near-English pronunciation even by people familiar with English: it would be regarded as affected not only because it is not supported by the spelling, but also because of the widely divergent sound systems. In consequence, transliteration into a different alphabetical system inevitably obscures to a lesser or greater degree the 'Englishness' of Anglicisms and, hence, greatly contributes to their integration. Trendy neologisms in youth slang are usually marked as English on the basis of both form and meaning/style, e.g. *khard* 'porno', *khaĭ* 'in style', *feĭs* (E *face*), *sori* (E sorry), *speshŭl* (contrasting with the standard adjective *spetsialen*) (E *special*), *kilŭr* (E *killer*), *khepi* (E *happy*), etc.

The rendition of the Bulgarian letter<Ъ> (>/ə/) requires special mention. The general practice is to transliterate it either as <ă>, or as < ŭ > (cf the Roman spelling of the name Bulgaria: the first syllable is pronounced /bəl-/ both in the English word and in the Bulgarian forms *Bŭlgariya, bŭlgarski*). For the purposes of the *Dictionary of European Anglicisms* it was decided to use the symbol < ŭ> so as to remain close to the internationally known form *Bulgaria*, on the one hand, and on the other, to distinguish the written symbol for /ə/ from either <a> or <u>.

Although Anglicisms in Bulgarian function as a rule in a transliterated form, some loans preserve the English spelling. Well-established examples are *WC* and *Change*, used as signs for 'convenience' and 'exchange office'. *Change* is also a widely known colloquialism, transcribed, and transliterated, as *cheĭndzh*, *che(ĭ)nch*. Over the past few years the preservation of Roman letters has become a fashionable trend, especially in shop signs (*Coca-Cola*, *Fast Food*), in company names in general, in journalese, and in the informal register. The pronunciation of acronyms (*CD*, *PC*, *US*, etc.) or items like *made in* varies between the more modern English and the more customary one based on the tradition of reading the Roman letters, e.g. *CD* pronounced as /si di/ or /tse de/. The spelling pronunciation of *made in* is now stigmatized.

13.3 Morphology

13.3.1 Introduction

(Stoyanov 1983; Molhova 1979; Alexieva 1977, 1983)

As pointed out in s. 13.1.1, present-day Bulgarian is analytical, and thus structurally similar to English, a fact which facilitates the integration of Anglicisms. But although Bulgarian has lost its nominal case inflections (except for the vocative), its system of inflectional and derivational morphemes for nouns, verbs, and adjectives is incomparably richer than that of English.

13.3.2 Nouns

Bulgarian nouns are characterized by three regular grammatical categories: gender, number, and definiteness.

13.3.2.1 Gender

Every noun is marked for one of the three basic gender forms: M(asculine), F(eminine), and N(euter), which are normally assigned on the basis of the word-final phoneme of the singular form. Since nouns ending in a consonant (*C*) or the glide /*j*/ are as a rule M, most loanwords from English are thus classified (e.g. *blŭf* < E *bluff*, *gol* < E *goal*, *bar(man)*, *brich* < E *breeches*). The same applies to all loans ending in *-s*, in which E *-s* is interpreted as a part of the root, as in *keks* (E *cake*), *klips* (E *clip*), *blus* (E *blues*), and *chips* (a collective noun in Bulgarian).

Nouns ending in *-a*, *-ya* in the singular are typically F in Bulgarian. As there are few such nouns in English, the number of these Anglicisms is very low. Examples are *koka-kola* (E *Coca-Cola*) and *bazuka* (E *bazooka*). An interesting case of reinterpretation is provided by the widely used word *mediya*, which is treated as a singular F noun with a regular Bulgarian plural form *medii*. Semantic factors may, however, interfere. Thus *mis* 'miss' is F; other words add *-a* to indicate F gender: e.g. *gŭrla* 'easy female' (from E *girl*), *styuardesa* (E *stewardess*), *mokasina* (E *moccasin*) (the general Bulgarian word for 'shoe' is F), and *disketa* (E *diskette*) (loans in *-ette* always add *-a*).

By far the most interesting group comprises Anglicisms which end in *-i*, replacing English *-y*, as in *poni* (E *pony*), *parti* (E *party*), *lobi* (E *lobby*), *khobi* (E *hobby*), *khipi* (E *hippie*), *yanki* (E *Yankee*), *zhuri* (E *jury*), *zombi* (E *zombie*), *beĭbi* (E *baby*), and *rali* (E *rally*). Such loans are normally N, the category for native nouns ending in *-o*, *-e* and for loanwords ending either in *-o*, *-e*, or in *-i*, *-(y)u*, e.g. *video*, *polo*, *rege* (E *reggae*), *barbekyu* (E *barbecue*).

When, however, the loan names a person, it may be N, or M/F (e.g. *beĭbi* (F), *dendi* (M), *bobi* (E *bobby*) and *zombi* (N or M), *khipi* (N, M, or F). The clash between M or F and the N form is usually resolved syntactically with the help of an attributive adjective or numeral in the respective gender form, e.g. *mlad* (M)/ *mlada* (F) *yanki* 'a young Yankee'. The contradiction between N form and natural gender marks the otherwise well-known loan as 'foreign', i.e. not completely integratable.

The Bulgarian system also includes the category of Common gender, applied to names of persons irrespective of their formal ending. So, the above examples could be treated rather as exponents of this group. The trendy loan *model* 'a person posing or displaying clothes', although predominantly used of women, linguistically functions as an M noun. In this sense *model* joins the class of native and borrowed nouns designating occupations and titles which are M or F according to context (e.g. *profesor*, *doktor*, etc.).

13.3.2.2 Number

The three basic gender categories (M, F, N) have different endings for the plural. Masculine gender can create problems for the integration of the most frequent class of Anglicisms. As a rule monosyllabic M nouns form their plural by adding *-ove* (e.g. *chek + ove* (E *cheque + s*), and polysyllabics by *-i* (e.g. *printer + i*). But the rule fails with some native and borrowed words: the loans *film*, *snob*, *fakt* (E *fact*), etc. add *-i*, whereas *skeĭtbord* (E *skateboard*) and other *-bord* words take the *-ove* pl., obviously by analogy with monosyllabic *bord* (E *board*). Bulgarian inanimate M nouns also have a plural form in *-a*, used when the noun is accompanied by a numeral. This is the reason for providing such Bulgarian M entries in the *Dictionary of European Anglicisms* with two plural forms: *-a/-ove*. Loans like *brichove* 'women's saddlebags' (from E *breeches*) and *shorti* (E *shorts*) have replaced the English plural with a native one. F loans ending in *-a* are treated like native words replacing *-a* with *-i*, e.g. *gŭrla—gŭrli*, and *relsa* 'rail'—*relsi*. The word *gupi* (E *guppy*) is an example of morphological reinterpretation of the final vowel as a plural marker, thus 'backderiving' the singular form *gupa*.

N Anglicisms ending in *-o* substitute the plural inflection *-a*, e.g. *video—videa*, *polo* 'polo neck'—*pola*. Most informants find this plural form awkward with recent loans and prefer using a phrase, e.g. *kombo* (sg.)—*kombo sŭstavi* 'combo groups'.

The more numerous group of loans ending in *-i* tend to add the plural marker *-ta*, thus *ponita* (E *ponies*), *partita* (E *parties*), or *khipita* (E *hippies*). But when the semantic element [male] or [female] is conspicuous, as in the case of *yanki*, the word remains unchanged in the plural. Its final *-i* is semantically in harmony rather with the M and F plural ending *-i* than with the N singular ending.

13.3.2.3 Definiteness

Unlike English, Bulgarian does not have an indefinite article, and definiteness is marked by an enclitic, a feature which also contrasts with the other Slavonic languages. The form of this marker depends on the noun's gender and number. Thus *-a* is attached to the final consonant of M nouns (*klana* 'the clan'), and *-ta* and *-to* to the final vowels of F and N nouns (*disketata* 'the diskette', *uiskito* 'the whisky'). *Yanki* is an interesting exception: its M/F gender meaning interferes semantically with N *-to*, while its final *-i* blocks formally the addition of the M/F morphemes. All this makes it impossible for *yanki* to take a definite article. When there is a need to express definiteness, this is met syntactically, by attaching the appropriate form of the article to a preceding attribute (thus: *seksapilnata yanki* (F); but when the adjective is uninflectable (*seksi*), even this strategy fails (see s. 13.3.3). The same holds for *mis* (E *miss*).

The plural definite article is *-te* for M and F nouns and *-ta* for N nouns, observing the principle of vowel harmony, e.g. *snobite* 'the snobs', *disketite* 'the diskettes', vs. *uiskitata* 'the whiskies'. The plural definite *-te* is the only possible inflexion for *yanki*—thus *yankite* (pl.), which provides morphological proof of the M/F interpretation of this loan.

In the *Dictionary of European Anglicisms*, as regards the application of the degrees of integration ((1)/(2) or (3)) to borrowed nouns, those that are adapted morphologically as a result of reinterpretation are assigned grade (3), e.g. *blus*, *gŭrla*, *shorti*, and *dzhinsi*.

13.3.3 Adjectives

Most Bulgarian adjectives are derived from nouns. This also holds for well-integrated adjectives based on borrowed nouns. Because of their derivative nature they are discussed under s. 13.3.6. As a rule Bulgarian adjectives are inflected for gender and number, showing concord with the noun modified. The typical adjectival grammatical endings are ø (M), *-a* (F), *-o* (N), *-i* (pl.), the three vowel endings being added to a base identical with the M form.

Although the number of directly borrowed adjectives is not large, most are widely current as colloquial and youth slang words. Typical examples are: *grogi* (E *groggy*), *seksi* (E *sexy*), *kreĭzi* (E *crazy*), *sori* (E *sorry*), *khepi* (E *happy*), *khevi* (E *heavy*), *soft*, *khard* 'porno', from E *hard*, etc. Most contain the typical ending *-i*, which has an English 'feel' for Bulgarian users and is exploited in playful modifications or translations of proper names (e.g. *Sŭni Biĭch*, Bulgarian *Slŭnchev bryag* 'Sunny Beach', a well-known seaside resort).

These adjectives are invariant, that is, they remain morphologically unintegratable in the class of the inflected Bulgarian adjectives. The new category is well integrated syntactically—all its members can function predicatively, can take the degrees of comparison, and some are also regularly found in attributive position (*seksi*, *khard*, *speshŭl*).

These invariant adjectives, in combination with the principle of language economy, appear to have paved the way for another innovation. The characteristic English attributive pattern noun + noun, which is alien to the structure of Bulgarian, is now rapidly gaining ground. Examples are: *soul muzika* (E *soul music*), *ofis tekhnika* 'office equipment'. Possibly well-established loans like *biznes*, *tenis*, *pop*, *rok*, and *seks*, which have never added a Bulgarian adjectival morpheme, have made the pattern acceptable (see s. 13.3.7). The fact that the attributed noun is invariant affects the position of the definite article, which is added to the head noun, thus *ekshŭn idola* 'the action film idol'. (On the relation of this phenomenon to the much increased productivity of compounding, see s. 13.3.7.)

13.3.4 Adverbs

Most adverbs in Bulgarian are derived from adjectives; there are no direct English borrowings with the suffix *-ly*. For the same reason adverbs based on loan adjectives are further discussed under s. 13.3.6. As adverbs are themselves uninflected, the integration of the few cases of direct adverbial loans does not cause any morphological problems. Examples are: *nonstop*, *tiptop*, and *khaĭ*, from E *high* 'in style', in youth slang.

13.3.5 Verbs

Bulgarian verbs are inflected for person, number, tense, voice, mood, and aspect. Most native verbs are basically imperfective, leaving a smaller group as originally perfective. By adding suffixes and prefixes verbs can change from one group to the other. Verbs in Bulgarian are either reflexive or non-reflexive in form. Reflexives are derived from both transitive and intransitive verbs by means of the reflexive pronouns *se* and *si*, and can express a variety of other functions in addition to the reflexive meaning proper and the passive. This process affects also derivative loan verbs, e.g. *boksiram se*, from E *to box* 'to practice boxing'. When this verb (like other sports verbs) is employed in a strictly terminological sense ('to fight in a certain way'), it is used without *se*.

The non-finite forms of Bulgarian verbs include participles (present and past, which can be both active and passive, e.g. *izkrejzil* 'gone daft', from *crazy*, *linch-uvan*, 'lynched'), deverbal nouns (see s. 13.3.6), and a remnant of an infinitive, used only in some dialects. In standard Bulgarian (unlike the other Slavonic languages) the infinitive is replaced by the particle *da* and a finite form in the appropriate person, number, and tense. Verbs in the *Dictionary of European Anglicisms* are given in their conventional dictionary form: first person, singular, present tense, as in the cited examples above. (For denominal verbs see s. 13.3.6.)

In conclusion, the data on morphological integration permit the following observations:

(i) when a loanword can find a niche in the appropriate morphological class, i.e. when there is at least a partial formal compatibility, it is assimilated by being made to conform to Bulgarian rules;

(ii) but when the form is entirely alien, it functions as an uninflected exoticism. However, a sufficient number of such loans (e.g. invariant adjectives ending in *-i*) begin to be perceived as members of a new class. Thus they set up a formal model of their own, constituting a grammatical innovation. The new model facilitates the adaptation of future importations of the same type by offering them the necessary morphological niche.

13.3.6 Derivation (selection)

The participation of borrowings in the word-formation process of the receptor language is an unmistakable sign of their integration. Although most loans conform to the rules of the host language, leading to hybrid derivation, they can also affect the system by stimulating certain derivational models (e.g. compounding, see s. 13.3.7) at the expense of others (adjectival suffixation, see ss. 13.3.3, 13.3.6, 13.3.7).

Gender specification. Bulgarian personal F nouns are derived from M nouns by the addition of the highly productive gender suffix *-ka*. This rule applies to loans as well, e.g. *biznesmenka* 'businesswoman', *fenka* from *fan*, *dizaǐnerka* from *designer*, and *modelka* from *model*. Sometimes *-ka* is felt as colloquial, or contains a pejorative nuance. In such cases derivation is avoided either by adding no suffix at all, or by using a lexical alternative, as in *biznesdama* 'business lady'.

Agent nouns. Bulgarian has several agentive suffixes, both native and borrowed. One of them is -*er* (*dok<u>er</u>* 'docker'), in some (usually indirect) loans modified to -*yor*, under the influence of French -*eur* (*sprint<u>yor</u>* 'sprinter'). The English agentive (and instrumental) -*er* is fully transparent as a suffix in Anglicisms only when accompanied by structurally simpler cognates, e.g. *dok*, *sprint*, *dizaĭn* and *kombaĭn* 'combine'. The same holds for -*yor*, whether the words are borrowed through French (*blŭf<u>yor</u>* 'bluffer', *boks<u>yor</u>* 'boxer'), or are independently derived in Bulgarian (*reket<u>yor</u>* 'racketeer', *rekord<u>yor</u>* 'record-holder'). But -*er* is not generally felt as a suffix in loans like *mikser* 'mixer', *toster* 'toaster', because of the restricted usage of *miks* (only a musical term) and the novelty of *tost* 'toasted slice'. In *report<u>er</u>* (arch. *report<u>yor</u>*) its agent interpretation is supported by the French loan *reportage*, but in *broker* the understanding of -*er* as agentive depends on the overall 'professional' meaning of the word. This is even more so in the case of phonetic reduction of -*er* to /ər/, as in *dilŭr* 'dealer' and *bukmeĭkŭr* 'bookmaker'. The suffixal meaning is completely lost, however, in many inanimates, which are interpreted as simple base words (with or without reduction of -*er*), e.g. *konteĭner* 'container', *konveyer* 'conveyor belt', *trilŭr* 'thriller', *kompyutŭr* 'computer', and *bestselŭr* 'bestseller'. Unlike in English, there is no verbal base connected with the loans.

Some Anglicisms add the Bulgarian suffix -*ar* either to express an agentive meaning (*blus<u>ar</u>* 'a performer of blues' and *kŭmping<u>ar</u>* 'camper') or to strengthen the meaning of animateness, sometimes with a pejorative nuance (*khip<u>ar</u>*, along with *khipi* 'hippie', and *snob<u>ar</u>*, *pŭnk<u>ar</u>*, along with *snob*, *pŭnk*).

The Bulgarian suffix -*ist* is very productive and is again found in mediated Anglicisms (*futbolist* 'footballer', through Russian), and as a result of Bulgarian derivation (*sportist* 'sportsman', *sŭrfist* 'windsurfer', *softuerist* 'software specialist').

Some native derivatives acquire a colloquial or pejorative nuance, when their bases add the very productive agentive suffix of Turkish origin -*(a)dzhiya* as in *cheĭnchadzhiya* 'one involved in illegal foreign currency exchange', *mitingadzhiya* 'one frequenting rallies', and *kompyutŭrdzhiya* 'computer specialist'.

Denominal and deadjectival verbs. All loan verbs in Bulgarian are derived by suffixation mainly from borrowed nouns. The two suffixes commonly used in Anglicisms are -*uva*- (e.g. *flirtuvam* 'to flirt', *sportuvam* 'to engage in sport', and *mitinguvam* 'to participate in a rally'—from *meeting*) and the even more productive -*ira*- (*parkiram* 'to park', *shutiram* 'to shoot', *stopiram*, *startiram*, and *shokiram* 'to shock').

New adjectives. The two most productive Bulgarian adjectival suffixes -*ov* and -*en*, both used with inanimates, are in a competitive relationship. Some examples are *naĭlon<u>ov</u>* from *nylon*, *kesh<u>ov</u>* from *cash*, *stres<u>ov</u>* from *stress*, *futbol<u>en</u>* from *football*, *kompyutŭr<u>en</u>* from *computer*, and *barter<u>en</u>* from *barter*. Recent loan nouns, therefore, are faced with a difficult choice. There was noticeable hesitation on the part of informants when asked to derive adjectives from new borrowings.

The third productive suffix -*ski* is used mainly with animate (agent) nouns, e.g. *broker<u>ski</u>* from *broker* and *dzhentŭlmen<u>ski</u>* from *gentleman*. Some colloquial adjectives are based on active and passive past participles, the only representatives of defective verb paradigms (*grogyasal* 'exhausted' from *groggy* and *izbaran* 'dressed up' from *bar*).

Deadjectival, denominal, and deverbal nouns. Abstract nouns can be coined from well-integrated adjectives with the suffix -*nost* (*seksapilnost* from *sex appeal*), from other nouns with -*stvo* (*dzhentŭlmenstvo* and *liderstvo* from *gentleman* and *leader*), and from all verbs with the extremely productive suffix -*ne* (*flirtuvane*, *parkirane*, etc., see s. 13.3.5). Bulgarian -*ne* matches English deverbal -*ing* in function and productivity.

The international suffix -*ism* is also productive, or if it is part of the English loan, it is transparent, often in contrast to the root (*iskeĭpizŭm* 'escapism').

Deadjectival adverbs. Bulgarian adverbs are derived from adjectives chiefly by means of the suffix -*o*, which coincides with their N singular form. This applies also to adverbs based on adjectives which are derived from loan nouns (e.g. *seksapilno* from *sex appeal*). Adverbs like *sportsmenski* and *snobski* 'in a sportsmanly, snob-bish way' are based on adjectives derived from animate borrowed nouns; the suffix -*ski* in this case coincides with the M form of the adjective. (As is to be expected, adverbs derived from uninflected adjectives share the only form available, e.g. *seksi* from *sexy*.)

Another derivational model, clipping, has become noticeably productive in recent years. The most popular forms are *fest* (← *festival*) and *folk* (← *folklor*). While the first is preferred as a modish journalese variant of the 'colourless' full form, the second now designates 'modern songs appealing to the popular taste'.

13.3.7 Compounds and combining forms

Compounding (without a vowel linking the two roots) is increasingly productive in modern Bulgarian. It has received a powerful boost from the daily influx (mainly through the media) of compound Anglicisms, whose bimorphemic structure is transparent to most users. The components of many compounds are used by themselves, so that it is often difficult to draw a line between compounds borrowed wholesale and native creations; examples are *seksskandal*, *folkzvezda* 'folkstar', *biznes-shkola* 'business-school', *pornofilm*, and *pop-pevets* 'pop-singer'. Their spell-ing varies as in English: they may appear with or without a hyphen, and quite often as two separate lexemes (compare *tenis raketa* 'tennis racket', *tenis-kort* 'tennis court', and *tenisturnir* 'tennis tournament'). There are also cases of structural reinterpretation: E *false start* > *falstart*, which is seen as derived from *fal* + *start* 'foul start'.

There is an obvious connection between the two-word spelling of compounds and the new attributive model noun + noun (see s. 13.3.3). The noticeable increase in the productivity of compounding (and the related n. + n. model) in present-day Bulgarian can be explained by the fact that it is seen as a major means to achieve a higher degree of language economy by avoiding lengthy, although more explicit, phrases. Compounding and the n. + n. model also help Bulgarian speakers to avoid the choice between the two competing adjectival suffixes -*en* and -*ov* (s. 13.3.6) by using the first noun as an uninflected modifier (*doping control* 'drug control', *top khonorar* 'top fee').

13.3.8 Calques (loan translations, cf. s. 13.6)

The analytical feature of modern Bulgarian is being reinforced by borrowing from
English, especially in the domain of compounding and the appearance of the new
model n. + n. (s. 13.3.7). Thus loan translation is normally easy. The linking of the
two roots of a compound with a vowel (*nebostŭrgach* = 'skyscraper') is giving way
to compounds like *kavŭrversiya* = 'coverversion'. Loan translation affects equally
acronyms, compounds, and phrases (see s. 13.6).

13.4 Meaning

(Danchev 1981, 1986; Alexieva 1986, 1987, 1994; Molhova 1976, 1982)

In a contact situation usually only one meaning is borrowed, especially if the loan
designates a new object or phenomenon (typically in terminological use). In
polysemous etymons the loan carries over only one of a whole range of meanings
(e.g. 'defensive player' is the only sense of Bulgarian *bek*).

Another regular feature is the change in the meaning of a loan from general to
specific: thus *dog* and *miting* designate a particular type of *dog* and *meeting*, namely
'Great Dane' and 'rally', as Bulgarian has its own generic terms.

When borrowed, a lexeme breaks away from its native semantic field and the
loan meaning is typically unmotivated (contrast *bek* and *back*, *spreĭ* 'atomizer' and
spray in English where 'atomizer' is the third, metonymically derived, meaning).
The examples illustrate the general principle of loss of semantic motivation, i.e.
transparency. It is even more apparent when derivatives are borrowed: *lider*
'leader', *snaĭper*, 'sniper', *trilŭr*, 'thriller', *dilŭr* 'dealer', and many other loans
containing the suffix -*er* are simple-base words in Bulgarian.

The same principle holds when compounds are borrowed wholesale: the Bulgarian Anglicism *penkiler* 'jack-of-all-trades' serves to illustrate the semantic development of opaque compound loans. English *painkiller* was borrowed about a century
ago as the name of an imported medicine. The motivation of its meaning, however,
was inevitably lost on the users of the loan *penkiler*. The product went out of use,
but the word remained, extending its meaning to designate 'an all-purpose object'.
The present-day sense, with a typical ironic connotation, applies mostly to
humans. This widely current colloquialism also illustrates the independent lexical
development of integrated loans, which can create their own figurative meanings in
the receptor language.

The loss of derivational motivation in the borrowing of compounds is found to
affect the structure of the respective loans, as exemplified by a group of -*ing* loans
in Bulgarian: *parking* 'parking-lot', *dansing* 'dancing-floor', *kŭmping* 'camping-
site', etc. These, and similar loans, structurally simplified in French, but preserving
the meanings of the English compounds, were later handed on to other languages,
including Bulgarian. This results in English-looking items, which in English itself
do not, and cannot, have the meanings of the full forms. A similar mechanism must
have been at work in the case of the Anglicism *displeĭ*, deriving from *visual display
unit*, which eventually has come to mean 'a computer screen', and in that of *flopi*,
which carries the meaning of the entire phrase *floppy disk drive*.

Loans like *displeĭ* and *flopi*, which are not isolated cases, also illustrate the effect of structural simplification on the meanings of technical terms, even of recent ones, as in the domain of computing. This phenomenon, resulting in the creation of *faux amis*, is at variance with the necessity to preserve the identity of denotation of the loan and its etymon, which is of crucial importance for international terminological practice.

Comparing the figurative meanings of loans with those of the English etymons often reveals generalization and extension. For example, the Bulgarian *shou* ('show'), which enjoys immense popularity at present, has extended its basic meaning 'performance' to embrace all sorts of activities and human behaviour, which can be characterized with semantic features like 'big circus', 'fun', 'striking'. By contrast the extended senses of E *show* 'pomp, grandness' are obviously dependent on the basic meaning 'exhibition'. Similarly, the colloquial sense 'women's saddlebags' has been metaphorically derived from *brichove* 'breeches', the sense 'platform shoes' of *tankove* (pl.) from the military meaning of *tank*, and that of 'a man's pot belly' from the technical meaning of *boĭler* 'boiler'.

If borrowing can radically change the denotational meaning of some etymons, it can obviously affect connotation as well: *nou-khau* in Bulgarian is a specific technical term, with the 'feel' of a prestigious, English-sounding, modern loan, in contrast to the colloquial connotation of the etymon. A reversed relationship (neutral source word—colloquial Anglicism) holds between E *change* 'money exchange' and Bulgarian *che(ĭ)nch*. In this spelling (and pronunciation) it has the pejorative connotation 'illegal'. However, the alternative form *cheĭndzh* is not pejorative.

13.5 Usage

The basic domains of present-day English lexical influence in Bulgarian, are:

1. technical terms in various scientific and technological vocabularies (those in maritime and aviation terminologies functioning within professional bilingualism);
2. colloquial or slang loans, characteristic of spoken use and found mainly in youth language and journalese;
3. loans which conveniently fill lexical gaps by replacing longer and unwieldy native phrases (*uikend* 'weekend', *reĭting* 'rating', *imidzh* 'image', and *nou-khau* 'know-how'). Designations of new (fashionable) electronic devices such as *organaĭzer* 'organizer', *peĭdzhŭr* 'pager', and some other computer terms and of new professions and phenomena connected with technological progress or market economy, such as *broker*, *dilŭr* 'dealer', *menidzhŭr* 'manager', and *reket* 'racket', are widely current in the speech community. They fulfil not only denotational needs, but also the role of sociolinguistic markers of prestige. Their frequency is increasing noticeably (e.g. *fen* 'fan', *kesh* 'cash', *bodi* 'body stocking', *nou-khau* 'know-how', *sekŭndkhend* 'secondhand', and *dzhakpot* 'jackpot').

The increasing adaptation of the new loans in writing manifests itself in dropping hyphens and quotation marks which used to accompany such words (e.g. *pleĭ-*

of > *pleĭof* 'playoff') and in using the original English spelling, especially in signs, advertisements, and in journalism. This practice has aroused apprehensions and stimulated puristic attitudes.

13.6 Forms of linguistic borrowing and their categorization

Borrowing proper, i.e. taking over of the form and (part of) the content of foreign words, is by far the most frequent type of lexical impact on a receptor language. This general impression is supported unequivocally by the number of Bulgarian loan translations in the *Dictionary of European Anglicisms* (some 150) in relation to that of the loans proper (about 1,600), i.e. the two groups are in the ratio of almost 1 to 11.

1. *Borrowings* can be divided into three types:

    (*a*) items which are unadapted and hence not felt to be part of Bulgarian; these include quotation words, foreignisms, ad hoc loans (typically in media usage), and instances of code-switching characteristic of the current language practice and an unambiguous attestation of the strong lexical impact;

    (*b*) words which still look foreign in form or are insufficiently adapted phonologically and morphologically (*foreign words, aliens*);

    (*c*) fully integrated items (*borrowings, denizens*). The foreign concept can also be rendered with native resources.

2. *Replacement* (*calquing*) is of four types:

    (*a*) translation, rendering as closely as possible the components of the complex etymon. In many cases only one part is translated, the result being a *semi-calque* (see examples in group A below);

    (*b*) rendering, which provides looser equivalents for a part of the foreign item or changes the order of the components as required by Bulgarian structure (see examples in group B);

    (*c*) creations: formally independent equivalents which are coinages prompted by foreign items. The influence of a foreign etymon is often difficult to prove (see examples in group C below);

    (*d*) semantic loans; an existing item in Bulgarian, whether native or previously borrowed, takes over one meaning of the foreign partial equivalent (see examples in group D below).

A *Translations*

1. Successful

    skyscraper < nebostŭrgach, crossword < krŭstoslovitsa, black box < cherna kutiya, UFO < NLO, Iron Curtain < Zhelyazna zavesa, round table < krŭgla masa, number one < nomer edno, time is money < vremeto e pari

2. Coexisting

    freestyle = fristaĭl/svoboden stil

3. Semi-calques

   brains trust = mozŭchen trŭst, coverversion = kavŭrversiya, safe sex = bezopasen seks, big business = edriya biznes, flying start = letyasht start

4. Coexisting

   PC = personalen kompyutŭr/pisi/PC

B *Renderings*

1. Successful

   brain drain < iztichane na mozŭtsi, AIDS < SPIN, self-service < na samoob-sluzhvane, flying saucer < letyashta chiniya, do-it-yourself < napravi si sam

C *Creations*

1. Successful

   cornflakes < zŭrneni yadki, freelance < na svobodna praktika

2. Coexisting

   fast food = bŭrza zakuska, public relations = vrŭzki s obshtestvenostta/pŭblik rileĭshŭns, feŭrpleĭ = sportsmenska igra

D *Semantic loans*

1. Successful

   mouse < mishka, memory < pamet, shuttle < sovalka, batch < paket

3. *Pseudo-loans*

   A receptor language uses borrowed items productively, thus coining new linguistic units, which only formally resemble English words.

   (*a*) lexical pseudo-loans, which are made with combinations of English morphemic material (e.g. *vatman* 'tramdriver', coined in French on the pattern of English compounds with -*man*, and borrowed by Bulgarian, *softlaĭner*, the lexical opposite of *khardlaĭner* 'hardliner', *avtogol* 'own goal');

   (*b*) morphological pseudo-loans, which are shortenings of items ranging from simple words (*krimi < kriminalen* 'criminal', *boks <* 'boxing', *fest < festival*), through compounds (*khepiend <* 'happy ending', *parking <* 'parking-lot', and other -*ing* loans and *super*, a colloquial variant of *supermarket*), to phrases (*kokteĭl <* 'cocktail party', *kŭntri <* 'country music'—see s. 13.4.);

   (*c*) semantic pseudo-loans, where the Anglicism develops a meaning in Bulgarian that is absent from the etymon (*bikini* 'scanty women's briefs', *suing* 'an extravagant loafer' from *swing*, and *tankove* 'platform shoes' from the plural of *tank*).

13.7 The future of Anglicisms

Bulgarian will undoubtedly remain within the orbit of the English linguistic influence for the foreseeable future. My observations on the attitudes of speakers of different ages, cultural backgrounds, and educational levels lead to the conclusion that Bulgarian, as a stable, well-developed national language, is not in danger of having its basic word stock changed dramatically or of being congested with Anglicisms. On the whole, there is a healthy public awareness (shared by younger users too) of how appropriate the use of Anglicisms is in different social spheres and situations. This is basically due to the mature attitude to linguistic matters of a small literate nation, which for generations has had a stable interest in acquiring foreign languages. The Bulgarian language community is critical of the excessive, showy usage of 'foreign words' and this attitude is undoubtedly due to purist activities, which, though moderate on the whole, have permanently influenced public opinion.

As shown above, the influx of Anglicisms, especially recently, has led to innovations also in the largely closed phonological and morphological systems. It can be expected that a greater number of Anglicisms will be accepted sharing the formal features of the new models (see s. 13.2.3). Fashionable adoptions will probably be short-lived, unless they manage to assert themselves as more permanently useful for at least a section of the speech community.

13.8 Research

Proper research on Anglicisms in Bulgarian started in the early 1970s. It was preceded by mostly purist comments on isolated loans by linguists publishing mainly in the serial journal *Bulgarian Language* (Andreĭchin and Stankov 1951–   ), in language columns in newspapers and collections of articles on so-called 'language-building'. Research has centred on the phonological, morphological, syntactic, and lexico-semantic adaptation of Anglicisms. There are also some sociolinguistic studies, which started in the 1980s, and some contrastive ones involving a third language. There are several compilations of English loans in special vocabularies (sport, mining and geology, veterinary, and maritime terminologies, tourism, medicine) (see s. 13.9, and the *Annotated Bibliography of European Anglicisms*). A dictionary of sports borrowings is being compiled. Anglicisms figure more and more prominently in successive editions of dictionaries of foreign words.

13.9 Bibliography

The list includes the titles referred to in the chapter. For full evidence see the *Annotated Bibliography of European Anglicisms*, where the more important titles are accompanied by short summaries.

ALEXIEVA, NEVENA (1977), 'Gramatichni i semantichni faktori pri opredelyane roda na angliĭskite zaemki v bŭlgarski ezik' (Grammatical and Semantic Factors in Determining the Gender of English Loanwords in Bulgarian), *Byuletin za sŭpostavitelno izsledvane na bŭlgarskiya ezik s drugi ezitsi*, 2: 4–5, 44–54.
—— (1983), 'Derivational Characteristics of English Loanwords in Bulgarian', *University of Sofia English Papers*, 2: 29–58.

——(1986), 'Some Observations on the Lexico-Semantic Assimilation of English Loanwords in Bulgarian', *Godishnik na Sofiĭskiya universitet/Annuaire de l'Université de Sofia*, 75: 96–128.

——(1987), 'English Synchronic and Diachronic Loanwords in Bulgarian', *University of Sofia English Papers*, 3: 29–41.

——(1994), 'New, Metaphorically Extended, Meanings of Anglicisms in Bulgarian', *Chuzhdoezikovo obuchenie/Foreign Language Teaching*, 1: 61–64.

ANDREĬCHIN, LYUBOMIR, and STANKOV, VALENTIN (1951–), *Bŭlgarski ezik* (The Bulgarian Language) (Sofia: BAN/The Bulgarian Academy of Sciences Publishers).

DANCHEV, ANDREI (1981), '*Anglitsizmite v bŭlgarskiya ezik*' (Anglicisms in Bulgarian), *Sŭpostavitelno ezikoznanie/Contrastive Linguistics*, 6: 190–204.

——(1986), 'The English Element in Bulgarian', in W. Viereck and W.-D. Bald (eds.), *English in Contact with Other Languages* (Budapest: Akadémiai Kiadó), 7–23.

——(1989), 'On the Contrastive Phonology of the Stressed Vowels in English and Bulgarian', in Jacek Fisiak (ed.), *Papers and Studies in Contrastive Linguistics*, 25: 156–75.

——(1994), *Bŭlgarska transkriptsiya na angliĭski imena* (Bulgarian Transcription of English Names), 3rd edn. (Sofia: Open Society Fund Publishers).

DOBREVA, DENKA (1987), 'Angliĭskite zaemki v bŭlgarskata veterinarno-zootkhnicheska leksika' (English Loanwords in the Bulgarian Veterinary-Zootechnical Terminology), unpub. Ph.D. thesis (University of Plovdiv).

GABEROFF, IVAN (1999), *Rechnik na chuzhdite dumi v bŭlgarski* (Dictionary of Foreign Words in Bulgarian), 3rd edn. (Sofia).

ILCHEV, STEPHAN, FILIPOVA-BAĬROVA, MARIA, et al. (eds.) (1982), *Rechnik na chuzhdite dumi v bŭlgarskiya ezik* (Dictionary of Foreign Words in Bulgarian) (Sofia: BAN/The Bulgarian Academy of Sciences Publishers).

KABUROV, GEORGI (ed.) (1983), *Terminologichen rechnik po fizicheska kultura i sport* (Dictionary of Physical Culture and Sports Terms) (Sofia).

KONDOVA, VERA (1984), 'Anglitsizmite v terminologichniya rechnik po fizicheska kultura i sport' (Anglicisms in the Dictionary of Physical Culture and Sports Terms), *Nauchni trudove*, 25: 35–8.

——(1986), 'Nyakoi nablyudeniya vŭrkhu upotrebata na anglitsizmi v bŭlgarskata sportna terminologiya' (Some Observations on the Use of Anglicisms in Bulgarian Sports Terminology), in *Proceedings of the Second National Conference on the Theory and Practice of Scientific and Scientific-Technical Texts* (Sofia: University of Sofia), 168–73.

MASLOV, YURIĬ (1982), *Gramatika na bŭlgarskiya ezik* (A Grammar of the Bulgarian Language) (Sofia: Naouka i izkoustvo Publishers).

MILEV, ALEKSANDŬr, et al. (1978), *Rechnik na chuzhdite dumi v bŭlgarskiya ezik* (Dictionary of Foreign Words in Bulgarian), 4th edn. (Sofia: Naouka i izkoustvo Publishers).

MOLHOVA, JANA (1976), *Outlines of English Lexicology*, 3rd edn. (Sofia: Naouka i izkoustvo Publishers).

——(1979), 'Angliĭskite zaemki v bŭlgarskiya ezik' (English Loanwords in Bulgarian), in Khristo Pŭrvev (ed.), *Pomagalo po bŭlgarska leksikologiya* (Sofia: Naouka i izkoustvo Publishers), 227–38.

——(1982), 'English Borrowings in Bulgarian', *Proceedings of the Bulgarian-American Conference. Boston, 11–14 Oct. 1982*.

MOSKOV, MOSKO (1958), *Borbata protiv chuzhdite dumi v bŭlgarskiya knizhoven ezik* (The Struggle against Foreign Words in the Bulgarian Literary Language) (Sofia: BAN/The Bulgarian Academy of Sciences Publishers).

PASHOVA, GALINA, NAIMUSHIN, B. and VELEVA, B. (2001), *Rechnik na chuzhdite dumi v bŭlgarskiya ezik* (Dictionary of Foreign Words in Bulgarian) (Sofia: Hermes Publ.).

PAVLOVA, ANNA (1991), 'Leksikalni ekvivalenti v bŭlgarski, angliĭski i frenski ezik s nachalen element *avto-/auto-*' (Lexical Equivalents in Bulgarian, English and French with *avto-/auto-* as their Initial Element), *Godishnik na Sofiĭskiya universitet: Annuaire de l'Université de Sofia*, 80: 62–115.

——(1992), 'Mezhduezikova leksikalna ekvivalentnost i nyakoi ot neĭnite proyavi v rechnika na turizma' (Lexical Equivalence across Languages and Some of its Manifestations in the Vocabulary of Tourism), *Philologia* (Sofia), 25: 127–37.

PETKOVA, VYARA (1977), 'Angliĭskite zaemki v bŭlgarskata morska terminologiya sled Vtorata svetovna voĭna i tyahnata semantichna konfiguratsiya' (The English Borrowings in the Bulgarian Maritime Terminology after the Second World War and their Semantic Configuration), *Sŭpostavitelno ezikoznanie/Contrastive Linguistics* (Sofia), 2: 170–9.

——(1988a), 'Bulgarian–English Language Contacts in Maritime Communication', unpub. Ph.D. thesis (University of Sofia).

——(1988b), 'Kalkirane na angliĭski morski termini v bŭlgarskata morska terminologiya' (Loan Translation of English Maritime Terms in the Bulgarian Maritime Terminology), *Trudove na VNVMU*, 22: 1–42.

STOYANOV, STOYAN (ed.) (1983), *Gramatika na sŭvremenniya bŭlgarski knizhoven ezik (Morfologiya 2)* (A Grammar of the Contemporary Bulgarian Literary Language (Morphology 2)) (Sofia: BAN/The Bulgarian Academy of Sciences Publishers).

TASEVA, YOANA (1994), 'Phonological Adaptation of English Loanwords in Modern Japanese and Bulgarian', unpub. MA thesis (University of Sofia).

TILKOV, DIMITŬR (ed.) (1982), *Gramatika na sŭrvremenniya bŭlgarski knizhoven ezik (Fonetika 1)* (A Grammar of the Contemporary Bulgarian Literary Language (Phonetics 1)) (Sofia: BAN/The Bulgarian Academy of Sciences Publishers).

TSVETANOVA, YANKA (1978), 'English Borrowing in the Tourist Industry', unpub. MA thesis (University of Sofia).

VANKOV, LYUBOMIR (1971), 'Rannite zaemki ot angliĭski ezik v bŭlgarski' (The Early Borrowings from English into Bulgarian), *Godishnik na Sofiĭskiya universitet/Annuaire de l'Université de Sofia*, 65: 297–324.

VIDENOV, MIKHAIL (1982), *Sotsiolingvistika: Bŭlgarski sotsiolingvisticheski problemi* (Sociolinguistics: Bulgarian Sociolinguistic Problems) (Sofia: Naouka i izkoustvo Publishers).

14

FINNISH

Keith Battarbee

14.1 History of language contact: historical and sociocultural factors

14.1.1 Chronology of intensive influences

The impact of English upon the vocabulary of Finnish prior to industrialization in the nineteenth century was minimal. The most significant lexical field was that of navigation, and even here the immediate source of the loans was Swedish. No instance appears to exist of a traditional nautical term borrowed directly from English.

English influence in the period of industrialization was reinforced by the migration to Finland (as to other areas around the Baltic littoral) of English-speaking entrepreneurs and engineers, especially from Scotland. Scots names such as Crichton, Ramsay, and Finlayson resonate powerfully in Finland's economic history (*Finlayson* eventually generating the felicitously domesticated textile trademark *Finla*).

On the other hand, the co-occurrence of industrialization with Romantic nationalism powered a strong motive to build on indigenous Finnish lexis to meet the needs of the new society, and most of the industrial vocabulary dating from the latter nineteenth or early twentieth centuries is indigenous, not loaned.

During the period between the two world wars, AmE influences (especially in the world of entertainment) were evidently largely insulated from the pressures of linguistic nationalism, and the lexis of music, dancing, cinema, etc. displays a

An earlier draft of some of the material in this article appeared in *Essayes and Explorations: A Freundschrift for Liisa Dahl* (Turku, 1996). I am also very grateful to my colleagues in the Departments of Finnish at the University of Turku and Åbo Akademi University for their support and comments.

high proportion of Anglicisms. The same trends have been powerfully intensified since the advent towards the end of the twentieth century of mass markets for recorded music, cinema, and television.

Foreign-language films and television programmes in Finland are subtitled, not dubbed; on any day of the year, soundtracks in English comprise a major proportion of the broadcasting on all four national television channels. An examination of the nationwide television broadcasting in Finland during one week (15–21 September 1997) revealed that English-language material accounts for just over 40 per cent of all broadcasting time on all channels, varying from 18.3 per cent (on the publicly owned TV-1 at the weekend), through 30–50 per cent on the three major channels at most times of the week, and reaching 80 per cent on the recently established commercial Channel 4. Material in English comprises over ten times as much as that in Swedish (the second official national language), and only 10 per cent less than that in Finnish. Most of the English-language material consists of fiction (feature films and various serials) ranging from humour to thrillers, but it also includes programmes on science and the arts, and twice a day the 20–minute English-language version of EuroNews.

In practice, this predicted impact is difficult to recognize on a lexical level in the *Dictionary of European Anglicisms* data, and is certainly not confirmed by the evidence from Finland. It might therefore be speculated that high exposure to American material on television may contribute to an ongoing shift of preference from a British to an American model of English, and may well reinforce the acquisition of English as a foreign language, but where there are powerful pressures in operation to maintain the 'integrity' of the local language, mere exposure even to a prestigious foreign language is not by itself sufficient to trigger off large-scale lexical loans.

During the 1980s and 1990s, the culture of Finnish society shifted extremely rapidly into an urban, high-technology, postmodern mode. At the time of writing (1997), Finland has the highest *per capita* densities in the world of cellular mobile telephones and of Internet connections. Yet even the intensity of this transition has not reversed the project for an indigenous lexis: the evidence in the *Dictionary of European Anglicisms* indicates, for instance, that no other language of the sixteen in the sample uses such a high proportion of indigenous vocabulary as Finnish for fields such as computing.

14.1.2 Types of influence

Since written Finnish is highly phonetic, loans from other languages usually raise problems concerning assimilation from the spoken or the written form.

Among the oldest stratum of loanwords found in Finnish, one of the best known is *kuningas* 'king', virtually unaltered from the proto-Germanic **kuningaz*. The survival of a few items such as this with minimal adaptation is striking, but it would be seriously misleading to envisage Finnish as a kind of linguistic aspic in which proto-Germanic flies have been preserved. This particular word happens to have been compatible with the phonological patterns of the early Finnish language, and may arguably also have been more resistant to change on account of the high status of its meaning. In a more democratic age, contemporary Finnish also has the parallel affectionate/diminutive form *kunkku*.

It is clear that there are real and significant differences and incompatibilities between the phonological systems of Finnish and Indo-European languages. This is vividly illustrated in the assimilation of Christian names. *Petros*, for instance, reached the Finnish-speaking community by several routes, presumably including German, Swedish, Latin, and Russian, and is now found in a range of forms ranging from the archaic/sacral *Pietari* (used for St Peter and thus also for St Petersburg) through *Petteri/Petri* to the demotic, and now predominant, *Pekka*.

14.1.3 Linguistic purism in Finnish

The process by which Finnish has developed from a peasant vernacular to a sophisticated standard language has been steered by an ideological agenda. Notwithstanding the centuries of borrowing from adjacent Indo-European languages, in the nineteenth century a goal of lexical self-sufficiency was adopted, the equivalent in linguistic terms of ethnic Finnishness in poetry (Lönnrot's recension of the *Kalevala*), in painting (Gallen-Kallela's integration of *Kalevala* motifs into an Art Nouveau aesthetic) and in music (Sibelius). There has therefore been an ongoing project to create Finnish terminology for new lexical needs, reminiscent of that in German, Icelandic, or French; and contemporary Finnish contains a striking range of indigenously coined vocabulary, from *puhelin* ('speech-instrument') for 'telephone' to *ohjelmisto* ('program-matter') for 'computer software'.

On the other hand, modernity has impacted on Finnish society as a process of internationalization, as in any other minority or peripheral culture, and the adoption of 'international' vocabulary has therefore been reinforced by powerful hegemonic pressures. Consequently, alongside the national coinages cited above, loaned terms abound, such as *radio* and *televisio*, *ministeri* and *direktiivi*, *poliisi* ('police') and *mafia*.

The geopolitical location has determined the circumstances of linguistic interaction as well. Until 1809, Finnish was a peasant vernacular within the Swedish state, not suppressed, but with minimal official standing; the ruling elites all used Swedish. By historical accident, the subsequent tsarist period coincided both with the beginnings of an industrial economy, and (as elsewhere in Europe) with the impact of Romantic nationalism. The Swedish-speaking elites in Finland came to see themselves as differentiated from the people of Sweden, yet counterposed to the Russification policies intermittently pursued by the Tsar's government. 'Swedes we are no longer; Russians we will not become; therefore let us be Finns.'

It has been repeatedly argued by the Finnish historian Matti Klinge that it is precisely this paradoxical situation of Finland in the nineteenth century, poised culturally and politically between its western inheritance and its eastern sovereign, which created the conditions in which it could evolve from a peripheral province to a coherent polity. Finland was so different—culturally, economically, socially, jurisprudentially—that the Tsar could not incorporate it into Russia; but in order for it to function as a semi-distinct polity, it needed a working infrastructure. The nineteenth-century networks of public communications (especially rail and post), radiating from the new capital in Helsinki, offer a vivid illustration of this transformation, which was then further reinforced by the creation of a social infrastructure, above all of schools, and eventually (in 1906, still under tsarist sovereignty) of universal adult suffrage (the first enacted in Europe) for a unicameral Parliament.

In this political context, the commitment of many members of the Swedish-speaking elites to a Finnish identity went beyond the literary nationalism of (say) the Anglo-Irish; to 'canonize' the Finnish language was a concrete means of expressing and reinforcing the cultural autonomy of the people of Finland. The establishment of the Finnish Literature Society and similar organizations and the spread of the Finnish press in the 1840s and 1850s, for instance, represented a major commitment to a 'national project', of which linguistic purism was a logical expression.

The existence of a political agenda, however, is no guarantee of its implementation. For a speech community, control of the language always remains ultimately in the hands of the collectivity of speakers, and attempts to impose linguistic guidelines from above may well be ideologically counterproductive. The decisive factors which promoted the transformation not only of Finland into a viable independent republic, but of Finnish into a viable modern language, depend upon the support of the speech community as a whole, and here the political projects of the twentieth century have been vitally important.

Despite the introduction of parliamentary democracy, Finland at the beginning of the twentieth century was still in social and economic terms a hierarchically stratified society, with a large proletariat both in the urban industrial economy and also, much more extensively, in the countryside. After independence, civil war broke out within Finland between the Reds (affiliated to the Bolshevik Comintern) and the conservative Whites. Following the defeat of the Reds, the White state, anxious to avert future confrontations, embarked on a major and largely successful project to reshape rural society and replace the manor-house agricultural economy by an agrarian democracy. The image and to a large extent the reality of Finland was recast as an egalitarian community of Little Houses in the Big Woods. Consequently, even the subsequent major economic transformation after the Second World War into a welfare state, on a social democratic model, can be seen as a continuation of an egalitarian project with a wide national base. During and after the Second World War, the successful repulsion (both military and subsequently political) of Soviet attempts at domination merely served to strengthen further the loyalty of the population to the social order and to their national identity.

The evident will of the Finnish speech community to maintain the autonomy of their language (language purism) can thus be seen as analogous to their determination to maintain their political sovereignty. On the other hand, in order to maintain political sovereignty it was essential that Finland should have a modern economy, and the implications of this logic are in contradiction to protectionism. Particularly since the decline throughout the West of the post-Second World War welfare state and the emergence of neoliberal economic doctrines, and with the membership of Finland since 1995 in the European Union, the ideological parameters have now shifted radically, and 'internationalization' is a very powerful slogan in Finnish society and culture in the 1990s. At present, the Finnish government is firmly committed to joining the first round of European Monetary Union. Irrespective of the economic arguments, the symbolic impact of replacing the national currency (the mark, obtained as a major concession under Russian rule in the mid-nineteenth century) by the euro is profoundly antinationalistic.

14.1.4 Regional differences

One of the major areas of differentiation between western and eastern dialects of Finnish relates to the much heavier influence of Swedish in the west, not only in lexis but also in grammar. To a much less significant extent, the converse holds true for Russian influence in the east. With respect to Anglicisms, however, no evidence has emerged of any such differentiation, nor would this be expected, since the major impact of English borrowings has occurred during the twentieth century and in conjunction with cultural influences equally affecting east and west. However, the polarization of Finnish society between city and country has constituted a major dimension of differentiation and tension throughout the twentieth century, as was recently graphically illustrated in the referendum on European Union membership (supported in the cities, opposed in rural areas). There can be little doubt that Anglicisms are very significantly more frequent among the urban populations.

14.1.5 Stylistic differences

Stylistic differences predominantly occur in two registers: the technical and the colloquial. This observation is particularly evident in situations where two alternative terms are available, one an Anglicism and the other indigenous. In such cases the predominant pattern is that the Anglicism is colloquial, but for formal purposes the indigenous term will be preferred (e.g. colloquial *disketti* vs. formal *levyke* for 'computer diskette').

During the 1990s, a vogue has arisen for using English interjections in colloquial spoken Finnish, especially (though not exclusively) among the young: e.g. *Yes!* ([jes:], a cry of triumph); or ... *about* ('approximately', usually postpositionally: e.g. *kolme viikkoa about* 'three weeks approximately'). This usage projects an image of modernity, and displays little relation to background factors such as level of education, though it probably correlates to some extent with urban versus rural speakers.

On the other hand, the 'insider' register of many occupational communities (particularly those with international connections) tends to include many internationalisms and Anglicisms, the use of which correlates with 'insiderness'. In a few cases unassimilated Anglicisms constitute the only terms available, as in the advertising industry: *copywriter*, *AD* ('art designer'), etc. In Finnish it is much more typical, however, for parallel indigenously coined terms also to be available, and these are likely to be used both by 'outsiders' in general and also in the media.

Thus, where a stylistic differentiation or opposition between an Anglicism and indigenous lexis is available, Anglicisms may be deployed to convey a range of different social messages; the predominant implications are of youth and/or modernity versus tradition, of insider status versus outsiders, or of colloquialism versus formality.

14.1.6 Innovation and obsolescence

Since the great bulk of Anglicisms in Finnish are of relatively recent provenance, obsolescence is of minor relevance. A few cases can be noted, however, where an Anglicism or internationalism has subsequently been largely or even totally displaced by an indigenous coinage (i.e. not even permitting stylistic or register differentiation): e.g. *telefooni*, which evidently survived into the 1930s, but nowadays sounds either archaic or humorous, having been totally displaced by *puhelin*. Similarly, *gramofooni* has entirely yielded to *levysoitin* 'record-player', and *soitin* ('playing-instrument') is also exclusively used for more recent innovations in sound reproduction technology such as *CD-soitin* 'CD-player'. There is, however, considerable arbitrariness in these developments, and *mikrofooni*, now *mikrofoni/ mikki* 'microphone', remains totally unchallenged.

As the foregoing examples illustrate, the processes by which one Anglicism survives and another is abandoned are unpredictable and inconsistent. In a recent comment, a representative of the National Bureau for Indigenous Languages emphasized that it is the language community which ultimately collectively opts for a solution: 'A word either becomes absorbed into the Finnish language, or it doesn't; it's the users who decide.'[1]

No simple link has been established between technological innovation as such and the use of Anglicisms.

14.1.7 English in schools

English played a relatively small part in language instruction in schools in Finland until after the Second World War. For one reason, in a bilingual country the first priority in language instruction is to ensure a command of the second national language: for Finnish-speakers, Swedish; for Swedish-speakers, Finnish. Earlier, under the tsarist regime, secondary schools (restricted in that period to the elite) also needed to offer Russian. Furthermore, Finland has since medieval times belonged to the periphery of the German-dominated cultural region, and German continued to be the foreign language of preference even beyond the end of the Second World War. English was, like French, an extra.

Since the rise of the anglophone countries to their present hegemony in world culture, however, Finland has followed the international trends and English has

---

[1] Anneli Räikkälä, quoted in Niiles (1997), a weekend magazine article based on Jouko Vesikansa's 1978 handbook to lexical purism, *Miljoona sanaa* (A Million Words). Vesikansa's own position is considerably more polemic, as Niiles's following quotation illustrates: 'As more and more words are adopted from English, it should be borne in mind that every one of these is (to use a medical term) a *corpus alienum*, a foreign body, which physicians recommend should be surgically removed.'

since the 1970s been the foreign language of first preference for approximately 95 per cent of secondary school students. (The second national language continues to be obligatory, and most schools also offer German and French; much less widely, Russian and Latin may be available.)

14.2 Pronunciation and spelling

14.2.1 Pronunciation

The major phonological hindrance to the uptake of Anglicisms in Finnish relates to sounds systemically recognized in English but not in Finnish. The most striking instances of English phonemes not occurring in Finnish are the variant sibilants. Standard Finnish recognizes only the unvoiced /s/; an English voiced /z/, / ʃ /, and /ʒ/, therefore, all tend to be realized in Finnish as [s], with no voicing contrast. Correspondingly, /tʃ/ and /dʒ/ are both realized as [ts]. In a fully systemic Finnish rendering, for example (with the addition of a nominative -*i* ending), English *chock* and *jock* would both be realized as [tsɔk:i], and *shock* as [sɔk:i].

Under the competing influence of Finnish orthography, on the other hand, the letter <z> for the voiced sibilant /z/ may either be reduced to the unvoiced [s], or be associated with the /ts/ value carried by the letter <z> in Finnish: thus *zombie* might be realized either as [sɔmbi] (spoken assimilation) or as [tsɔmbi] (written assimilation).

A fundamental feature of Finnish consonant phonology is the gemination of certain consonants. Gemination is found in English only at word boundaries (e.g. *hot tea* [hɒ t:iː]). In the assimilation of Anglicisms, the impact of this phenomenon is that in certain environments (particularly, perhaps, at the boundary between a word stem and its inflections) a single consonant in the English word will be subject to pressure to geminate; for instance, *cent* > *sentti*.

The voiced plosives /b, d, g/ and the unvoiced fricative /f/ do not occur in traditional Finnish phonology. Although in contemporary Finnish they now occur fairly frequently (mainly in loanwords), there is a tendency for them to be realized in speech as unvoiced plosives [p, t, k] and as a voiced fricative [v] respectively. Intriguingly, contemporary Finnish slang does have quite a number of words with initial voiced plosives and unvoiced /f/. Several of these are evidently derived from other languages, but have been considerably altered en route: e.g. *bailata* 'to party', *biisi* 'piece of music', *bileet* 'a party' (either from Swedish *biljett* from French *billet* 'ticket', or from Sw from Latin *jubileum* 'celebration'); *bisse* 'glass of beer' (allegedly from Italian *birra*); *donitsi* 'doughnut' (with a central hole, as opposed to *munkki* 'solid doughnut'), *duuni* 'a job' (from Sw *dona* 'to be busy'); *femma* 'a five-mark coin' from Sw *fem* 'five'. Despite the fact that many speakers still tend towards realizing a written <b> as [p], for instance, it can therefore be argued that word-initial /b/, /d/, and /f/ are now becoming integrated into the phonology of Finnish.

Finnish also traditionally never permits a word-initial consonant cluster. This restriction leads to loanwords such as *stressi* 'stress' being realized in colloquial

speech as [res:i], although in more careful speech the whole cluster will be pronounced: [stres:i]. Both /θ/ and /ð/ are normally realized as the Finnish unvoiced,
non-aspirated [t], possibly with slight voicing.

In the vowels, Finnish phonology observes systemic vowel harmony, according
to which 'back' and 'front' vowels may not occur in the same word, but the
'neutral' vowels /i/ and /e/ may co-occur with both. The requirement for vowel
harmony means, for instance, that many morphological endings for nouns or verbs
occur in two parallel forms: e.g. the inessive case -ssa/-ssä ('in . . .'), or the third
person plural verb ending -vat/-vät. In compound words, however, vowel harmony
operates independently in the separate elements (e.g. kahvi+pöytä 'coffee-table', or
sähkö+posti 'e-mail'). Nonetheless, vowel harmony does cause difficulties with
loanwords, the most notorious example probably being olympialaiset kisat 'the
Olympic Games', very widely pronounced with vowel harmony as [ɔlʉmp:iɑlɑiset]
rather than [ɔlympiɑlɑiset] as the orthography would indicate.

The English vowel phonemes /æ/ and /ʌ/ (typically written as <a> and <u>)
overlap phonetically with the Finnish phonemes /æ/ and /ɑ/ respectively (written as
<ä> and <a>), and where words with these phonemes are borrowed from Eng-
lish, either the spoken or the written form may prove to be decisive: e.g. lämäri
from slam shot in ice hockey (influenced by the indigenous Finnish verb lämätä 'to
strike') as against slammata from slamming 'rendering concrete'. In the case of the
letter <u>, the written form seems more likely to determine the phonetic realization of the loanword; e.g. dumpata [dʉmpɑtɑ] from to dump 'discard surplus stock'.
This outcome illustrates an important feature of loans in a literate age: that the
orthography and the phonology may exercise distinct and even contradictory
impacts, offering alternative pathways towards incorporation (cf. grunge 'grunge
music', widely pronounced [gruŋge] rather than the English [grʌndʒ], vs. luuseri
'loser', adopted as a spoken word [lu:zeri] and given the according Finnish spelling).

Nonetheless, there is no good reason for positing a significantly higher phonological threshold for contemporary Finnish than for the other languages participating in the Dictionary of European Anglicisms project. Undoubtedly the
phonological system of Finnish has features not widely found in other European
languages, such as vowel harmony, or a high vowel/consonant index. On the other
hand, the phonemic restraints and intonation patterns of French, for example,
located very close to English both geographically, culturally, and in terms of
language development, present very considerable problems for the full assimilation
of English vocabulary.

14.2.2 Orthographic integration

Finnish uses a Latin alphabet, like English, but (like many European languages)
with some modifications. The consonant graphemes <b, c, f, q, w, x, z> are only in
limited use, occurring mainly in more recent loanwords. The vowel range is
augmented with the fronted versions of <a, o>, written as <ä> and <ö> respectively, <y> being used (as in Swedish) for fronted /y/. The Finnish alphabet also
includes one vowel from the Swedish alphabet, <å> /o:/, which occurs in proper

names of both people and places. The characters <å, ä, ö> are treated as graphemes, and are separately alphabetized in that order following <z>.

Until the end of the nineteenth century, <w> was used for the phoneme /v/, and in texts around the beginning of the twentieth century, confusion persisted about <v> vis-à-vis <w>. This problem has effectively disappeared today, but much confusion still occurs with the alternatives to the letter <k>. Within conventional Finnish phonology, the only velar plosive is /k/; hence Finnish has no indigenous need for the letters <c, g, q>. Since these three letters all resemble each other graphically in having a rounded central shape, in sharp contrast to the angularities of the letter <k>, and traditional Finnish phonology does not motivate any distinction between them, they are easily confused by less educated or less careful writers.

The major orthographic problem with Anglicisms, however, relates to the fact that Finnish is spelt highly phonetically. If unassimilated loans are disregarded, the only significant element in Finnish speech not represented in the orthography is a glottal stop which occurs at the end of certain words as a reduction of a now lost yogh-type guttural; e.g. *osoite* 'address' from **osoite^k* or *vyöhyke* 'address' from **vyöhyke^k*. It may therefore be assumed that literate Finnish speakers (and the literacy rate in Finland is very high) will hold a different attitude towards the relationship between speech and writing from that found in a language like English.

The assimilation of Anglicisms into Finnish thus presents two alternative solutions, one based on the pronunciation and the other derived from a Finnish reading of the spelling. Among the most interesting outcomes are hybrids such as *gentleman*, pronounced [tsentlemɑn], where the initial [ts] is an adaptation of the English pronunciation, but the [tle] sequence in the middle of the word is derived from the spelling.

14.3 Morphology

14.3.1 Introduction

Despite the fact that Finnish belongs to the Finno-Ugric family of languages, and might therefore be expected to display very different linguistic constructions in comparison with those found in Indo-European, the structures of contemporary Finnish are in many ways very similar to patterns found within the Indo-European family. Indeed, the 'language family' concept, so crucial for understanding diachronic language history, is of limited relevance for synchronic classification of the lexical, grammatical, phonological, or orthographic structures of contemporary languages. The variation on these parameters within the Indo-European family is as wide as that between Indo-European and Finno-Ugric.

Finnish is a highly inflected language, with a complex morphology of endings both for verbs and for nouns and adjectives. Verbs are inflected for person, number, tense and mood. Nouns and adjectives inflect both for syntactic role (e.g. accusative objects in assertive clauses) and for semantic function: genitive, partitive, three locative series ('at'/'in'/'on' mapped onto 'motion-towards'/'position-at'/'motion-from'), instrumentality, and association. Many cases thus correspond semantically to prepositional constructions in contemporary Indo-European languages. Many of the overall principles governing morphological inflection in Finnish are very similar to those for Indo-European languages such as Latin; indeed for verbs three of the basic principles (person, number, and tense) outlined above are identical, though the pattern of tenses is different.

On the other hand, in some important respects Finnish is simpler than Latin; for instance, the absence of grammatical gender. Moreover, although certain groups of nouns and verbs mutate on similar distinctive patterns, it would be misleading to speak of separate declensions or conjugations.

Clearly, languages with inflectional grammar need to be able to inflect loanwords as well, and potentially this could comprise a serious barrier to the incorporation of new words from other languages. The solutions adopted in Finnish will therefore be discussed.

14.3.2 Nouns

With nouns, Finnish is highly tolerant as to the form of the nominative. Where the need is felt, a default-value declension can be deployed using -i- as the vowel needed to articulate case endings; in speech -i is also often attached to loanwords in the nominative (older, already assimilated loans also frequently have other vocalic stems, such as *litra* 'litre', or the much older *koulu* 'school'). For instance, the word *center* (typically found in proper names of commercial and similar institutions) is always spelt thus (in the AmE spelling) in the nominative, but is pronounced [se̱nter] or [se̱nt:eri], and when declined, takes -i-: e.g. *centerissä* 'in/at the centre'.

Finnish does not face difficulties in absorbing English nouns with respect to concepts of number. In Finnish all nouns, countable or not, can be used with a non-count/mass aspect in the partitive case. Formation of the partitive is therefore necessary for semantic reasons. Moreover, since the partitive singular is also used for numeral constructions (Finnish says *kuusitoista kieltä*, literally 'sixteen of-language', rather than 'sixteen language-s'), it is necessary for all imported nouns to be able to form a partitive singular case, which involves an ending in -a/-ä, with an inserted -t- where necessary.

In a few cases, an English plural form appears to have been taken over almost accidentally and treated as a singular, possibly for reasons of euphony; a striking recent case of this is *pinssi* 'a brooch pin'. The mechanism may in some way resemble that by which German earlier adopted English *cake* in a pseudo-plural form as *Keks* 'biscuit' (from which Finnish, like many other languages in the *Dictionary of European Anglicisms* project, in turn acquired *keksi*).

Like English, Finnish has a number of pluralia tantum nouns for which no singular form occurs, and such loans often end up with two plural endings in succession, one from English (-s) and one for Finnish (-it): e.g. *shortsit* 'shorts', or (in a recent television discussion of power politics within the European Union), *insit ja outsit* 'the ins and the outs'.

14.3.3 Adjectives

Adjectives are slightly more problematic than nouns: the largest class of Finnish adjectives have a nominative ending in *-nen*, but many loanword adjectives are not amenable to the addition of *-nen*. One available strategy involves adding *-(i)lainen*, *-(i)mainen*, or *-(i)nainen*, which indicate various shades of meaning suggesting 'like' or 'associated with' and can be used very widely to generate ad hoc adjectives; e.g. *thatcherimainen* 'Thatcherite'.

A solution which obviates the need for inflection deploys the loanword in a manner analogous to a small class of Finnish uninflected adverbs used quasi-adjectivally, such as *auki* 'open', *kiinni* 'closed', or *rikki* 'broken'; e.g. the loans *on-line* or *off-road*. Somewhat similar is the use of compound elements, e.g. *hifi*, or postpositive qualifiers such as *classic* or *light/lite* 'low in calorie content': e.g. *hifilaitteet* 'hi-fi equipment', or *Cola Lite*, *1836 Classic* (commercial brands of cola drink and lager).

14.3.4 Adverbs

No adverb in *-ly* is adopted as such into Finnish. Adverbs can be formed from adjective Anglicisms in the usual Finnish manner, mainly using the standard ending *-sti*. As mentioned above, the adverb *about* has recently been borrowed and deployed postpositively; *OK* also occurs not only as an interjection of assent (pronounced ['ɔkei]) but also adverbially with the quasi-adjectival meaning 'in working order, acceptable' (pronounced ['oː'koː]).

14.3.5 Verbs

The inflection of loan verbs is for the most part unproblematic, since the default-value conjugation pattern in *-ata/-ätä* can almost always be added without difficulty to the base form of the English word; e.g. *faksata* 'to fax', *liisata* 'to lease', *printata* 'to print out'. Verbs from English with standardized endings in *-ise/-ize*, *-ify*, etc., are readily assimilated to the patterns already existing for previous loans, e.g. *privatisoida* 'to privatize', *stilisoida* 'to stylize/to edit for style', or *ratifioida* 'to ratify'. The *-oida* ending recognizable in these last two patterns can also be deployed independently, as in *konsultoida* 'to consult/to act as a consultant' or *markkinoida* 'to market'.

Once equipped with a Finnish verb articulation, loan verbs are capable of conjugating all the standard forms of the Finnish verb (number and person, tense, non-finite forms) and even when required of generating ergative derivatives; this is achieved in Finnish by morphological means, e.g. the loanword *orientoida* 'to orientate' can generate *orientoitua* 'to adopt an orientation' (i.e. 'to become oriented') just as the indigenous verb *kirjoittaa* 'to write' generates *kirjoittautua* 'to register' (i.e. 'to become written'). Similarly, one can without difficulty generate *printtauttaa* 'to have something printed' from *printata* 'to print'.

14.3.7–8 Compounds and calques

Finnish lexis includes a very large number of compound nouns. These are formed in most cases with a first element either in the nominative (e.g. *moottori+tie* 'motor|way') or in the genitive (e.g. *viikon+loppu* [week's|end] 'weekend'); there does not appear to be any clear semantic principle underlying the choice of either construction. The genitive construction is arguably more 'indigenous' in feel, and appears to be more rare with loanwords.

Once a word has been adopted into Finnish and has undergone morphological assimilation, it becomes capable of participating in the formation of compounds. There does appear to be a slight preference in general for compounds with loans as first element rather than as second element. One exception to this tendency in commercial language, however, is the use of items such as *-center* with a wide variety of first elements (non-commercial institutions are more likely to be called by the Finnish equivalent term *-keskus*). Thus a horticultural enterprise might be called *Garden Center* or *Puutarhacenter* or *Puutarhakeskus* or indeed *Gardenkeskus*.

As in the case of German, the frequency of such compound nouns in Finnish, their ease of formation, and the elegance of their semantic transparency render it in many cases extremely difficult to evaluate whether a particular item should be classified as a calque from English or some other language, or as a spontaneous parallel formation in Finnish—for example, the many compounds with the element *-kortti* ('card'), such as *pankki+kortti* 'bank card', *luotto+kortti* 'credit card', *puhelin+kortti* 'phone card', etc.; these all correspond closely with the English terms, but Finnish also has *ajo+kortti* [driving+card], i.e. 'driving licence', and, most recently, *äly+kortti* [intelligence+card] 'smart card'.

14.4 Meaning

There are cases where the meaning of a loanword may undergo modification when adopted in Finnish. This appears to have occurred most noticeably in cases where the loanword occurs in coexistence with an indigenous term, allowing the possibility either of total or virtually total synonymy (probably with differentiation by register or style), or of denotative differentiation. Examples of both developments are discussed elsewhere in this article: e.g. synonymy in *printteri* vis-à-vis *kirjoitin,* both meaning 'computer printer' but used on different stylistic levels, versus the lexical distinction in *traileri* 'vehicle-towed trailer for transporting a boat etc.' vis-à-vis *peräkärry* for all other trailers of similar size. Such denotative differentiation is relatively rare, however, and stylistic differentiation far more common.

14.5 Usage

Questions of usage are particularly relevant in the consideration of Anglicisms in Finnish in those cases where the loan and a corresponding indigenous term coexist and are used virtually synonymously, thus allowing differentiation with regard to stylistic level of discourse, or to the persons being addressed.

The domains where loanwords are more frequent are in general terms the same for Finnish as for the other languages examined in the *Dictionary of European Anglicisms*, since they are determined by the prevailing transnational trends in western culture. However, a number of fields stand out in the *Dictionary* material as having a markedly more indigenous vocabulary in Finnish than in other languages: e.g. the language of tennis and football. Similarly, the major applications of advanced technology in contemporary society, such as computing, telecommunications, transport, which are of central economic and indeed crucial symbolic significance in Finland today, are *all* characterized by a marked preference for indigenous Finnish vocabulary.

Similar patterns could be adduced for the lexical domains of high-speed trains (currently being introduced in Finland) or for road and air transport. Abbreviations derived from English, whether wordlike acronymics or not, seem to stand a noticeably better chance of being adopted: in motor vehicles, for instance, *ABS* 'Automatic Braking System' has been accepted, whereas an airbag is an *ilma+tyyny* [air+cushion]. Virtually all the standard components in motor vehicles have indigenous terms, usually unchallenged by rival Anglicisms. Indeed, German would appear to have been a more important source language than English in the early years of motor vehicle technology: e.g. *kaasutin* [gasifier] presumably from Ge *Vergaser* rather than having any connection with the opaque English *carburettor*. Only in sports vehicles have Anglicisms a slightly more established place: e.g. *spoileri* 'spoiler' or *bokseri* for the boxer arrangement of the firing cylinders.

puhelin	telephone
matkapuhelin ['travel|phone']	mobile phone [formal]
kännykkä ['hand'+]	mobile phone [colloquial]
fax/faksi	fax [colloquial]
telekopio	fax [formal]
modeemi	modem
liittymä	(electronic) connection
käyttöliittymä ['use|connection']	interface
viivakoodi ['bar|code']	barcode
lukija ['reader']	reader device (for barcodes, CDs, etc.)
verkko = *netti*	net, Internet
pääte ['head'+]	(computer) terminal
terminaali	(transportation) terminal
nauha	tape (most forms of tape)
teippi	adhesive tape (only)

The + symbol here indicates use of an appropriate standard word-formation suffix.

It might also be noted here that there are hardly any tools named by Anglicisms. Many older names of implements have been borrowed from other languages, sometimes a very long time ago (e.g. *saha* 'saw' from Sw *såg*, or *vasara* 'hammer' from early Aryan). Even where the terms for relatively recently introduced tools such as *iskuporakone* [impact+drill+machine] 'percussion drill' could be interpreted as calques, they can equally be seen as having the quality of transparency which is one of the most striking benefits of purist indigenous lexis for the majority of speakers. In a few cases, an Anglicism may occur in a restricted sense alongside a more widely used indigenous term (cf. *teippi* cited in the table above): e.g. *kultivaattori* 'tractor-attachment cultivator' versus *jyrsin* 'garden cultivator', or *traileri* [treileri] 'trailer for transporting a boat etc.' versus *peräkärry* (behind-cart) or *perävaunu* (behind-wagon) for all other goods trailers towed by motor vehicles.

Since the *Dictionary of European Anglicisms* is specifically a dictionary of usage, its compilation has necessarily relied heavily on the subjective judgement of the contributors. For the Finnish contribution, in addition to myself three students were recruited—Mari Koski, Heli Sarlin, and Henriikka Sotamaa—who were all studying both English and Finnish language to an advanced level, and guidelines for their work were agreed in advance with the Department of Finnish Language at Turku University. The contributors from Finland thus represented older and younger, male and female, anglophone immigrant and native-speaker competences in Finnish. In many cases, it emerged that one member alone of the team was familiar with the use in Finnish of a particular Anglicism, to which other members reacted with surprise, antipathy, or incredulity. Since the aim of such a project must be descriptive and not normative, however, the confident evidence of even one contributor was taken as sufficient evidence that the term in question had penetrated the language. Undoubtedly, with a larger team we might also have reported a wider uptake of Anglicisms; the same applies, of course, to the other languages represented in the *Dictionary of European Anglicisms*.

The team made full use of the dictionaries available, including specialist dictionaries for particular fields, but it follows from the nature of the enquiry that a dictionary can only evidence the occurrence of items known to and accepted by the lexicographers. Usage in speech, recent adoptions, and usage in language varieties which happen to be poorly documented for the lexicographers will not be found in the pages of dictionaries. Moreover, Finnish dictionaries are fairly clearly seen— both by their compilers and their users—as fulfilling a prescriptive role. Usages regarded as unacceptable, which in recent monolingual English dictionaries may be listed but tagged as 'vulgar' or the like, are more likely to be totally omitted from dictionaries of Finnish.

On the other hand, there is a long tradition of Finnish needing to adopt terms from other languages for special purposes relating to content or style. The oldest borrowings date from before written records, and many were taken from Ur-Germanic and from the Baltic languages. In recent centuries, loans have come from many sources: through Swedish, German, French, Russian, from Latin and Greek. If their usage becomes firmly established among the educated elites, they become defined in Finnish as *sivistyssanoja*—literally, 'culture words'—and one of our sources for documentation was the *Sivistyssanakirja*, a dictionary of terms used by educated people. The closest equivalent for English is probably Hutchinson's *Dictionary of Difficult Words*. The *Sivistyssanakirja* is however a relatively conservative work; its task is to increase access to firmly established but difficult vocabulary of foreign origin in high registers. The overlap between its lexicon of Anglicisms and that of contemporary usage is therefore necessarily rather limited.

14.7 The future of Anglicisms

If the argument offered here has any validity—i.e. that it is these overlapping ideological formations on the interface between East and West which provide the most convincing explanation for the strength of Finnish linguistic purism—then the twenty-first century may bring with it a significant weakening of the lexical distinctiveness of the Finnish national speech community. On the other hand, I would not be surprised if the very impact of the international and pan-European innovations being introduced in other fields of society and culture serves as a further reinforcement for guarding and promoting the lexical sovereignty of the language.

14.8 Research

The major research undertaken specifically on Anglicisms in Finnish was the Anglicism Project at the Department of English, University of Jyväskylä, which was launched in the 1970s (Sajavaara et al. 1978). More recently, no new systematic research seems to have been undertaken until the Turku team began to prepare the Finnish material for the *Dictionary of European Anglicisms*. Other than the Jyväskylä project, the main source of researched findings has been the various publications on loanwords more generally, most of which (as discussed above) are written from a purist rather than a descriptive perspective.

14.9 Bibliography

AALTONEN, ANJA (1989), *Korkeakoulusanastoa suomeksi ja englanniksi* (University Terminology in Finnish and English) (Helsinki: Yliopistopaino).

ALANNE, V. S. (1968), *Suomalais–englantilainen suursanakijrja* (Finnish–English Dictionary) (Porvoo: WSOY).

ALHONIEMI, ALHO (1974), 'Sivistyssanastoa' (Culture-Words), in Ikola (1974a).

ESKOLA, MATTI (1990), *Sivistyssanakirja: 19,000 hakusanaa* (Dictionary of 'Culture-Words': 19,000 headwords) (Keuruu: Otava).

HAKULINEN, AULIKKI, and KARLSSON FRED (1979), *Nykysuomen lauseoppia* (Finnish Syntax) (Helsinki: Suomen kirjallisuuden seuran toimituksia 350).

HAKULINEN, LAURI (1961), *The Structure and Development of the Finnish Language* (Bloomington, Ind.).

——(1979), *Suomen kielen rakenne ja kehitys*, 4th edn. (Keuruu: Otava).

——(1973), *Suomen sanaston käännöslainoja* (Calques in the Finnish Lexis) (Helsinki: Suomen kirjallisuuden seuran toimituksia 293).

HENDELL-AUTERINEN, LAURI (1967), *Sivistyssanakirja: 27660 hakusanaa* (Dictionary of 'Culture-Words': 27,660 Headwords), 11th edn. (Helsinki: Otava).

HURME, RAIJA, et al. (1973), *Englantilais–suomalainen suursanakirja* (English–Finnish General Dictionary) (Porvoo: WSOY).

——et al. (1984), *Uusi suomi–englanti suursanakirja* (New Finnish–English General Dictionary) (Porvoo: WSOY).

——et al. (1994), *Agricolasta nykykieleen* (From Agricola to Modern Finnish) (Porvoo: WSOY).

——et al. (1996), *Suomalaisten esihistoria kielitieteen valossa* (Finnish Prehistory in the Light of Linguistics), Tietolipas 174 (Helsinki: Suomen kirjallisuuden seura).

IKOLA, OSMO (ed.) (1974d), *Nykysuomen käsikirja* (Handbook of Modern Finnish) (Helsinki: Weilin and Göös).

——(1974b), 'Suomen kielioppi ja oikeakielisyysopas' (Finnish Grammar and Guide to Correct Usage), in Ikola 1974a.

LEINO, ANTTI, and LEINO, PIRKKO (1990), *Synonyymisanasto* (Dictionary of Synonyms) (Helsinki: Otava).

NIILES, MIKKO (1997), 'Moposta ei tullut nopsoa: Kielitoimisto ei sanoista määrää' (The Moped Didn't Become a *Nopso*: The Language Bureau Doesn't Lay Down Rules for Words), *Turun Sanomat, Extra* supplement, 20 Sept.: 8.

NURMI, TIMO, et al. (2001), *Gummeruksen suuri sivistyssanakirja* (The Gummerus Comprehensive Dictionary of Loanwords) (Jyväskylä and Helsinki : Gummerus).

Nykysuomen sanakirja (1973) (Dictionary of Modern Finnish), 4th edn. (Porvoo: WSOY). (3rd edn. 1961.)

RINTALA, PÄIVI (1974), 'Tyyliopin perusteita' (Basics of Stylistics), in Ikola 1974a.

ROINE, SIRKKA-LIISA, and SIPILÄ, LEENA-MARI (1988), *Sijoittajan sanasto* (A Glossary for Investors) (Helsinki: Taloustieto Oy).

SAJAVAARA, KARI, et al. (1978), *The Anglicism Project* (Reports from the Department of English) (University of Jyväskylä).

TALVITIE, JYRKI K., HYTÖNEN, AHTI, and PALOVUORI, TAPANI (1987), *Suomalais–englantilainen tekniikan ja kaupan sanakirja* (Finnish–English Dictionary for Technology and Commerce), 2nd edn. (Espoo: Tietoteos).

TIRRI, RAUNO, et al. (1993), *Biologian sanakirja* (Dictionary of Biology) (Helsinki: Otava).

TOIVONEN, Y. H. (1978), *Suomen kielen etymologinen sanakirja* (Etymological Dictionary of Finnish), 3rd impression, Lexica Societatis Fenno-Ugricae XII/1–6 (Helsinki: Suomalais-ugrilainen seura).

TURTIA, KAARINA (2001), *Sivistyssanat* (Loanwords) (Helsinki : Otava).

Vakuutusalan sanakirja (Insurance Glossary English–Finnish–Swedish) (1986) (Helsinki: Vakuutusalan kustannus Oy).

VALPOLA, VELI, (2000), *Suuri sivistyssanakirja* (Comprehensive Dictionary of Loanwords) (Helsinki: WSOY).

VESIKANSA, JOUKO (1978), *Miljoona sanaa* (A Million Words) (Helsinki: WSOY).

15

HUNGARIAN

Judit Farkas and Veronika Kniezsa

15.1 History of language contact

15.1.1 Chronology of intensive influences

Hungarian linguists have studied foreign elements in the native lexicon for almost two centuries. The impact of most of the major European languages (mainly Latin, German, and French) has been investigated, and also the influence of the languages of the neighbouring countries (principally Slavic languages). However, English has hardly been investigated as one of the sources of foreign elements in the Hungarian lexicon. Consequently, studies, surveys, and wordlists of English loans are extremely rare compared to those of other European languages.

The geographical fact that England and Hungary are far away from each other excluded English until recently as a close-contact source of borrowings. Recently, English has become the most important source of foreign elements which have contributed to the Hungarian vocabulary.

There are, therefore, difficulties in studying Anglicisms in Hungarian. For one thing, the topic has only recently become an important field of research, stimulated by the fact that more and more English words have entered Hungarian: dozens of new Anglicisms have appeared every month. Hungarian has reached a point where there is almost no domain without English words and expressions, whether in the written or spoken language.

The first loanwords from English were found two hundred years before the 'Age of Reform', i.e. before the nineteenth century. The political situation explains the rarity of seventeenth-century loans (when only five were recorded): there was no direct contact between Hungary, part of the Catholic Habsburg Empire, and the

The Hungarian project was made possible by the grant of the National Science Research Foundation (OTKA).

westernmost Protestant country, England. Two words belong to politics (*parlament* 'parliament', *puritán* 'Puritan'); the other three words are *druida* 'druid', *jacht* 'yacht', and *flanell*. Their origins have been debated, but they seem to have entered Hungarian via English, whatever their original etymology.

The eighteenth century shows a more varied picture. English words started flowing into the language particularly in the second half, in governmental institutions, social life, philosophy, fashion and clothing, culinary art, agriculture, transport, medicine, warfare, and various sciences; many of these were foreignisms, including some exotic words from the USA, Australia, and Asia.

The Age of Reform (1820–49) can be considered as the first era of boom. It is interesting and new compared to earlier periods that words now borrowed were accepted very soon after their appearance in the donor language. Another important feature is that the words—some 150 or more—were no longer restricted to the 'luxury' stock of the upper classes but were assimilated to the everyday vocabulary of the people.

New areas included sports (boxing and horse-racing), technical and monetary terms, and some set phrases. In the subsequent period until the end of the First World War Hungary discovered English culture. By 1920 some 400 'newcomers' were integrated into the language of most social classes. Additional fields now included philosophy and religion, lifestyle, behaviour, occupation, economics, industry, culinary terms, medicine, entertainment, literature, agriculture, transport, sciences, sports (especially football, hockey, tennis), and politics.

Whereas in the previous centuries the influx of English words can be considered as an evenly evolving process, the period between the two wars saw the adoption of some 160 new Anglicisms (but also the loss of earlier ones). Another important feature is that Viennese German ceased to be the mediating language. Most of the new English words were direct borrowings, and many came from spoken English, a consequence of the advent of the radio. The fields affected were still the same, but the number of words entering one or the other was different. Most spectacular was the decrease of political and legal terms and the big increase in economic terms. Words with abstract denotation did not increase in number, but seem to have been more permanently integrated in the Hungarian lexicon than those with concrete denotation.

The decades between the end of the Second World War and the 1980s saw a complete change in the social and political system, and with it, the lexicon. The influx of English words increased dramatically, but there was also a strong tendency for the purging of English elements for obvious political reasons. One major characteristic of new adoptions is that they were mainly internationalisms, and most came—often through Britain—from the United States.

The fields most affected included clothing and the textile industry, catering, tourism, transport, information techniques, cybernetics and other sciences, architecture, agriculture, warfare, economics, sociology and psychology, medicine, sports, arts, entertainment, and youth culture.

The 1980s deserve a separate chapter because of the social and political changes. During this period there was a clear opening towards the West, reflected by increasing tourism (to and from the country), easier travel, and the availability of scholarships, and satellite TV channels, commercials, videocassettes, and so on. All these developments led to an unprecedented boom in the adoption of English words in almost all areas of life.

New dimensions opened up after 1989. Joint-venture companies, more and more western enterpreneurs, chain-stores, shops, restaurants, pubs, music centres, cosmetic agencies, information and computer agencies, banks, and tourist offices suddenly appeared. With these, many new trademarks and jingles from commercials established themselves, too, expressing a real 'Anglomania'. Anglicisms are pouring into the country and tend to assimilate to Hungarian (or assimilate Hungarian) very quickly. It is obvious that different fields are affected as well as different age groups. Youngsters are by far the most ready to accept them and assimilate them. In the schools (s. 15.1.9), English has become the most popular foreign language.

15.1.2 Origins of influence

Before the Second World War in Hungary BrE words dominated, while after 1945—for political as well as economic reasons—AmE became more prominent; it has gained greater popularity mainly through the media.

15.1.3 Types of influence

With Hungarian we face the same problem as with other languages in deciding what is to be considered an Anglicism. Usually (see Országh 1977: 12) four categories are set up. Since English loanwords in Hungarian are an extremely heterogenous set, and their morphological form and semantic content as well as the socio-stylistical layers to which they belong are different, four criteria can help in structuring the discussion:[1]

1. *Origins.* Anglicisms represent words with a wide range of origin, those of English (<Germanic) etymology like *know-how* or words like *finis* 'finish', ultimately French, and English coinages from foreign (mainly Latin or Greek) elements which do not exist in such form in the original donor language(s) (e.g. *agitátor, detektív, kombájn*).

2. *Change of word class.* English proper names and product names can become common words. Such words have lower-case initial letters in Hungarian (e.g. *graham, szendvics.*

3. *Derivation and idioms.* Derivatives of the English loanwords (e.g. *sport-* as a first or *-sport* as second element). This group contains also some set phrases and idioms which were commonly used in Hungarian (e.g. *goddam* 'God damn' (before the nineteenth century), *last (but) not least, struggle for life* (nineteenth century)).

4. *Style.* The classification of words can be based on three oppositions: frequency vs. occasional occurrence, common vs. technical language, and their status

---

[1] Note that the classification here suggested is not the one followed in the *Dictionary of European Anglicisms* which defines as Anglicisms words of English origin (excluding neoclassical words) and those transmitted through English if these have something English in their forms.

as loanwords vs. foreignisms. It is quite obvious that in the first opposition the frequent words are counted. In the second opposition not only words occurring in the common language are considered but also technical terms which first occurred in one or other field of science and later became part and parcel of the common lexicon. In the third opposition it is extremely difficult to draw any borderline between the two kinds of terms. Perhaps those can be considered as loanwords which have become entirely integrated into Hungarian (e.g. *gól, klub*), and to distinguish from those which have remained alien (referring to a foreign culture for instance: e.g. *lord, mayor*). These are the so-called 'localisms', e.g. *bushel, homestead, Ku-Klux Klan*. Those which came to be used to describe Hungarian ideas, things, etc. (e.g. *speaker, lady*) became real loanwords.

15.1.4 Chronology of purist phases

The first purist phase occurred in the 1920s and 1930s when a number of dictionaries appeared with the aim of 'purging the Hungarian language of foreign terms'. These achieved little success, except in the field of sports terminology. The Hungarian equivalents became generally accepted by the 1950s, so that many Anglicisms disappeared. What is interesting, however, is that with the recent revival of some sports such as tennis, and due to the impact of foreign media, many original English terms have been reintroduced (e.g. in tennis *to serve* → Hu: *szervál* → *adogat* → *szervál*).

A real resistance against English (as well as against German and French) lexis began with the influence of the Soviet Union in the 1940s. This was not a kind of purely linguistically motivated 'purism': the policy to stop English words from entering Hungarian went together with a complete change in social, political, and economic institutions. With the loss of formerly existing concepts, words denoting them disappeared, too; e.g. *civillista* (E *civilian*), *havelok* (E *havelock*), *komfartabilis* (E *comfortable*) etc. Moreover, there was an (undeclared) ban on Western European books and newspapers. These languages were almost completely expelled from school curricula for some twenty years: for forty years Russian became the first foreign language in the schools. From the 1960s Western European languages—among them English—returned to secondary and higher education.

15.1.5 Regional differences

Apart from the language of the Hungarian minorities living all over the world—which is beyond the scope of the present study—we cannot speak about regional differences in Hungarian. We can, however, speak of social and stylistic differences.

15.1.6 Stylistic differences

The earliest Anglicisms in Hungarian related to a specialized stylistic layer—that of politics and law; e.g. *parlamentarizmus*. The situation is almost the same as in German; exceptions are the very first Anglicisms (pre-nineteenth century) which dominated politics and law.

Before 1918 English words entered Hungarian through the written media, and thus were known and accepted mainly by the intelligentsia, the aristocracy, and tradesmen. In later developments, when technical terms became the most frequently borrowed category, loanwords were assimilated first by the relevant special interest groups. Some of these words have never become more generally known.

After 1918 media involving speech began to play an important role in the adoption of new English words when first radio transmissions in English became available. Political and legal terms now became fewer, while more and more words were introduced in the different branches of industry as well as everyday life. In the present-day flood of English words similar tendencies can be observed: special interest groups connected with e.g. trade, economics, computation, or new sports adopt the new words first. In addition, youth language is full of Anglicisms—sometimes slang or special jargon—and the Anglicized lexis of music and drugs has started to affect the general lexicon.

15.1.7 Innovation and obsolescence

It is clear from the age and character of English words in Hungarian, as well as from the influence of social stratification in their adaptation, that the process of obsolescence has always existed.

The causes are very similar to those in other European languages. They include:

1. changes in social structure/political institutions;
2. the disappearance of objects as a consequence of new technological developments;
3. the replacement by Hungarian calques, especially in sports terminology, and conscious efforts to replace foreignisms with Hungarian equivalents in other sections of everyday speech.

On the other hand, the continuing influx of English words was due to:

4. new notions and objects introduced from Britain or the USA, and the lack of a native word for a foreign product or innovation; this applies in particular to new sciences and newly introduced sports;
5. fashion (or snobbery) which has played an important role, especially from the 1980s onward, when English/American product names, shop labels, etc. were considered more desirable (mirroring the 'designer label' phenomenon in western countries).

Unfortunately no statistics on the increase and loss of Anglicisms have ever been compiled; an objective picture has become difficult to obtain especially in recent years, when hundreds of Anglicisms have appeared, the permanence of which cannot be predicted.

15.1.8 Mediating languages

As a consequence of geographical remoteness and historical/political factors, direct contact between Hungary and Britain started relatively late. This explains why many of the early Anglicisms entered Hungarian via Viennese German (e.g. *sport*). The other mediating language was French, the language of the aristocracy (e.g. *zsüri* 'jury', adopted with French pronunciation as in other languages).

15.1.9 English in education

Before 1914 the compulsory foreign languages in schools were Latin and German. English was first introduced in 1924 in twenty-five secondary schools, but this did not have a direct influence on the number of Anglicisms entering the language.

After 1945, the change of political orientation led to the banning from school curricula of English, and indeed all other West European languages. The 1956 revolution brought a short revival among the youth, but, following the failure of the uprising, English remained peripheral up to the 1960s, when it began to be reintroduced as an optional foreign language after Russian. Since then, and especially since the late 1980s, it has become the most popular foreign language in Hungary. It is now the first choice in the school curriculum; there are even some secondary schools where most subjects are taught in English. These facts have greatly contributed to the unprecedented flood of recent Anglicisms.

15.2 Pronunciation and Spelling

15.2.1 Pronunciation

During the integration of a loanword, its phonetic/phonemic make-up undergoes segmental and suprasegmental changes. There can be differences in stress, pitch, and quantity relationships between the donor language (DL) and the borrowing language (BL).

Loanwords usually start their lives in the BL with the pronunciation carried over from the DL. There are exceptions when the source is written rather than spoken, or when a loanword contains phonemes or clusters lacking in the BL. In this case substitution occurs: the missing element is replaced by the item nearest in phonemic shape. This process was called 'transphonemisation' by Filipović (1960: 37–8). It has two major forms; the substitution can be based on pronunciation or on the written form.

Variants of the same phoneme differing in phonetic features are easily adapted by the replacement of the native equivalent. Thus, stops are aspirated in some contexts in English but not in Hungarian, and the 'dark l' allophone of English /l/ is replaced by the clear /l/ of Hungarian. English flapped initial and intervocalic /r/ are replaced by their Hungarian trilled equivalent. The influence of the written form is likely to be responsible for the fact that postvocalic <r> is rendered by Hungarian /r/, sometimes accompanied by shortening of the vowel: *park* [park]. Syllabic nasals and /l/ develop excrescent vowels in Hungarian: *bicycle* becomes *bicikli*; *jungle*, *dzsungel*.

The problem is more complicated if the DL has phonemes lacking equivalents in the BL. In such cases the nearest phoneme renders the original; thus /θ/ is replaced by [t]: *Margaret Thatcher* > Hungarian [tetʃer]. The English bilabial semivowel /w/ is regularly replaced by the voiced labiodental fricative /v/ as in Germanic languages *W(ater) C(loset)* > *vécé*.

A less predictable development is represented by consonant lengthening. Whereas in most European languages consonant quantity is no longer distinctive, in Hungarian minimal pairs are regular: e.g. *ál* 'false' vs. *áll* 'chin'. In word-final and intervocalic position stops both are written and pronounced long: *tipp, tippel* from *tip, stopp, stoppol* from *stop*. This applies also to fricatives and affricates: *meccs* from *match*, *dressz* from *dress*; and to liquids and nasals: *szlemm* from *slam*, *halló* from *hallo*. (Some of these may represent spelling pronunciations, as in *hallo*.)

Major problems are found in the vowels of English loanwords. Although monophthongs are more or less easily replaced by their native Hungarian counterparts, greater difficulties are caused by /u/-diphthongs, which are not part of the Hungarian vowel system. Though there are some words with [au], especially of Latin origin such as *augusztus* or *autó*, new items with the diphthong are treated in a peculiar way. In TV advertisements, the sweet *BOUNTY* is usually trisyllabic [bo-un-ti]. Alternatively, such diphthongs are pronounced as monophthongs: *gól* from *goal*; two variants are found in Hu [no̱-hau] from *know-how*.

In Hungarian there is no real quantitative opposition in low back vowels: the long one is unrounded, similar to other /aː/ sounds, the short one, however, is rounded. Since there are no central vowels, [ʌ] has a variety of substitutions, depending on time of borrowing, whether the word came through a mediating language, or was adopted through the written form. Thus, the renderings are most frequently either [ø]: *dömper* from *dumper*, *löncs* from *lunch* (due to German transmission and suggestions in grammars) or [u]: Hungarian *rum, dzsungel* from *rum, jungle* (probably influenced by the written form). By contrast, the expected [a] is rare: *ramsztek* from *rumpsteak*; sometimes also [e]: *lemberdzsek* from *lumberjack*; or [y]: *tübbing* from *tubing* are found.

In some cases a shortening of English vowels also occurs, as in *ramsztek* from *rumpsteak*, *rosztbif* from *roastbeef*, etc.

Hungarian has no 'unstressed' syllables with a 'schwa'. Though Hungarian has bound lexical stress on the first syllable, there is no strong contrast between stressed and unstressed syllables: contrastive vowel quantity and quality also occur in unstressed syllables. This is why even in English words second syllables are pronounced with a full vowel, usually reflecting the one signalled by the written form: *dollár* [dollaːr] from *dollar*, *morze* [morze] from *Morse*, *nelzon* [nelzon] from *Nelson*, *huligán* [huligaːn] from *hooligan*.

15.2.2 Graphemic integration

Hungarian orthography is morphophonemic, with an almost complete correlation of phonemes and graphemes. This principle differs from a phonetic spelling in that the various combinative changes, such as assimilation, dissimilation, and sound deletions are not represented. The Latin 'letters' are used in their general medieval *potestas*, and eventual changes in pronunciation are gradually introduced in updates of the orthographic rules, without basic changes to the orthographic system.

In earlier times when Hungarians largely lacked spoken knowledge of English they tended to pronounce written English words according to the Hungarian conventions, thus producing spelling pronunciation in Hungarian *fotbal* [futbal] < *football* (hence the diminutive, Hungarian *foci*).

In later periods the usual observation is that frequent and established loans are also orthographically adapted. Since Hungarian and English use the same set of 'letters' but with different conventions, loanwords usually go through a three-step assimilatory development:

1. the English spelling is preserved: <know-how>;
2. there is an interference between the spelling form of English and Hungarian: <roastbeef> adopted as <rostbeaf>, etc. leading to <rosztbif>;
3. the loanword is assimilated to the Hungarian orthography: <back> first <back> (1899), then <beck> (1911), and finally <bekk> (1913).

In Phase 1 (etymological spelling) and Phase 3 (morphophonemic spelling) the written form is stable; in Phase 2 there can be transitory forms. Some of these are due to a lack of knowledge of English. This phase may be passed over if the pronunciation and spelling are fairly close in both languages: *box* adopted as Hu <box>, later <boksz>, *farmer* as <farmer>.

In the development of the written form the spelling and pronuncation of mediating languages can also play a role: *reaction* was adopted as <reactio> (due to Latin influence in medical language).

In general, the supposition is that the older the lexical element, the better incorporated it will be into the Hungarian system; in consequence, its spelling follows the native rules. However, the most recent examples show that it is not necessarily so, and even very new special terms can obtain a Hungarian spelling quickly, as in *laser* which was adopted as <lézer>.

15.3 Morphology

15.3.1 Introduction

In Hungarian there is no gender distinction in the case of nouns, pronouns, or adjectives. The only marked categories of the noun are number and case. Verbs are inflected for person, number, tense, and mood. Loanwords are normally fully integrated.

15.3.2 Nouns

Any analysis of English borrowings into Hungarian shows that, unsurprisingly, nouns are in the majority: they represent some 80 per cent of the English words. It seems that new things and notions are more frequently adopted than words designating qualities or actions. Nouns are accepted more or less spontaneously as labels of new things and notions, other parts of speech requiring a greater effort of abstraction.

English borrowings in Hungarian become naturalized as members of a single part of speech. Polyfunctional words are very rare; an example is *patent* which is a noun ('snap fastener') and an adjective ('clever, ingenious').

Changes in part of speech is rare, and may be caused by clipping, as in *tonic* and *rocky*: *Ő ivott egy tonikot én egy rockyt* 'He drank a tonic water and I drank a Rocky Cellar beer.'

Loans from English take the usual grammatical markers for number and case: (sg. = Ø, pl. = *k*): e.g.: *klub—klubok, klubban—klubokban* (club—clubs, in a club—in clubs).

Some early borrowings with German mediation appear in their English plural forms but with singular meaning: *keksz* 'biscuit' and *koksz* 'coke'. These words take an additional -*k* marker if pluralized, as in *kekszek* 'biscuits'.

15.3.3 Adjectives

Very few adjectives have been borrowed, possibly because they usually do not represent new ideas, but highlight already known characteristics of a thing or a notion. Many English adjectives are affective/subjective rather than descriptive. Some are only used predicatively: *tipp-topp*. The great majority of English adjectives are used primarily attributively and never as predicates themselves: *objektív* 'objective'.

All introduced adjectives can freely be used in the comparative (adding -*bb*), and the superlative (*leg-. . . -bb*), as in *up-to-date, up-to-date-abb, leg-up-to-date-abb*.

New adjectives can be derived from nouns and names by adding -*i*: for example, *oxford-i*.

15.3.4 Adverbs

Every borrowed adjective can be used in adverbial function either with the addition of the formative element -*án/én* or -*ul/ül*- (*pozitívan, unfairül*) or with the addition of the adverb *módon* (*tipp-topp módon*).

There are few examples of borrowed adverbs and numerals, and none of pronouns. There are no forms with -*ly*. Only one adverb is used in tennis and volleyball: *out*. The numerals *fifteen* and *thirty* occur in tennis. The adverb *fifti-fifti* is used attributively: *A hasznot fifti-fifti alapon osztottuk meg* 'We shared the profit on a fifty-fifty basis.'

15.3.5 Verbs

There are very few borrowed verbs; most verbs are derived in Hungarian from a previously borrowed noun or adjective. All are marked by -*zik* or -*l*, e.g.: *hokizik* 'to play hockey' and *trimmel* 'to trim', *realizál* 'to realize', *shoppingol* 'to do shopping'.

A considerable proportion of these verbs are intransitive: *bokszol, sztrájkol*; and many express sports activities: *hokizik, startol*. In early borrowings with German as a mediator the infix *-ir-* is found: *fixíroz*.

15.3.6 Derivation

Gender specification. In certain cases the original English feminine forms have been taken over: *stewardess, hostess*. *Szportsman* and *szportslédi* (since the English term is *sportswoman*, the *sportslédi* is also an example of a pseudo-loan, cf. s.15.6) reflect the English gender distinction. In most cases feminine sex is expressed by the Hungarian suffix *-nő* ('woman') as in *riporternő*.

Agent nouns. English nouns in *-er* are treated as base forms: thus *tréner* is perceived as monomorphemic. (The English verb *to train* has not been borrowed into Hungarian—the relevant verb *tréningez* is derived from the *-ing* form.)

Usually agent nouns are the result of multiple derivation: English noun + Hungarian verb-forming element + Hungarian deverbal agentive element: *-ó, -ő*: e.g. *boksz* + *ol* + *ó* = 'boxer', *tréning* + *ez* + *ő* = 'trainee'.

In the case of nouns which are of non-Germanic or Latin origin, the *-ist* is frequently replaced by the Hungarian relatinized form *-ista*, as in *biciklista*.

Denominal verbs. All the English loan verbs in Hungarian belong to this category. The process has been described under s.15.3.5.

New adjectives. English adjectives with *-ble* are relatinized to *-bilis*: *kompatibilis* 'compatible'. New adjectives can be derived from borrowed nouns as in *pizsamás* 'wearing pyjamas' or from proper names (geographical or personal) with *-i*: *oxfordi, thatcheri* '(something) of Thatcher'.

Deadjectival nouns. The few words recorded in this category are treated as base forms, for example *fitness*.

Deverbal nouns/adjectives. In Hungarian *-ing* forms are borrowed as base forms from which verbs, verbal nouns, and adjectives are derived: *training* > *tréning* 'training' → *tréningez* 'to train' → *tréningezés* 'training' → *tréningező* 'trainee'.

15.3.7 Compounds and combining forms

Recently, hybrid compounds have become very popular, though these are mainly found as names/shop signs (and not yet as proper words): *Pólus Center* (the name of a new shopping mall), *Divat Shop* 'Fashion Shop', *Babilon Cipő Diszkont* 'Babilon Shoe Discount Store', *Saláta and Drink* 'Salads and Drinks'. In all these cases the foreignness of the English element is very apparent.

15.3.8 Calques (loan translations)

Since the morphological structure of English and Hungarian composition (especially noun + noun and adjective + noun compounds) is identical, i.e. the sequence is determinans followed by determinatum, translation is easy; e.g. *béka* + *ember* 'frogman', *hét* + *vége* 'weekend', *felhő* + *karcoló* 'skyscraper', *közép* + *csatár* 'centre-forward'. In this last instance Hungarian *köszép* equals 'centre' and *csatár* equals E *forward* 'an attacking player in football, ice hockey, etc.'

15.4 Meaning

In borrowing, words normally preserve the original meaning or have their meaning narrowed. There are, of course, a few special cases.

In monosemic words, Hungarian normally preserves the original meanings especially in polysyllabic technical terms: e.g. *agnosztik* 'agnostic', *szentimentális* 'sentimental'. This applies also to some colloquial words, as in *sznob* 'snob', *klán* 'clan', *cowboy*, etc.

In English polysemic words, a single sense is normally borrowed: *görl* 'showgirl', *gól* 'goal' (in football), *lift* 'elevator'; *toast* was borrowed as *tószt* 'speech' quite early, and again as 'roasted bread' in very modern usage.

In a few cases the English meaning has been extended: *sál* from *shawl* in Hungarian designates all kinds of scarf.

Narrowing and widening are combined in Hungarian *dzsem* (from *jam*), which refers to a 'mass made of fruits', but not to a 'traffic. On the other hand, in Hungarian it also means the 'flesh of exotic fruits'.

In a few cases, there is no apparent connection between the Hungarian meaning and the original English one, as in *gém* + *kapocs* 'paperclip' (from English *gem* + Hungarian *kapocs* 'clip').

In Hungarian it has to be considered whether the word is used in everyday language or only peripherally (in some special fields). The more colloquial or accepted a word is, the more probable it is that it has been affected by changes of meaning, e.g. *boy* now means 'messenger'.

15.5 Usage

There is not sufficient information concerning sociolinguistic and stylistic aspects of the use of English loanwords in Hungarian. However, the numerical majority are found in special fields, as in sports, medical language, fashion, cinematography, advertisements, computation techniques, banking and trade, and brand names. In youth language Anglicisms are found especially in the field of popular music and rock, as in other European languages.

15.6 Forms of linguistic borrowing and their categorization

Hungarian exhibits the same categories as English influence on other European languages; we here provide a few specimens to illustrate pseudo-loans. Lexical pseudo-loans include *dzseki* 'jacket' from *jacket*, *lumberjack* (also *jackie, jacky*); the shortened form does not seem to exist in English.

Also compare other un-English clippings, as in *profi* from *professional* (via German), *pulcsi* from *pullover* (cf. German *Pulli*), and *farmer*, which in Hungarian means 'blue jeans'.

Calquing has frequently been attempted in Hungarian; not all of the new coinages have proved successful. The following examples serve to illustrate the phenomenon.

A *Translations*

1. Successful

brainwashing < agymosás, maiden speech < szűzbeszéd, penalty-kick < büntető rúgás, semi-conductor < félvezető, flying saucer < repülő csészealj, Iron Curtain < Vasfüggöny, mixed double < vegyes páros, time is money < az idő pénz

2. Coexisting

bodyguard = testőr, pacemaker = ritmusszabályozó, Big Brother = a Nagy Testvér, old boy = öreg fiú, first class = első osztályú, do-it-yourself = csináld magad

3. Failures

beefsteak > marhasült, roast beef > rostélyos marhasült, self-made man > önalkotta ember, garden party > kerti összejövetel

B *Renderings*

1. Successful

roller-skate < görkorcsolya, skyscraper < felhőkarcoló, greenhorn < zöldfülű, overtime < túlmunka, dead heat < pokoli hőség, no comment < kommentár nélkül, my home is my castle < az én házam az én váram, be in the same boat < egy csónakban evezni

2. Coexisting

ham and eggs = sonka tojással, cross-country = mezei futás, goodbye = viszlát, for ever! = örökké! (sports), *soft porn = puha pornó*

3. Failures

pen top > toll alapú számítógép, happy end(ing) > szerencsés vég

C *Creations*

1. Successful

steeplechase < akadályfutás, space shuttle < űrkomp, black box < fekete doboz, globetrotter < világjáró, work-to-rule < lassító sztrájk, struggle for life < létért való küzdelem

2. Coexisting

(blue) jeans = farmer, topless = meztelen felső

3. Failures

public relations > közkapcsolatok, grapefruit > citrancs

D *Semantic loans*

1. Successful

mouse < egér, to fire < tüzel, to feed < betáplál, soap opera < szappan opera, make money < pénzt csinál, mad cow disease < kerge marha kór

2. Coexisting

xerox = fénymásoló, computer = számítógép, up-to-date = korszerű, peep show = kukkoló show

3. Failures

brainstorming > agyvihar, marketing > piacelemzés, goodwill > vevőkör, topless bar > félmeztelen bár, mountain bike > hegyi bringa

15.7 The future of Anglicisms

Since the greatest influx of English words started in the 1980s in all fields of life, these Anglicisms have not been in the language for a long time. Therefore, it is impossible to predict whether they are here to stay. The further import of Anglicisms will depend on various extralinguistic factors: politics, fashions, purism, and attitudes in general.

15.8 Research

An extensive study of Hungarian Anglicisms started relatively late compared to other European languages, in fact as late as the 1960s, but even then individual investigations covered usually only one special field (e.g. sports or medicine). The first monograph focusing on Anglicisms in Hungarian in historical as well as semantic perspective appeared in 1977 (Ország 1977); since then there have not been many further studies in this field (as the *Annotated Bibliography of European Anglicisms* shows).

Even though hundreds of English words started to flow in from the 1980s in everyday usage as well as in special fields, this influx has not so far stimulated an extensive survey, nor a field-oriented or a sociolinguistic study.

We have asked some of our students to collect material in different fields, but this has not yet resulted in any comprehensive and systematic research. Therefore, the present chapter represents a first attempt at a coherent description for which our work on the *Dictionary of European Anglicisms* and editorial advice has been very helpful.

15.9 Bibliography

BAKOS, FERENC (1994), *Idegen szavak és kifejezések kéziszótára* (A Dictionary of Foreign Words and Expressions) (Budapest: Akadémiai Kiadó).

BÁRCZI, GÉZA (1958), *A magyar szókincs eredete* (Origins of the Hungarian Lexicon), Egyetemi magyar nyelvészeti füzetek (Budapest: Tankönyvkiadó).

FILIPOVIĆ, R. (1960), *The Phonemic Analysis of English in Croatian* (Zagreb).

KÁLMÁN, BÉLA (1970), 'Amerikai magyarok' (American Hungarians), *Magyar Nyelvőr*, 94: 377–86.

KISS, LAJOS (1966), 'Műveltségszók, vándorszók, nemzetközi szók' (Cultural Words, Wandering Words, International Words), *Magyar Nyelv*, 62: 179–88.

KONTRA, MIKLÓS (1975), 'Javaslatok orvosi nyelvünk angol szavainak fonetikai átírására' (Suggestions for the Phonetic Transcription of the English Words in our Medical Language), *Magyar Nyelvőr*, 99: 37–41.

——(1981), *A nyelvek közötti kölcsönzés néhány kérdéséről, különös tekintettel 'elangolosodó' orvosi nyelvünkre* (On the Question of Borrowing from Different Languages, with Special Respect to our 'Anglicized' Medical Jargon), Nyelvtudományi Értekezések 109 (Budapest: Akadémiai Kiadó).

ORSZÁGH, LÁSZLÓ (1977), *Angol eredetű elemek a magyar szókészletben* (English Elements in the Hungarian Lexicon), Nyelvtudományi Értekezések 93 (Budapest: Akadémiai Kiadó) (review: Kálmán, 'Szemle', *Magyar Nyelv*, 74 (1978), 107–9).

16

ALBANIAN

Rolf Ködderitzsch and Manfred Görlach

Prolegomena

Among the sixteen languages here included Albanian is not only the one least affected by English influences, it is also remarkable for the total absence of relevant literature: the virtual omission of a section in the *Annotated Bibliography of European Anglicisms* is easily explained by the fact that there was hardly anything to report. When discussing the situation with the contributor of the lexical data for Albanian, T. Ködderitzsch, we came to the conclusion that rather than omitting a chapter in this volume, too, the special status of the language would be much more adequately reflected by a provisional chapter which may, hopefully, encourage research in the field of Anglicisms so that in a second edition of the book a fuller account can be given. It may be useful to list a few desiderata; many of them have to do with data collection which could be done by research students, for degrees at the universities in Albania, Kosovo, and Macedonia with no great need for technological equipment:

1. a careful documentation of incoming Anglicisms (corpus-based collections using newpapers, radio and TV, noting pronunciations, spellings, inflections, and meanings);
2. a contrastive study of existing (and persisting) regional differences between Albania and Kosovo/Western Macedonia/Southern Montenegro, where the English influence started much earlier and was more thorough than in Albania, which was effectively cut off from the rest of the world (and certainly from western influences) for much of the period after 1945—the time when the greatest impact of the English language happened in the other countries;
3. sociolinguistic surveys (on however small a scale) to test how widespread the new English words are in various sections of the community, and how well understood, to establish approximate values for their style and status.

In the absence of such studies, and of text corpora and modern and comprehensive dictionaries, any account of Anglicisms in Albanian must be very provisional and incomplete. It is hoped that the following account reflects the situation at least as well as the minimal number of attestations of Anglicisms in the *Dictionary of European Anglicisms* does.

16.1 History of language contact

16.1.1 Chronology of intensive influences

Albanian is now spoken by some 6 million people of which the majority (3.5 million) live in the modern state of Albania. The remainder are found in the neighbouring provinces of Kosovo (1.5–1.8 million), Western Macedonia, and Southern Montenegro. Medieval settlements in Greece and Italy have (now) no considerable numbers of speakers left, nor have emigrant communities in the USA and Australia. Albanian is traditionally spoken in two major dialects, Geg in northern Albania and Kosovo and Tosk in the south.

Albania was the last territory in the Balkans to achieve independence from the Turks. The early history of the Albanians was characterized by domination by more powerful neighbours; this has resulted in various language contacts which have caused the replacement of much of the lexis inherited from Indo-European: various stages of Greek, Latin, Italian, Slavic, and Turkish influence left Albanian with an exceptional number of loanwords. Political developments of the twentieth century detailed below have led to a reversal of this trend, Albanian being possibly the one European language *least* affected by loanwords from French in the nineteenth century, and from English in the twentieth century (There was considerable French influence later, in the twentieth century, co-occurring with a substantial impact of Italian.)

Modern Albania effectively came into existence in 1912 when Ismail Qemal bej Vlora proclaimed an independent state, ending a period of Turkish rule which had lasted for more than 500 years. The new state comprised only half of all ethnic Albanians and was recognized by the great powers with a great deal of hesitation. When the Austrians who had occupied the northern half in the First World War moved out, the Italians extended their dominance to the entire state—an influence which culminated in the conquest of 1939. After Italy's capitulation in 1943, the Germans took over for a year, until the Communists under Enver Hoxha came to power in the (economically and culturally) underdeveloped country, in which there were few schools and some 80 per cent of the population were illiterate. The close affiliation with Tito's Yugoslavia came to an end in 1948, and Albania became a close ally of Moscow (until the break in 1961) and then of China (until the break in 1978). After 1978 Albania was almost completely isolated until 1991.

Much of the Communist cultural effort after 1945 was devoted to literacy campaigns, but the policy was largely xenophobic: foreign languages and foreign books were treated as suspect or were downright forbidden. Even when English was slowly replacing the restricted teaching of Russian from the 1960s onwards this meant using materials home produced for the Albanian market. On the other hand, literacy campaigns by the Albanian authorities had effectively spread the standard language based on the southern Tosk dialect to the masses—a unique opportunity to manipulate them by means of an authoritarian prescriptive usage which did not allow any deviation (and which passed over in silence the great tradition of writers in the Geg dialect). Since Geg was also spoken in Kosovo, the policy also impaired whatever desires there might have been for a Greater Albania (even though in 1968 Kosovo Albanians opted for accepting the Tosk-based standard language).

16.1.2 Origins of influence

Britain and the United States were never much interested in Albania, and the patriarchal structures of Albanian society did not have much in common with western ideas and ideals. Contacts with English were therefore marginal before 1991. Although many Albanians had emigrated to the USA around the turn of the century, and some 10,000 returned from there after independence, their influence on the language was limited. Italian had a much greater impact, including the mediation of a few English words (often changed to an extent that their English provenance is impossible to prove). A handful of Anglicisms (*combine*, *dispatcher*, etc.) were spread to Albanian through Russian mediation—as they were to other Eastern European countries.

16.1.3 Types of influence

The small number of Anglicisms, and the fact that almost all were mediated through Italian (and partly through French), has meant that the linguistic structure of Albanian has remained unaffected by English influence. It seems too early to say what consequences the massive importation of English words (and concepts) after 1991 will have.

16.1.4 Chronology of purist phases

There were a few purist moves by members of the 'National Renaissance' (*Rilindja Kombëtare*) in the nineteenth century; these were directed against Turkish, but the ideas had an impact on the thinking of Enver Hoxha. The formation and cultivation of the standard language which happened after 1948 under increasingly xenophobic conditions meant that concepts not in accord with the dominant ideology were not admitted (so that there was no need to name them, either). Names for necessary items from technology and science in particular tended to be translated—the twofold screening of things and expressions resulted in an extreme purist language planning. Regionalisms and other non-standard usages were also purged, as were older loanwords (a policy which considerably reduced the lexis of standard Albanian).

There is no information on whether there have been any recent purist reactions to the post-1991 influx of foreign words, but it is likely that the prestige of these newcomers is too high for any purist move to be effective.

Although not generally motivated by purist concerns, the remarkable capability of Albanian to integrate foreign loans phonetically and phonologically has left a large number of Anglicisms (Gallicisms etc.) without any formal indication of their provenance. Whether this system will work with a rapidly increasing number of modern loanwords taken from spoken youth and media language, or leave newly imported colloquialisms unadapted, remains to be seen—no recent evidence is available for reliable conclusions or predictions.

16.1.5 Regional differences

Up to 1945 there were several written standards: one based on northern Geg (which includes Kosovo Albanian), another on southern Tosk, a third on a southern variety of Geg based on the dialect of Elbasan close to the dialect boundary. This diversity is not reflected in the adoption of Anglicisms. Since even the coherent settlement area of Albanian is divided between states of different social and political histories, it is to be expected that major differences exist. Although the distribution of Anglicisms in Macedonian and Greek Albanian communities have not been investigated, we can say that there is a marked difference between Tirana and the Kosovo region which (for all its Communist regime) remained relatively open to the West—albeit that the many guest workers went not to an English-speaking country but mainly to Germany. However, since Kosovo Albanians decided in 1968 to adopt the Tosk-based standard, the written forms are now determined by the Academy at Tirana. Therefore in the *Dictionary of European Anglicisms* entries the label 'regionally restricted' (1 reg) always refers to the currency of a word in Kosovo Albanian (where its status is substandard or colloquial, not being sanctioned by the Academy). It will be interesting to see whether the political opening of Albania will level many of these differences in the course of the next few years.

16.1.6 Stylistic differences

The tiny number of Anglicisms taken in before 1991 were mainly technical in character; these have now been supplemented through the influence of the media, with items from slang, youth language, and various aspects of modern lifestyle. However, it would seem that members of the educated classes avoid Anglicisms, and dictionaries published after 1991 and recent linguistic publications show that paraphrases and calques are preferred to borrowed terms from English. In the absence of empirical investigations of recent linguistic developments statements cannot be more than hunches—the basis for hypotheses which need confirmation by fieldwork.

16.1.7 Innovation and obsolescence

The overturning of the old ideological terminology and the influx of words expressing modern conditions are likely to be dramatic, even more drastic than in other East European countries. While the outgoing lexis is largely Albanian bureaucratese, the incoming lexis is likely to have a considerable English component in it.

16.1.8 Mediating languages

The dominance of Italian between 1916 and 1943 leads us to expect that English words would have been handed on through Italian. However, the number of Anglicisms in pre-1945 Italian was not very large, and the few English words borrowed directly from Britain and North America, or transmitted through French, German, or Russian, do not make an impressive list either. As in other European languages, Albanian *biftek* and *vagon* were borrowed through French (but *buxhet* [bud̠ʒet] and *juri* were not); Albanian *keks* and *koks*, both masculine singular, were transmitted through German.

16.1.9 English in education

As mentioned above, English took over from Russian as the first foreign language in the 1960s. However, the number of schools in which English was taught was small, and the teaching was impaired by the facts that teachers had no proper training, native speakers of English were not available, and discussion of western concepts was not allowed. The demand for English is huge in post-1991 Albania but there is insufficient information on the ELT situation in the country to allow any discussion of trend at this point.

16.2 Pronunciation and spelling

16.2.1 Pronunciation

The integration of loanwords from English is complicated by a few structural differences between the two languages; these are less grievous as far as consonants are concerned:

1. There is a phonemic contrast between /r/ and /r:/, spelt <r> and <rr>. Postvocalic [r] in English is always pronounced in loanwords [barmen̠, apɛr-kat̠].
2. A phonemic contrast between alveolar [l] = <l> and alveolar-dental [ɫ] = <ll> is reflected in the loanwords *lord* and *futboll* (where it renders English allophones). There are no syllabic /l̩/ and [r̩] which explain Albanian [tunɛl, dʒɛntəlmɛn, akər].
3. [ŋ] is allophonic, occurring before [g, k] so that *-ing* words have regular [-ŋg].
4. /w/ is not a regular feature of the Albanian system; it occurs only in interjections and in a few loanwords like *kuarc* [kwarts]. Its representation in Anglicisms is variable; contrast [v] in *vikend* and *vestern* with [w] in *uiski, sanduiç*, and *tuist* (the dance).

5. Albanian consonants which have no equivalent in English—[c] = <q> and
[ɟ] = <gj> are used in the loanwords *qëndër* 'centre' and *kolegj*.

Where the expected correspondence between the English etymon and the
Albanian loanword does not hold, borrowing may be from written forms or
transmitted through another language (frequently via French or particularly
Italian).

The adaptation of vowels is more difficult: the Albanian standard language (and
the Tosk dialect) have seven vowels: a, i, e, o, u, y, ə <ë>; quantity is not
phonemic. In addition, there are a great number of rising and falling diphthongs
and triphthongs which are considered phoneme sequences by many linguists. The
English vowel system is very different, and many phonemes are not consistently
rendered, in particular:

5. [ou] is represented by <ou> (a unique grapheme sequence to render [ʊ] as in
kloun 'clown' or *shou* 'show') or by <o> = [ɔ], as in *kod* 'code', *gol* 'goal', and
koks 'coke'.
6. [ʌ] is represented by [ɔ] as in *blof* 'bluff', by [a] as in *aperkat* or *baterflaj*, or by
[u] as in *klub* or *tunel*.
7. [ɜː] is represented by [ər] as in *tishërt*, by [ɛr] as in *derbi* or by [ir] as in *flirt*.
8. [æ] can be [ɛ] as in *bek* 'back' or [a] as in *kamp* or *gangster*.

Many of these differences are explained by the age of the loanwords, their transmission through another language, or their adoption from written versus spoken
English.

Distributional differences between English and Albanian include the devoicing
of word-final stops; however, in contrast to other receiving languages, voiced stops
are preserved in modern loanwords in Albanian, as in *klub*, *kod* 'code', and in
sibilants like *bluz* 'blues'. Consonant clusters do not present difficulties for the
integration of loanwords, but note that word-final <x> = [dz] has not been found
in the standard language so far. Word stress is not phonemic; it normally falls on
the final syllable of words ending in a consonant or in *-i*, on the penultimate in the
other classes. The same pattern applies to all loanwords, too.

16.2.2 Graphemic integration

The modern spelling system in Albanian was settled at a conference in Monastir
(present-day Bitola) in 1908, when the so-called *Bashkimi* alphabet was finally
accepted with a few modifications. This was developed by the literary society of
Shkodër and was successful because it was necessary to add only two new letters
to the traditional Latin alphabet: <ç> = /tʃ/ and <ë> = /ə/, and even these were
easy to handle with a French keyboard. Nasalized vowels (in Geg) were indicated
by a circumflex. In addition, a number of digraphs and 'superfluous' graphemes
were used to render specific Albanian phonemes. Since the spelling used for
Modern Albanian is largely phonemic no phonetic transcription is generally
necessary.

16.3 Morphology

16.3.1 Introduction

Albanian inflects for gender, case, and number in pronouns, adjectives, and nouns; verbs inflect for person, mood, diathesis, and tense. All loanwords are integrated— there are only few uninflected forms even in the most recent Anglicisms as in *uiski*, *poni*, and *blu*; even some abbreviations (e.g. *CIA*) are inflected. A postposed definite article is added to loanwords as it is to native nouns.

16.3.2 Nouns

The major problem for loanwords is gender allocation. Since neuter is a tiny relic category, loanwords are normally treated as masculine (if ending in a consonant) or feminine (if ending in a vowel); the latter include words ending in <-ë> which is normally mute. This makes the distinction between masculines and feminines difficult, except where the absence of devoicing gives a clue, as in *bombë* [bomb] 'lamp'.

This phonological pattern made *mis* 'miss' masculine, whereas *kombajnë* 'combine harvester' is feminine, although it is masculine in the transmitting languages Russian and Serbian. Semantic/analogic factors have made *grejpfrutë* feminine (adapted to *frutë* 'fruit'). In the case of *stjuardesë* an *-ë* was added to produce a feminine form. In the case of *biznesmen* a new opposition is formed in Albanian by the derivation of *biznesmene* 'businesswoman'. There are also some cases of heterogeny by which gender differs in the singular and plural (*mis* M/F, as also in *koktej* 'cocktail', *sanduiç*, and *kolegj*).

There are five cases, of which the ablative is mainly used to form attributes (to modify indefinites, whereas definites are modified by genitives). Case is marked by inflection; a very few loanwords are uninflected (see above). Plural is indicated by various allomorphs; the choice is largely unpredictable.

The word *jeans* can serve to illustrate the process of integration. It is undeclined in *pantallona xhins*, but M sg. indeterm. in *një xhins* 'a (pair of) jeans', determ. sg. in *xhinsi* and F pl. *xhinse*.

16.3.3 Adjectives

There are three classes: those with preposed article, and those without; finally, there are uninflected adjectives which include all words borrowed from English, such as *seksi/seks* 'sexy'.

16.3.4 Adverbs

Since Albanian adverbs are normally not marked, adjectives borrowed from English also function as adverbs.

16.3.5 Verbs

As in other Balkan languages, there is no infinitive in Albanian; therefore the first person or third present is lemmatized (*dribloj* 'I dribble'). Verbs are categorized into three conjugations of which the *-oj* class is regular and fully productive; accordingly, borrowed verbs are integrated in this class. Note that *bëj boks* 'to box' is exceptional. All the synthetic and analytic forms—of which there are many—are inflected as in native verbs.

16.3.6 Derivation

Derived verbs. Albanian has three conjugation classes. New words are inflected according to the first class in *-oj*, as in *dribloj, kidnapoj, stopoj*; note exceptional *bëjboks* 'to box'.

  Agent nouns. It is similarly easy to derive agent nouns in *-ues* (originally a present participle suffix); this also frequently replaces the E equivalent in *-er*: *driblues, kidnapues*. Other derivations can be made on *-ist*, especially in combinations with *-bollist* (*volej-, basket-*); note that this pattern may have been borrowed—it is widespread in Eastern European languages. By contrast, the suffixes *-er* and *-man* have not established themselves, although they are found in a few loanwords (*biznesmen, barmen* vs. *kameraman*, and *bojler, buldozer, boksier* vs. *mjeshtër* 'master'.

  Feminine agents are now commonly derived on *-e* (*inxhiniere* 'female engineer', *biznesmene* 'businesswoman'), whereas formerly (and in modern written Albanian) *-eshë* was preferred (*profesoreshë*).

  Action nouns. Verbs in *-oj* permit the derivation of action nouns in *-im*; the suffix is also frequently used to replace E. *-ing*: *driblim, kidnapim*. However, unadapted forms like *miting* occur.

  New adjectives. There are three classes of adjectives; the few Anglicisms are normally adopted into the third uninflected class: *seksi, seks* both 'sexy'.

  New adverbs. The only borrowed interjections/adverbs are the almost universal *okej* and *stop*.

16.3.7 Compounds

The normal sequence in Albanian is opposite to the English pattern—the *determinans* follows the *determinatum*. However, there are a few exceptions, as in *bukë+pjek+ës* 'bread+bak+er', *keq+bër+ës* 'evildoer' or *at+dhe* 'fatherland'. This pattern is also followed in some English-based calques like *qendër+sulm+ues* 'centre-forward'.

16.4 Meaning

Attributed genitives are joined to their heads by a 'link article' which conforms with the head according to gender, case, and number, as in *slogani i fermerëve* 'the slogan of the farmers'. The pattern is also formed in calques as in *fund(i) i javës* '(the) end of the week'. In other formations, ablatives are used as in *goditje+dënimi* 'kick+penalty (abl.)'.

16.5 Usage

English loanwords have been so marginal in Albanian until recently, and developments so uncertain that even cautious statements on the topic are not yet possible.

16.6 Linguistic borrowing

The evident need to fill lexical gaps is met by borrowing and (to a very great extent) by calquing. Since developments are quite recent as far as Anglicisms are concerned it is too early to say what the proportion of the two is, and whether the calques (and which forms in the case of alternatives) will survive. A few recent items can serve as illustrations:

1. translations: *weekend* → *fund+javë*, *fund+jave*, or *fund i javës*; *skyscraper* → *qiell+gërvishtës*; *flying saucer* → *disk fluturues*, *Iron Curtain* → *perde e hekurt*;
2. rendition: *know-how* → *njohuri e saktë* 'exact knowledge' (or: *nou-hau*);
3. semi-calques: *cruise missile* → *raketë kruiz*; *television* → *shikim TV-je* (or: *televizion*).

In some cases various calques coexist; thus *brainwashing* can be translated as *shpëlarje (ideologjike) trush* or paraphrased as *topitje (çoroditje) mendore* 'psychological intimidation'.

16.7 The future of Anglicisms

Everything will depend on how soon the country regains its stability, on the reinstatement of foreign teaching in the school system, and on the extent to which a regular flow of international communication and exchange of technological know-how are established. Since such communication is mainly through English, Anglicisms are certain to increase, but it is not possible to predict how quickly and how thoroughly this will happen. It is, however, obvious that Albanian will remain the European language least affected by Anglicisms for some time to come.

16.8 Research

There has been next to no research into Anglicisms in Albanian; the two dictionaries cited below may be helpful although they are not up to date, and do not reflect recent developments, missing the impact of English after 1991.

16.9 Bibliography

NDRECA, MIKEL (1986), *Fjalor fjalësh e shprehjesh të huaja* (Dictionary of Foreign Words and Expressions) (Prishtinë).
Fjalor i fjalëve të huaja (Dictionary of Foreign Words) (1988) (Prishtinë).

17

MODERN GREEK

Ekaterini Stathi

17.1 History of language contact: historical and sociocultural factors

17.1.1 Chronology of intensive influences

Intensive contact between Greek and English dates from the beginning of the nineteenth century, when British travellers first visited Greece. After the foundation of the Greek state in 1832 and throughout the nineteenth century, contact was maintained through the presence of travellers, diplomats, archaeologists and scholars. As the nineteenth century progressed, the influence of English on Greek became more intensive and was accompanied by heavier lexical borrowing. The Industrial Revolution in Britain during the nineteenth century had an impact on Greece; new techniques and products were introduced together with their designations.

In the early twentieth century, Greeks found British social life and culture attractive. Many early Anglicisms date precisely from this period, when terms for sports (football, tennis), clothing, textiles, etc. were imported together with the objects and concepts. Around 1900, Greek emigration to the United States inaugurated the contact between Greek and AmE. The immigrants adopted and transferred back home (through letters and visits) a lot of vocabulary associated with their new life in the American environment. Meanwhile, Greek in Cyprus borrowed words from British English, after the island became a crown colony (1878–1959).

Since the Second World War, American influence on Greece has been, as elsewhere, enormous. The USA became the leading power in the domains of economy, military matters (Greece joined NATO in 1952), commerce, and technology. It was also the source of terms relating to cinema, dance, and music. Furthermore, the emergence of tourism enhanced the need for communication in

English. From 1974 (at the end of the dictatorship) Greece has steadily opened up towards the West. In 1981 Greece became a member of the EEC.

Nowadays, the impact of AmE on Greek is very significant for a number of reasons. The massive importation of goods and technological inventions is accompanied by the importation of their names (the role played by advertising is not negligible in this regard). Television and the press constitute the main sources of input. Since the 1980s, when the first private radio and TV channels started, American style and the American way of life have entered Greek households. In the press, most translated articles are from British and American newspapers and magazines. In the domain of entertainment, the cinema is dominated by American movies which contribute both music and an auditory input (films are shown in their original language in Greece). The evolution of computer technology has made English terminology widely available. English is also the language of science worldwide. This is clearly reflected in the terminology which often remains untranslated in scientific texts. Many Greeks receive their higher education in Great Britain or America and import current theory, method, and terminology into Greece. Since English now has the status of a worldwide lingua franca, it is regarded in Greece as an indispensable tool for everyone.

17.1.2 Origins of influence

Since the provenance of Anglicisms is normally not distinguishable by their form, a judgement on whether an item was borrowed from AmE or BrE has to be based on extralinguistic factors. British influence was dominant until 1920 (revealed by loans such as *golf*, *lady*, *lord*, *gentleman*, football terminology, etc.). During the inter-war years, Modern Greek borrowed increasingly more from AmE; since 1945 the majority of loans have been American in origin (e.g. *gangster*, *jazz*, *star*, *jeans*), but, even now, while American culture is dominant, ties with Great Britain remain important: BrE is still taught in schools and institutes; it has prestige due to its classical literary tradition; both countries are members of the European Union; and many Greeks choose Great Britain for their studies.

17.1.3 Types of influence

Language contact can influence all levels of language: spelling, pronunciation, morphology, syntax, and especially vocabulary.

The spelling of Modern Greek is influenced by English in so far as direct loans are often introduced into Greek texts written in the Latin alphabet, an ever more popular practice (on the graphemic integration of loans see s. 17.2.2). Pronunciation has not been affected by English to a great extent: Modern Greek has not borrowed phonemes or sequences of phonemes from English except in the loans themselves (on phonological integration of loans see s. 17.2.1). Modern Greek has not adopted any morphological elements such as affixes from English. English influence is, however, apparent in the structure of some combining forms (see s. 17.3.7) and in the coining of acronyms. According to Anastassiadis-Syméonidis (1986: 246), the emergence of acronyms in Modern Greek is attributable to foreign, in particular Anglo-American influence, especially after 1974, when their number drastically increased. As expected, it is vocabulary which shows the greatest influence from English, either through the adoption of direct loans or through the coining of native equivalents (loan translations and semantic loans). The influence of English can be detected particularly in the expansion of the number of lexemes which belong to scientific or other technical vocabularies. These filter into the general vocabulary, as aspects of science become popularized.

17.1.4 Chronology of purist phases

The purist tradition in Greece goes back to the end of the first century AD, when the movement called *Atticism* emerged. Atticist scholars refused to write in the spoken language of their time, the Hellenistic *koiné*, but imitated instead the language of the classical Attic writers of the fifth and fourth centuries BC. The assumption behind this practice was that the contemporary language was the product of decay and inferior to that of classical times (a view which is still popular, see below). Later Christian writers adhered to the same principle, and archaic language was used for the next thousand years in the written medium. The diglossic situation which was thus created continued during the Byzantine era.

In the years of Turkish rule the language known as *katharevusa* emerged. This was something between the archaic language used in Byzantium and the contemporary spoken language. Even before the Revolution in 1821, when the idea of ethnic consciousness arose, there began the search for a language which was intended to lead the Greek nation out of its 'mental darkness'. A dispute started between scholars who proposed a simple language and those who used an archaic variety. Once again, the views of the latter predominated: it was claimed that the spoken language was vulgar and inappropriate for scientific and literary purposes, because the Greek nation had lost 'its' proper language. In order to revive the past glory, the uncultivated nation had to learn the Ancient Greek language. *Katharevusa* became the official language of Greece and was used by the state (in the administration, army, press, and education) and by the Church, while the spoken language, the *dhimotiki*, was used for all other purposes. This diglossic situation was ended by law in 1976 when the *dhimotiki*, the language of the people, became the official language.

Supporters of *katharevusa* also saw it as their task to 'protect' and 'purify' the language from 'intruding' foreign elements which 'harmed' it. Consequently, loans from Italian, Turkish, and French were avoided through the coining of equivalents from native elements (most of them were actually from Ancient Greek). Scientific terms, imported mainly from French, were rendered by means of loan translations. Even proper names were transformed and integrated morphophonologically. The loans which came in through the written language were replaced by loan translations or semantic loans, which resulted in many polysemous lexemes.

Even now, after more than twenty years, purist views are still popular. On the one hand, language change is regarded as decay, and on the other, the 'intrusion' of Anglicisms is said to 'destroy' the language. Purists use expressions like 'decay, pollution, destruction, bad quality' and want to 'save' the language. They do not realize that the overall number of loans which are actually used is small, and that most of them are restricted to specialist fields. Officially, the Bureau of Scientific Terms and Neologisms of the Academy of Athens provide translations and native equivalents for scientific terminology and terms of other specialist fields which are proposed in their *Reports*; these may replace the loans more or less successfully.

17.1.5 Regional differences

Very little can be said about regional differences in the adoption of Anglicisms within Greece. We should, however, distinguish between mainland Greek and Cypriot Greek, which came into direct contact with BrE (see s. 17.1.1) and which contains many official terms of administration which mainland Greek lacks. Studies on regional differences in loans are not available, but cf. Swanson (1958: nn. 3 and 4), who refers to two studies concerning Crete.

17.1.6 Stylistic differences

The entries in the *Dictionary of European Anglicisms* clearly show that the majority of Anglicisms in Modern Greek belong to the technical and colloquial registers. The technical register includes the terminology of domains such as sports, industrial products, music and entertainment, economy, journalism, computers, drugs, and fashion. During the last few years, some of these parts of modern life have become popularized and available to people other than experts. The technical vocabulary has become part of the community vocabulary in fields such as sports, computer technology, and journalism. Colloquial usage of Anglicisms is reflected in youth language which is characterized by its great number of Anglicisms. These are in general not integrated phonogically and morphologically and reveal knowledge of and a positive attitude towards English. Contrary to the general belief, such items are short-lived: they tend to become obsolete very quickly as new ones are adopted or created. The creation of pseudo-Anglicisms or words and expressions modelled on English is common, but these are also usually short-lived. On the other hand, there are some established loans which are in everybody's lexicon. These are either relatively old (*supermarket*, *sorts* 'shorts', *tzin* 'jeans', *trolei* 'trolley bus', etc.) or refer to new, but widely known, concepts and objects (*kobiuter* 'computer', *khaburger* 'hamburger', *erkodision* 'air conditioner', etc.).

17.1.7 Innovation and obsolescence

There is a great discrepancy between the loans that actually exist or have existed and those listed in dictionaries. Older dictionaries contain very few Anglicisms, because most lexicographers were influenced by the purist tradition or were purists themselves. A large number of loans which were once actually used have apparently not survived. This is the reason why older texts and lists (e.g. Swanson 1958) are particularly valuable sources of information about loans. Furthermore, most dictionaries hardly mention calques, i.e. they do not specify that a particular word is a translation of a foreign item, especially when it contains a Greek or Latin element. Thus, it is difficult to estimate the overall influence of English. But it can be argued that the impact has risen constantly and is reaching a new peak.

Lexemes tend to become obsolete when the objects or concepts they refer to are replaced by new technological inventions (e.g. *vintsi* 'winch', *skuna* 'schooner') or because life changes. Thus the games *rami* 'rummy' and *stikaman* (or *stekaman*) 'stick 'em up' cited by Swanson (1958: 33) are no longer known; Swanson himself refers to the card-game *wist* (or *uist*) 'whist' as obsolescent (1958: 34). Younger generations do not use the same Anglicisms in their speech as did their parents: the word *tedibois* 'teddyboy' which was popular in the middle of the century is known to young people only from Greek films of that period, and is no longer in use. Of course, words may reappear in the language when the referent is reintroduced, as is sometimes the case with fashion: e.g. the terms *redigota* 'riding coat', *tuid* 'tweed' reappeared in the 1990s because the items they denote were again in vogue.

The shape of the loans may change through time and new word forms may arise as loans become steadily integrated into the system. But the reverse is also true: a more English-style pronunciation can replace an older one. Swanson (1958: 34) lists *tseki* 'cheque' which is only marginally attested today and has been practically replaced by the form *tsek* in nearly all parts of the population. The older learned form *ledhi* [le̯ði] 'lady' is now pronounced [le̯di]. Words which at the time of their introduction fluctuated between two forms have gained a stable form: Swanson (1958: 32) cites the loan *clown* as *klawn* and remarks that it is also heard as *klown* (his transcription), but only the form *kloun* has survived.

Finally, an Anglicism may disappear because it is replaced by a native equivalent, or a loan from another language. Many Anglicisms in Greek have been replaced by successful native loan translations (e.g. *revolver* by *peristrofo*, cf. also s. 17.6). Swanson's list (1958: 31) contains the loan *frejm* 'frame' (of picture) which has been replaced by *kadhro* (from Italian *quadro*).

17.1.8 Mediating languages

Many Anglicisms were not borrowed directly, but transmitted via French and Italian. Modern Greek has borrowed extensively from French, in both the lexical and the grammatical sphere (see Contossopoulos 1978; Anastassiadis-Syméonidis 1994). It is thus not surprising that French has also mediated in the transmission of Anglicisms, a fact which is evident from the following characteristics of some loanwords (Anastassiadis-Syméonidis 1994: 57–64):

1. The loan is a shortened form of the English word (compound or idiom) which also exists in French: Greek *khapi ed* < French *happy end* < English *happy ending*; Greek *kats* < French *catch* < English *catch-as-catch-can*; Greek *kabing* < French *camping* < English *camping ground/site*.
2. The Anglicism has the same meaning in Greek as the corresponding loan in French and both differ from that of the English etymon. In particular, the

meaning tends to become more specialized and therefore more restricted: Greek *pikap* 'record-player' < French *pick-up*, Greek *spiker* 'announcer' < French *speaker*.

3. The morphophonological shape of the loan resembles that of the Anglicism in French. In all the following examples the accent is on the ultima: Greek *rosbif* < Fr *rosbif*, Greek *reglan/raglan* < Fr *raglan*, and Greek *rekor* < French *record*. In Greek *striptizez* < French *stripteaseuse* the presence of the French suffix is clear evidence of mediation.

There are cases where more than one criterion applies, e.g. in *pikap* 'record-player' both the semantic restriction and the accent are indicative. In others, two alternative forms exist: Greek *iderviu* through French or *iderviu* directly from English; in this case the first pronunciation may be older. French may also have played a role in the variation found with the noun *shorts*: an older form of the loan is *sorts*, but there is also a recent form *sort*. Both are singular nouns. Anastassiadis-Syméonidis (1994: 61) argues that the recent form is attributable to French mediation (French has *short*). But it may also have occurred independently due to reanalysis of the word as knowledge of English improved (see s. 17.3.2). Modern Greek has also borrowed pseudo-Anglicisms from French: Greek *rekordman* and *sabuan* < from *shampooing*.

Some English loans have also filtered through Italian, from which Modern Greek has borrowed extensively. This class contains very old loans which are morphophonologically fully integrated such as *fanela* 'flannel, undershirt', *sterlina* '(pound) sterling', and *kotero* 'cutter'.

17.1.9 English in education

In 1836, four years after the foundation of the Greek state, French was introduced into schools as the only foreign language. Triantaphyllidis reports (1965: 412) that French was already taught in the first newly founded gymnasium in Nauplion in 1833. It was only in 1931 that English made its first appearance in education: it was introduced into the private schools in parts of Athens where foreign communities resided. English was introduced into public gymnasiums in 1945, but until 1957 it was taught by people with limited knowledge of English. From 1958 the teachers were university graduates. Nowadays, English is obligatory in the *ghymnasio* and *lykio* as a first foreign language, the second being French or German. In 1987–8 English was also introduced into primary schools.

Outside the state schools many private language institutes are responsible for the spread of foreign language skills. This is also one of the main duties of institutes like the British Council and the Hellenic-American Union. The latter was founded in 1957 and offers language courses and cultural events. The British Council in Athens has existed officially since 1951. It now hosts about 2,500 pupils per year and also organizes the examinations for various certificates. According to recent statistics, the number of people obtaining the Cambridge Certificate of Proficiency in English has risen by more than a factor of ten during the past fifteen years (612 in 1981, 1,624 in 1985, 6,246 in 1990, 10,848 in 1995,

7,070 in 1997). English is now the most taught and learned foreign language. It can be assumed that it is spoken by a large section of the younger generation.

17.2 Pronunciation and spelling

17.2.1 Pronunciation

The pronunciation of English loans is a very problematic issue, since it is characterized by considerable variation ranging from English or near-English pronunciation (*importation* according to Haugen (1950)) to full morphophonological adaptation. An exact reproduction of the loan is rare. The degree of phonological adaptation depends on the individual speaker's knowledge of English, their age, sex, the attitudes of their peers towards English, whether it is seen as a prestigious language, the topic and setting, the addressee, and so on. A loan will most often be integrated into the Greek phonological system when it is used by monolingual speakers. Its ultimate form is also dependent upon the channel through which it enters the language—i.e. the spoken or the written medium (acoustic vs. optic loan)—although variation and fluctuation between similar forms of the same lexical item are frequent, especially at the start of its introduction into the system. In a first stage, a correspondence between the phonemes or graphemes is established. Once the loan becomes more widespread, it may be further subject to the phonological rules and processes of Greek. Morphological adaptation tends to proceed simultaneously. According to Setatos (1974: 5) the segmental adaptation is more important than adaptation to the syllabic structure of Modern Greek or the morphological system (with the exception of the popular language, where loans are always fully integrated, e.g. *to trami* for *tram* < English *tramway*).

The phonological systems of the two languages vary considerably; in particular, Modern Greek has far fewer phonemes than English.

17.2.1.1 Consonants

Table 17.1 compares the consonantal sounds of two languages. Modern Greek has eighteen consonantal phonemes as opposed to English which has twenty-four. Table 17.2 illustrates the differences (English phonemes not found in Greek are italicized whereas phonemes peculiar to Greek are in boldface).

The major allophones and phonological processes of the consonantal phonemes of Modern Greek are the following:

1. Voicing
   (*a*) Nasal + /p t k/ → Nasal + /b d g/ (word-medially and at word boundaries)
   (*b*) /f/ > [v]/ – [+ voiced] (e.g. [ev loɣos])
   (*c*) /s/ > [z]/ – [+ voiced] (e.g. [tuz loɣus])

2. Denasalization: [mb, nd, ng] → [b, d, g]
3. Palatalization: /k g x ɤ/ → [c, ɟ, ç, j]/ – /i, e/. Other consonants are palatalized before a raising diphthong, e.g. /n l/ → /ɲ ʎ/

Table 17.1. The consonants of Greek and English

	labial	dental	alveolar	palatoalv.	palatal	velar	glottal
Greek							
Plosive	p b	t d			c ɟ	k g	
Fricative	f v	θ ð	s z		ç ʝ	x ɣ	
Nasals	m		n		ɲ	ŋ	
Trill			r				
Lateral			l		ʎ		
Approx.					j		
English							
Plosive	p b		t d			k g	ʔ
Fricative	f v	θ ð	s z	ʃ ʒ			h
Nasals	m		n			ŋ	
Lateral			l			ɫ	
Approx.	w		ɹ		j	w	
Affricate			tʃ dʒ				

Table 17.2. English and Greek phoneme inventories compared

	Modern Greek	English
Plosives	/p/ /t/ /k/ – /b/ /d/ /g/	/p/ /t/ /k/ – /b/ /d/ /g/
Fricatives	/f/ /v/ – /θ/ /ð/ – /x/ /ɣ/ – /s/ /z/	/f/ /v/ – /θ/ /ð/ – /h/ – /s/ /z/ /ʃ/ /ʒ/
Nasals	/m/ /n/	/m/ /n/ /ŋ/[1]
Lateral	/l/	/l/
Trill	/r/	
Approximants		/r/ /w/ /j/[2]
Affricates	**ts dz**[3]	/tʃ/ /dʒ/

4. /n/ → [ŋ]/ – /k, ɣ, x/
   → [m]/ – /p, b/
5. /m/ → [ɱ]/ – /f, v/

Where Greek has a corresponding phoneme (in articulatory and/or auditory terms), it is substituted for the English one (*phonemic substitution*):

English	**Greek**	**Example**
/p/	/p/	/pank/ 'punk'
/t/	/t/	/top/ 'top'

[1] This sound has the status of an allophone of /n/ in Greek before a velar stop or fricative.

[2] The corresponding fricative sound /j/ is the allophone of both the fricative /x/ before the front vowels /i/ and /e/ and before i + V; it is also the allophone of the vowel /i/ in the environment voiced C + i + V where /i/ is unstressed.

[3] Their status as affricates is disputed, but this discussion is not relevant to our analysis, since they do not pose any problem to the integration of the loans.

/k/	/k/	/kul/ 'cool'
/f/	/f/	/flis/ 'fleece'
/v/	/v/	/kover gerl/ 'cover girl'
/θ/	/θ/	/θriler/ 'thriller'
/ð/	/ð/	/on ðe roks/ 'on the rocks'
/h/	/x/	/xol/ 'hall'
/m/	/m/	/motel/ 'motel'
/n/	/n/	/nokaut/ 'knock out'
/l/	/l/	/lifting/ 'lifting'
/r/	/r/	/rok/ 'rock'
/tʃ/	/ts/[4]	/tsarleston/ 'charleston'
/dʒ/	/dz/	/dzaz/ 'jazz', /dzidzer/ 'ginger'

Lack of correspondence between the phonemes of the two languages results in *phonemic underdifferentiation* (where Modern Greek lacks a corresponding phoneme) or *phonemic overdifferentiation* (when one English phoneme is equivalent to more than one in Greek).

Phonemic underdifferentiation

English	Greek	Example
/ʃ/	/s/	/sou/ 'show', /flas/ 'flash'
/s/	/s/	/set/ 'set'
/ʒ/	/z/	/kazual/ 'casual'
/z/	/z/	/zum/ 'zoom', /zapiŋ/ 'zapping', /bleizer/ 'blazer'

Phonemic overdifferentiation

English	Greek	Example
/ʃ/	/s/	/sou/ 'show', /erkodision/ 'airconditioning'
	/ts/	/aktsion/ 'action' (this correspondence emerges due to the presence of the consonant)
/w/	/u/	/suiŋ/ 'swing', /kuiz/ 'quiz', /uiski/ 'whisky', /skuos/ 'squash', /saduits/ 'sandwich', /tuid/ 'tweed', /tuist/ 'twist'
	/x(u)/	/patsɣuork/ 'patchwork', /xuokman/ 'wakman', /forɣuord/ 'forward'

(see below for another outcome of /w/ in Greek)

These correspondences do not seem to pose any serious problem, since they are relatively straightforward. But other consonants vary according to the medium which was used when they were transferred into Greek. The series of the voiced plosives is such an instance. E /b/, /d/, and /g/ are nowadays rendered as the corresponding /b/, /d/, and /g/ in Greek respectively:

---

[4] The outcome /ts/ in Greek can also go back to English /t + s/ at morpheme boundaries, as e.g. in (*hot*) *pants*.

/b/	/b/	/barman/ 'barman', /bebis/ '(male) baby'
/d/	/d/	/dopiŋ/ 'doping', /adapter/ 'adapter'
/g/	/g/	/gangster/ 'gangster', /galop/ 'gallup', /golf/ 'golf'

But the data contain also some older loans, among other scientific terms, which were introduced by the written medium and were matched to the graphemes < βδ x > and to the voiced fricatives /v ð x/ which they represent:[5]

/b/	/v/	/vermuða/ 'bermuda shorts'
/d/	/ð/	/ðanðis/ 'dandy', /leði/ 'lady', /jarða/ 'yard'
/g/	/x/	/xaloni/ 'gallon', /xarðenia/ 'gardenia' (but cf. /garden parti/ 'garden party')

The phoneme /w/ is rendered as /v/ in older loans:

| /w/ | /v/ | /vintsi/ 'winch', /tramvai/ 'tramway', /bugi vugi/ 'boogie woogie' (cf. German) |

In the case of /j/ and /ŋ/ which are phonemes in English but allophones in Greek, *dephonemization* occurs, i.e. the English phoneme is substituted for the phone which in Greek has the status of an allophone (cf. Apostolou-Panara 1985: 181–2):

| /ŋ/ | [ŋ] or [ŋg] (allophone of /n/): [parkiŋ(g)] 'parking', [gaŋ(g)ster] 'gangster', [maŋgo] 'mango' |
| /j/ | [j] (allophone of /x/): [japis] 'yupee', [jot] 'yacht' |

During the phonological integration of the loan, minor articulatory differences remain because the sounds are articulated as in Greek. For instance, the plosives /t/ and /d/ which are alveolar in English are realized as dental in Greek. The voiceless plosives which are aspirated in English lose their aspiration because this feature is totally absent from Greek. Furthermore, the quality of the phoneme /r/ varies considerably in the two languages: in Greek it is always a trill while in English it is normally an approximant or a tap. Loss of lateral and nasal plosion is also observed. In addition, the allophonic variations of English are lost (cf. the allophonic variations of /l/). Instead, the phonemes enter into the allophonic distinctions that exist in Greek, e.g. /k/, /g/ and /x/ are palatalized before /e, i/: [kul] 'cool', [kol jerl] 'call girl', [kastiŋ] 'casting' but [ceterin] 'catering', [cibord] 'keyboard'; [glamur] 'glamour' but [jest star/jestar] 'guest star', [jinea] 'guinea', [xot] 'hot' but [çumor] 'humor', [çit] 'hit'. The sequence [nj] is rendered as [ɲ]: [ɲukamer] 'newcomer', [ɲuz] 'news', [ɲu luk] 'new look'.

---

[5] In the case of these loans which were introduced through the written language, the orthography determined the pronunciation. The scholars at the time of *katharevusa* transliterated the < b > as < β >, because the < β > of Ancient Greek words or roots in Western European languages was transferred as < b > (Mackridge 1990: 49). But they did not know that the pronunciation had changed and that the < β > was pronounced as /b/ in Ancient Greek. As a consequence, the sounds /v ð x/ which nowadays are represented by the letters < β δ γ > were then considered as learned and 'ancient-like' and were therefore used in the transliteration and, consequently, in the pronunciation of the loans. Notice that even early loans (like *bebis/beba* 'male/female baby') not introduced through writing retained the voiced plosive.

During or after its integration, a loan may be affected by the regular phonological rules of Modern Greek. These may alter its phonological shape considerably in relation to the English etymon. Only the most frequent ones will be referred
to here (cf. also Apostolou-Panara 1985 and Anastassiadis-Syméonidis 1994).

Assimilation. In Modern Greek /s/ becomes [z] before a voiced consonant
(voicing). This rule seems to have operated on some older and established loans
like /smokin/ [zmokin] 'smoking jacket', /rosbif/ [rozbif] 'roast beef', [zmol] 'small',
[zlip] 'slip' but it does not apply to all loans (e.g [slogan] not *[zlogan]), so variation
is still observable. Note that assimilation is regressive in Modern Greek, so that
plural forms which have been adopted and which are subject to the progressive
assimilation of English contain an [-s] not [-z]: [klabs] instead of [klabz] 'clubs',
[slaids] (and with regressive assimilation [slaits]) instead of [slaidz], [slams] instead
of [slamz] 'slums'.

([n + p] > [mb], [n + t] > [nd], [n + k] > [ŋg]) as in *camping* > /kambing/
[kambiŋg] (or [ka^mbiŋg] with prenasalization which is a free variant) are combinations which tend to be further simplified (denasalized): [mb > b, nd > d, ŋg > g],
e.g. [kabig]. Prenasalization seems not to be very frequent with loans although the
suffix *-ing* is very productive in loans from English. But there is the tendency to
preserve the consonant clusters *-mp-*, *-nt-*, and *-nk-* in loans (cf. especially loans
from French like *champagne* > [sampana] or [sabana]). Normally, loans fluctuate
between the two forms during the first stages of their introduction into the system,
e.g. with *container* both [konteiner] and [kodeiner] are frequent. The two possible
forms, with voiceless or voiced plosive, differ in style and are sociolinguistically
relevant. But there are also cases where the one or the other form is established, as
in *center*. The Greek word is *kentro*, pronounced [cedro] or [ce^ndro]. Greek
borrowed at the beginning of the century the English *centre* '(football) the middle
player' which is usually heard as [seder]. Recently, *centre* was reborrowed as the
second element of compounds, but in this case the [-nt-] is retained in the pronunciation, at least for the moment: [sopiŋ senter] 'shopping centre'. Finally, [-nt-] is the
normal pronunciation in *cent* [sent], *joint* [dzoint], and *point system* [point sistem]
(which is a pseudo-Anglicism).

There is also assimilation with regard to the place of articulation, e.g. *canvas* >
/kamvas/ [kaɱvas], *convoy* > /komvoi/ [koɱvoi], *press conference* > /pres komfe-
rens/ [pres koɱferens].

Dissimilation. Dissimilation of voicing is observed in loans like /dripla/ 'dribbling', /dzokin(g)/ 'jogging', /rakbi/ 'rugby'.

Simplification of consonant clusters. Complex clusters of several consonants are
simplified, e.g. [sauntrak] 'soundtrack', [jestar] 'guest star', [rozbif] 'roast beef',
[bakraud] 'background', [partaim] 'part time', [oltaimer] 'oldtimer' etc.

Table 17.3 summarizes the relationship between the consonants of the two
languages. It shows the outcomes in Greek and their possible English source(s).

17.2.1.2 Vowels

Modern Greek has a simple five-vowel system as opposed to English which has
twelve vowel phonemes. Greek vowels are not distinguished according to length,

Table 17.3. Summary of consonant
correspondences

Modern Greek	English
/p/	/p/
/l/	/l/
/t/	/t/
/r/	/r/
/k/	/k/
ts	/tʃ/, /ʃ/, /t+s/
/f/	/f/
dz	/dʒ/
/v/	/v/ (/b/, /w/)
/s/	/ʃ/, /s/
/θ/	/θ/
/b/	/b/, (mp)
/ð/	/ð/
/d/	/d/, /nd/, (nt)
/z/	/z/, /ʒ/
/g/	/g/, /ŋ/, (ng)
/x/	/h/
/ɣ/	/w/, (/g/)
/m/	/m/
j	/j/
/n/	/n/, (/ŋ/)
/u/	/w/

i.e. they are short (stressed vowels tend to be slightly longer except in the ultima).
Furthermore, the English vowels can be divided into tense (those that have been
assigned a length mark) and lax vowels, a distinction which is absent from Greek.
In English nearly all vowels (except /ɔ/, /ʊ/, /u/, and the diphthongs /aʊ/ and /ɔɪ/)
can reduce to [ə] in unstressed reduced syllables. The following graph illustrates the
differences.

Greek vowels: /i/, /u/, /e/, /o/, /a/
English vowels: /iː/, /ɪ/, /uː/, /ʊ/, /ɛ/, /ɜː/, /ə/, /ʌ/, /ɔː/, /œ/, /ɑː/, /æ/

The Greek phoneme /i/ has three allophones, namely [i], [j], and [ʝ] (Setatos 1974:
8). The English phoneme /ɜː/ is usually rhotacized in AmE (3ʲ).

Phonological integration of loans leads to the subtraction of the characteristic of
length in vowels, as is required in Greek. Where the two languages have a corresponding phoneme, *phonemic substitution* takes place:

English	Greek	Example
/ɛ/	/e/	/tenis/ 'tennis'

But since the vocalic inventory of English is much more complex, *phonemic underdifferentiation* takes place with the following phonemes:

English	Greek	Examples
/iː/	/i/	/spiker/ 'speaker'
/ɪ/	/i/	/biznes/ 'business'
/uː/	/u/	/bum/ 'boom', /kul/ 'cool'
/ʊ/	/u/	/futbol/ 'football'
/ɔː/	/o/	/ɣuokman/ 'walkman'
/ɒ/	/o/	/top/ 'top'
/æ/	/a/	/bak/ 'back'
/aː/	/a/	/parti/ 'party'
/ʌ/	/a/	/kari/ 'curry', /rami/ 'rummy', /brants/ 'brunch', /dram/ 'drum'

/ɜː/ (or /ɜʳ/) is represented by /er/ in Greek (presumably analysed into the two components, the vowel and the rhoticization, or probably because of the presence of < r > in the spelling):

/ɜː/	/er/	/erbag/ 'airbag', /erbas/ 'airbus', 'erkodision' 'air condition(ing)', /berger/ 'burger', /kersoras/ 'cursor', /ser/ 'sir', /flert/ 'flirt', /ferst ledi/ 'first lady'

/ə/ which is the most central vowel always assumes the value of the grapheme which represents it (optic loans):

English	Greek	Examples
/ə/	/or/	/akselereitor/ 'accelerator', /sponsor/ 'sponsor'
	/r/	/akr/ 'acre'
	/o/	/aktsion/ 'action', /beikon/ 'bacon', /galop/ 'gallop', /oridzinal/ 'original', /salmonela/ 'salmonella'
	/er/	/adapter/ 'adapter', /θriler/ 'thriller', /mikser/ 'mixer', /afterseif/ 'aftershave (lotion)', /internet/ 'Internet', /evergrin/ 'evergreen',
	/a/	/american futbol/ 'American football', /ekstasi/ 'Ecstasy', /asembler/ 'assembler', /editorial/ 'editorial'
	/u/	/kukuning/ 'cocooning'
	/ar/	/tsedar/ 'cheddar'
	/ur/	/glamur/ 'glamour'

17.2.1.3 Diphthongs and vowel combinations

The major diphthongs of English are /eɪ, aɪ, ʌɪ, ɔɪ, aʊ, ɔʊ/əʊ, ɪə, ʊə/. Modern Greek has fewer diphthongs, /oi, ai/ being the most common phonemic units. Other diphthongs such as [ei̯, ii̯, ui̯] are products of fast speech, while the rising diphthongs (/i̯i/, /i̯e/, /i̯o/, /i̯u/, /i̯a/) occur mainly in the sequence consonant+r+i+vowel (Setatos 1974: 10; Petrounias 1984: 397). The diphthongs of English loans are rendered as the simple phonemes of which they consist:

Ekaterini Stathi

English	Greek	Examples
/eɪ/	/ei/	/eids/ 'AIDS', /beikin/ 'baking (powder)', /korn-fleiks/ 'cornflakes', /beididol/ 'baby doll' But: /bebis/ 'baby (male)', probably with mono-phthongization; /cetering/ 'catering' due to misin-terpretation of the value of < a > as [æ], /data/ 'data' is an optic loan.
/ɔɪ/	/oi/	/boiler/ 'boiler', /boikotaro/ 'to boycott', /dzoint/ 'joint'
/aɪ/	/ai/	/olrait/ 'all right'
/ʌɪ/	/ai/[6]	/erlain/ 'airline', /baipas/ 'bypass', /bait/ 'byte', /kopirait/ 'copyright', /drai/ 'dry', /ofsaid/ 'offside'
/oʊ/	/ou/	/bouling/ 'bowling', /bangalou/ 'bungalow', /kas flou/ 'cash flow', /roudster/ 'roadster', /kouts/ 'coach', /xoum peidz/ 'homepage', /noutbuk/ 'note-book', /soul/ 'soul'
	/o/	is found: in optic loans /dikoder/ 'decoder', /band-zo/ 'banjo', /broker/ 'broker', /slogan/ 'slogan'; in older acoustic loans: /buldoza/ 'bulldozer', /bol/ 'bowl', /tsok/ 'choke', /kok/ 'coke', /gol/ 'goal'; in /klonos/ 'clone' due to Greek origin of the root.
/ʊə/	/er/	/berbon/ 'bourbon'
/iə/	/i/	/kliring/ 'clearing', /sirial/ 'serial'
	/ia/	/midia/ 'media', /sirial/ 'serial'
	/iu/	/midium/ 'medium'
	/ir/	/pirsing/ 'piercing'

Triphthongs are also common in English. In Modern Greek combinations of three or four vowels are not uncommon. In loans, the triphthongs are represented by the corresponding simple phonemes in sequence. The *Dictionary of European Anglicisms* corpus contains one loan with four successive vowels: /leiaut/ 'layout'.

17.2.1.4 Syllable structure

Modern Greek as well as English allows consonant clusters consisting of max-imally three consonants in word-initial position. Word-medially (at morpheme boundaries) Modern Greek allows a wide range of consonantal combinations (see Setatos 1974), which are motivated by derivation and compounding. In this position it is open to new consonant clusters. What deserves more attention is the structure of word-final syllables where the two languages differ. Greek words may end only in a vowel, an /s/ or /n/ (found in particles). On the other hand English allows complex consonantal combinations of up to four consonants word-finally, mainly a product of inflectional and derivational morphology. But even in

---

[6] *Phonemic underdifferentiation.*

Greek, word-final consonant clusters are not uncommon since *katharevusa* introduced a great number of consonant combinations through loans from Ancient
Greek. More recent loans from French and English have preserved their phonological structure, so that in loans much more consonant clusters are possible.
According to Apostolou-Panara (1985: 252), the most significant new syllable
schemes in final position are CVi, CCiV, CCVCC, CViC.

17.2.1.5 Stress

Stress in loans from English is a complex issue. According a rule of Modern
Greek, stress must fall on one of the last three syllables (trisyllabic rule). Consequently, if the loan is stressed on one of these syllables the stress is retained at that
position. But very often, especially when the stress exceeds the antepenultima, it
shifts to the right (e.g. /akselereitor/ 'accelerator' instead of */akselereitor/, /ampli-
faier/ 'amplifier' instead of */amplifaier/). Stress in compounds is problematic,
since they carry a primary and a secondary stress in English. Retention of the
double stress is indicative of a low degree of integration, because normally one
stress is lost (/kornflau(e)r/ 'cornflour', /livingrum/ 'living room', /kopirait/ 'copyright'). However, some loans have alternative forms: /basketbol/ or /basketbol/
'basketball'. Finally, the trisyllabic stress rule is violated in the lexeme 'cameraman' which is pronounced /kameraman/ or /kameraman/.

17.2.2 Graphemic integration

The graphemic integration of loans is of particular interest, since Modern Greek
uses the Greek alphabet. Loans appear either in the Latin alphabet or transliterated into the Greek. Latin spelling is maintained in many cases, even in otherwise
Greek texts, particularly in the press (and on TV). The proportion of such
items varies according to the readership and attitudes (magazines which address
young people contain many graphemically unadapted loans; so do specialized
magazines in car technology, musical equipment, sports, etc.). The names of
imported products also tend to preserve their orthography, which is partly attributable to the role which advertising plays in their distribution. In scientific texts,
terminology is also given in the Latin alphabet, usually in parentheses after the
Greek equivalent. Furthermore, proper names (not only English ones), which were
transliterated formerly (see s. 17.1.4 and below), are now preferred in their original
form.

   Usually, loans remain in their original spelling during the first stages of their
introduction and are represented by the native alphabet as they become more
widespread and established, although a fluctuation between one form and another
is observable, sometimes even within the same text. During the past few years, even
old and well-established loans which once were written in Greek letters now remain
in the Latin alphabet.

   When loans are transliterated into Greek, they usually obey the existing orthographic rules for loans which are proposed by the *Neoelliniki Ghrammatiki (tis
Dhimotikis)* 1941. These rules account for the simplified orthography of loans,

which receive a quasi-phonemic transcription, while native words preserve the historical orthography (Anastassiadis-Syméonidis 1994: 172–5, 177–9).

17.2.2.1 The transliteration of Greek graphemes in the Dictionary of European Anglicisms

In the *Dictionary of European Anglicisms* the Greek alphabet is transliterated for the benefit of readers who are unfamiliar with Greek. Table 17.4 shows the transliteration conventions that have been adopted.

According to the orthographic rules proposed for loans double consonants are avoided word-medially (*ten(n)is*) and disallowed word-finally (*biznes, futbol, gril,* etc.).

17.2.2.2 The transliteration of Greek vowel graphemes in the Dictionary of European Anglicisms

According to the spelling rules, loans ought to contain only simple vowel graphemes, i.e. loans from English containing an /i/ should be written with < ι > (not with < η, ει, οι, υ >, which also represent /i/ and result from the historical orthography). Likewise, the phoneme /e/ in loans should be written < ε >, not < αι >, the phoneme /o/ written < o >, not < ω >. These rules are largely followed, but one often finds examples of an effort to reproduce the English spelling more faithfully by distinguishing orthographically between short and long English phonemes: the

Table 17.4. Transliteration of Greek consonant graphemes in the *Dictionary of European Anglicisms*

Phoneme in Greek	Grapheme	Transliteration in *Dictionary*
/p/	< π >	< p >
/t/	< τ >	< t >
/k/	< κ >	< k >
/b/	< μπ >	< b >
/d/	< ντ >	< d >
/g/	< γκ, γγ >	< g >
/f/	< φ, ευ, αυ >	< f, ef, af >
/v/	< β, ευ, αυ >	< v, ef, af >
/θ/	< θ >	< th >
/ð/	< δ >	< dh >
/x/	< χ >	< kh >
/ɣ/	< γ >	< gh >
/s/	< σ, ς >	< s >
/z/	< ζ, σ >	< z >
/m/	< μ >	< m >
/n/	< ν >	< n >
/l/	< λ >	< l >
/r/	< ρ >	< r >
ts	< τσ >	< ts >
dz	< τζ >	< tz >

Table 17.5. Transliteration of Greek vowels

Phoneme in Greek	Grapheme	Transliteration in *Dictionary*
/i/	< ι >	< i >
	< η >	< i >
	< υ >	< y >
/e/	< ε >	< e >
	< αι >	< e >
/u/	< ου >	< u >
/o/	< o >	< o >
	< ω >	< o >
/a/	< α >	< a >

English phoneme /i:/ is sometimes (and was especially during the era of *katharevusa*) written as < η > (which in Ancient Greek symbolized /ε:/). Examples are: *beatnik* < μπητνικ >, *speaker* < σπηκερ >. The spelling < αι > instead of < ε > is retained in words where the first element is *air-*, because *air-* is equated to Greek *aer-*: thus *airbus* is < αιρμπας >. < υ > is often used where English has < y >, and is obligatory if the base is Greek or Latin.

17.3 Morphology

17.3.1 Introduction

Modern Greek inflects for gender, case, and number in nouns, pronouns, adjectives, and articles, and for person, number, tense, aspect, and mood in verbs. Borrowed verbs are normally fully integrated. Nouns, on the other hand, can show differing degrees of integration, ranging from minimal (in which case they remain morphologically unadapted, but are obligatorily assigned gender) to maximal (through participation in one of the inflectional paradigms). Adjectives remain totally unadapted (and therefore uninflected).

17.3.2 Nouns

17.3.2.1 Gender

The attribution of gender is obligatory in Modern Greek. Loanwords are assigned gender according to a series of rules which apply in a fixed order:

1. Animates (in particular human beings) receive the grammatical gender corresponding to the natural sex, irrespective of whether the nouns are morphophonologically integrated (*o tedibois* M 'teddyboy', *i mazoreta* F 'majorette') or not (*o golkiper* M 'goalkeeper', *i beibisiter* F 'baby-sitter', *o/i star* M/F 'star'). Exceptions are: *to kol gerl* 'call girl', *to top model*, N (discussed below).
2. Inanimates can be classified into two categories: those which are morphophonologically adapted and those which are not. Morphophonological

adaptation is the result of two processes. An inflectional ending is added to English loanwords which end in a consonant, allowing them to enter into an existing inflectional paradigm and to adopt the corresponding gender: *to rum-i* N 'rum', *i ints-a* F 'inch'. The selection of a particular inflectional ending may be motivated by the existence of a synonym, as in the case of *i sterlin-a* F < *sterling* after *i lira* 'pound', an older loan (Apostolou-Panara 1986: 101). English words which end in a vowel and resemble Greek nouns in form can be matched to native ones and be either F or N: *i skuna* F 'schooner', *i buldoza* F 'bulldozer'; *to parti* N 'party', *to penalti* N 'penalty', *to uiski* N 'whisky', *to polo* N 'polo'. The phonological shape is also decisive for words which end in an Ancient Greek or Latin suffix. These are easily analysed and adapted: e.g. *-ism* > *-ismos* M.

Morphophonologically unadapted loans (most of them ending in a consonant) are most commonly assigned to the neuter gender; this happens quasi-automatically when they are introduced for the first time: *to basketbol* 'basketball', *to saduits* 'sandwich', *to brifing* 'briefing', *to marketing* 'marketing', etc. Subsequent integration into the system may cause a change in gender. On the other hand, a noun may take on the gender of a near-synonym or hyperonym in Modern Greek. This strategy of 'semantic analogy' (in Anastassiadis-Syméonidis's terms) may lead to instability in the gender of some loans, for instance *to kobiuter* N/*o kobiuter* M 'computer' after the loan rendition (and therefore synonymous) *o (ilektronikos) ypologhistis* M.

Sometimes two genders compete as in *i rok* F (due to the F gender of the hyperonym *i musiki* 'rock music') and *to rok* N, which may be N either by default or because of a difference in hyperonym and hence in meaning. The neuter term may refer to rock music as a movement (*to kinima* N). The above-mentioned exceptions *to kol gerl* N 'call girl' and *to top model* N are best explained by semantic analogy to *to koritsi* 'girl' and *to fotomodelo* 'model' which are both N. The word *aktsion* 'action' has never been attested with an article. Theoretically, it could be either N or F (the Greek equivalent is *i dhrasi* F). Finally, the loan may remain morphologically unadapted and hence be N (*to tsoper* 'chopper'), but then develop an adapted form (*i tsoperia* F with affective meaning).

17.3.2.2 Case

Adapted loans (e.g. *sponsor-as*, *bodibilder-as*, *politsman-os*, *kauboi-s*) show the endings of their respective declension; case is marked by means of the case endings of the declensions, both in singular and plural (e.g. singular: nominative *o sponsor-as*, genitive *tu sponsor-a*, accusative *to(n) sponsor-a*; plural: nominative *i sponsor-es*, accusative *tus sponsor-es*; the genitive case sounds odd and is highly unlikely. Those which are unadapted remain uninflected. Case can then only be signalled by means of the article and modifiers (adjectives, possessives, quantifiers, etc.) which in Greek obligatorily agree with the noun in gender, case, and number.

17.3.2.3 Number

Adapted loans show the plural endings of their inflectional class (see above). Unadapted loans normally remain uninflected: e.g. **to** *film* (N sg.)—**ta** *film*

(N pl.). As with case, number can be expressed by the article and modifiers. Many recent unadapted loans also have the English plural inflection -*s*: *to film* N, *ta film(s)*; *oli reporter* M/F, *i reporter(s)*; *to klab* N 'club', *ta klab(s)*; *to sou* N 'show', *ta sou(s)*; *olto kobiuter* M/N 'computer', *ilta kobiuter(s)* etc. Forms with -*s* have arisen because the recent widespread knowledge of English permits speakers to analyse the forms, and to show off foreign language skills. Which of the forms will be used is largely determined by extralinguistic factors, such as age of speakers, attitudes towards English and purism, the speech situation, and fashion. Some nouns are used only in the plural (pluralia tantum), exactly as in English, e.g: *ta kornfleiks* N 'cornflakes', *ta tsips* N 'chips', *sixtis* 'sixties', *ta midia* N 'mass media'; *konektsions* 'connection' is more frequent in the plural. A few nouns were adopted in their plural form but with a singular meaning: *to tanks* N 'tank', *to slaids* N 'slide', *to klips* N 'clip', *to pampers* 'panty', *to sorts* N 'shorts'. However, increasing knowledge of English and awareness of its morphology has led to a reanalysis of these old loans, so that sometimes the forms *to tank, to slaid*, and the hypercorrect form *to sort* appear in the press (the form *sort* may also be due to French influence, see s. 17.1.8). It is evident that -*s* has now been recognized as a plural marker by Greek speakers, resulting in its appearance in recent loans and in a few older loans which were formerly totally uninflected according to the rules of Modern Greek, and by contrast its (partial) disappearance in loans which showed it also in the singular (e.g. *to tank* 'thank'). Agent nouns in -*man*/-*woman* follow the English pattern (*o barman, i barmen*) or remain unchanged.

The case of the noun *business* is noteworthy. This occurs as in the neuter form *to biznes*, but since the ending -*es* is the nominative/accusative plural ending for some classes of M and most of the F nouns, the form is interpreted as F pl. (as in *ellinoservikes biznes* 'Greek-Serbian business'). Probably in analogy of Greek F nouns with this plural ending, the corresponding singular form *i bizna* emerged. Apostolou-Panara (1986: 102) also gives the form *i biznes* F sg., which I too have heard. This form is probably produced by the rule that unadapted loans are uninflected (i.e. show the same form in sg. and pl.).

17.3.3 Adjectives

In contrast to native adjectives which are inflected to agree with the nouns in gender, case, and number in attributive as well as predicative use, adjectives borrowed from English are integrated only at the phonological level, and thus remain uninflected, e.g: *i spesial ekpobi* 'the special show', *i mini fusta* 'the mini skirt', *to top estiatorio* 'the top restaurant'.

17.3.4 Adverbs

The following adverbs have been borrowed from English (see *Dictionary of European Anglicisms* entries): *by night, backstage, full-time, non-stop, out* (sport), *over*; *on-line* and *cash* are also used as adverbs in Greek. Adverbs can also be formed from derived adjectives (see s. 17.3.6) by means of the native suffix -*a*: *gangsterikos* > *gangsterika* 'like a gangster'.

17.3.5 Verbs

Most verbs are obligatorily integrated morphologically by the suffix -*aro* (an early borrowing from Italian/Venetian) which is attached to the stem of the borrowed verb, thus *kodrol-aro* 'to control', *tsek-aro* 'to check', *skor-aro* 'to score', *sut-aro* 'to shoot'. Usually, the corresponding noun is also borrowed: *to kodrol* N 'control', *to skor* N 'score', *to sut* N 'shoot(ing)' are also found. Exceptions are *exitaro* 'to excite' and *fliparo* 'to flip out' (Anastassiadis-Syméonidis 1994: 198). Another strategy for introducing verbs is to use the verb *kano* 'to do' plus a nominal form of the verb, usually the *-ing* form, e.g. *kano tzokin(g)* 'to jog'. For some verbs alternative forms exist: *kano bakap/bakaparo* 'to back up' are both found. Once a verb is available, a perfect passive participle (used adjectivally) can be easily coined by the addition of the suffix -*ismenos/i/o*. Examples are: *tsek-ar-ismenos* 'checked', *flip-ar-ismenos* 'flipped out', *rilax-ar-ismenos* 'relaxed', *lynts-ar-ismenos* 'lynched'.

17.3.6 Derivation

Gender specification. Modern Greek does not require personal nouns to distinguish feminine forms. Many occupational terms have only one form for both sexes, the distinction being made (if at all) by the article: *o/i reporter* M/F 'reporter', *o/i manatzer* M/F 'manager', *o/i dizainer* M/F 'designer', etc. In some cases, Modern Greek has borrowed both forms from English, especially in the case of nouns ending in -*man/-woman*: *biznesman* M/*biznesghuman* F 'businessman/business-woman'. In others, it has derived a feminine counterpart on the model of the Greek ending -*issa*. This happens when the English base is assigned to masculine nouns ending in -*is*: *o kauboi(s)* M/i *kauboissa* F 'cowboy/cowgirl', *o khipis* M/i *khipissa* F 'hippy'. In still other cases, Modern Greek differentiates natural gender although English does not: *o bebis* M/i *beba* (or *bebeka*) F 'male baby/female baby' and recently (in modish, colloquial, and journalese registers) *o modelos* M/i *modela* F 'male model/female model' in addition to N *(top) model*.

Agent nouns ending in -*er* are borrowed unchanged and can be either M or F, or both, e.g: *diler* 'dealer', *beibisiter* 'babysitter', *gangster*. In addition to borrowing agent nouns, Modern Greek also derives them by means of native suffixes: -*istas* M/-*istria* F (itself from French -*iste* and going back to Ancient Greek -*istēs*), is the most common, yielding *tenistas* M 'tennis player', *basketbolistas* M 'basketball player', *voleibolistas* M 'volleyball player', or *serfistas* 'surfer' parallel to *serfer* M, *dzazistas* M 'jazzman', and many more.

Other agent suffixes denoting occupation in Modern Greek can be attached to a base of English origin. One is -*tzis* (from Turkish -*ci*), F -*tzu*, yielding the following derivations: *gol* N 'goal' > *goltzis* M 'a football player who scores regularly', *pulman* N 'pullman' > *pulmatzis* 'bus driver', *striptiz* N 'striptease' > *striptitzu* F 'stripteaser'. Another is -*as* M, yielding *saduitsas* M 'sandwich seller' < *saduits* N 'sandwich', *rokas* M 'rocker' < *rok* F/N 'rock', *khevimetalas* M 'heavy metal fan' < *khevi metal* F/N 'heavy metal'.

Denominal verbs are also formed by the addition of -*aro*: *snobaro* < *snob*. There is one example of a verb derived from an adjective: *fularo* 'to fill completely' < *ful* 'full'.

New adjectives. New adjectives can be formed from nominal stems by the suffix
-ikos/i/o (one of the most productive suffixes in Modern Greek), but they are rare:
gangsterikos '(typical) of gangsters' < *gangster*, *thatserikos* 'belonging to/of Margaret Thatcher' and, with an acronym *NATOikos* or *natoikos* 'belonging to/of
NATO', *internetikos* 'belonging to/of the Internet'. The suffix *-istikos/i/o* can also
attach to an English base, e.g: *kauboistikos* 'like a cowboy'.

Deadjectival nouns. Derivatives (in *-ness*) do not occur. In Modern Greek *duty
free* is a N noun (from English *duty free shop* through clipping). Also *to mini* 'mini
skirt' is more often used nominally.

Deverbal nouns (N in gender) can easily be formed from verbs ending in *-aro* by
the nominalizing suffix *-(ar)isma* as in *doparisma* 'the act of doping', *stoparisma*
'the act of stopping (football)', *parkarisma* 'the act of parking', and *snifarisma* 'the
act of sniffing', etc.

Other derivations include the following: the English suffix *-ing* is used with
nouns of English origin for the derivation of a neuter abstract noun: *to clubbing*
'the act of visiting clubs', or *to autobanking* 'the use of autobanks'.

The suffix *-adhiko* (meaning 'place' and producing N nouns) may combine with a
noun base of English origin to form a (colloquial) noun designating a type of place:
fastfud-adhiko N 'fast-food restaurant', *tost-adhiko* N 'snack bar' (from toast),
striptiz-adhiko N 'cabaret'.

The diminutive ending *-aki* is used in the formation of N nouns from English
loans; in most cases the suffix assigns affective meaning to the loan. In this way
some doublets are produced, e.g: *to bar* N/*to baraki* N 'bar', *to tsoper* N/*to
tsoperaki* 'chopper'. Sometimes the base and derivative differ in meaning, e.g: *to
kobiuter* N 'computer' vs. *to kobiuter-aki* N 'calculator'.

Augmentatives are formed by the suffix *-ara* which produces F nouns, e.g: *to gol* N
'goal'/*i golara* F 'a great/nice goal'. Such pairs of words differ at the pragmatic level.

17.3.7 Compounds and combining forms

Loanwords can be used in compounds irrespective of their morphophonological
integration into Modern Greek. But usage in compounding indicates that the loan
is well established.

Greek has borrowed compounds and phrases straight from English. Examples
are *tsizkeik* 'cheesecake', *erbag* 'airbag', *biznesman* 'businessman', *afterseiv* 'aftershave', *gril rum* 'grill room', *beibisiter* 'babysitter', *sidi pleier* 'CD player'. These are
treated as non-transparent, monomorphemic units in Modern Greek (Anastassiadis-Syméonidis 1994) both with respect to their morphophonological integration
and in compounding.

Many compounds are coined in Modern Greek as loan translations, e.g. *tyroghlyko* 'cheesecake', *aerosakos* 'airbag', *uranoxystis* 'skyscraper', *aerodhromio* 'airport'.

Loans themselves can be combined freely with native elements, e.g. *mats* 'match'
+ *filos*: *matsofilos* M 'someone who loves matches' (Anastassiadis-Syméonidis
1994: 202). The element *afto-* (*auto-*) combines with *gol* 'goal' to give *aftogol* N
'own goal'.

Another category of compounds consists mainly of loan translations and renditions (calques), which are formed in the following two ways (see Anastassiadis-Syméonidis 1986):

(*a*) noun + noun-genitive: *farma omorfias* 'beauty farm', *pyrghos eleghkhu* 'control tower', *eleghkhos gheniseon* 'birth control', etc.
(*b*) adjective + noun: *adisyliptiko khapi* 'antibaby pill', *aeroviki ghymnastiki* 'aerobics', *iptamenos dhiskos* 'flying saucer', *pistotiki karta* 'credit card'.

17.3.8 Calques (loan translations)

The majority of the designations of new concepts and objects in Modern Greek are loan translations (comprising loan renditions and loan creations). Many were created when *katharevusa* was the official language of the state (see s. 17.1.4) in order to designate achievements of science and technology. During the last years their number has increased enormously. In contrast to the direct loans, loan translations are normally transparent and are not felt as foreign to the language (they obey the word-formation rules of Modern Greek).

This is particularly true for loan translations of scientific and technical terms composed of Ancient Greek or Latin elements which are translated very easily back into Modern Greek and are felt as native (*re-migrants* in Swanson's terms). One such element is E -*ism* < AGr -*ismos*, which in Modern Greek is also -*ismos*. Loan translations have led to a revival, as it were, of many 'scholarly' elements from Ancient Greek such as *auto-* (*afto-*), *anti-* (*adi-*), *mikro-*, *makro-*, *ana-*, *tele-* (*tile-*), *oiko-* (*iko-*), and *bio-* (*vio-*). Often it cannot be determined whether the source of the loan translation is English or French, since such words spread across many countries at the same time, and in several directions.

17.4 Meaning

Most commonly loans are monosemous, since normally only one meaning is taken over from polysemous etymons during borrowing. Lexemes which tend to exhibit this characteristic are as follows:

1. Loans which belong to technical or scientific terminologies and have a stable and concrete referent (new inventions, apparatuses, etc.) usually retain the meaning of the etymon (e.g. *erkodision* N 'air conditioner', *erbag* N 'air bag', *kobiuter* N 'computer', *ailainer* N 'eyeliner').
2. Other words may also be adopted with one meaning only, and indeed this is the case with the majority of loans thus: *star* M/F 'star' (a famous or brilliant person), *korner* N 'corner' 'free kick or hit from a corner (football and hockey)', *basketbol* N 'basketball' (the game).

Polysemy in the receiving language emerges for the following reasons:

3. More than one meaning of the English etymon may be borrowed directly, e.g. English *back-up* > Greek *bakap* N ('a procedure for making security copies of data'; 'copy of data'), English *clips* > Greek *klip(s)* N ('a device for holding things together', 'a piece of jewellery fastened by a clip').

4. Once the loan is integrated into the language, it is subject to semantic extensions, since it is part of a new system. For instance, *bleizer* N 'blazer' which in addition to the meaning '(dark blue) summer jacket (esp. men's)' as in English also refers in Greek to a 'summer jacket for women'. The word *doping* N, in addition to meaning 'administering drugs to increase athletic performance' as in English, also means 'taking drugs to increase athletic performance', and 'a stimulant for support during sport competitions'— senses which English lacks. The adjective *khai* 'high' is adopted with the meaning 'intoxicated by alcohol or drugs', but in Greek it has the additional meaning 'in style' (this is also true for Bulgarian).

Semantic extensions are often preceded by and attributable to metaphorical uses of particular words. In Modern Greek metaphorical use of Anglicisms is observable particularly in the press, where it is often indicated by quotation marks. These metaphorical meanings may spread and lead to polysemy. The following examples illustrate the case: *lifting* N has as its only loan meaning 'tightening of skin', but it is also used metaphorically, e.g. *'lifting' tis kyvernisis* 'lifting of the government' to refer to a new government scheme; *doparo* v. originally meaning to 'administer dope to, drug' is used outside the domain of sports with the meaning 'stimulate'.

5. Polysemy may be also due to reborrowing, i.e. a lexical item is borrowed with a specific meaning and reborrowed with another meaning after a time gap. The word *centre* (mentioned in s. 17.2.1.1) was borrowed with its sporting meaning of 'centre forward' at the beginning of the twentieth century and reborrowed at the end of the twentieth century with the meaning 'place or group of buildings forming a central point'). Another example is *film* N which according to Anastassiadis-Syméonidis (1994: 63–4) was borrowed in order to denote 'a filmed story'. Later it was reborrowed with the meaning of 'a strip covered with light-sensitive emulsion' (photography).

Finally, in Greek the meaning of a loan may not be attested in English at all: during the borrowing process the meaning can change completely. Sometimes the mediation of another language is responsible for this discrepancy. In Modern Greek many lexical items carry the meaning of the corresponding French item, i.e. meaning change has in these cases already occurred in French and is taken over into Greek (see s. 17.1.8).

17.5 Usage

Sociolinguistic and stylistic analyses of the subject are, so far, completely lacking, but it is obvious that the impact of English on Greek does not affect the whole range of the vocabulary to the same extent. Loans are characterized by variability in their domains of usage, degree of formality, technicality, frequency, and according to social variables (age, sex, education, region, and cultural attitudes). There is also considerable variation in pronunciation, spelling, morphology, meaning, and style. The correlation between such social and linguistic variables remains to be properly investigated.

For the moment, *Dictionary of European Anglicisms* data enable us to make some preliminary generalizations. In Greek, most loanwords belong either to technical or to colloquial and slang registers. Technical loans are restricted to the terminologies of science, technology, and other similar jargons; they tend to be infrequent, written, and attitudinally neutral. They may enter the general vocabulary if the field with which they are associated is popularized. Colloquial or slang terms are found predominantly in youth language, journalism, and advertising; they are frequent in the spoken language, with often unpredictable or changing meanings, and they are generally short-lived. They are usually poorly integrated, with English or near-English pronunciation prevailing.

In general, there is a remarkable discrepancy between the great number of Anglicisms in spoken Greek and the smaller number found in the written language—some magazines excepted.

17.6 Forms of linguistic borrowing and their categorization

Language contact can lead to various forms of expansion in the receiver language; the most frequent type is the takeover of the form and (parts of) the content of the foreign word:

1. *Borrowing*
   - (a) Totally unadapted words not felt to be part of Greek (quotation words, code-switching, foreignisms);
   - (b) words still looking foreign in form or unadapted;
   - (c) fully integrated items.

There is a continuum between the categories 1 (b) and 1 (c), words being placed closer to one of the two ends (with differences between individual users and usually developing from 1(b) to 1 (c). However, there are various ways of rendering the foreign concept with the resources of the recipient language; all these types can be subsumed under 'replacement'.

2. *Replacement*
   - (a) Translation (*metafrastiko dhanio*): reflects the morphological structure of the English complex item as closely as the structure of Greek permits. In many cases, only part of the foreign word is translated (constituting a *semi-calque*). For examples see group A 1–3 below.
   - (b) Rendering: translates only part of the foreign item but provides looser equivalents for others. See group B below for examples.

(c) Creation: a formally independent equivalent whose coinage was, however, prompted by the foreign item; see group C below.

(d) Semantic loan, an existing Greek item taking over one meaning of the foreign partial equivalent; see group D below.

3. *Pseudo-loans*

These are English-looking items which do not exist in English itself.

(a) Lexical pseudo-loans, which forge (combinations of) English word material into new linguistic units that do not exist in the donor language (Greek *auto bank, point system*);

(b) *morphological pseudo-loans*, i.e. the shortening of items ranging from compounds (Greek *bantzi* < English *bungee jumping*, Greek *blok* < English *block-note*) to phrases and phraseologisms (Gr *tzin tonik* < English *gin and tonic*) and to blends made from Greek and English elements (*afto-gol*);

(c) semantic pseudo-loans, where the Anglicism develops a meaning in Greek that is absent from English (see 4).

Categories 2(a–2(d) (replacements) can be illustrated with Greek specimens, distinguishing between successful attempts and proposals which have not been fully accepted.

A *Translations*

1. Successful

brainwashing < *plysi egefalu, maiden speech* < *parthenikos loghos, pacemaker* < *vimatodhotis, flying saucer* < *iptamenos dhiskos, Iron Curtain* < *Sidhirun Parapetasma, mixed double* < *mikto dhiplo, time is money* < *o khronos ine khrima, Big Brother* < *Meghalos Adhelfos*

2. Coexisting

basketball = *kalathosferisi*
public relations ≧ *dhimosies skhesis*
multimedia = *polymesa*
Internet ≧ *dhiadhiktyo*

3. Failures

airbus > *aeroporiko leoforio/aeroleoforio*
fast-food (restaurant) > *takhyfaghio/takhytrofio*
supermarket > *yperaghora*
cornflower > *anthos aravositu*
crash test > *dhokimi sygrusis*

B *Renderings*

1. Successful

skyscraper < *uranoxystis*
antibaby pill < *adisyliptiko khapi*
airport < *aerodhromio*

2. Coexisting

on-line ≥ *se liturghia*

3. Failures

cameraman > *ikonoliptis, khiritis kameras*
CD > *psifiakos dhiskos*

C *Creations*

1. Successful

all risk < *kata pados kindhynu*

2. Coexisting

air condition(ing) = *klimatismos*
topless = *ghymnostithi*
computer = *ilektronikos ypologhistis*

3. Failures

lifting > *rytidhektomi*
joystick > *mokhlos eleghkhu*
laptop > *ypologhistis tsadas*

D *Semantic loans*

1. Successful

mouse < *podiki*
make money < *kano lefta*
to cover (TV) < *kalypto*

2. Coexisting

live = *zodani metadhosi/zodana*

17.7 The future of Anglicisms

Although it is not the task of the linguist to prognosticate, some general predictions are possible at this stage. Considering the current political and sociocultural setting, it is to be expected that English will continue to exert great influence upon Modern Greek. Membership in the unified Europe will manifest itself in the coining of corresponding terms in all the relevant languages (Kalamvoka 1993) and the dominance of the USA in many fields and the attractiveness of the American way of life will presumably continue to constitute another source of the enrichment of Greek vocabulary. This influence need not mean that the number of direct loans will increase dramatically, since loan translation in Greek is also a widely used technique. But the number of English borrowings (adapted or unadapted) which will enter dictionaries in the near future may rise considerably: many loans which already exist are likely to become institutionalized. What is of particular interest for linguists is whether heavy lexical borrowing will result in the adoption of phonemes or grammatical elements (e.g. affixes) like those taken over from French, Italian, and Turkish in earlier periods.

17.8 Research

Anglicisms in Modern Greek have not yet attracted the interest of many scholars. Relevant studies are listed and commented on in the *Annotated Bibliography of European Anglicisms*. The influence of French on Greek has received much greater attention (cf. Contossopoulos 1978). In 1905 Manolis Triantaphyllidis wrote an excellent monograph on loanwords in Greek, expressing very progressive arguments as to why they should not be expunged from the language by purist activities. On Anglicisms in particular, Swanson (1958) provides an interesting compilation of material accompanied by a preliminary analysis. Anastassiadis-Syméonidis (1994) has recently given us insightful studies of both French and English loanwords based on a large corpus. It is undoubtedly of paramount importance that her work, which is lexicological, continues. But there is scope for much further research.

The compilation of data should continue and include all styles and domains; the linguistic analysis of the material (phonology, morphology, semantics, syntax) still has new results to offer, since the situation is changing continuously.

Other areas which require detailed attention are sociolinguistic analysis (variation according to age, sex, social class, education); variation according to region; loans in written texts other than the press (literature, poetry, theatre); a complete study of loan translations and loan meanings; and the integration of insights from all this research into dictionaries and lexicographical studies.

17.9 Bibliography[7]

ANASTASSIADIS-SYMÉONIDIS, ANNA (1986), *I neologhia stin kini neoelliniki* (Neologism in Modern Greek) (Thessaloniki: School of Philosophy Yearbook, Univ. of Thessaloniki, 65).

——(1990), 'To ghenos ton syghkhronon danion tis NE' (The Gender of Recent Loans in Modern Greek), *Studies in Greek Linguistics: Proceedings of the 10th Annual Meeting of the Department of Linguistics, Faculty of Philosophy* (Aristotelian University of Thessaloniki, 9–11 May 1989, Thessaloniki: Kyriakides), 155–77.

——(1994), *Neologhikos dhanismos tis Neoellinikis: Amesa dhania apo ti Ghalliki ke anglo-amerikaniki. Morphophonologhiki analysi.* (Neological Borrowing in Modern Greek: Direct Loans from French and Angloamerican. Morphophonological Analysis) (Thessaloniki).

ANDRIOTIS, N. P. (1983), *Etymologhiko Lexiko tis Kinis Neoellinikis* (Etymological Dictionary of Modern Greek), 3rd edn. (Thessaloniki: INS).

ANGELOUSSI, CHRISTINA (1984), 'Brief Historical Background to the Language Question in Greece until the Close of the 19th Century', *Parousia B*: 351–68.

APOSTOLOU-PANARA, ATHENA-MARIA (1985), 'Ta dhania tis Neas Ellinikis apo tin Agliki: Fonologhiki edaksi ke afomiosi' (The Phonological Integration of English Loanwords into Modern Greek), unpub. diss. (Athens).

---

[7] Names of Greek authors are transliterated according to their own practice or in the way they are usually transliterated by others.

328 Ekaterini Stathi

APOSTOLOU-PANARA, ATHENA-MARIA (1986), 'Gender Assignment of English Substantives in Modern Greek', *Parousia D*: 97–104.
——(1988–9), 'The Significance of English Graphophonemic Relationships for English Loanword Integration into Modern Greek', *Glossologia* (1988–9), 7–8: 193–205.
CHARALABAKIS, CHISTOPHOROS (1992), 'Metafrastika dhania tis Neas Ellinikis apo evropaikes ghlosses' (Loan Translations from European Languages in Modern Greek), in *Neoellinikos Loghos* (Athens: Nefeli).
CHRISTAKIS, LEONIDAS, and EPARATOS, MARKOS (1995), *To lexiko tis daglas* (Athens: Opera).
The Complete Idiot's Guide to Computer Terms (1994) (Greek translation, Athens: Giurdas).
CONTOSSOPOULOS, NICOLAS (1978), *L'Influence du français sur le grec: Emprunts lexicaux et calques phraséologiques* (Athens).
Dheltio Epistimonikis Orologhias ke Neologhismon (1997), (Report of Scientific Terminology and Neologisms) vol. vi (Athens: Academy of Athens, Bureau of Scientific Terms and Neologisms).
EKLUND, BO-LENNART (1993), 'Modern Greek on the Microcomputer: The "GREVOC" Project', in Philippaki-Warburton, Nicolaidis, and Sifianou 1993: 499–506.
FRAGOUDAKI, ANNA (1987), *Ghlossa ke Idheologhia: Kinoniologhiki prosegisi tis ellinikis ghlossas* (Language and Ideology: A Sociological Approach to the Greek Language) (Athens: Odysseas).
HAUGEN, EINAR (1950), 'The Analysis of Linguistic Borrowing', *Language*, 26: 210–31.
HORROCKS, GEOFFRY (1997), *Greek: A History of the Language and its Speakers* (London: Longman).
KALAMVOKA, PANAGIOTA (1993), 'Greek Terminology with the Multilingual Environment of EURIDICAUTOM', in Philippaki-Warburton, Nicolaidis, and Sifianou 1993: 491–7.
KALIORIS, JANNIS M. (1993), *O ghlossikos afellinismos* (The Linguistic Dehellenization) (Athens: Armos).
KAMAROUDIS, S. (1985), 'Style chaise longue: Simplifications orthographiques récentes en grec moderne', *Studies in Greek Linguistics, Proceedings of the 6th Annual Meeting of the Dept. of Linguistics* (Faculty of Philosophy, Aristotle University of Thessaloniki).
KRIARAS, EMMANOUEL (1995), *Neo Elliniko Lexiko* (Modern Greek Dictionary) (Athens: Ekdhotiki Athinon).
KOURMOUSIS, GIORGOS A. (1992), *Lexiko Marketing: Aglo-Elliniko* (English–Greek Marketing Dictionary) (Athens: Interbooks).
MACKRIDGE, PETER (1990), *The Modern Greek Language* (Greek translation, Athens: Patakis).
Neoelliniki Ghrammatiki tis Dhimotikis (Modern Greek Grammar of Dhimotiki) (1996), 4th edn. (Thessaloniki: INS). (1st edn. 1941.)
NEWTON, BRIAN (1963), 'The Grammatical Integration of Italian and Turkish into Modern Greek', *Word*, 19/1: 20–30.
PETROUNIAS, EVAGELOS (1984), *Neoelliniki Ghrammatiki ke Sygritiki ('Adiparathetiki') Analysi* (Modern Greek Grammar and Comparative ('Contrastive') Analysis), vol. i: *Theory* (Thessaloniki: University Studio Press).
PHILIPPAKI-WARBURTON, NICOLAIDIS, I. K., and SIFIANOU, M. (eds.) (1993), *Themes in Greek Linguistics: Papers from the First International Conference on Greek Linguistics* (London: John Benjamins).
SETATOS, M. (1974), *Fonologhia tis Kinis Neoellinikis* (The Phonology of Modern Greek) (Athens: Papazisi).
SWANSON, DONALD C. (1958), 'English Loanwords in Modern Greek', *Word*, 14: 26–46.

TRIANTAPHYLLIDIS, MANOLIS (1963), *Xenilasia i isotelia?* (Expunction or Equality?), Apada (Thessaloniki: INS), 1–297. (1st edn. 1905.)

—— (1965), *I xenes ghlosses ke i aghoghi* (Foreign Languages and Education), Apada 7: 407–562.

TZERMIAS, PAVLOS (1993), *Neugriechische Geschichte: Eine Einführung*, 2nd edn. (Tübingen: Franke).

WEINREICH, URIEL (1968), *Languages in Contact: Findings and Problems*, 2nd edn. (The Hague: Mouton).

Subject Index

INDEX OF NAMES

INDEX OF WORDS

DATE DUE
